D0907372

Saint Jerome in the Renaissance

The Johns Hopkins Symposia in Comparative History

The Johns Hopkins Symposia in Comparative History are occasional volumes sponsored by the Department of History at the Johns Hopkins University and the Johns Hopkins University Press comprising original essays by leading scholars in the United States and other countries. Each volume considers, from a comparative perspective, an important topic of current historical interest. The present volume is the thirteenth. Its preparation has been assisted by the James S. Schouler Lecture Fund.

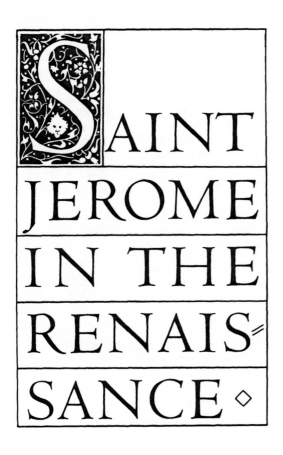

SAINT JEROME IN THE RENAISSANCE ◇

Eugene F. Rice, Jr.

The Johns Hopkins University Press
Baltimore and London

To Paul Oskar Kristeller

This book has been brought to publication with the generous
assistance of the National Endowment for the Humanities.

© 1985 The Johns Hopkins University Press
All rights reserved. Published 1985
Printed in the United States of America

Johns Hopkins Paperbacks edition, 1988

The Johns Hopkins University Press, 701 West 40th Street,
Baltimore, Maryland 21211
The Johns Hopkins Press Ltd., London

The paper used in this publication meets the minimum requirements of
American National Standard for Information Sciences—Permanence of Paper
for Printed Library Materials, ANSI Z39.48-1984.

Photographs were provided by the owners of the works reproduced except the
following:
Alinari: Figs. 8, 14, 23, 34.
Foto Grassi, Siena: Fig. 40.
Gabinetto Fotografico Nazionale, Rome: Fig. 51.
Lichtbildwerkstatte "Alpenland," Vienna: Fig. 12.
Ronald E. Musto: Fig. 41.
Louise Rice: Fig. 4.

Library of Congress Cataloging-in-Publication Data

Rice, Eugene F.
  Saint Jerome in the Renaissance.

  (The Johns Hopkins symposia in comparative history)
  Bibliography: p. 265
  Includes index.
  1. Jerome, Saint, d. 419 or 20—Influence. 2. Renaissance. I. Title. II. Series.
BR1720.J5R53   1985   270.5   84-21324
ISBN 0-8018-2381-1 (alk. paper)
ISBN 0-8018-3747-2 (pbk.)

Contents

Illustrations

Preface & Acknowledgments

THE following pages are a revised and expanded version of the James S. Schouler Lectures that I had the honor to give at the Johns Hopkins University in the fall of 1977. The occasion remains in my memory as a particularly happy one, and I am grateful to my old and new friends in the Department of History at Hopkins for inviting me to talk to them and to their colleagues and students.

I began to collect the material on which the lectures were eventually based at the Biblioteca Apostolica Vaticana in 1974–1975. For the opportunity to enjoy the unclouded happiness of that year in Rome I warmly thank the National Endowment for the Humanities, which generously doubled my sabbatical salary, and the director and staff of the American Academy in Rome, who gave my wife and me a home on the summit of the Gianicolo, an enchanted spot protected by the Aurelian wall and hedged with laurel.

I turned the lectures into a book during subsequent summers in Oxford. It gives me much pleasure to be able to record here my gratitude to the members of the Senior Common Room of Lincoln College for their many kindnesses and to Bodley's Librarian and his colleagues who for more than thirty years have allowed me (as they have allowed so many other foreigners) to read in the Bodleian Library as freely as if I were a member of their own community.

Like every scholar, I owe most to colleagues and students of my own university and to friends everywhere who answered my questions, sent me photographs, and supplied me with pieces of information from their own reading I would otherwise have missed. I shall deeply regret it if the following list is incomplete: Pamela Biel, Anne Beresford Clarke, Catherine Carbelleira, Sigmund Diamond, Colin Eisler, Richard Goldthwaite, Kenneth Jorgensen, James Hankins, Howard Hibbard, Richard Kagan, Patricia Lorcin, John Monfasani, John Mundy, Ronald Musto, John O'Malley, Myra D. Orth, Ronald Rainey, Orest Ranum,

Inge Jackson Reist, John Rice, Louise Rice, Juergen Schulz, and Robert Somerville. The scholar I have long most admired is my colleague Paul Kristeller; so I am happy that he has agreed to accept the dedication of this book.

I hope I am right in thinking that the book itself requires no introduction. My intention has been to follow the varying fortunes of one of the principal fathers of the Latin church from his death in 420 until the early seventeenth century, giving closest attention to the three centuries when his cult was liveliest, his popular reputation at its height, and his representations in the visual arts most numerous and original. I use the word "Renaissance" in my title to denote the period from the beginning of the fourteenth century to about the year 1620.

Saint Jerome in the Renaissance

Fig. 1.   School of Corbie, *Beatus Hieronimus presbyter,* eighth century. The earliest surviving full-figure representation of St. Jerome, a miniature from an early Carolingian manuscript of his letters copied at the Abbey of Corbie.

I
The Historical Jerome

AINT Jerome[1] (his Latin names, Eusebius Hieronymus, derive from the Greek and mean "devout" and "of sacred name") (fig. 1) was born around A.D. 345[2] of well-to-do Christian parents at Stridon, in Dalmatia, a town so efficiently sacked by the Goths (in 379 perhaps, after they had shattered the imperial army at Adrianople) that we can be fairly sure only that it was in what is today Yugoslavia and within comfortable reach of Aquileia, the large commercial, military, and administrative port at the head of the Adriatic. When he was about twelve, his father sent him to Rome to continue his education at the best secondary school in the Empire, that of the grammarian Aelius Donatus, a first step to what the father no doubt hoped would be a rewarding career for his son. After finishing the course of study in Donatus's school (he was then probably sixteen or seventeen), Jerome enrolled in a Roman school of rhetoric, the nearest fourth-century equivalent of an Anglo-Saxon undergraduate college of maximum prestige. Here he was trained in the art of public speaking and debate, normal preparation for law or the civil service.

Although Jerome and his contemporaries called their education liberal and took for granted that no one could become truly human without it,[3] their training was in fact extraordinarily narrow. Jerome received no formal instruction in philosophy, science, or history. He learned some Greek, but not much. Even among Latin authors, he studied in detail only Vergil, Cicero, Sallust, and Terence, though he read in others as well: Plautus, for example, Horace and Quintilian. Not only was his education almost exclusively literary, it was narrowly classical, like that of Chinese mandarins and the affluent pupils of Renaissance humanists, an ostensibly practical training designed to polish future servants of the state yet based on the study of authors already dead for several centuries.[4]

It was of course pagan as well; although Jerome himself, born a Christian, had begun during these student years in Rome to take a more observant interest in his own religion. He and his friends used to visit the catacombs, the subterranean cemeteries near Rome that had recently become the sites of pilgrimages and services in honor of the apostles and martyrs believed to have been buried there. "On Sundays, when I was a boy studying the liberal arts in Rome," he recalled many years later,

> my friends and I often toured the tombs of the apostles and martyrs. We entered those crypts which have been dug out of the depths of the earth and which, along the walls on either side of the passages, contain the bodies of buried people. They were so dark it almost seemed that the prophecy of the Psalmist was fulfilled: *Let them go down alive into Hell* [Ps. 54:16]. Only here and there did a ray of light penetrate from above and relieve the horror of blackness. . . . Then we would grope our way back through the darkness, remembering Vergil's line: "Everywhere dread grips my heart; even the silence frightens me."(*Aen.* 2, 755)[5]

A more significant fact is that he offered himself for baptism (sometime before 366),[6] a serious step in the fourth century, one commonly postponed until old age and understood as a sign of deepening commitment, even of a break with the world.

Jerome spent his early and middle twenties for the most part in Trier (the administrative capital of the Western Empire and between 367 and 383 the principal residence of the Emperors Valentinian I and Gratian), perhaps employed there in the sort of bureaucratic job for which he had been trained in Rome, and in Aquileia, where he became a member of a circle of devoutly ascetic clerics.[7] During these years the competing satisfactions of the Christian religion and pagan literature seem to have possessed his heart in relative harmony. Vergil remained often on his lips (indeed, he very likely knew most of the *Aeneid* by heart); he kept always by him favorite works of Plautus and Cicero. At the same time, he refined his knowledge of Scripture, followed contemporary theological debate, and added a growing variety of Christian texts to the personal library of pagan authors he had begun to collect while he was a student.[8] Gradually the balance of his commitment shifted. Radical ascetic ideals hostile to the values inculcated by his formal education began powerfully to shape his aspirations. He remained proudly Roman (*homo Romanus* he would call himself later in a letter to Pope Damasus),[9] but the magnetic pull of a very different fatherland began to attract him even more. The world, he came to believe, was plunging each day deeper into sin.[10] His sense of his own unworthiness deepened also. His early letters are piteously repetitive: "You know how slippery is the path of youth; I too have fallen on it"; "I am soiled with every sinful baseness"; "I lie prostrate in the tomb of my crimes, bound by the fetters of my sins."[11]

He resolved to change his life. About the year 372, when he was twenty-seven, Jerome embarked on a pilgrimage to the East and to Jerusalem, taking his library with him. He stopped first in Antioch, where he was the guest of Evagrius, a Christian priest of wealth and influence, translator of Athanasius's *Life of Anthony,* whom he had met earlier in Aquileia. Here he began seriously to learn Greek. With the help of a tutor he read some of Aristotle's logical works and commentaries on Aristotle by Alexander of Aphrodisias.[12] From his host he learned more of the sophisticated controversies about the doctrine of the Trinity then agitating the Eastern churches. He observed the austerities of the Eastern anchorites. In this novel, intellectually and emotionally charged environment, the latent tension between the claims of his two cultural inheritances, Christian and classical, became explicit and acute. He prayed, fasted, and wept for his sins; then he read Cicero. When he picked up his Bible, the language of the prophets repelled him as uncouth. Chronic ill health exacerbated his unease. His mounting anxiety brought on a spiritual crisis. It took the form of a dream (figs. 2 and 3).

One night, during Lent (probably in 374), when his body was so weakened by fever that death seemed near, he was suddenly caught up in the spirit, *subito raptus in spiritu.* He dreamed that he was called before the supreme Judge. "What condition of man are you?" asked Christ the Judge. "I am a Christian," replied Jerome. "You lie," thundered the Judge. "Ciceronianus es, non Christianus: you are a Ciceronian, a disciple of Cicero, not a Christian. Where your treasure is, there your heart is also." The Judge ordered him to be flogged. Smarting from the blows and even more from the burning of his own conscience, he cried out, "Have pity, Lord, have pity." Even the bystanders now fell on their knees and asked the Judge to forgive Jerome's youthful errors and allow him to do penance. Jerome himself swore a solemn oath: "Lord, if ever again I possess worldly books, if ever again I read them, I shall have denied you." He woke up, his eyes wet with tears and his shoulders bruised and swollen from the divine chastisement, clear physical evidence of the objective reality of his experience.[13]

Fig. 2. Francesco d'Antonio, *The Dream of St. Jerome,* c. 1430. Predella panel from an altarpiece commissioned by the Florentine banker Rinieri di Lucca di Piero Rinieri, probably for the Florentine community of the Gesuati (see fig. 29). On the left, Jerome, much weakened by illness, lies asleep; on the right, he is beaten by an angel.

Jerome's problem was not new. Paul's was the earliest antithesis: What has light, he had asked, in common with darkness? Christ with Belial?[14] Early in the third century, Tertullian sharpened the question: "What has Athens to do with Jerusalem, the Church with the Academy, Christians with heretics?";[15] Jerome echoed him: "What has Horace in common with the Psalter? Vergil with the gospels? Cicero with the Apostle Paul?" Or at the end of his life: "Quid Aristoteli et Paulo? Quid Platoni et Petro?" At the day of judgment "foolish Plato" will go to hell; so will Aristotle, with all his subtle arguments; but the poor unlettered Christian, *pauper et rusticanus,* will laugh and go to heaven.[16]

Outright rejection of classical culture was not to be Jerome's ultimate solution of the problem. Rufinus, the loved friend of his youth and vilified enemy of his old age, called him a perjurer because he found in Jerome's later writings Vergilian reminiscences, phrases like "our Tully" or "our Flaccus," and boastful references to Chrysippus, Aristides, or Empedocles. Jerome even claimed to have read Pythagoras, an impudent falsehood, according to Rufinus, because no book by Pythagoras survived.[17] Jerome did in fact remain sensible both to the aesthetic attraction of classical literature and the Christian's continuing need for useful secular knowledge. He justified his mature opinion by citing the precept of

Fig. 3.   Sano di Pietro, *The Dream of St. Jerome*. Predella panel from a polyptych, signed and dated 1444, painted for the Gesuati church of S. Girolamo in Siena.

Deuteronomy (21:10–13) that a Jew may marry a captive Gentile woman if he has first shaved her head and eyebrows and clipped her nails. "What is so surprising then about my wish to treat secular wisdom, which I admire for the beauty of its content and the elegance of its style, like this captive maiden, that is, to make her an Israelite once she has been clipped and shorn of idolatry, error, and lust?"[18] But it was the dream, not this more balanced judgment, that was to be longer remembered, a weapon ever ready to the hand of enemies of the classics and an embarrassment to defenders of the humanities. The ingenious efforts of Renaissance humanists to minimize its significance or transform its meaning was to become a comic but instructive episode in the history of exegesis.

At the time, the dream was a shattering experience, akin both to an ecstatic vision and to a conversion more profound than the earlier ones that had led him to put on at baptism the *vestimenta Christi*, the robe of Christ, and to abandon his home, family, and career for a pilgrimage to the Holy Land. He resolved to change his life again, even more radically. He postponed his trip to Jerusalem. In order better to fulfill his oath to the supreme Judge, mitigate his fear of hell, and do penance for his past sins he made a vow of solitude and became a hermit in the Syrian desert, somewhere in the neighborhood of Chalcis, between Antioch and Palmyra.

He summarized his two or three years in the wilderness (374–376) in the passage from his work most often quoted in the Middle Ages and in the Renaissance. "O quotiens in heremo constitutus et in illa vasta solitudine," it begins. "O how often, when I was living in the sun-scorched solitude of the desert, which offers monks a savage hospitality, how often I imagined myself back among the pleasures of Rome!" He covered his wasted limbs with sackcloth. His companions were scorpions and wild beasts. He slept on the bare ground, drank only water, and spurned cooked foods as an unacceptable luxury. He wept, groaned, prayed, and mortified a body tormented by visions of Roman dancing girls (fig. 4).

> When all else failed, I lay down at Jesus's feet, watered them with my tears, and wiped them with my hair. I subdued my rebellious flesh with weeks of fasting. . . . I remember crying out for days and nights together; and I beat my breast without stopping until the Lord vouchsafed me some tranquility. I came to dread my own cell, as though even it were aware of my unclean thoughts. Filled with stiff anger against myself, I went out into the desert alone. Wherever I found a deep valley or rough mountainside or rocky precipice, I made it my place of prayer and of torture for my unhappy flesh. The Lord himself is my witness, after many tears, I fixed my eyes on Heaven and seemed to find myself among the angelic hosts. Then, full of joy and happiness, I would sing out: "I run after you in the fragrance of your perfumes."[19]

In the catacombs he had remembered Vergil; in the desert he quoted the Song of Songs (*Cant.* 1:3) (fig. 5).

Because, like all hermits, Jerome wished to live an angelic life in permanent communion with God, to live in the body as though he had no body, his spirituality was profoundly dualistic. Eating, drinking, and sleeping nourish and support the body; they must be reduced to a minimum. No guilt harrowed Jerome more fiercely than the memory of the "sweet fires of sensual pleasure"[20] that had made a purgatory of his adolescence and early manhood. No practice that moderates the *flamma carnis* is too extreme (castration was not unknown).[21] No virtue is more desirable than chastity, no possession more precious than virginity. By reducing the body to the insensibility of a stone, the hermit becomes

Fig. 4.   Stefano Magiore, *St. Jerome in the Wilderness Tormented by Memories of the Dancing Girls of Rome*. An engraving after one of Domenichino's frescoes of 1604/1605, commissioned by Cardinal Girolamo Agucchi for S. Onofrio, the Roman convent of the Poor Hermits of St. Jerome. Amidst the austerities of the desert, Jerome reported to Eustochium, he remembered the delights of Rome and often thought that he was watching young girls dancing (*Ep.* 22, 7). Here Jerome's guardian angel protects him against sexual desires inspired by the devil. "His power," said Job (40:11) about the devil, "is in the loins, his strength in the navel." Jerome explained the verse later in the same letter: "*Loins* and *navel* were Job's modest way of designating the male and female genitals. This is why he says that the whole power of the devil over men is in their loins, over women in their navel" (*Ep.* 22, 11).

literally dead to the world. Then his soul, free at last, sometimes sees the angelic hosts and enjoys, in rare moments of contemplation, an ecstasy akin to the mystic's vision.

Rejection of the body was also a rejection of the family and the *civitas*, the urban taproot of ancient civilization. Jerome could be chillingly ruthless: "Even if your mother, her hair undone, tears open her dress to show you the breasts that nourished you," he wrote, urging a boyhood friend to break with the world and follow him into the desert, "even if your father tries to stop you by lying across the threshold, trample him under foot and with dry eyes fly to the standard of the Cross."[22] His

Fig. 5.   Sano di Pietro, *The Penitent St. Jerome in the Wilderness,* 1444

abandonment of the earthly city for a *civitas nova,* the citizens of which meditate night and day on Scripture and God's law, was equally explicit. The wilderness and solitude, he thought, are lovelier than any city. Indeed, he believed the *civitas* incompatible with Christianity: *quicumque in civitate sunt, Christiani non sunt.*[23] From the remotest antiquity, urban living had distinguished the civilized from everything savage, rustic, and barbarous. Jerome's reversal of traditional values could hardly have been sharper.

Yet, mortification and rejection were not the whole Jerome, even during his years in the desert. His austerities were mild compared with the picturesque excesses of the Syrian anchorites around him. These "athletes of wisdom" were usually simple peasants, often illiterate, ignorant of Greek, speaking only Syriac. One lived in a hole in the ground hardly larger than a fox's burrow. A second survived the forty days of Lent on fifteen dried figs. All of them were filthy and hairy, skeleton-thin, their skins wrinkled by exposure to wind, rain, snow, and sun. They wore a goatskin, or plaited palm fronds, or nothing at all. Their common penitential practice was to load themselves with iron chains. A

9

hermit named Eusebius festooned himself with 250 pounds of them. Another kept himself bent almost double, his eyes fixed permanently and humbly on the ground, by attaching the chains he wore about his waist to an iron band riveted around his neck. He endured this penance for over forty years. In order to avoid importunate visitors demanding blessings and cures, the most extravagant protected their lives of solitary prayer by retreating to the tops of columns, hoping in this way to quit the world below and like the birds and clouds fly nearer to God.[24]

Although Jerome probably did live in a natural cave, it must have been a spacious one, because he tells us himself that he brought his considerable library into the desert with him. Nor was he always alone. Other hermits were close by, Evagrius was a frequent visitor, and he specifically mentions his *alumni*, probably young monks who could read and write and were in some fashion in his service, whom he kept busy copying books and taking his dictation.[25] He wrote and received letters. His fasts and vigils punctuated systematic intellectual work, for he continued to build in these years the linguistic and scholarly foundation of his permanent achievements as a translator of and commentator on the Bible. He improved his spoken Greek and learned some Syriac. With the help of a Christian convert from Judaism, he began his heroic effort to master Hebrew. "After the subtlety of Quintilian, the eloquence of Cicero, the majesty of Fronto, the smooth grace of Pliny," he wrote later, "I set myself to learn an alien alphabet and strove to pronounce hissing, aspirate words. What labor! What difficulties to conquer! How often I despaired! How often I gave up, only to swear stubbornly again that I would learn it."[26] Eventually he did. No Christian writer before him (not even Origen) and no Christian-born writer for many centuries after him (possibly not until the seventeenth century) possessed a comparable command of Hebrew, and therefore of the Old Testament in its original language.

Jerome's last months in the desert were soured by quarrels with his ascetic neighbors about the Trinity and the authority of the bishop of Rome. He left in disgust for Antioch, where he was ordained priest by the orthodox bishop Paulinus (on condition that he retain the freedom of a monk and not be tied to the ministry in a particular church) and wrote his first surviving book, a brief *Life of Paul the First Hermit,* an ascetic romance, full of marvels credulously imagined. During the next several years, spent in Antioch and Constantinople, he continued to work on Hebrew. He perfected his Greek and deepened his knowledge of Eastern theology, especially that of Origen, the greatest thinker the church had yet produced. In Antioch, he attended the lectures of Apollinarius, bishop of Laodicea; in Constantinople, he became acquainted with Gregory of Nyssa and Gregory Nazianzen (whom he would often proudly call "my teacher")[27] and followed the turbulent sessions of the Second Ecumenical Council of the church, meeting between May and July, 381. The apprentice was becoming a master, ready for the great work of his maturity: to pass on to the Latin world the religious knowledge of the Greeks and Hebrews.[28] He gave his newly clarified aim in life an initial substance with a translation and continuation of the *Chronicle* of Eusebius of Caesarea and translations of Origen's *Homilies* on Jeremiah and Ezekiel, earliest in a series of influential Latin versions of works by the man he then considered "second only to the Apostles as teacher of the churches."[29]

In the late summer of 382, Paulinus of Antioch and Epiphanius, bishop of Salamis (now Famagusta) in Cyprus, left Constantinople to attend a council that Ambrose of Milan had persuaded the Emperor Gratian to convoke in Rome. Jerome accompanied them as interpreter and adviser. The synod was a failure, but Jerome, noticed and favored by Pope Damasus (366–384), stayed on in Rome. This second Roman period, from the fall of 382 to August 385, was one of the happiest and most productive of his life. Damasus consulted him on the interpretation of difficult points of Scripture and used him to draft his correspondence with the churches of the Greek East. Most important of all, he commissioned him to revise the Latin text of the Gospels according to the Greek original.[30]

A standard, uniform, dependable text was badly needed. The books of the New Testament were circulating in a variety of Old Latin translations of varying quality. By the later fourth century, the different versions had become chaotically mixed and much disordered by the corruption to which texts are inevitably condemned in a scribal culture. Copying a text accurately is difficult; careless scribes multiply error at each recopying. Add to this natural degeneration the "improvements" of the ignorant and, among the early Christians, the unresisted temptation to harmonize the Gospels or bring them into line with current orthodoxy, and the result is what Jerome described to the pope in his dedicatory epistle: there are as many forms of the biblical text in circulation as there are manuscripts.[31] Jerome's revision was conservative. The changes he made in the Old Latin text were relatively few and largely confined to places where the sense had diverged from the Greek or where the slavish literalness of the original translators made it unintelligible. What was to be important for the future was his emphasis on the primacy of the Greek original (*Graeca veritas*) and the fact that the Greek manuscripts he used were older and better than any that survive today. Jerome presented his new standard version of the Gospels to Damasus in 384. It was the first installment of what would come to be known in the Middle Ages as "our translation" (*nostra tralatio, nostra usitata editio*) or "the translation commonly used in our churches" (*ea tralatio qua nostrae ecclesiae passim utuntur*) and in the sixteenth century as the Vulgate Bible (*Biblia Sacra vulgatae editionis*).[32] The vast enterprise of revising or retranslating the whole Bible (a task he never finished) was to occupy him at intervals for the next twenty years.

Revising a traditional religious text is no way to make friends. Jerome was blamed for disdaining the authority of the ancients and the opinion of the world. Still, if he had stuck to biblical scholarship, he would have avoided even more serious trouble. Instead, he satirized the Roman clergy for their hypocritical piety, lisping effeminacy, avarice, gluttony, and luxury (they looked more like bridegrooms than clerics, he said). At the same time he campaigned passionately in favor of Oriental ascetic ideas and practices, urging the superiority of virginity to marriage and the monastic to civic life. He thus offended both the clergy and the laity, especially the senatorial aristocracy, many of whom considered celibacy antisocial, degrading, and unnatural. Their hostility sharpened when Jerome became the center of an ascetic circle that included several aristocratic women: Marcella, the first Roman woman of rank converted to the asceticism of the East; Asella (dedicated to virginity from birth by her father on the authority of a dream); and Paula and her daughters Blesilla and Eustochium. These women had established what were virtually domestic nunneries in their palaces on the Aventine, where the small communities of noble ladies and their household slaves vowed themselves to chastity and biblical study, fasted, and wore coarse clothing in order to look as unattractive as possible (Paula rarely bathed and slept on the floor). Jerome, who had an unusual gift for attracting the devotion of women, encouraged their ascetic seclusion, sexual abstinence, and biblical readings (fig. 6).[33] Several of them were to become his most loyal disciples and correspondents.

When Pope Damasus died in December 384, removing the support that had kept Jerome's enemies at bay, Jerome was left alone to face the resentments aroused by his revision of the Gospels, his reforming zeal, his

Fig. 6.   Francisco de Zurbarán, *St. Jerome Explains the Bible to Paula and Eustochium,* c. 1638–1640. The subject goes back to the mid-ninth century at least: see the middle register of the Jerome frontispiece from the First Bible of Charles the Bald (fig. 9). A mosaic in S. Maria Maggiore in Rome of about 1300 (destroyed in the eighteenth century but identifiable from drawings and prints) showed Jerome reading with Paula and Eustochium over the inscription, *S. Hieronymus sermonem fecit ad Paulam et Eustochium.* Probably painted for the Hieronymite nuns of Santa Paula in Seville.

tactless pen, and his spiritual sway over women of rank and money. Once, he reported bitterly, people called me holy, humble, and learned and said that I was worthy to become pope. Now they think me a scoundrel, trickster, liar, and criminal allied to the devil.[34] Exactly how the Roman clergy got rid of him is not clear. What seems to have happened is that a rumor circulated insinuating improprieties in his relationship with Paula. A commission of inquiry investigated, presumably cleared him, but pressed him to leave the city. With his younger brother and a small group of monks, he sailed from Portus, the harbor of Rome, in August 385 (see fig. 9, upper register).

Paula, accompanied by Eustochium, soon followed him. On the quay her little son Toxotius held out supplicant arms, and her adolescent daughter Rufina tearfully begged her mother not to leave her before she married. But Paula, vanquishing love for her children with love of God, turned dry eyes to heaven (the phrase is a reminiscence of Horace) and sailed away.[35] She and Eustochium joined Jerome in Antioch. For the next year their two parties exhaustively toured the Holy Land and the hermitages and monasteries of Nitria, the cradle of monasticism in the Nile Delta south of Alexandria.[36]

In Jerusalem, Jerome found his friend Rufinus and the celebrated Melania the Elder, another noble, rich, and pious Roman matron. Some ten years previously Melania and Rufinus had together founded on the Mount of Olives the first Latin monasteries in the Holy Land, one for men, another for women. Paula and Jerome, because of their special devotion to the infant Jesus and his mother, decided to establish similar foundations in Bethlehem.[37] The money came from Paula. During the next three years (386–389), she erected a convent for women near the Church of the Nativity, built nearly a century before by Constantine and the empress Helena, his mother, over the grotto where Jesus was born; a monastery for men; and a hospice for pilgrims "next to the main road." Paula ruled the convent, Jerome the monastery.

We know little directly about the daily life of the monastery. Epiphanius, in a letter to the bishop of Jerusalem in 394, speaks of a "multitude of pious brothers,"[38] but how many brothers made a multitude is uncertain. Most of them were Latins, though there were a few Greek-speaking monks as well. They met at regular hours to pray and chant the psalms. They read the Bible, the food of the soul. On Sundays and holy days they heard Mass in the Basilica. Jerome was later to translate the *Rule* of Pachomius (c. 290–346), reputed founder of cenobitic monasticism in

Egypt. If we can accept it as a rough guide to the routine of his own monastery, the monks lived in separate cells but came together for silent meals, religious instruction, and prayer. They obeyed their superior because they had exchanged worldly liberty for servitude to Christ. They were chaste because they had given their bodies to God. They held all things in common. They combined intellectual with manual labor, copying books, working in the garden, and weaving mats and baskets from rushes and palm leaves.[39]

As far as we know, Jerome did no manual labor himself, however warmly he recommended it to others. But he could have said with Napoleon that he had known the limits of his eyes and legs, but never the limits of his work. He preached; supervised the hospice; acted as spiritual adviser to Paula, Eustochium, and their nuns; instructed candidates for baptism; ran a school for children where he taught them Vergil, the comic and lyric poets, and the historians; and continued to study Hebrew with Jewish tutors. He went often to Jerusalem and occasionally to the great library at Caesarea to consult the original of Origen's *Hexapla,* his colossal edition of the Old Testament in Greek and Hebrew in six parallel columns: the Hebrew text in Hebrew characters, the Hebrew text transliterated into Greek, the Greek translation of Aquila (c. 132), the Greek translation of Symmachus (late second century), the Septuagint corrected from the Hebrew, and, finally, the Greek translation of Theodotion. In the midst of all this, he maintained a stupefying literary productivity. Apart from the odd saint's life, biographies (the *De viris inlustribus,* a catalogue of Christian writers, one of the most widely read of all his works in later centuries), reference books (a gazeteer of places mentioned in Scripture and an etymological dictionary of biblical proper names), and more translations from the Greek (Didymus's *On the Holy Spirit,* for example), his own oeuvre falls into three main parts: the translation of the Hebrew Old Testament; biblical commentaries, mostly on books of the Old Testament; and polemics against heretics.

Jerome's Latin translation from the Hebrew of the canonical books of the Old Testament (c. 391–c. 405) was his most distinguished achievement (fig. 7). He did not recognize at once the superiority of the Hebrew to the Greek translation known as the Septuagint. So-called because seventy different translators, locked up in seventy noncommunicating cells in Alexandria, separately translated the Pentateuch, only to find that their seventy versions were identical, a sure sign their labors were divinely inspired (Jerome mocked this legend with his customary mordancy),[40]

Fig. 7. Liuthard, *St. Jerome Translating the Psalms*, c. 860. The inscription reads, *"Nobilis interpres Hieronimus atque sacerdos/Nobiliter pollens transscripsit iura Davidis.* Jerome, noble translator and mighty priest, nobly translates the Psalms of David."

the Septuagint enjoyed in the fourth century the same superstitious reverence sixteenth-century conservatives would claim for the Vulgate. Yet despite its antiquity and substantial merits, it was only a translation, while the current Latin Old Testament, itself translated from the Septuagint, was the translation of a translation. Jerome argued that both translations were secondary authorities and that only the Hebrew text (the *Hebraeica veritas*) could claim primacy and divine inspiration: "When the Latins face a problem caused by variant readings in different copies of the New Testament," he wrote, "they return to the Greek, the language in which the New Testament was written; in the same way, we must consult the Hebrew original when Greeks and Latins disagree about an Old Testament text. Only in this way will the little streams that flow from the original spring retain their purity."[41] So although he began his work on the Old Testament simply by revising the Latin translation of the Septuagint, comparing it with other Greek versions and with the Hebrew verity,[42] he came eventually to see that this was not enough and that the primacy of the Hebrew text dictated an altogether different strategy: to translate the canonical books of the Old Testament anew from the Hebrew.

Jerome was the greatest translator of antiquity, and he had definite ideas about the art. He knew that good translations rest on philological expertise, erudition, and literary skill, not on the inspiration of the Holy Spirit.[43] He believed, as had Cicero and Horace, that the good translator does not translate word for word but sense for sense, avoiding servile fidelity in order to express the idiom of the original in phrases appropriate to the genius of his own language;[44] or, as the poet Dryden would wittily paraphrase him, "A translator should not lackey by his author, but mount up beside him." He was equally aware that a translation of the Bible serves a special purpose and addresses a special audience. Translators of Scripture should not strain for secular eloquence but adopt a popular, colloquial style, for they are not addressing scholars or philosophers but "the whole human race."[45] Scripture, moreover, is inexhaustible and sublime. Its word order is itself a mystery, indeed every word of it is sacred and mysterious. It therefore demands a more scrupulous attention to the letter than other texts.[46] In practice, Jerome steered a middle course between the cramping literalism of earlier versions of the Bible and the freedom advocated by the Roman rhetorical tradition. Explaining his procedure to Augustine, he argued that his translation of the Hebrew was the more faithful precisely because he had extracted the true sense and not tried to retain the exact order of the words.[47] The result, especially in the historical books of the Old Testament, was a version more accurate and more beautiful than any Latin Christians had had before.

In words and for reasons that uncannily foreshadow the controversies of the sixteenth century, Jerome was furiously attacked for irreverently tampering with the familiar text of the Old Testament. His version was said to be tainted with Judaism. His rejection of the Septuagint denied the verbal inspiration of the seventy translators and undermined the faith of the laity. Many of his changes seemed unnecessary. Even Augustine sided with the opposition. Jerome gave as good as he got: his critics were "yelping dogs," envious "backbiters," "two-legged asses," "filthy swine who grunt as they trample on pearls."[48] Not surprisingly, acceptance of his great achievement came very slowly, long after his death. Only in the ninth century was the victory of his superior text secure (and the Old Latin continued to be copied even in the thirteenth century).[49]

Jerome coupled his translation of the Bible with scriptural commentaries: on four Pauline epistles (Galatians, Ephesians, Philemon, and Titus) (387–388), Ecclesiastes (c. 389), the Gospel of Matthew (398), and, much more important and valuable, on the prophetic books of the Old Testament, the twelve minor prophets (c. 391–406), and—the masterpieces of his old age—the four major prophets, Daniel (407), Isaiah (408–410), Ezekiel (410–415), and Jeremiah (415–420). His exegetical method was as straightforward, in principle, as his strategy as translator. "The purpose of a commentator is not to show off his own eloquence but to enable his reader to understand the exact meaning of the original author";[50] or again: the commentator's task is "to explain what has been said by others and make clear in plain language what had been written obscurely."[51] Readers of Scripture are especially in need of a guide, for the Bible, particularly the Old Testament, is full of obscurities.[52] To help them, Jerome first cleaned up the text, discussing the translation he was using and comparing it with others and with the original Greek or Hebrew; next, he explained the literal meaning of the passage, what he called the historical verity (*historiae veritas* or simply *historia*); finally, he probed its figurative and allegorical meaning in order to unfold the "secrets of spiritual understanding" (*spiritualis intelligentiae sacramenta*) it contained.[53]

Jerome's commentaries are eclectic compendia, and he shamelessly plundered past and contemporary writers for them, sometimes acknowledging his source, more often not. He had read widely. He had experienced directly the methods and principles of the major exegetical schools of the Greek East: that of Antioch (with Apollinarius), the Cappadocian (with Gregory Nazianzen and Gregory of Nyssa), and, most recently, the Alexandrian (he had spent a month with Didymus the Blind, a fervent admirer of Origen, questioning him "about the things I found obscure in every part of Scripture");[54] and through his studies with one Bar-ḥanina[55] and other learned Jews he was becoming increasingly familiar with what he called the "traditions of the Hebrews" (*auctoritas Hebraeorum*).[56] His principal sources were Origen and the rabbinical scholars living in Palestine in his own day. The rabbis helped him understand the historical meaning of Old Testament texts; Origen and the other Greek fathers spelled out in detail their prophetic meaning for Christians. For of course Jerome took it for granted that what "was carnally promised to the Jews has been and is now being fullfilled spiritually among us."[57] On this double foundation of Jewish *historia* and Christian typology, Jerome erected a lasting and influential exegetical edifice furnished with a prodigally miscellaneous learning. Indeed, it was largely through his commentaries, often dictated hastily to secretaries, sometimes in bursts of as many as a thousand lines a day,[58] that the scriptural scholarship of the Greek fathers and the Jewish rabbinate was transmitted to the medieval West.

Jerome spent almost as much time in doctrinal and personal dispute as in translating and commenting on the Bible. Against Helvidius, who argued that after the birth of Jesus his mother lived a normal life and therefore that celibacy and marriage are equal in dignity, Jerome defended the perpetual virginity of Mary and the superiority of celibacy. Against Jovinian's criticism of works and of the notion that superior merit can be acquired by fasting and chastity (because faith and baptism have made all men equal), he asserted that sexual intercourse is defiling and that a perfect Christian life is impossible without abstinence and ascetic practices. He blasted Vigilantius, a priest from Gaul, for attacking the cult of relics, the veneration of martyrs, and all-night vigils. His ferocious attacks on Bishop John of Jerusalem and Rufinus grew out of the controversy over Origen, which boiled up during the 390s in both East and West, at once an episode in the definition of heresy and orthodoxy, a complex episcopal power struggle, and, most narrowly, a jurisdictional quarrel between the monks of Bethlehem and their ecclesiastical superior, the bishop of Jerusalem. Both Rufinus and Jerome had long rightly admired Origen and translated his work; but while Rufinus, blinded by partiality, persuaded himself that Origen's "errors" had been interpolated into his work by cunning heretics, Jerome had come to believe that although Origen was an admirable biblical commentator, he was a dangerously heretical theologian. There were other no doubt good reasons for the break between the two old friends, but the unrelenting venom with which it was conducted was mostly Jerome's. Even after Rufinus was dead, Jerome was still calling him "scorpion," "serpent," the "grunting pig." The last to feel his satire and invective was Pelagius, who had arrived in the Holy Land in 411. In his *Dialogue against the Pelagians* (415), Jerome attacked with undiminished brio and coarseness Pelagius's denial of inherited original sin, his claim that men and women can live without sin if they will only try, and his generous conception of free will.[59]

Jerome's last years were shadowed by the deaths of Paula (404) and Eustochium (418), grievous losses deeply mourned, and by the misfortunes of the Latin monasteries in Bethlehem. Paula's money had been dissipated even before she died; on occasion the monks and nuns were on the verge of starvation. Marauding bands of Bedouin or Isaurian tribesmen forced them to build a fortified tower for defense. In 416 a mob (probably monks, supporters of Pelagius) attacked the monasteries, fired the buildings, and assaulted the inmates.[60] For a time Jerome and Eustochium were driven out and their quarters occupied by the raiders.[61] Jerome may have lost his library in the flames. The political and military news from the West was equally ominous. "For days and nights I could think of nothing but the universal safety," he wrote on hearing of Alaric's sack of Rome in August 410. "Now that the glorious light of the world has been put out, now that the very head of the Roman empire has been cut off, now that the whole world has perished in this single city, 'I am dumb, and am humbled, and kept silent' [Ps. 38:3]."[62] It was a time only for tears.[63] As his world collapsed while sinners flourished, he foresaw the approach of the Antichrist and the end of all things.[64] Crowds of refugees from the West besieged the monastery, taxing its scanty resources and putting another drain on Jerome's time and energy, so vast a crowd, he explained, apologizing for taking so long to finish his *Commentary on Ezekiel,* that "we shall either have to shut our gates or else abandon the study of the Scriptures, even though it was for this purpose that our monastery was established in the first place. I can only steal time to work during the nights, now lengthening with the approach of winter, and dictate what I can by lamp light, trying to overcome the weariness of a distracted mind by commenting on the Bible."[65] So the old

Fig. 8.   Fra Filippo Lippi, *The Death of St. Jerome,* c. 1452. The dead saint is mourned
by his monks. Beside the bier, a cripple is about to recover the use of his limbs by touching the corpse. To his right is the donor, Geminiano Inghirami da Prato (d. 1460), a
leading ecclesiastic in the town. In the background, from left to right: the Holy Family
beside the manger, a reference to Jerome's devotion to the infant Jesus and his place of
burial beside the crib; St. Jerome's vision of the Trinity; and the apparition of St. Jerome
to St. Augustine.

lion worked on. He was almost blind. But the "great ardor for learning" that he had confessed in his youth[66] was undiminished; and despite a lifetime of valetudinarian complaints he had reached his seventies with a mind as sharp as ever. His last illness overtook him in the middle of his *Commentary on Jeremiah.* According to Prosper of Aquitaine,[67] his much younger contemporary, he died on 30 September. The year was almost certainly 420 (fig. 8).

2

From History to Legend

EDIEVAL Christians learned about Jerome's life from several short biographies written between the late eighth and the end of the thirteenth centuries: an anonymous life no later than the middle of the ninth century known from its first two words as *Hieronymus noster;*[1] a second anonymous life of approximately the same date beginning *Plerosque nimirum*[2] (neither of these works is a source of the other, while all subsequent biographers pillaged both of them freely); the *Vita sancti Hieronymi collecta ex tractatibus eius ac sanctorum Augustini, Damasi, Gregorii, Gelasii, et aliorum patrum sanctorum* by Nicolò Maniacoria (or Nicola Maniacutia),[3] a biblical scholar active in Rome in the middle of the twelfth century whose sound historical method is outlined in the title of his book; the notice of Jerome in the *Speculum historiale* of the thirteenth-century encyclopedist Vincent of Beauvais, itself unoriginal but accompanied by a rich and much-used collection of passages from Jerome's works;[4] and the life of the saint that Jacopo da Varazze (Jacobus de Voragine), a Dominican friar and archbishop of Genoa, included in his *Legenda sanctorum* (c. 1260), a book of readings about the saints so popular (over 500 manuscripts survive and more than 150 editions from the first century of printing) that it became known as the Golden Legend.[5]

These lives contain trustworthy information derived ultimately from Jerome's authentic letters and prefaces and from the autobiographical note with which he ended *Famous Men.*[6] They add to the historical record two convincing but unverifiable facts: first, that Jerome's monastery in Bethlehem was "a humble structure located north of the town's west gate,"[7] information possibly derived from a reliable source now lost; second, that Jerome was buried under the Basilica of the Nativity in Bethlehem in a tomb cut from the rock of the narrow entrance to the cave where Jesus was born, a statement based on a good early tradition preserved in the *Itinerarium* of Antoninus of Piacenza, who about 570 toured the Holy Land.[8] They quote testimonials to Jerome's character and learning culled from authentic works of late ancient and early medieval authors: St. Augustine, Sulpicius Severus (c. 363–c. 425), Cassian (c. 360–435), Prosper of Aquitaine (c. 390–c. 455), the *Chronicle* of Marcellinus Comes (first half of the sixth century), Cassiodorus (c. 485–c. 580), Pope Gregory the Great (c. 540–604), and Isidore of Seville (c. 560–636).[9] Their more obvious characteristic is a wish to show Jerome in the best possible light. Disobliging incidents are omitted or refuted, uplifting ones detailed at disproportionate length, a pattern of selection and emphasis inclining to hyperbole. Memorable sayings and deeds of other saints are attributed to Jerome. Baroque explanations are invented to solve puzzles of motive or action. Imaginary facts are added: some plausible but untrue, others less plausible and also untrue, still others anachronistic and absurd. Tendrils of legend insinuate themselves into the narrative. The author of *Plerosque nimirum* credited Jerome with a miracle; Jacopo da Varazze devoted one-third of his space to it.

From remote antiquity, similarities of sound and the conviction that there exists a quasi-magical relationship between a man and his name had tempted biographers to attribute probity, for example, to the Roman emperor Probus or to derive Seneca's name from *se necans* because he was to commit suicide. Jerome's biographers followed ancient precedent. They took *hiero* (correctly) to mean *sanctus* or *sacer* and *nymus* (wrongly) to mean *noma* (!), that is, *nomos = lex = law,* and so concluded that Hieronymus meant *sacra lex,* "holy law."[10] Jacopo da Varazze imagined freer associations. He suggested that *nymus* might equally derive from *nemus,* "grove" or "woods" (the correct derivation is from *onoma,* "name"), a fancy that may help explain why so many literal-minded artists in Venice and early sixteenth-century Germany were to picture Jerome in luxuriantly wooded landscapes. Jacopo commented on "holy law" and "sacred grove" at some length: "[Jerome] was holy, that is, he was firm, or clean, or dipped in blood, or set aside for sacred usage (as vessels used in church are called holy because set aside for sacred uses). For he was firm in good works by his patience and steadfastness, clean in mind because of his purity, dipped in blood by his contemplation of the Passion of our Lord, and set aside for sacred usage by his exposition and interpretation of Holy Scripture. He is called a grove after the grove in which he lived for some time [as a hermit], and a law because of the rule and discipline that he taught his monks, or because he set forth and explained the Holy Law." Next he gave a mystical sense to Jerome's name. *Hierony-mus* can also mean a sight or vision of beauty (*visio pulchritudinis*; cautiously, he offered no etymological evidence for this), a derivation that encouraged him to distinguish spiritual, moral, intellectual, supersubstantial, and divine beauty and to attribute each of these five beauties to Jerome. Last, *Hieronymus* means "judge of words"; for Jerome himself used words carefully, while at the same time approving the true words of others, confuting their erroneous words and explaining doubtful locutions, an oblique tribute to the philologist and man of letters.[11]

The most persistent error in the early lives is a disordered chronology. The confusion originated in the *Chronicle* of Marcellinus Comes: "Our Jerome," he wrote, "mastered Greek and Latin literature in Rome, and also was ordained a priest there. Later the young man went to Bethlehem, where he decided to remain, like a prudent animal, beside our Lord's crib."[12] The authors of *Hieronymus noster* and *Plerosque nimirum* adopted Marcellinus's chronological framework the more confidently because they too misunderstood Jerome's statement that he had "put on the robe of Christ" in Rome to mean that he had been ordained there, neglecting to notice his explicit statement elsewhere that he had been ordained in Antioch by Bishop Paulinus, a lapse caused by their ignorance of the way early Christians were baptized—stripped almost naked, immersed wholly or partially in water, then reclothed in a white garment, the *vestimenta candida* that symbolized their rebirth in Christ.[13] Later authors had no reason to distrust the earlier accounts: they attached little importance to chronology for its own sake; none of the purposes for which they wrote and for which their readers valued their narratives demanded chronological nicety; while the obstacles to constructing a more accurate chronology were formidable—the data were scattered throughout Jerome's letters and prefaces, and although manuscripts of his works were widely diffused in the Middle Ages, few libraries possessed all, or even most, of them. Until the sixteenth century, everyone agreed that Jerome had spent the first documented period of his life in Rome, where he was educated and became a priest, and that he then went to the East and remained there until his death.

Telescoping into a single period Jerome's student years in Rome (c. 357–c. 367) and his later years of service there under Pope Damasus (382–385) caused difficulties. Was he a boy in Rome, or an adolescent, or a young man? Was he ordained at twenty, at twenty-nine, or at thirty-nine? Where had he been and what had he been doing in the twenty, or

25

twenty-nine, or thirty-nine years before his Roman ordination? Who was pope: Damasus (366–384), a supposition supported by the texts, or Liberius (352–366), which seemed to make better sense chronologically? Jerome's own well-known statement that he spent three years in Rome (he was referring only to his second period in the city)[14] made matters worse by forcing his biographers to crowd within those three short years his grammatical and rhetorical education, Ciceronian dream, and ordination; the crystallization of his monastic vocation; revision of the New Testament for Pope Damasus; his early association with Paula and Eustochium and their friends; and his efforts to reform the Roman clergy.

For the much longer second period of Jerome's life, his biographers constructed a simplified scheme. He was still a young man when he left Rome for the East. He went first to Constantinople, where he was the "docile pupil" of Gregory Nazianzen; next to Syria where he met Evagrius; four years of penitence in the desert followed; finally, he settled in Bethlehem. With the permission of the bishop of Jerusalem, mistakenly identified as Cyril instead of as his less-familiar successor John (Cyril had died in March 386 before the historical Jerome arrived in Bethlehem), he founded a monastery; and there for the next fifty-six years and six months or until his death at eighty-eight (or at other ages ranging from eighty-eight and six months to ninety-nine) he translated the Old Testament, wrote commentaries, and defended the orthodox faith against heretics.

The same chronology and emphasis are reflected in two Carolingian pictorial cycles, frontispieces from the First Bible of Charles the Bald, copied about 845 at the monastery of St. Martin of Tours, and the Bible of San Paolo fuori le mura in Rome (c. 868, possibly from Rheims). The ultimate pictorial source of both bibles was probably an illustrated bible produced in Italy in the fifth century. In the upper register of the Jerome frontispiece in the Bible from St. Martin of Tours (fig. 9), (a) Jerome, wearing Carolingian vestments, a long tunic, handsome dalmatic, chasuble and stole, and carrying a crozier, leaves Rome (personified by the female figure standing in the walled city behind him) and embarks for the East; (b) in Jerusalem he gives coins to his Hebrew teacher. In the middle register, (a) he interprets scripture for Paula and Eustochium and their nuns in Bethlehem; (b) a fellow priest (perhaps his disciple Eusebius of Cremona) takes down Jerome's words, while behind him two monks begin to multiply the text, one reading from the archetype, the other taking his dictation. In the bottom register, Jerome distributes copies of

Fig. 9. School of Tours, *The Jerome Frontispiece from the First Bible of Charles the Bald*, c. 845.

the Latin Bible to monks who return with them to their own monasteries. The San Paolo Bible contains an additional scene in which Jerome disputes with two monks whom the caption identifies as Pelagian heretics.[15]

Within this chronological frame, the narrative gradually acquired an alien encrustation, like an amphora on the bed of the Mediterranean. About Jerome's Roman education we learn not only that he studied grammar with Donatus but also that he studied rhetoric with the orator Victorinus, a detail suggested by a misreading of Jerome's preface to his *Commentary on Galatians* and confirmed by the conviction that if the best teacher were available, Jerome was sure to have been his pupil.[16]

Why Jerome had been forced to leave Rome despite the fact that everyone considered him worthy of the papacy was a problem of a different order and one that long puzzled his admirers. Jerome himself had said only that "certain persons" had accused him of every sort of crime.[17] The author of *Hieronymus noster* plausibly identified these enemies as gluttonous clergy who, bent on revenging themselves for Jerome's criticism of their vices, laid a trap for him (*insidias paraverunt*).[18] He did not specify what the trap was. The author of *Plerosque nimirum* offered a different explanation. He knew from the *Liber pontificalis* that the emperor Constantius had been an Arian; so he surmised that Jerome left the "splendid and most sacred city of Peter" because the Roman people were tainted with the emperor's heresy. He did not mention the trap.[19] By the middle of the twelfth century, Johannes Beleth, a pupil of Gilbert de la Porrée and the author of liturgical works, was able to identify the *insidiae* casually, in passing, as "a woman's garment."[20] Nicolò Maniacoria identified Jerome's enemies as pseudopriests, monks, and heretics and justified his departure for the east by citing Matthew 10:23: "But when they persecute you in this city, flee ye into another."[21] Naming Beleth as his authority and using Maniacoria without naming him, Jacopo da Varazze told the ludicrous story in full. Certain Roman pseudopriests and monks, furious at Jerome for attacking their lasciviousness, "placed near his bed a woman's garment. The saint, getting up in the dark to go to matins, reached out and put it on, mistaking it for his own; and thus scandalously appareled he made his way to church. His enemies played this trick on him so that the people would think he had spent the night with a woman"[22] (fig. 10).

Readers were curious about the circumstances of Jerome's death. In the early fourteenth century, forged letters allegedly written by St.

Fig. 10. Jean de Limbourg, *St. Jerome Tricked into Wearing Female Dress to Matins,* 1408–1409. On the right, a malicious monk places a woman's garment beside the sleeping saint. On the left, Jerome enters the choir in woman's dress.

Fig. 11.   Francesco d'Antonio, *(left) St. Jerome's Vision of the Trinity; (right) St. Jerome, during His Last Illness, Lifts Himself Up in Bed by a Cord Suspended from the Ceiling,* c. 1430. A predella panel from the Rinieri Altarpiece (see fig. 29).

Augustine, St. Cyril of Jerusalem, and Eusebius of Cremona would satisfy copiously this thirst for detail. In the meantime, the author of *Hieronymus noster* provided a touching glimpse of Jerome during his last illness: "He was so weak at the end that he grasped a rope suspended from a beam in the ceiling and used it to lift himself up in bed in order to participate as much as he could in the monastic office" (fig. 11). Maniacoria supplied the hour of his death: sunset.[23]

Other elaborations of the record reflect less the wish to fill gaps or add verisimilitude by concrete imaginary detail than the need to meet the community's rising expectations about the qualities, behavior, character, and rank of so venerated and holy a person. By the early seventh century Jerome was a saint; by the middle of the eighth, a father and doctor of the church; in the ninth century he acquired a miracle; in the twelfth he became a cardinal.

The word "saint" took on a Christian meaning only gradually. Among the pagans it had described divine and human powers, moral perfection, fidelity to family duties, or piety toward the gods. Christians of the first centuries called bishops, priests, and monks *hagioi* or *sancti*, by which they meant persons belonging to God or consecrated to his service.[24] The word received a more technical meaning from its association with the cult of martyrs. Martyrs were the heroes of the early church. Because their agonies were a second baptism, a baptism of blood that

removed even the hint of sin, God conferred on them the same blessing he had conferred on the patriarchs and the apostles: admission without delay to his presence and the contemplation of his glory. The church also honored spiritual martyrs, those who "witnessed" or "confessed" the faith, not by their deaths, but by rigorous observance of the commandments and the exercise of heroic virtue.[25] In the fourth century, Christian communities began to offer spiritual martyrs or "confessors" the same homage they offered those who had died for the faith: a public cult sanctioned by custom, tradition, and ecclesiastical authority. They commemorated the anniversary of their death or burial (depositio), the day, that is, when, reborn, they entered into glory and became immortal. They celebrated them in the liturgy, listened to panegyrics on their deeds and virtues, recalled their miracles, honored their relics, and raised shrines and altars over their tombs. They prayed to them for protection and intercession. They called them saints, and in time the honorific title came regularly to precede their names. Finally, in a decisive narrowing of the meaning, the noun sanctus came to denote martyrs and confessors only, while at the same time the idea of sanctity itself became indissolubly linked to the practice of public liturgical commemoration. Henceforth, "saint" and "cult figure" were to be rigorously synonymous.[26]

To ask, therefore, when Jerome began to be venerated as a saint is to ask when he became the object of a public cult recognized by the church.

The answer is simple in principle: when the authors of martyrologies included his name in their lists.

A martyrology is a catalogue that lists martyrs and confessors in the order of their anniversaries. The first important Latin martyrology appeared in northern Italy toward the middle of the fifth century. The original compiler (or possibly a later editor) prefaced it with an apocryphal exchange of letters between Jerome and bishops Chromatius of Aquileia and Heliodrous of Atinum (historical correspondents of Jerome), falsely claiming Jerome as author of the work. Whether Pseudo-Jerome was innocent enough or impudent enough to include the historical Jerome in the original list of saints is uncertain. The archetype of the oldest surviving manuscripts of the "Martyrology of St. Jerome" (which date from the early eighth century) represents a revised text prepared and copied in Gaul around A.D. 600. The archetype and its numerous progeny do list Jerome: "30 September: In the territory of Palestine, in the hill town of Bethlehem, was buried the presbyter Jerome."[27] By at least the beginning of the seventh century, then, Jerome was venerated as a saint. The martyrologies of the eighth and ninth centuries—those of Bede, Florus of Lyons, Rhabanus Maurus of Fulda, Wandelbert of Prüm, Ado of Vienne, and Usuard—confirm his cult and summarize his titles to veneration: he was *sanctissimus,* most learned (*eruditissimus*), skilled in every branch of letters (*omnium studia litterarum adeptus*), an exemplary monk, translator of the divine books from Hebrew into Latin, the commentator who explained the allegorical meaning of the prophets, hammer of heretics, and a holy man whose manner of life was perfect and pleasing to God.[28]

Jerome was acquiring other titles as well. Writing to Pope Gregory the Great at the end of the sixth century, Bishop Licinianus of Cartagena called certain earlier Christian writers remarkable for their breadth of learning, knowledge of Scripture, theological insight, and holiness of life "fathers," "doctors," and "defenders of the church": *eximie doctrine sancti antiqui patres, doctores defensoresque ecclesie.*[29] Early lists of the doctors named Augustine, Hilary of Poitiers, Cyprian, Ambrose, Jerome, Gregory Nazianzen, and Pope Gregory himself; but by the end of the eighth century four Latin fathers had begun clearly to emerge as preeminent: Gregory, Ambrose, Augustine, and Jerome. By the eleventh century, medieval authors regularly associated these four with the four major prophets, the four evangelists, and the four cardinal virtues. They were said to be learned in all things divine and human, a classical definition of wisdom. Their eloquence was likened to the four rivers of Paradise. They were "true lights of the world," "athletes of God," "princes of the Christian faith," "mouths of the Lord" transmitting to posterity the "word of truth."[30] Their double title of father and doctor was confirmed by Pope Boniface VIII in a decretal of 20 September 1295 which instructed the faithful to celebrate these four confessor saints with the same solemnity previously accorded the patriarchs and apostles, for "their flowing discourse, fed by streams of heavenly grace, solves scriptural puzzles, unties knots, explains obscurities, and resolves doubts. Like precious stones, their beautiful and profound works ornament the spacious structure of the church, which shines forth the more gloriously as it is raised high by their eloquence."[31]

It was as a father and doctor of the church that artists before 1300 almost always represented Jerome. His attributes, like those of other doctors, were a book, symbolizing his work as translator, exegete, and teacher; a pen (the writer); a model of a church (the spiritual edifice he illumined by his teaching, or the monastery he had founded in Bethlehem, or, in later centuries a convent of one of the congregations that bore his name). Like the evangelists, he was typically shown seated on a chair or throne, made more comfortable by a cushion, his feet on a stool, reading from a book propped on a lectern, writing, dictating to a scribe or *notarius,* handing out copies of his translation of the Bible, or instructing one or two small figures, monks or clerics, who sit below him. In the oldest miniature painting of him to have come down to us (see fig. 1), he sits on a wine-red throne framed by an arcade. The miniaturist identifies him by name, *Beatus Hieronimus presbyter,* and pictures him as an old man with a short white beard, his bald head circled by a halo. He wears a Byzantine tunic and a short mantle and holds a wax tablet in his left hand and a stylus in his right.[32] The painter of a marginally later miniature (from a book copied at Salzburg) shows the same hieratic figure standing and labels him *Sanctus Hieronimus* (fig. 12). He wears a toga and holds a closed book in his left hand and raises his right in blessing. But whereas he is represented as bearded and bald in the manuscript from Corbie, the painter of the Salzburg miniature shows him as a beardless youth with a good head of hair.[33] The two traditions, young and old, bearded or clean shaven, will be observable in future representations of the saint. An author-portrait by Liuthard, principal painter at the court school of Charles the Bald (d. 869), in a Psalter executed for the king's personal use, was modeled like the others on representations of the evangelists and is a

Fig. 12.   School of Salzburg, *St. Jerome*, c. 800

wholly typical (and influential) image (see fig. 7). It shows a haloed, beardless, and tonsured Jerome, "nobilis interpres," at work translating the Psalms. Richly dressed, seated on a cushioned throne under a canopied arcade, he grasps with his left hand the lectern on which his open book is lying and with his right dips his pen into an inkpot.[34] Later artists often show Jerome as a monk. Apart from that change, there were to be no iconographical innovations of consequence before the fourteenth century.

Medieval Christians automatically ranked the four doctors and fathers of the church. Gregory was first in dignity because he had been pope. The two bishops, Ambrose and Augustine, came next. Jerome, a simple monk and priest, came last. But when the emergence of the cardinalate created an ecclesiastical dignity between those of bishop and pope, symmetry and appropriateness suggested the desirability of promoting Jerome to the new rank. The author of *Plerosque nimirum* had called Jerome a "cardinal priest." By the twelfth century anachronistic piety assigned him two *tituli*: Maniacoria named him cardinal priest with the title of S. Anastasia; others assigned him S. Lorenzo in Damaso (fig. 13).[35]

Jerome's promotion paralleled the inflation in meaning of the word "cardinal" itself. The phrase "cardinal priest" occurs in a letter of Pope Pelagius I (555–560) and several times in the letters of Gregory the Great. They used it in a sense entirely different from what it came to mean later: to denote a priest authorized to perform liturgical functions in a parish or church other than the one in which he had been originally ordained. The word was not applied to members of the Roman clergy before the second half of the eighth century. Its meaning remained the same. The senior priests of the Roman *tituli*, or quasi parishes of the city, and the bishops of seven suffragan sees began then to be called cardinal priests and cardinal bishops because they took turns conducting weekly services in the city's four great basilicas, St. Peter's, S. Paolo fuori le mura, S. Maria Maggiore, and the Lateran, while remaining tied to the churches of their original ordination.[36] This is what the author of *Plerosque nimirum* meant when he called Jerome a cardinal priest.

Etymology, however, suggested different and broader meanings for *cardinalis*. A *cardo* is a hinge. Ancient astronomers spoke of cardinal points, astrologers of cardinal signs, geographers of the cardinal winds, suggesting by the adjective that these were in some sense nature's hinges. In a more figurative sense, *cardo* and *cardinalis* meant chief, of special significance, essential, fundamental, that on which all else hinges or

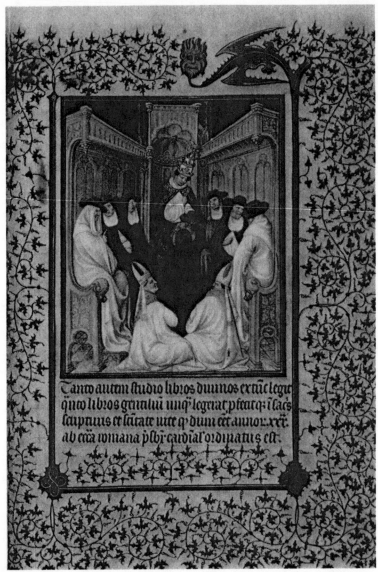

Fig. 13. The Limbourg brothers, *St. Jerome Ordained a Cardinal*, 1408–1409. Two of the cardinals wear red *cappas*, the others are in blue or white. Jerome wears a coarse brown monastic habit.

depends. As the actual political and jurisdictional powers of the occupants of the Roman *tituli* vastly expanded during the great reform movement of the eleventh century, these connotations of status, exalted rank, and dignity gradually usurped the original pastoral and liturgical meaning of the word. The cardinals were now senators of the church (*spirituales ecclesiae universalis senatores*). "Like an immovable hinge which sends the door back and forth," wrote Leo IX (1048–1054) to the patriarch of Constantinople, "Peter and his successors have sovereign judgment over the entire church. . . . Therefore his clerics are named cardinals, for they belong more closely to the hinge by which everything else is moved." Deusdedit, cardinal of S. Pietro in Vincoli, went a step further. The cardinals, he wrote in 1087, are themselves "hinges" who rule and guide God's people.[37]

The anachronism of making Jerome a member of a Sacred College that had taken institutional shape in Rome only at the end of the eleventh century gave him a place in the hierarchy and government of the church commensurate with his sanctity and learning: he became a "spiritual senator," a papal elector and prince of the church, below only the pope in rank and dignity. This is what Maniacoria had in mind when he called him cardinal priest of S. Anastasia.

So ingrained became the habit of thinking of Jerome as a cardinal in the meaning (and the dress) that the office carried in later centuries, that the red hat, the *galerus ruber* prescribed for cardinals by Pope Innocent IV at the Council of Lyons in 1245, became after the middle of the fourteenth century one of Jerome's two most familiar attributes in the visual arts. His second attribute was a lion, the subject of his earliest, and for many centuries his only, miracle.

"Late one afternoon, when blessed Jerome sat reading and explaining scripture to his brother monks, as is customary in monasteries, a huge lion limped into the courtyard on three legs, holding the fourth up in the air. Some of the brothers, overcome by human frailty, fled in terror; but St. Jerome went boldly to meet him, as though the lion were his guest. The lion, because it could not speak, silently held out its wounded paw to the holy man. Jerome called the brothers back and asked them to wash the lion's foot and find out why he limped. When they examined the paw, they found thorns embedded in it. Once the wound was cared for and the lion fed, he quickly recovered. Not only that: he laid aside his brutish wildness and from then on remained tamely with the monks, a tranquil domesticated animal" (fig. 14).[38]

Fig. 14.   Benozzo Gozzoli, *St. Jerome Extracts a Thorn from the Lion's Paw*, 1452. One scene of a fresco cycle "in honor of glorious Jerome."

Plerosque nimirum is the earliest surviving text in which Jerome is the hero of this legendary anecdote; the tale itself, both in its details and in its general structure, is much older. It appears complete as one of Aesop's fables, "The Lion and the Shepherd,"[39] and in the more familiar story of Androclus and the lion. Androclus, a runaway slave, removed a sharp root from a lion's paw. The lion was so grateful that for three years he allowed his benefactor to share his lair in the Libyan desert and gave him half the prey he brought back from the hunt. (The lion ate his meat raw; Androclus cooked his on a rock heated by the desert sun.) Eventually, man and lion were separately captured. The slave was thrown to the wild beasts in the circus; the lion, one of the beasts, recognized Androclus and joyfully licked his hand and protected him from the other animals.[40]

The story was Christianized in the Greek East. Its earliest surviving occurrence in a Christian context is as an incident in Cyril of Scythopolis's mid-sixth-century life of St. Sabas of Palestine (439–532), a monk and hermit venerated throughout the Greek world and also in Italy—at Naples, Monte Cassino, and Rome, where early in the seventh century monks from St. Sabas's own monastery in the Judaean hills settled on the Little Aventine in a house that may have belonged to Gregory the Great's mother. One day, near the sacred river Jordan, St. Sabas met a huge lion limping in pain. The lion showed him his paw. Sabas sat down, examined the paw, and pulled out a thorn embedded in it. During all the days of Lent, the lion followed the old man like a faithful slave.[41]

The same incident occurs in the legend of another Palestinian ascetic, St. Gerasimus. Gerasimus had arrived in Jerusalem about 451; he lived as a hermit in the rocky desert near the Dead Sea and later founded a laura, a community of anchorites who lived in separate cells under the rule of a superior, near the Jordan. Walking one day along the river bank, he too met a lion with a thorn in its paw. The lion offered its paw; the saint sat down, extracted the thorn, drained the wound of pus, and bandaged the foot. The tamed lion, who henceforth ate only bread and boiled vegetables, remained with him as his "loving disciple" until the saint's death.[42]

Taming a lion is a metaphor for taming the bestial in man, for the triumph of law over unregimented nature, of morality over passion and instinct, of civilization over savagery. In a Christian perspective, it represents the victory of love, holiness, and grace over the sinfulness of unredeemed and fallen nature. The thorn is sin, whether in the paw of the lion or in the crown that bloodied the head of Christ; the holy man who tames a lion by removing the thorn from its paw possesses divine powers and is a type of Christ, who conquers sin and death.[43]

The removal of the thorn signifies more particularly the washing away of original sin in baptism. The compiler of the *Gesta Romanorum,* a collection of moralizing tales put together toward the end of the thirteenth century, preserves a version of the story in which the hero is a knight who has become an outlaw in the forest. Some years after the knight had extracted a thorn from a lion's infected paw, the king captured them both, kept the lion in a pit without food for a week, then threw the knight in with him. The lion fawned on his benefactor and licked his hands. The astonished king pardoned the knight and sent the lion back to the forest. The moral is this: "The knight is the worldly man who daily strives to acquire as many of the world's goods as he can. The limping lion is the whole human race, which limps because of the sin of our first parents; the thorn is original sin drawn out by baptism and cured by the ointment of good works."[44]

The connection of lions with Christian baptism (lions were carved on early medieval baptismal fonts)[45] is attested as early as the apocryphal *Acts of Paul* (second century). On his way from Smyrna to Ephesus, St. Paul paused near a river to pray. A great and terrible lion, "large as a horse," approached him and lay down at his feet. "I [St. Paul is speaking] was filled with the Spirit (and) looked upon him, (and) said to him: 'Lion, what wilt thou?' But he said: 'I wish to be baptized.' I glorified God, who had given speech to the beast and salvation to his servant. . . . When I had prayed thus, I took [the lion] by his mane (and) in the name of Jesus Christ immersed him three times. But when he came up out of the water he shook his mane and said to me: 'Grace be with thee!' And I said to him: 'And likewise with thee.' The lion ran off to the country rejoicing (for this was revealed to me in my heart). A lioness met him, and he did not yield himself to her but . . . ran off."[46] The next day Paul delivered a sermon in Ephesus in which he described his conversion and the baptism of the lion. He was arrested and at the demand of the people thrown to the beasts. Among the animals in the amphitheater was the lion Paul had baptized. "Borne along by faith Paul said: 'Lion, was it thou whom I baptized? And the lion in answer said to Paul: 'Yes,'" and did not harm him but lay down against his legs, docile as a lamb. Soon after a violent hailstorm fell from heaven, dispersed the crowd in the circus, tore off the proconsul's ear, but did not touch Paul or the lion. They took leave of one another and each went safely away.[47]

The story of Jerome and the lion has other episodes. Jerome assigned the lion the job of guarding the ass used by the monks to bring firewood from a nearby forest. One day the lion fell asleep while the ass grazed in the pasture. Merchants, riding past on camelback, on their way to Egypt to buy oil, seeing the ass unguarded, stole it. The monks assumed that the lion had eaten the ass, and Jerome ordered him to take on the ass's work, a burden he bore with patient fortitude. Months later, "alerted from on high," the lion spotted the caravan on its return trip. He fell on it with fierce roars and forced merchants, camels, and ass to the gates of the monastery. "*Ecce pastorem nostrum,* Behold our shepherd," said the penitent monks, and returned the lion to favor. The merchants begged Jerome's forgiveness, gave him half of their oil for the lamps of the church and the use of the brothers, and promised to furnish them and their successors forever with a generous yearly measure of olive oil[48] (fig. 15).

Combining the motif of guardianship with those of gratitude for benefits received, taming the rude and savage, turning a lecherous carnivore into a chaste vegetarian, and curing a lapsed humanity gives the story a monastic cast. It was commonly believed that lions sleep with their eyes open,[49] a characteristic that preeminently fitted them to be guardians of sacred precincts and sacred objects. A pair of golden lions guarded the entrance to Alexander's burial chamber. Lions were carved on palace gates, in the courtyards of temples, on church doors and bishops' thrones. They ornament the covers of bibles.[50] In the same fashion, Jerome's lion guarded the monastery's ass—inefficiently, to be sure. But by patiently suffering adversity, obeying his superior, and bending his proud neck to a regular discipline of work and service, he proved himself a model of the monastic virtues. He learned humility, became weak in order to be truly strong, exchanged the freedom of the world for servitude to Christ, and abandoned the law of nature and submitted to the law of grace. When the monks saluted him after his trial as a "good shepherd," they paid homage not only to the good monk but to an ideal of the guardian abbot as well. Indeed, turns of phrase recurring regularly in the lives suggest that the lion came to signify Jerome's own monastic vocation and his role as founder and custodian of a monastic community. For when the biographers mention Jerome's decision to settle permanently in Bethlehem as a monk, they call him, following Marcellinus Comes, a *prudens animal;* and when the reborn lion decides to remain in the monastery, they call him a *domesticum et tranquillum animal*—man and beast have each tamed their animal nature in and for the Lord's service.[51]

Fig. 15. Jean de Limbourg, *Episodes from the Legend of the Lion*, 1408–1409. *In the middle distance*, the lion sleeps while the ass grazes; *above left*, the lion performs the stolen ass's work; *below*, the lion has found the missing ass and forces the thieving merchants to the door of the monastery.

How, when, where, and by whom the miracle of the lion was assigned to St. Jerome is uncertain. Several associations of motif and idea made it appropriate for him to have one. He had defended the purity of the faith against heretics with lion-hearted courage and leonine roars.[52] His qualities as a monk and cleric, as a careful and perfect man (*vir cautelosus et perfectus*), as one called to rule and govern others by doctrine and example, reflected other characteristics commonly attributed to lions: virtue, firmness, love of humanity, and sagacity. Pierre Bersuire, in his *Reductorium morale*, alleged that lions fear fire and confuse pursuers by wiping out their footprints with their tails; the perfect man fears the fires of hell and foils pursuing demons by wiping out his sins in confession.[53] Jerome had been a hermit in the desert, and hermit saints, like Orpheus,[54] typically tamed the wild beasts who were their companions in the wilderness. Lions dug the sandy graves of St. Anthony, St. Mary the Egyptian, and the hermit Paul of Thebes (Jerome himself described the scene in his life of Paul).[55] St. Mammas, a Cappadocian shepherd, preached the Gospel to lions and made cheese from their milk, which he gave to imprisoned coreligionists. The local magistrate ordered him smeared with honey and bound to a tree swarming with ants. A lion freed him, licked the honey from his limbs, and tried to persuade him to come away and live with him in the forest.[56] When St. Zosimus of Anazarbus in Cilicia refused to sacrifice to the gods, his tormentors suspended him upside down with a rock tied around his neck. A friendly lion appeared and held up the rock; threatened with death, the lion spoke in a human voice and said that he rejoiced to shed his blood for Christ.[57]

The author of *Plerosque nimirum* supplies scraps of more direct evidence. He reports that the miracle took place in Jerome's monastery in Bethlehem; that accounts of it, passed down from generation to generation, were current "among the inhabitants of that place"; and that the story was brought back to the West by pilgrims to the Holy Land. More important, he notes that the story is similar to incidents reported in the lives of other "ancient fathers."[58] One of those ancient fathers was certainly St. Gerasimus; and it is the uniquely close correspondence of the later episodes of their two stories—and the absence of these episodes in the other tales about lions and humans which have come down to us[59]—that points to the immediate source of Jerome's miracle. For Gerasimus's laura also owned an ass—the monks used it to transport their drinking water from the Jordan, a mile away. Gerasimus too assigned his lion the task of guarding the ass while it pastured on the river bank. One day the inattentive lion allowed the ass to wander off, and a camel driver from Arabia stole it. Gerasimus thought the lion had eaten the ass. "Since you ate the ass," he told him, "you shall do his work." From then on the obedient lion patiently carried water from the Jordan in four amphoras. Sometime later, the lion spotted the camel driver (now on his way to sell wheat in Jerusalem) as the caravan, led by the ass, was crossing the Jordan. He seized the ass's halter and dragged him and three camels to the monastery. Gerasimus named the lion "Jordan" and made him his inseparable companion.[60]

The story of St. Gerasimus and the lion is one of several hundred tales about famous ascetics collected by yet another Palestinian hermit: Johannes Moschus.[61] Moschus was born in Damascus about 550, became a monk in the monastery of St. Theodosius near Jerusalem, then lived for many years as an anchorite in the Judean desert and in the so-called New Laura founded by St. Sabas. He spent his later life visiting monasteries and hermitages. When the Persians captured Jerusalem in 614, he fled to Rome, followed soon by a host of coreligionists driven out by the Muslim conquest of the East. The refugees brought with them Eastern relics, customs, feasts, devotions, legends, and iconographical motifs: the heads of St. Anastasius and St. George; from Bethlehem, Jesus' crib, installed in S. Maria Maggiore; and three feasts of the Virgin—her Nativity, Annunciation, and Dormition—imported at the end of the seventh century by the Syrian pope Sergius I (between 678 and 741, eleven of the thirteen popes were of Syrian or Greek descent).[62] The story of Gerasimus and the lion arrived in Rome in the same way and at the same time, one of the many miraculous incidents and sayings Moschus had collected while traveling among the monastic communities of his day. He made a book of them in Rome and called it the *Spiritual Meadow*.

It is unlikely that the author of *Plerosque nimirum* had read the *Spiritual Meadow*: very probably he knew no Greek, and the relevant chapter of the work was not translated into Latin until the fifteenth century.[63] Nor is it likely that it was he who transferred the story of the lion from Gerasimus to Jerome: he tells us that his account is condensed, presumably therefore from a version, whether written or oral, not his own. What more probably happened is that the similarity of "Gerasimus" to "Geronimus," the late Latin form of Jerome's name,[64] had earlier triggered the common hagiographic tendency (with its love of puns, wordplay, and fanciful etymology) of assigning the same incidents to saints with similar names. I conjecture—and it is no more than conjecture—that Greek monks in Rome (like those of S. Saba, a very plausible house for Moschus to have visited) preserved a copy of the *Spiritual Meadow*; that its contents gradually became known to a wider circle; that a Latin-speaking cleric, an admirer of St. Jerome at home in the environment of Greek monasticism in Rome, made St. Geronimus the hero of a story he had heard about St. Gerasimus; and that the author of *Plerosque nimirum*, attracted by a story at once so picturesque, so apparently appropriate, and so resonant in suggestion and meaning, and under the impression that its source was pilgrims who had been told it in Bethlehem, included it in his life of a favorite saint otherwise bereft of miracle.

As the faithful more widely admired the polyglot translator, biblical scholar, and polemicist and venerated the saint, ascetic, and miraculous lion-tamer, a growing number of spurious works became attached to his name, shaping and distorting in yet another way the conception people had of him. Some of these were authentic letters and treatises of minor contemporaries like Eutropius (c. 400), Gregory of Elvira (died after 392), or Niceta of Remesiana (died after 414), assigned to Jerome for the often-observed reason that the ignorant tend to attribute works of unfamiliar authors to better-known ones. Others were works by authors of dubious orthodoxy—homilies of Origen or treatises by Pelagius, the butt of Jerome's last savage polemic—for which their defenders were seeking the shelter of respectable patronage. Still others were works as well known as Rufinus's *Historia monachorum*, Athanasius's *Life of Anthony*, or the *Life of St. Macharius* by Palladius, given to Jerome for no better reason than that he too had been a desert hermit and wrote saints' lives. Many, though, were deliberate forgeries and confirm Cassiodorus's observation that anyone who wants to pass off a fake assigns to it the authority of a glorious name.[65] They range in date from the fifth to the fourteenth century and are extremely heterogeneous: prologues and prefaces to the Latin Bible, scriptural commentaries, sermons and orations, liturgical and ecclesiological works, baptismal rites and creeds, monastic rules, philosophical and theological treatises, saints' lives, translations from the Greek, works by authors claiming a knowledge of Hebrew, letters, and poems. Their titles and contents are equally varied: on the seven gifts of the Holy Spirit, the necessity of fleeing women, honoring one's parents; against the Jews; on the Incarnation and resurrection, fasting and virginity, penitence, musical instruments, the chains of St. Peter, the ten temptations of the people of Israel in the desert, and the secret meaning of the letters of the Hebrew alphabet; a mirror of sins, verses in praise of Vergil—and very many more.[66]

The most popular and influential of these texts contributed important elements to the Hieronymite legend. Writing to Eustochium, the historical Jerome reported that in the desert when he fixed his eyes on heaven he "seemed to find himself among the angelic hosts";[67] an unidentified author pretending to be Jerome claimed to have been vouchsafed a vision of the Trinity (see figs. 8 and 11).[68] The historical Jerome was devoted to Mary and argued the case for her perpetual virginity (his book is the foundation stone of Western Mariology); a Carolingian Pseudo-Jerome claimed to have translated from the Hebrew a secret Gospel of Matthew about the Blessed Virgin's birth and her life before the Annunciation,[69] while another writer, posing as Jerome but identified by modern scholars as Paschasius Radbertus, abbot of Corbie (d. 865), told the same story more briefly, omitting offensive details found in the earlier version (the story of Joseph's first marriage, for example).[70] The two works were to exert an immense influence on later literature and art. Paschasius Radbertus (again under the name of St. Jerome) also taught the corporeal assumption of Mary in a letter magnificently exalting her virtues, dignity, and glory. Passages from it were later used to associate Jerome with the doctrine of Mary's Immaculate Conception as well.[71] The historical Jerome translated the Rule of Pachomius and organized the liturgical routine of his monastery in Bethlehem (though no description of this routine has come down to us). An early falsifier attributed the first lectionary to Jerome (lectionaries list the verses from the prophets, gospels, and epistles to be read at Mass on Sundays and feast days throughout the year) and claimed that Jerome had instituted the monastic practice both of reciting all 150 psalms each week (allotting psalms to each day and to each of the canonical hours) and of ending the recital of a psalm with the doxology: *Gloria patri et filio et spiritui sancto, sicut erat in principio et nunc et semper in saecula saeculorum. Amen.*[72] The historical Jerome meditated often on the fragility of human life: "Think every day that you are about to die," he wrote the recently widowed Roman aristocrat Furia.[73] An apocalyptic Pseudo-Jerome of the tenth century made meditation on death more awesome by imagining fifteen signs or tokens that will herald the end of the world and the Last Judgment.[74]

Yet in spite of the facile pens of the fakers and the fancy of hagiographers, in spite of anachronism, a disordered chronology, and errors of biographical fact, the image of Jerome which literate Europeans shared toward the end of the thirteenth century was by and large a sober one. His authentic works were very widely diffused among the learned.[75] The threefold character of his achievement—as a scholar and man of letters, as a doctor of the church, teacher, and expounder of holy Scripture, and as an ascetic monk—was clearly recognized and given a balanced respect. Alcuin had called him *maximus doctor*, "greatest of teachers" and defender of the Catholic faith.[76] Hincmar, archbishop of Rheims, said that he had penetrated "to the marrow and very vitals of sacred scripture."[77] John of Salisbury appreciated his literary quality and introduced into his own writings elegant expressions that he had taken directly from the letters.[78] And although the scholastics of the thirteenth century appreciated him less than had the scholars of the Carolingian age or the twelfth-century Renaissance (he was neither a philosopher nor a systematic theologian, while they were little interested in the Roman tradition of *eloquentia*, valued logic more highly than grammar and rhetoric, neglected the classics, and were unpersuaded of the need to learn Greek or Hebrew), they nevertheless considered his translations as good as the originals, used his commentaries (he was now the uncontested authority on the literal or historical sense of Scripture, as Gregory was on the moral, Ambrose on the allegorical, and Augustine on the anagogical), and quoted as authoritative the doctrinal statements scattered through his polemical works and letters. In the *Summa theologiae*, St. Thomas Aquinas used the biblical commentaries, many of the letters, *Adversus Jovinianum*, *Contra Vigilantium*, and *Adversus Helvidium*. Phrases like "sicut beatus Hieronymus dicit" or "beato Hieronymo testante" flowed easily from every scholar's pen; and from the sixth through the thirteenth century, his admirers regularly cited Augustine's and Cassian's flattering comparison of him to a divine lamp lighting the whole world.[79]

His medieval admirers were not without critical sense. The learned Guigue du Châtel, fifth prior of the Grande-Chartreuse (1083–1137), prepared an edition of Jerome's letters and treatises. He prefaced it with a letter explaining why he had omitted several texts traditionally accepted as genuine. On the authority of Augustine, he assigned one to Pelagius and implied, correctly, that several others were by Pelagius as well. He noted discrepancies of style and doctrine. He rejected as spurious a dialogue on the origin of souls put into the mouths of Augustine and Jerome on the ground that in life the two doctors had never met.[80] Even Jacopo da Varazze, generally so reluctant to sacrifice edification to evidence, corrected enthusiasts by pointing out that Jerome himself had said that he was not a virgin.[81]

Nor were they miracle mongers. The contrast with St. Ambrose is instructive. When Ambrose was in his cradle, the same bees that had already deposited honey in the mouths of Pindar and Plato alighted on his mouth to foretell his future eloquence and the sweetness of his doctrine.[82] He cured the painfully inflamed foot of the notary Nicetus by accidentally stepping on it. He performed another "contact miracle" when he resuscitated a dead child by touching it with his right hand. He expelled demons. As he preached to the people, a newborn baby cried out, "Ambrose bishop," an omen soon confirmed by Ambrose's accession to the see of Milan. Once when saying Mass, he fell asleep on the altar and dreamed that he was participating in the funeral of St. Martin of Tours. He knew in advance the date of his own death.[83] Seven miracles; Jerome had performed only one.

This balanced admiration was to be abandoned in the early fourteenth century. A dramatically charged image of Jerome emerged, a superhuman miracle worker, the object of a magnetic cult, and the focus of a powerful surge of reverence, ascetic spirituality, and superstition. A phrase in Maniacoria's twelfth-century *Vita Hieronymi* adumbrated what was to come. "Who will deny," he asked, "that Jerome was rather an angel than a man?"[84]

3
The Cult

HE Renaissance Jerome emerged first as an ascetic virtuoso and a miracle worker.

Three influential pseudographs by a single author began to circulate early in the fourteenth century. The first is a long letter, purportedly from Jerome's disciple and successor as "abbot" of the Bethlehem monastery, Eusebius of Cremona, to Damasus, bishop of Portus, and Theodosius, a Roman senator. It describes Jerome's last hours and death. The second is a letter from a Pseudo-Augustine to a Pseudo-Cyril of Jerusalem about Jerome's *magnificentiae*, his titles to glory and veneration. The third, Pseudo-Cyril's reply to Pseudo-Augustine, enumerates Jerome's miracles before and after his death.[1] In their original Latin, these forgeries had a prodigious diffusion in manuscript and print. Their success in Tuscan and Sicilian, German, Dutch, French, Spanish, Catalan, Danish, and English dress was hardly less.[2] Pietro Calo da Chioggia incorporated them almost word for word in his *Legendae de sanctis* (before 1340),[3] and they were thoroughly mined by Pietro de' Natali for his notice of Jerome in his *Catalogus sanctorum* (1372),[4] after the *Golden Legend* the collection of abbreviated saints' lives for private reading most widely used before the more critical legendaries of the Counter-Reformation superseded them. So dense a circulation made the apocryphal letters reasonably accessible to anyone who was literate, and since preachers used many of their episodes in sermons, and artists represented them in frescoes, panel paintings, and manuscript illuminations, the letters became familiar as well to some who were not.[5]

Their common purposes were to gratify the wish of the pious for more numerous and more marvelous details about the saint they venerated; to fill gaps in the earlier lives, particularly their lack of information about Jerome's death and miracles; to promote his cult by emphasizing the effectiveness of his intercession and the power of his relics, name, and image; and to raise him to the position of premier Christian saint, inferior to none, superior to most, and equal in all things to John the Baptist and the apostles. Their more general purpose was to glorify Jerome. In antiquity glory had crowned the acts of courage and valor of victorious athletes and soldiers. Jerome is glorious in heaven because in life he was an "athlete of the Christian faith" and a "powerful warrior against heretics." The martyr's crown symbolized the glory of Christian victors in the age of persecution. Jerome's contempt for his body and for the world has won him a similar crown. Glory, said Cicero,[6] is a reward of virtue. Jerome acquired *gloria virtutis* by self-conquest. More important than these is his posthumous glory; because men and women are rewarded according to their works and merits, Jerome is one of the first citizens of the heavenly Jerusalem. Like the Roman *imperator* and the early martyrs, he is *gloriosissimus*.[7] From the early fourteenth century to the end of the sixteenth, *doctor gloriosus* was to be his most common title.

Even before his death Jerome possessed more than human qualities. It was no longer enough that he had been trilingual in Latin, Greek, and Hebrew and able to speak some Aramaic and Syriac; now he was said to command Arabic and the languages and literatures of almost every other people in the world as well as if he had been born and educated in each of them. He had no equal in either the liberal arts or the sacred sciences. What he did not know about human nature, no one has known. He smoothed out all the difficulties of Scripture, allowing us to see the light by his light. He is therefore rightly called "light of the church," "fountain of saving wisdom," "teacher of truth and equity," "keystone, foundation and golden column of the whole church." Like a refulgent sun he still shines in the temple of the Lord, dispersing the darkness of error with the light of his knowledge and learning.[8]

The apocryphal letters paint an even more emphatic portrait of the monk and ascetic. So holy was he that he remained a virgin until his death at ninety-six, traditional exaggeration of both his age and his continence. He drank no wine and ate no meat or fish (indeed, he scarcely allowed even the words "meat" and "fish" to pass his lips) but lived entirely on uncooked fruit, greens, and roots. He wore a hair shirt under rags, slept on the bare ground, whipped himself three times a day until the blood flowed (a detail drawn from the life of St. Dominic), and patiently endured every imaginable abstinence, temptation, and mortification. When his monks undressed him as he lay dying, they found him so thin from fasting, his body so lacerated and misshapen by penitential austerities, that he looked like a leper.[9]

Fig. 16.   Francesco d'Antonio, *The Death of St. Jerome*, c. 1430. Predella panel from the Rinieri Altarpiece (see fig. 29). St. Jerome's *anima*, like a star, is on its way to heaven.

His death was holy. After he had received the last communion, he stretched out on the ground and crossed his hands on his breast. Suddenly a light as bright as the sun shone down from on high. Some of the bystanders saw angels in the light; others heard a voice saying, "Come, beloved, the time is at hand for you to receive the rewards of your labors"; still others only heard Jerome murmur, "Behold, I come to you, dear Jesus; receive the soul that you have ransomed with your blood." The light disappeared, and Jerome's saintly *anima*, like a star resplendent with all the virtues, left his body and went to heaven (fig. 16; see figs. 8, 35, and 36).[10]

So glorious was this hermit saint that he surpassed all the other fathers of the church in holiness. The falsifier makes even St. Augustine acknowledge Jerome's superiority. On the very day and at the very hour of Jerome's death in Bethlehem, Pseudo-Augustine was sitting at his desk in Hippo beginning a letter to him in which he begged for answers to several difficult questions: What is the nature and intensity of the glory enjoyed by the blessed? Can the souls of the blessed wish for things they are unable to obtain? Suddenly a heavenly light and an ineffable fragrance filled his cell, and from the light he heard a voice speaking: "I am the soul that in Bethlehem at this very moment has laid aside the burden of the flesh, . . . put on the garment of immortality, . . . and is on its way to the kingdom of heaven." For several hours Jerome's *anima* answered Augustine's questions and instructed him about the Trinity, the hierarchies of angels, and the pleasures and intuitions of the blessed. The grateful Augustine styled himself Jerome's "lowliest servant" and begged Jerome to intercede for him in heaven and to guide him on the path to salvation (fig 17; see figs. 8 and 30).[11]

On the same day, in far-away Tours, Sulpicius Severus, a disciple of St. Martin, and three companions were astonished by a heavenly symphony of voices, organ, and tympani, a light seven times brighter than the sun, and an aromatic scent. God, unwilling for the world to remain ignorant of Jerome's glorification, and wishing to remind those who imitate Jerome's sanctity and virtues of their promised reward, caused a voice to speak from the light and announce that the King of kings was on his way to meet Jerome and escort him into the kingdom of heaven, and that the angels, patriarchs, prophets, apostles, disciples, martyrs, confessors, holy virgins, and the Blessed Virgin Mary were festively preparing to celebrate the arrival of their "compatriot and fellow citizen" (fig. 18).[12] In the meantime, on the same day, at the same hour, in the Holy Land, Cyril of Jerusalem, in an ecstasy, saw the progress of the saint's soul from the monastery in Bethlehem to heaven. Crowds of angels in mellifluous song escorted him, each holding a lighted candle, so the whole host was brighter than the sun. The Savior himself was at Jerome's right hand (fig. 19).[13]

Four nights later, Augustine had a second vision, from which he learned more exactly the nature of Jerome's *gloria* and how he should appropriately be praised. He dreamed that two men appeared to him in the midst of a multitude of angels. They looked alike except that one wore a triple diadem of gold and precious stones, while the other wore a double one. The two men were John the Baptist and Jerome. John wore the triple diadem because he had shed his blood for the faith; Jerome wore the double diadem because he was a white, or spiritual, martyr. But in sanctity of life and glory after death, John told Augustine, he and Jerome were equal. John was a hermit in the desert; so was Jerome. John mortified the flesh; so did Jerome. John was a virgin "clean and pure"; so was Jerome. "What I can do, he can do; what I will, he wills; and in the same way that I see God, he too sees, knows and understands God, and in this consists all our glory and happiness and that of all the saints" (fig. 20; see figs. 18 and 27).[14] Augustine thus learned that Jerome's name must be magnified and published among the people; that he should be feared.

Fig. 17.   French school, *The Apparition of St. Jerome to St. Augustine,* c. 1475–1480.
Augustine has just written the salutation of his letter to Jerome: *Iheronimo presbytero
Augustinus salutem.* The text of Pseudo-Augustine to Pseudo-Cyril begins below: *Glo-
riosissimi christiane fidei athlete, sancte matris ecclesie lapidis angularis.* The naked infant wearing a red cardinal's hat is Jerome's *anima.*

Fig. 18. Sano di Pietro, *(left) The Apparition of St. Jerome to Sulpicius Severus and a Monk of St. Martin of Tours; (right) The Apparition of St. Jerome and St. John the Baptist to St. Augustine,* 1444

Fig. 19 Luca Signorelli, *The Apparition of St. Jerome to St. Cyril of Jerusalem,* c. 1520. Predella panel of an altarpiece commissioned for the Compagnia di S. Girolamo in Arezzo. Jesus Christ escorts Jerome to heaven accompanied by angels carrying lighted candles.

Fig. 20. Luca Signorelli, *The Apparition of St. Jerome and St. John the Baptist to St. Augustine*, c. 1520. From the same predella as the scene shown in fig. 19.

revered, and venerated; and that God will punish all detractors of his name or powers and protect all those who call on him for help.[15]

While Jerome's glorified *anima* contemplated the divine nature in heaven, his body remained on earth generating miracles. At the end of Pseudo-Cyril's letter is an account of Jerome's burial. Cyril had prepared a marble sarcophagus to receive the body, but Jerome warned him in a dream that he preferred to lie naked in the bare ground at the entrance to the cave where Jesus was born. (From the early Middle Ages ordinary people were buried underground; only the bodies of saints were placed in tombs above the ground. Jerome's wish to be buried below the ground emphasizes his humility and modesty.) Jerome continued: "Know, Cyril, that my body will not be lifted from the grave where it now lies until the city of Jerusalem falls to the infidel. At that time, it will be moved to Rome and rest there for many years."[16]

The falsifier is quoting as prophecy a document confected in the 1290s and known as the *Translatio corporis beati Hieronymi*.[17] The text states that Jerome, moved by a desire to leave Bethlehem, occupied now by the

Saracens, and moved also by his special devotion to the Virgin Mary and a wish to return to Rome where he had been a cardinal, appeared in a dream to a monk living in the East and ordered him to exhume his body, carry the remains intact to Rome, and rebury them in S. Maria Maggiore. The site was appropriate. Consecrated to Our Lady in memory of the declaration of the Council of Ephesus (431) that Mary was the Mother of God, S. Maria Maggiore had possessed since the fifth century a chapel designed to reproduce the grotto of the nativity. After the Arabs conquered Palestine in the the seventh century, the remains of the crib itself (five small boards of Levantine sycamore) were carried from Bethlehem to Rome and housed in the same chapel, hence the basilica's secondary name, S. Maria ad Praesepem. So when the monk and two companions brought Jerome's body secretly to Rome and, still secretly, after dark, and in the presence only of the canons and clergy of the basilica (in order to minimize the danger of pious larceny by Romans avid for relics) buried it in the floor next to the Chapel of the Presepio under an iron slab, they were deliberately approximating the character and location of his original burial place. During the burial service, those present smelled a scent of unspeakable sweetness and beheld a light more brilliant than any seen before in the church: the Virgin Mary, wreathed in roses and lilies, brighter than the moon and more radiant than the sun, stood resplendent near the tomb of her learned and devoted admirer.[18]

Jerome's body (in these circumstances, "body" need mean no more than a small bag of dust and a few bones) lay undisturbed under its iron slab until 1395 when the canons reburied it under an "altar of St. Jerome," newly erected near the Chapel of the Presepio and endowed with a gift of real estate by Stefano Ottaviani de' Guaschi, one of the canons, "because of his great and singular devotion" to Jerome. The chapter moved the remains again in 1428 after Cardinal Pietro Morosini left them 100 florins to buy a silver urn in which to keep the relics "so they may be venerated more honorably."[19] A generation later (c. 1463), Cardinal Guillaume d'Estouteville, archpriest of the basilica, commissioned from the workshop of the sculptor Mino da Fiesole an elaborate free-standing monument decorated with panels in low relief showing episodes from Jerome's life and legend.[20] Jerome rested undisturbed in Mino's monument for over a century. Then, in 1587, Felice Peretti, Pope Sixtus V, ordered his architect Domenico Fontana to dismantle it in order to clear the approaches to the vast new chapel he was building to house his own tomb. The sculpted panels joined the pope's collections in Villa

Montalto on the Esquiline. In a remarkable feat of engineering, the ancient Cappella del Presepio was strengthened with timbers on the inside and enclosed in wooden beams and iron bars, detached from its foundations and moved on wooden rollers about fifty feet from its former location behind the choir, then lifted into the air like a vast box and lowered beneath the floor, where it rested under an altar in the center of the pope's new Cappella Sistina (fig. 21).

What happened to Jerome's remains is uncertain. In the seventeenth century, Romans insinuated to their visitors that the pope and his nephew Cardinal Alessandro Peretti had wanted to remove the bones to their titular church of S. Girolamo degli Schiavoni at the Ripetta but that an alert canon of the basilica had foiled them by hiding the precious relic. More probably, the pope had intended to house the relic in the small chapel dedicated to St. Jerome and located in the Cappella Sistina to the left of the entrance. What is certain is that an intensive search of the ground under and around the dismantled monument failed to turn up the bones, and they were all but forgotten until the middle of the eighteenth century when a silver ossuary, without name or inscription, was found in the crypt under the high altar. On the feast day of St. Jerome in the jubilee year of 1750, Pope Benedict XIV confirmed the identification of the bones it contained as Jerome's and had them placed alongside the remains of St. Matthew the Evangelist under the magnificent new high altar he had come to S. Maria Maggiore that day to consecrate.[21]

Despite the assurance in the *Translatio corporis beati Hieronymi* that the saint's body had come intact (*integraliter*) from Bethlehem to Rome[22] and a letter from Pope Sixtus IV confirming that Jerome's "holy body" undoubtedly (*indubitanter*) rested in S. Maria Maggiore,[23] the actual geography of ownership showed the more typical pattern of extreme dispersion. In Rome the church of S. Cecilia claimed part of his tibia; the Gesù acquired an arm; S. Sabina, S. Anastasia, S. Marco, S. Maria in Trastevere, and S. Girolamo della Carità possessed relics. At St. Peter's, Gregory XIII deposited one relic in an altar dedicated to the Virgin and raised a new altar dedicated to St. Jerome over a part of his chin. Other relics found their way to Florence, Bologna, Bohemia, the Netherlands, England, and Spain. St. Albans had an arm, Tournai a big bone and a little one, Orléans a reliquary with Jerome's name on it so heavy it needed two men to lift it. By the end of the sixteenth century, the best collection outside of Rome was at the Escorial. The star of the collection was Jerome's head, acquired in 1593 by an emissary of Philip II from the abbess and nuns of

Fig. 21.   Domenico Fontana, *The Transportation of the Cappella del Presepio*, 1590. The Cappella del Presepio is lowered intact to its new position beneath the floor at the center of the Cappella Sistina in the basilica of S. Maria Maggiore in Rome. In the Cappella del Presepio was an altar containing in a lead casket the holy remains of the manger in which the Christ Child had lain.

the Augustinian convent of St. Mary Magdalen in Cologne. They had been persuaded to part with it by the argument that it was unsafe so near the territories of Protestant heretics.[24]

The relics of saints, like the sacraments, are material signs through which God's grace is conveyed to the faithful. They inspire devotion to the extent that they perform miracles and attract pilgrims. Jerome's relics, embarrassingly unhelpful for over eight hundred years, were suddenly asserted to have acquired marvelous powers. Before his burial in Bethlehem the blind, maimed, and mute regained their faculties by touching his corpse (fig. 22).[25] According to Pseudo-Cyril, Eusebius of Cremona raised three men from the dead by laying Jerome's cloak over them. The resuscitated trio described the pains of sinners in purgatory, the torments of the damned in hell, and the joys of the blessed in heaven, thus confuting the pestiferous heresy, common among the Greeks, that souls do not suffer the pains of hell or enjoy the happiness of heaven until reunited with their bodies at the Last Judgment (fig. 23).[26]

Jerome's name is magical and wonder-working. Those in danger have only to cry out, "Help, help, glorious Jerome," and he will come to their aid. Shortly after Jerome's death two young Romans were on their way to Bethlehem to venerate his remains. Near Constantinople they were wrongly suspected, accused, tried, convicted of murder, and condemned to death. The weeping youths called out to St. Jerome. When the executioners' swords descended, they bounced off necks miraculously become hard as porphyry. The executioners tried to burn the two young men but they remained safe and jocund in the flames. When the executioners tried to hang them, Jerome himself appeared and held up the young men so the ropes could not harm them. At last, the judge, executioners, spectators, and the vindicated youths praised the Creator and glorious Jerome (fig. 24).[27] Jerome's image was thought to be as powerful as his name. Demons feared to enter the cell of a nun who kept his picture on the wall. An Arian heretic stuck his sword through a representation of the saint in a church. A wave of blood flowed from the image. The enraged populace stoned the heretic.[28]

Events and narratives like these mark the transformation into a popular cult of a veneration expressed in earlier centuries chiefly in the liturgy. The structure of narrative and the pattern of events are unoriginal: the beginnings of new devotions are regularly accompanied by an "invention" of relics (the saint appears to someone in a dream and tells him where he can find his burial place), by a translation (the saint's bones,

Fig. 22. Jean de Limbourg, *The Miracles of Healing Accomplished by St. Jerome's Corpse before Its Burial,* 1408–1409. In the background, hermits watch Jerome's funeral procession from their caves. Bishop Cyril of Jerusalem, surrounded by his clergy, comes forward to meet the bier at the entrance to the Basilica of the Nativity in Bethlehem. In the foreground, the sick and maimed become well and whole by touching the saint's corpse.

Fig. 23. Francesco Bianchi Ferrari, *Eusebius of Cremona Resuscitates Three Dead Men by Laying St. Jerome's Cloak over Them,* 1505. Predella panel from Ferrari's *St. Jerome Altarpiece* (see fig. 34).

miraculously discovered, are moved at his instruction from one place to another and from one owner to another, a transaction that commonly takes the form of a pious theft, *furtum sacrum*), and by miracles. The new owners receive the saint with joy, raise altars and sanctuaries over his remains, splendidly celebrate his anniversary and the feast of his translation, and put their home, monastery, parish, or city and their lives and property under his protection. Theseus, for example, was buried on the island of Scyros. The Delphic oracle instructed the Athenians to retrieve his bones and preserve them in Athens. Cimon, son of Miltiades, led an expedition against Scyros and captured the island. When he began to look

Fig. 24. Attributed to Pietro Perugino, *St. Jerome Supports Two Youths Wrongly Condemned to Death by Hanging*, c. 1500

for Theseus's burial place, an eagle showed him where to dig. In Athens the citizens received the relics with celebration and sacrifices and placed them in a sanctuary in the city's center.[29] An account of a Christian *translatio* exactly contemporary with Jerome's and carried out for similar reasons is more nearly parallel: the removal from Nazareth on 10 March 1291 of the Holy House of Mary, the home of her parents Anna and Joachim, where the Virgin was immaculately conceived, spent her childhood, and received the Annunciation. In order to preserve the house from further profanation by infidels, angels picked it up and carried it away to Italy, ultimately depositing it in the village of Loreto in the Marches, where it soon attracted the liveliest devotion and became the object of one of the most successful pilgrimages in Europe.[30]

Although the founders of the Renaissance cult of St. Jerome covered their traces well, we may tentatively reconstruct the sequence of events as follows. One or more of the canons and chaplains of the basilica of S. Maria Maggiore were in the later thirteenth century especially devoted to St. Jerome, much as Nicolò Maniacoria had been a century and a half earlier—and for reasons that need not have included admiration for his scholarship (Maniacoria first venerated Jerome because his pregnant mother, who had been gravely ill while carrying him, was cured and safely delivered through Jerome's intercession).[31] The presence of the Holy Crib in their church, coupled with their knowledge that Jerome was still buried in Bethlehem at the entrance to the cave from which it had been removed so long ago, alerted them to the appropriateness and desirability of reuniting Jerome with the *presepio*.

In the psychology of pious fraud it is a short step from recognizing what is appropriate and potentially edifying to proclaiming it abroad as true. So we may further suppose that the canons, their imaginations stimulated by the fall to the Mamlūks on 29 May 1291 of Saint-Jean d'Acre, capital of what remained of the Latin Kingdom of Jerusalem, began to claim that Jerome was indeed buried in their church and no longer in Palestine, and that they then commissioned the author of the *Translatio corporis beati Hieronymi* to document this claim and advertise their acquisition of a powerful new relic. By God's mercy and providence, St. Jerome was now fully present in S. Maria Maggiore. The translation had made plain God's approval of the Roman see, the people of Rome, and the clergy of S. Maria Maggiore. The new guardians of the relic had in their gift Jerome's own powers of protection, exorcism, healing, and intercession. The letters attributed to Saints Eusebius of Cremona, Augustine, and Cyril of Jerusalem confirmed and magnified the thaumaturgic powers of his remains and popularized devotion to him. Because the letters are so close to the *Translatio* in purpose, motif, and style, they too were probably written in Rome, early in the fourteenth century, and in the circle of S. Maria Maggiore. Internal evidence points to an author in or close to the Dominican Order.[32]

Jerome's *potentia*, so copiously illustrated by documented miracles and answered prayers, at once attracted the reverence, homage, and offerings of the faithful. In 1292, Pope Nicholas IV asked to be buried next to him; and as early as 1295 an indulgence carrying plenary remission of sins was available by papal authority to pilgrims visiting Jerome's altar in the basilica on the feast of his translation (9 May). Pope Pius II confirmed the grant in perpetuity on 21 January 1459 and again on 1 June 1464. A wonderful event on Christmas Eve of 1517 confirms Jerome's continued presence in S. Maria Maggiore. St. Cajetan of Thiene was meditating on the Incarnation between the Chapel of the Presepio and the nearby "niche" containing Jerome's bones and ashes when the Virgin appeared to him holding the Christ Child. Jerome, Cajetan's special patron, appeared and beckoned him to approach the holy pair. He obeyed, and the Virgin Mother gently placed her Son in his outstretched arms.[33]

Reconstruction of the next stage in the development of the cult rests on direct evidence rather than conjecture. Between 1334 and 1346/47, Giovanni d'Andrea (Johannes Andreae), professor of law at the University of Bologna, the most famous canonist of his day, called *tuba et pater iuris canonici* by contemporaries, wrote a book entitled *Hieronymianus* or *De laudibus sancti Hieronymi*.[34] Giovanni was a layman, married and the father of three daughters and four legitimate and two illegitimate sons. With minor interruptions he taught canon law at Bologna from 1301 until his death in the great plague in 1348. His glosses of the Sext and Clementines became the *glossa ordinaria* of each of those collections. His masterpiece was a commentary on the Decretals of Gregory IX. By the time he compiled the *Hieronymianus*, a collection of biographical material from the earlier lives, *testimonia* in praise of Jerome, accounts of his ancient and more recent miracles, and a list of his writings and a selection of excerpts from them—similar, though smaller in scope, to the vast fourteenth-century corpus of Augustinian doctrine, the *Milleloquium veritatis S. Augustini* compiled by the Augustinian hermit Bartolomeo Carusi da Urbino—he was a very distinguished and a very rich man indeed.[35]

He does not tell us what first inspired his devotion to St. Jerome, but his statement that his conversion dated back twenty-five years, to about 1310, suggests that a reading of the letters of Pseudo-Eusebius, Augustine, and Cyril may have precipitated it. He was dismayed, he reports, by the lack of reverence for St. Jerome that he observed in Italy at that time. The apostles and the other doctors of the church are decently honored;

but Jerome, who teaches every Christian, through whose writings persons of every age, sex, condition, and occupation, whether ignorant or learned, rich or poor, noble or commoner, clerk or layman, learn what true faith and the Christian life are, is neglected (fig. 25). He decided to do something about it. Spurred on by the hope of salvation and knowing that a tiny spark can turn into a mighty flame, he began to venerate the glorious doctor; observe his feast day with a variety of services and celebrations; and implore his aid in each of his acts, in all his writings, and before beginning any new undertaking. In the leisure moments of a busy legal and academic career, he urged parents to name their sons Girolamo; he persuaded monks to call themselves Girolamo when they entered religion. He sometimes signed himself Giovanni d'Andrea di San Girolamo. He collected and distributed relics. He composed orations, prayers, hymns, and poems in his praise. Horrified to discover that in all Italy there were only three churches dedicated to his hero, he dedicated a chapel in the cathedral of Bologna to Jerome and endowed a priest to serve it; with his daughter-in-law he founded and endowed a pretty parish church on the road to Florence and contributed generously to founding a Carthusian monastery, both dedicated to his patron saint; and he urged others to dedicate altars, chapels, and churches to Jerome.[36]

"I have also," he wrote, "established the way he should be painted, namely, sitting in a chair, beside him the hat that cardinals wear nowadays [that is, the red hat or *galerus ruber*] and at his feet the tame lion; and I have caused many pictures of this sort to be set up in divers places."[37] Andrea's claim to have supplied Jerome with what were to remain his most familiar attributes in the visual arts appears to be sound. Jerome had been pictured as a cardinal before Andrea wrote, and an occasional thirteenth-century miniature or fresco shows him taking the thorn out of the lion's paw;[38] but only after the middle of the fourteenth century were a lion and cardinal's hat used simply and regularly as identifying attributes. Moreover, Andrea much enriched the iconography of St. Jerome by having had painted on the façade of his own house in Bologna a cycle of pictures, with explanatory verses, telling the story of Jerome's life. The paintings have disappeared; the verses survive to give us a clear idea of what episodes Andrea selected for illustration. This is the more interesting because it establishes the Italian iconographic repertory behind the earliest Renaissance cycle that does survive, the twelve full-page miniatures that show "the entire life of blessed Jerome in pictures" in the *Belles Heures* of John, duke of Berry, painted by the Limbourg brothers, Paul, Jean, and Her-

Fig. 25. Italian school, *St. Jerome Instructs Christians of All Conditions in Faith and Morals*, c. 1350. The first page of a manuscript of Giovanni d'Andrea's *Hieronymianus*. The prototype is a miniature by Niccolò di Giacomo in Bologna, Collegio di Spagna, MS. 278.

man, in 1408-1409.[39] It is impossible to be sure into how many separate scenes Andrea's façade painter divided his material, but the subjects he represented were the following: Jerome learns the three languages in Rome and is beaten by angels because of his excessive attachment to Cicero; he is consecrated a cardinal of the Roman church; he is tricked into wearing a woman's dress to church; he leaves Rome for the East and founds a monastery in Bethlehem; here he translates the Bible and composes masterly works; he tames a lion by extracting a thorn from its paw; the obedient lion carries firewood, mourns the theft of the ass, then joyfully brings back the stolen ass; Jerome's death and burial. The poem ends with a reference to the translation of Jerome's remains from Bethlehem to Rome: "Now Rome holds your bones and prays to you in a church dedicated to the Virgin."[40]

One of the three churches Andrea had found dedicated to St. Jerome was the Dominican monastery church at Troia in Apulia, built between 1310 and 1312. He heard the following account of its foundation from one Nicolaus Bardanus. There was living near the town for some years past a group of hermits. One of them, Brother Bellatus, was a man of great penitence and purity and simplicity of soul. One night Jerome came to him in a dream. He complained that no church was dedicated to him and commanded Bellatus to build a church on a specified spot in the town, to dedicate it to his name, and to have it serviced by Dominican friars (another bit of evidence of the Dominican role in the early history of the cult). Bellatus and other devout people set to work; but money being short, progress was slow. One day an opulent ecclesiastic passed by and asked what was going on. "We are building a church for St. Jerome," replied Bellatus. "Ha, ha," laughed the cleric, "you *have* found yourselves a new saint." Now the most glorious Jerome, most famous of all the ancient fathers, was irritated by this remark, as appears from what followed. For he immediately caused cattle grazing across the road to break loose and chase the offender to the edge of a nearby cliff. Teetering on the edge, the repentant cleric vowed to give all he had toward the construction of the church if St. Jerome would only free him from his present danger, which Jerome at once did. The miracle stimulated other contributions; church and monastery were soon finished and in 1315 dedicated to the glory of Jerome.[41]

The site became the scene of a host of other contemporary miracles: cripples were made whole, men and women blind from birth recovered their sight, demons were expelled from otherwise innocent children, and dead men were raised up. An infant named John fell into an oven. His sister prayed to Jerome and dragged him out unsinged. One of the friars was repairing the church roof. He fell off. On the way down he prayed to Jerome and landed safely. A French knight in the service of the prince of Taranto vowed to give the church a gold florin if Jerome cured his beautiful horse. The horse's pains disappeared and the knight fulfilled his vow. The truth of these things, asserts Andrea, has been vouched for by the sworn testimony of thirty-seven witnesses, including the bishop of Troia; ecclesiastical and civil judges; the dean, cantor, and eight friars from the Dominican convent; and ten notaries.[42]

The cult of St. Jerome acquired a firm institutional base during the second half of the fourteenth century with the foundation of five new monastic congregations named for him and dedicated to imitating his virtues and manner of life: the *Frati Gesuati di San Girolamo,* the Spanish Hieronymites, the *Frati eremiti di San Girolamo a Fiesole,* the *Poveri eremiti per amore di Gesù Cristo di Frate Pietro da Pisa,* and the *Monaci eremiti di San Girolamo dell'osservanza di Lombardia.* Hieronymite nuns, too, appear in the documents, as *Gesuate di San Girolamo* or *Romite di San Girolamo.* Their earliest foundations were in Florence and Siena.

Later generations of Hieronymites believed that Jerome had been himself a professed monk; that he had explicitly made the three vows of poverty, chastity, and obedience; that he was in fact and name the abbot and pastor of the monastery in Bethlehem; that when he died his disciple Eusebius of Cremona succeeded him as abbot; and that the convent had enjoyed a continuous existence until the Muslim conquest. The order, already named after its founder, then lived mystically underground, like a hidden river, only to rise again, clearer and fresher than ever, about the year 1350.[43]

The reality was less tidy. The later fourteenth and earlier fifteenth century was in Italy a period of marked religious revival. The peninsula swarmed with enthusiasts. Tommaso da Boiano, Franciscan bishop of Aquino, disappeared from his see in 1349 and resurfaced as leader of a band of disciples calling themselves the Evangelical Brethren.[44] Pilgrimages to Rome for the Jubilee of 1350 generated intense excitement and millenarian expectations. Public flagellation became a common form of voluntary penance. By the end of the fourteenth century, there were at least fifteen confraternities in Florence alone in which flagellation was the central devotional exercise. Around 1351, Giovanni dalle Celle (d. 1394), a cultivated monk at Vallambrosa, used magical arts to lure a young virgin to his cell and rape her. Appalled by his crime, he retired to a hermitage where for forty years he repented in prayer, fasting, vigils, and physical labor. His sincerity and spiritual counsel eventually won the respect of St. Catherine of Siena.[45] Giovanni Colombini (1304–1367), a rich Sienese patrician and cloth merchant, was converted in middle age by reading the life of St. Mary the Egyptian while he waited for his dinner. About 1355 he began to give away his property (his wife, who had formerly chided him for un-Christian stinginess, now complained that she had prayed for rain, not for the flood). He dressed in rags, performed the lowliest and most humiliating tasks, and preached poverty, repentance, and love of Christ in all the cities of Tuscany. He and his followers called themselves "Poveri per Gesù Cristo" and established a loosely organized congregation of laymen, the Apostolic Friars of St. Jerome, the future *Fratres Iesuati S. Hieronymi* or *Gesuati*.[46] "We have dedicated all our churches and oratories to St. Jerome," wrote a fifteenth-century friar, "because it is his teaching we imitate and follow."[47]

The other Hieronymite congregations began in much the same way. Tommasuccio da Foligno (1319–1377), a Franciscan tertiary, called ardently for repentance, reconciliation, and peace in the cities of Tuscany and Umbria, worked miracles, and in an ecstasy dictated prophetic verses castigating the vices of his contemporaries and foretelling the coming of a Man destined to reform the world.[48] To a mixed group of disciples, some Italian and some Spanish, he prophesied the descent of the Holy Spirit over Spain in the form of the new religious order. In obedience to his prophecy, a few hermits owning nothing but their shirts and tattered, undyed woolen overgarments went to Spain determined to magnify the name of St. Jerome by imitating his eremitical life in remote and inaccessible places. In 1370 one of their prominent Spanish converts, Fray Pedro Fernández Pecha, sometime royal *repostero mayor*, founded the congregation's first formal house, near Lupiana in the diocese of Toledo. (His brother, Alonso Pecha, had renounced the bishopric of Jaén to become the redactor of St. Birgitta of Sweden's *Revelations* and eventually a hermit near Genoa.) Pope Gregory XI confirmed the congregation in the bull *Salvatoris humani generis* of 15 October 1373. Although he put the brothers under the Augustinian Rule and instructed them to follow the usages and ceremonies and wear the habit of a congregation established earlier in the century at the convent and church of S. Maria del S. Sepolchro near

Florence, the members of which were especially attached to the cult of St. Augustine, he permitted the Spaniards to call themselves Hieronymites because of their special devotion to St. Jerome.

The Spanish Hieronymites were to have an extraordinary success, numbering twenty-five houses at the time of the first Chapter General in July 1415. Under the patronage of John I and John II of Castille, of Ferdinand and Isabella, and of the Habsburgs, the order embraced several of the richest, most splendid, most observant monasteries in the peninsula: Nuestra Señora de Guadalupe in Estramadura (site of a magnetic Marian pilgrimage), Yuste (to which the Emperor Charles V retired after his abdication), San Gerónimo el Real in Madrid (traditional setting for the rituals surrounding the accessions and burials of the Spanish kings), and the magnificent Escorial itself. In Portugal, the great monastery of Belém, near Lisbon, founded in 1499 by King Manuel I to commemorate the discovery of the sea route to India, was a Hieronymite house; and the order played an important role in the New World (there is a church dedicated to St. Jerome at Taos Pueblo in Arizona).[49]

Two other Hieronymite congregations began in Italy and remained there, to be joined early in the fifteenth century by an observant offshoot of the Spanish order. The earlier in date, the hermits of St. Jerome of Fiesole *(Fratres S. Hieronymi de Fesulis, Congregazione degli eremiti di S. Girolamo a Fiesole),* was founded by Carlo da Montegranelli (c. 1330–1417). A member of the family of the counts Guidi di Monte Granelli di Bagno in the Tuscan Romagna, Carlo was a soldier before he became a Franciscan tertiary and retired about 1360 to a tiny hermitage on the rocky hillside near Fiesole to lead a life of meditation and mortification. Disciples gathered around him, attracted by his reputation for holiness. On Saturdays citizens climbed the hill to participate in spiritual exercises under his direction. (Out of these informal meetings was to grow the lay "Company of St. Jerome," which met in the Buca di S. Girolamo near the church of the SS. Annunziata and to which many well-known Florentines belonged; similar companies existed in other Tuscan cities.) Powerful friends encouraged and supported Carlo's wish to found a new congregation, and in 1406 Innocent VII approved it under a rule described in the Bull as the "constitutiones S. Hieronymi," provisions confirmed by Gregory XII on 8 July 1415. When Clement IX suppressed the congregation in 1668 in order to raise money for war against the Turks, it had forty houses.[50]

In 1377 Pietro Gambacorta (1355–1435), a Pisan patrician, experienced a conversion similar to that of Carlo da Montegranelli and abandoned fatherland, parents, and riches for the sake of Christ. He built a solitary hut on a mountainside near Urbino and led there a life of heroic penitence and mortification, "in imitation," says his fifteenth-century biographer, "of St. Jerome, to whom his devotion and attachment were extreme." He too attracted disciples who wanted to live under his direction the same life of expiation and separation from the world. In due course, following the common pattern of mitigating the eremitical ideal by introducing some of the practical advantages of cenobitic life, they built a monastery, founded new communities and built new convents, and sought papal approval of their increasingly well-organized and respectable congregation. Pope Martin V officially recognized the Poor Hermits of St. Jerome or *Girolamini* in June 1421. The congregation then numbered nine houses. There were fifteen in 1440 and forty-eight at the end of the sixteenth century.[51]

The offshoot of the Spanish order was founded by Lope de Olmedo (1370–1433), sometime general of the Spanish Hieronymites. Dissatisfied with the Augustinian rule under which his order had hitherto lived, he composed a new rule as strict as that of the Carthusians and made up entirely of sentences from works by St. Jerome, the *Regula monachorum S. Hieronymi*. The rule discouraged study (*scientia inflat*), prohibited the eating of meat (*esus carnium seminarium libidinis*), and forbade women from entering even the churches of the congregation.[52] His attempt to impose the rule provoked a battle that he lost. He resigned the generalship and with his supporters came to Rome in 1424. Pope Martin V gave him the monastery of Saints Boniface and Alexis on the Aventine and on 26 May 1428 approved his rule and statutes. At the end of the sixteenth century, the congregation, now known as the observant *Monaci eremiti di S. Girolamo di Lombardia*, numbered seventeen houses in Italy (the Spanish houses were reunited with the main order in 1567).[53]

In a letter to Giovanni Colombini's *Poverelli* after the death of the founder, Giovanni dalle Celle located the distinguishing characteristic of Hieronymite spirituality in penitential exercise. He distinguished exercises of the body from those of the inner man. Among the former are fasting, weeping for one's sins, beating one's breast, frequent confession, vigils, silence, manual labor, vileness of dress, simplicity of food and drink, and avoidance of women, even holy ones. Other exercises of the body are less stereotyped: avoidance of Gentile books (*fuga de' libri de' pagani*), separation from one's fatherland (*dilungamento dal proprio paese*), and rejection of relatives and friends (*odio de' parenti e delli amici temporali*). The spiritual exercises of penance include fear of sin; remembrance of death, the Last Judgment and eternal punishment; remembrance of the disobedience and fall of Adam and of his punishment and that of his posterity; remembrance of all the things Christ has done for us, his passion, and the agonies he suffered for us; remembrance of the apostolic life (*memoria della vita apostolica*) and the torments of the martyrs; and a most burning hatred of one's own will and of the delights of the senses.[54] The program ultimately depends on the Benedictine Rule, Basil the Great's *Sermo de ascetica disciplina*, and above all and in detail on Jerome's letters describing the austerities and raptures of the solitary life, the letter to Heliodorus (*Ep.* 14), for example, or the even more famous *Ep.* 22 to Eustochium.

A nearer source of Hieronymite spirituality is identified by the fact that this section of Giovanni dalle Celle's letter is a word-for-word translation of a short Latin tract by Angelo Clareno (d. 1337),[55] the leader during the first decades of the fourteenth century of a dissident group of Italian Spiritual Franciscans, the so-called *Fraticelli de paupere vita*, hermit-friars persecuted by their ecclesiastical superiors for teaching that the perfect life requires a complete renunciation of possessions, for founding rival associations outside the parent order, and for prophesying the impending destruction of the hierarchical church and the coming of a New Age of grace, charity, and peace.

Although the Spiritual movement was no longer an institutional threat to the official church after the middle of the fourteenth century, the wish to live an evangelical life in literal accord with the Sermon on the Mount and the commitment to absolute poverty and to a total rejection of the world modeled on the eremiticism of the desert fathers remained as lively and urgent as before. Such radical impulses found alternate expression in a variety of related ways: in the lives of individual hermits or small groups of ascetics clustered about a charismatic personality, within monastic orders in the successful efforts of zealots to observe the rule strictly (in 1368 the minister general of the Friars Minor permitted Paoluccio de' Trinci and a few followers to lead what they understood to be an apostolic life at the desolate hermitage of Brugliano, on the borders of Umbria and the Marches, the beginning of the Franciscans of the Strict Observance), and in the foundation of the Hieronymite congregations. For not only

did the early communities of hermits which matured into the Hieronymite congregations share the aspirations of the Spiritual Franciscans, the
founders themselves typically were Franciscan tertiaries touched by the
intransigent idealism of the radicals of that order. The essential difference
lay in their docility to ecclesiastical authority: from the beginning, like
Paoluccio's observant Franciscans, they preached and practiced obedience
to bishops and the Holy See. In order to emphasize the orthodoxy and
obedience of his community, Colombini sometimes called his followers
poveri di Cristo e del santo Papa.[56]

Another difference was their special veneration for St. Jerome and their
explicit wish to live a stricter and more perfect life by imitating his life,
rule, and works. By thus adopting Jerome as their patron and protector
they were able to perpetuate rigorous Franciscan values under the shelter
of a patristic authority. The fundamental demand remained poverty, the
evangelical standard against which the Hieronymites, like both the Spiritual and the observant Franciscans, measured the church and society of
their day. But Hieronymites prudently grounded their practice of it on
the example of Jerome, citing his fondness for Luke 14:33 ("Whoever
does not renounce all he possesses cannot be my disciple"); his satirical
hatred of wealth and luxury, of any sort of individual appropriation of
money ("you are rich enough when you are poor with Christ" or "all
riches derive from iniquity");[57] and the legendary Jerome's injunction to
his monks on his deathbed: "Imitatores paupertatis estote," follow
poverty, the better to imitate Christ who was born poor and died desti-
tute.[58] It is impossible to be rich and follow Christ. Poverty guarantees
that our riches are wholly in Christ and that we are dependent on him
alone, day by day, for food, shelter, and dress. Evangelical poverty makes
us free: free of the world, free from desire for the things of the world, free
from every earthly affection. And since even some spiritual goods hinder
complete poverty and humility and so continue to tie their possessors to
the world, Hieronymites tended to refuse the priesthood, as indeed
Jerome himself had tried to do.[59] "O poverty, foundation of the faith,
abundance of peace, nourishment of hope and charity, mother of humility," wrote Giovanni dalle Celle, "you are the purgatory of sins, you
muzzle the senses and open the soul, you perfect men and make them
wish for the kingdom of heaven, you arm us against every vice, you fill
heaven and empty hell, you are loved by the wise and hated by worldly
fools."[60]

Religious rejection of the world dictated another attitude common among the radical ascetics of fourteenth- and early fifteenth-century Italy: hostility to secular culture. Petrarch, whose maturity coincided with the crystallization of Hieronymite spirituality, used the phrase *docta pietas* to describe the harmony he discerned between religion and a knowledge of the humanities. The ideal of the early Hieronymites was *sancta rusticitas*, an unlettered holiness, a phrase they found in Jerome, tacitly overlooking his scholarship and eloquence. Giovanni Colombini taught his followers that the natural sciences, moral philosophy, metaphysics, the liberal and mechanical arts, "comedies, tragedies, and histories" are all vanities and "a cloud that darkens the soul" (*una nube tenebrosa dell'anima*).[61] The office of a religious, wrote Lope de Olmedo, quoting Jerome, "is not learning, but weeping, mourning for the world and for himself and fearfully awaiting the coming of the Lord." Referring repeatedly to St. Francis and Franciscan practice, he urged his brothers to give their time to prayer and good works rather than to letters; for the kingdom of God is not reached by scaling the mountain tops of science but along the paths of humility, patience, and virtuous obedience.[62] Unsurprisingly, Hieronymites found in Jerome's Ciceronian dream a message meant especially for them, and they liked to have representations of it in their convents. They did not introduce the subject to the visual arts: Giovanni d'Andrea had had the scene painted on his house façade before 1334, and the earliest surviving example is apparently that in the *Belles Heures* of the duke of Berry. Many of the later examples, though, were commissioned for Hieronymite convents: the Gesuati of Florence, Siena, and Ferrara (see figs. 2 and 3); the Hermits of St. Jerome of Fiesole (see figs. 27 and 30); S. Onofrio on the Janiculum, the Roman house of the Poor Hermits of St. Jerome (a fresco by Domenichino); El Escorial (a painting by Juan Gomez of 1593); Nuestra Señora de Guadalupe, where Zurbarán's *Dream of St. Jerome* still hangs in the chapel adjacent to the sacristy; and the Hieronymite monastery of San Jerónimo de Buenavista in Seville (a painting by Valdés Leal, one of an ambitious series he painted for the monks in 1657–1658).[63] Literate friars, before the late fifteenth century, confined their reading to Scripture and the fathers, repressed the appetite for learning, and ran no schools (monks who had degrees were not permitted to use their titles), while the statutes encouraged the illiterate to believe that their ignorance of the knowledge that puffs up would help them to retain the purity of heart that fosters charity. (In the sixteenth century attitudes changed. The *Constitutiones* of the Girolamini approved by Pius V in 1571 called ignorance the "root and parent of all the vices"; they provided for a teacher of rhetoric and the humanities in each convent and for readers in philosophy and theology in four of the congregation's principal houses.)[64]

At the center of the spirituality associated with the cult of St. Jerome in the later fourteenth and fifteenth centuries was imitation of his austerities. Colombini wore sandals in summer and went barefooted in winter. Gambacorta and his followers fasted throughout Lent, during the ten days between Ascension Thursday and Pentecost, from 1 August to the Feast of the Assumption (15 August), from All Souls Day (1 November) to Christmas, and at all other times of the year every Monday, Wednesday, Friday, and Saturday. In order to imitate Jesus, who was flagellated for the sins of mankind, they whipped themselves daily during Lent and every Monday, Wednesday, Friday, and Saturday for the rest of the year. As they corrected their bodies for the sake of their souls, they recited in turn the *Miserere*, one of the seven penitential Psalms, a plea for God's mercy; the *De Profundis*, another of the penitential Psalms, an appeal for deliverance from the misery of sin; and the *Salve Regina*, one of the oldest and most popular Marian prayers. In the middle of every night they rose for Matins and prayed for two hours (in summer) or three hours (in winter). They ate only bread, fruit, and cooked vegetables. They slept the minimum nature required, on a straw pallet but more often on the floor. Under a simple habit of coarse, undyed wool, they wore a hair shirt.[65]

The notion that a person can partly atone for his sins by punishing himself is of course no more an invention of the fourteenth century than are the related ideas that ascetic practices can control and help eradicate the passions that tempt to sin or that retirement from the world helps to shield the penitent from further temptation. It does seem to be the case, however, that economic contraction and political insecurity, intensified by the scourges of plague and war, combined in the second half of the fourteenth century with symptoms of disarray like the great Schism to magnify beyond the ordinary many people's fears and their sense of sinfulness and guilt. And it is certainly the case that in central Italy especially there emerged as one way to atone for sin, mitigate fear, and win acquittal for the guilty a form of penitential piety the practitioners of which believed they were imitating the penitential practices of St. Jerome in the desert. Renaissance artists made vivid its austerities in hundreds of pictures of the penitent saint.

The image of the penitent St. Jerome in the wilderness was invented in Italy around 1400. It is not to be understood as a medieval image superseded by the Renaissance image of St. Jerome in his study; indeed, surviving images of St. Jerome in his study are earlier in date than the earliest penitent Jeromes. Both are Renaissance images and both post-date, though they do not entirely displace, the typical medieval representation of Jerome as a doctor of the church (see fig. 29, for example). It is possible to be even more specific. The penitent Jerome originated in Tuscany in the environment of the Hieronymite congregations.[66] An early example is a panel from the late 1420s by Giovanni di Francesco Toscani (fig. 26). Jerome stands in the desert, clothed in rough sackcloth, his only companions scorpions and wild beasts. His head is turned up to heaven in spiritual exaltation and he beats his breast with a stone. In his left hand he holds a scroll on which are fragments from the rules that governed the Hieronymites: "Subdue your flesh by fasting. A monk should avoid wine as if it were poison. To eat anything cooked is accounted self-indulgence." At the bottom right and left are the arms of two Florentine patrician families, the Gaddi and Ridolfi, a possible reference to the marriage in 1424 of Agnolo di Zanobi Gaddi and Maddalena di Niccolò di Antonio Ridolfi and a pledge of the couple's devotion to St. Jerome.[67]

A predella panel by Sano di Pietro, from a polyptych signed and dated 1444, painted for the Gesuati church of S. Girolamo in Siena, shows a variation of the same scene (see fig. 5).[68] Jerome kneels in front of a cave. The contrast of *civitas* and wilderness, of the walled towns on the horizon and Jerome's rocky retreat, is strongly marked, at once a literal illustration of the eremitical impulse in Hieronymite spirituality and a metaphor for the separation from the world that the penitent has won by his ascetic practices and for the truer freedom of a soul naked and alone with God. He weeps for his past sins and prays for strength to overcome the temptations of the flesh. He beats his breast like the publican in Luke because, as St. Jerome explained, the human breast is a treasure chest of impure thoughts; by bloodying his chest he punishes and tames his sinful heart.[69]

In an alterpiece by Francesco Botticini (c. 1470), the penitent Jerome is flanked on the left by Eusebius of Cremona and Pope Damasus and on his right by Paula and her daughter Eustochium (fig. 27). The altarpiece is still in its original frame and bears the arms of another great Florentine family, the Rucellai. The donor was probably Girolamo di Piero di Cardinale Rucellai, and he gave it in honor of his name-saint to the Hieronymite church of S. Girolamo in Fiesole, renovated in the 1450s at

Fig. 26.   Giovanni di Francesco Toscani, *The Penitent St. Jerome*, 1426–1430

Fig. 27. Francesco Botticini, *St. Jerome Altarpiece*, c. 1470. The predella shows the following scenes: *St. Jerome Extracts a Thorn from the Lion's Paw, The Dream of St. Jerome, The Death of St. Jerome,* and *The Apparition of St. Jerome and St. John the Baptist to St. Augustine.*

the expense of Giovanni de' Medici, the younger son of Cosimo *pater patriae*, who built for himself at the same time a suburban villa close by the monastery.[70] Donors and flanking saints do not venerate Jerome himself, but a picture of him, a real icon, the function of which in private devotion is to permit the worshipper to relive in a conscious act of meditation the symbolic narrative represented on the icon. "I used to lay down at Jesus's feet, watered them with my tears, and wiped them with my hair," Jerome had written to Eustochium. "I remember crying out for days and nights together; and I beat my breast without stopping until the Lord vouchsafed me some tranquility. Filled with stiff anger against myself, I went out into the desert alone. Wherever I found a deep valley or rough mountainside or rocky precipice, I made it my place of prayer and of torture for my unhappy flesh."[71]

When Jerome said that he "lay down at Jesus's feet," commentators and artists understood him to mean that he beat his breast before a crucifix, meditated on the Passion, and so participated in Christ's sufferings on earth (see figs. 27 and 28). Already in the *Golden Legend* Jacopo da Varazze had described Jerome as "dipped in blood by his contemplation of the Passion of our Lord."[72] In the fourteenth century, meditation on the Passion became a widely practiced devotion. St. Birgitta of Sweden, who was in Italy from 1349 until her death in Rome in 1373, was passionately attentive to the image of Christ crucified, lingering in her visions on each bloody detail, Christ's bloodshot eyes, his beard matted with dried blood, his face pale and blood-stained, his stomach cleaving to his backbone as though he had no intestines, his feet curled like door hinges around the nails that fixed him to the cross, his tender body bloodied from over five thousand wounds, splinters, and cuts.[73] St. Catherine of Siena (1347–1389) began her letters "in the name of Christ crucified" and regularly apostrophized the blood of Christ: "O sweet blood, you burn and consume the soul in the fire of divine love. . . . You comfort it in adversity. . . . O blood of Christ, wine that intoxicates the soul; the more of it one drinks, the more of it one wants to drink."[74] Hieronymites shared the same sensibility and devotion. After they broke their fasts, their "most delicate food" was meditation on the Passion. They beat themselves "per la memoria della passione di Cristo," a phrase that occurs in the statutes of every flagellant confraternity. Evangelizing Città di Castello, Giovanni Colombini observed exultantly that the whole city was shouting "Praise be Jesus Christ crucified! Oimè, oimè; wake up! Shout the name of Christ by day and by night, in every street and square. Long live the most holy name of Jesus! May tongues never tire nor hearts be weary of shouting Christ crucified."[75]

Contemporaries found the image of Christ crucified inexhaustibly moving and paradoxical. Death extinguished the life of Christ's body, but his death gives life to mankind. The hands nailed to the cross loose the bonds of sin. The very wood of the cross hides life in death. Since it came from the tree of knowledge in the Garden of Eden, it is a tree of death (artists often showed Jerome's crucifix attached to a blasted tree or rotting stump).[76] But because Christ's sacrifice atoned for Adam's sin, the cross is also a tree of life, a tree of all the virtues, an emblem of charity, piety, humility, truth, holiness, and innocence, a token of redemption and immortality, humanity's gateway to the kingdom of glory. It should be adored and venerated in silence and with penitential tears and acts. The cross is the light and salvation of the faithful, the death of death, the spring of resurrection. The blood of Christ nourishes the mystical body of the church. The Christian receives it through the sacraments and by imitating Christ, by conforming himself to Christ crucified, by living an evangelical life patterned on the cross, *cruciformis evangelica vita*. Franciscans "conformed" to the Gospel by imitating Francis; Hieronymites looked to Jerome. Jerome led an evangelical life by faithful imitation of Jesus' holy life; we can achieve an approximation of the same evangelical life by imitating Jerome's life and virtues in our body and soul. After his baptism, Jesus went into the desert and so did Jerome; like Jesus, Jerome lived in the flesh in spite of the flesh. By modeling our lives on the cross, as he did, we too may hold heavenly conversation with God.[77]

Contemporaries expressed most simply what they imagined Jerome to be saying and thinking as he knelt in penitence before a crucifix in the many prayers they attributed or addressed to him. A fifteenth-century *Office of St. Jerome* contains prayers that the anonymous author has put into the mouth of St. Jerome himself. He prays to Jesus Christ crucified for himself, a miserable sinner, and on behalf of his relatives and friends and all those who have confidence in his prayers and support him with alms. "Deign to free my soul from sin, turn my heart from wicked and depraved thoughts, free my body and soul from servitude to sin, drive concupiscence from me." He asks God to hear the psalms he chants in his honor and in honor of the Blessed Virgin Mary and all the saints and to forgive his many shameful sins as well as the sins of Christians who have commended themselves to him in their prayers. In the cadences of the Psalms he prays for mercy and eternal life and does penance for himself and for all Christian people. "Spare, O Lord, your people, whom you, Lord Jesus Christ, have redeemed with your blood; spare them and do not forget us in eternity."[78]

Even more helpful in understanding the purpose and rewards of venerating St. Jerome are the prayers addressed to him by ordinary Christians.

O lampas ecclesiae
  Et lumen solare,
Beate Ieronyme,
  Pro nobis precare.[79]

Or again: "Great lover of Christ, famous, glorious Jerome! Help us live uprightly and love God as you have taught us to in your books. Lover of chastity, whose purity of heart shaped a life of purity, make us chastise our body and weep for our sins. *Ora pro nobis, gloriose Hieronime.*"[80] Prayers specifically designed for the personal use of the laity can be found in the Books of Prayers that became common from the fourteenth century on. "O noblest doctor, light of the Church, blessed Jerome, lover of holy writ, pray to the Son of God for us, intercede with him on our behalf. Pray for us, O blessed father Jerome, that we may be found worthy of Christ's promises."[81] Then there were prayers for specific purposes: for safety on a trip; for the health of body and soul and a long life; for the release of a relative's soul from purgatory; for help in resisting life's temptations, in avoiding its perils, and in enduring its miseries.[82] Most common of all were prayers asking for the virtues that Jerome himself was supposed preeminently to have possessed: humility, chastity, patience, firm faith, and a "clear understanding of what we must know to do God's will"[83] (fig. 28).

However picturesque the practices and beliefs clustered around the veneration of St. Jerome may seem, they were not untypical. During the early Renaissance, the cult of saints became everywhere more intense and passionate than at any time since late antiquity. The pseudographs about Jerome are a very small part of a flood of hagiographical literature loosed in fourteenth-century Italy, the multiplication of his image but a single example of the astonishing proliferation of pictures of every popular saint: St. John the Baptist, St. Sebastian, St. Catherine of Alexandria, St. Anthony of Padua, St. Rocco, St. Bernard, St. Bernardino of Siena. Even Giovanni d'Andrea's advice to parents to name their sons Girolamo reflects (and helps explain) a more general phenomenon, the so-called "anthroponymic revolution" of the fourteenth and fifteenth centuries, the change from an earlier period when few Italians had a specifically Christian name to the end of the fifteenth century when almost all of them were named for Christian saints. For everyone knew he needed a powerful friend and protector in heaven. On earth, patrons were useful and necessary to success; in heaven, their advocacy was indispensable to both the living and the dead. The earthly client honored his spiritual patron with feasts and processions, sponsored masses at his altar, and prayed for favors before his image; the heavenly patron advanced his client's interests before the celestial Judge.[84]

By 1400, the cult of St. Jerome, in some of its expressions at any rate,

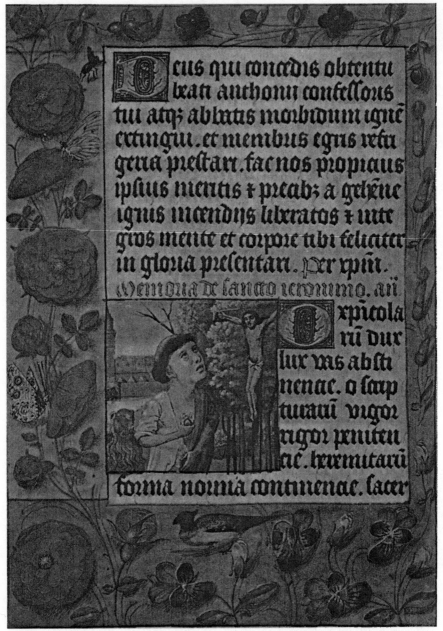

Fig. 28. Flemish school, *St. Jerome in Penitence*, c. 1510. A page from a Book of Hours. At the top, a prayer in the name of St. Anthony Abbot. Next to the miniature begins an antiphonal prayer to St. Jerome:

O Christicolarum dux, lux vas abstinencie!
O scripturarum vigor, rigor penitencie,
Heremitarum forma, norma continencie!

It concludes on the next page:
Sacerdos fidelissime lucens ardensque lucerna,
Ieronime clarissime nos tuere, nos guberna.

had become a popular devotion, popular in the sense that it was largely untouched by the technicalities of scholastic theology and speculative mysticism and increasingly communicated in the vernacular, or translated into it; popular, too, in the sense that its appeal was catholic: it spoke reassuringly in texts and images of varying levels of sophistication to monk and layman, rich and poor, learned and ignorant, patrician and artisan; popular, finally, in the sense that it could arouse the kind of mass emotion that animated the two hundred men and women who walked in procession through the streets of Pisa about 1364 in penitential sackcloth and ashes or Colombini's joyful audiences in almost every town of central Italy, singing lauds, shouting the name of Jesus, and dancing their love of Christ crucified. The piety associated with the cult was to this extent another attempt to meet the profoundest spiritual demand of the age, the layman's aspiration to participate more actively and seriously in religious life and worship.

At the same time, even Jerome's most ascetic disciples understood that his intellectual and literary interests were not as rudimentary as those of many of his devotees and that it was possible, for both clerks and laymen, to imitate him in other ways than by beating the chest and saying "peccavi, peccavi." On balance, the ascetic Jerome dominated the four-teenth century and remained a powerful image and model well into the seventeenth. But already the scholar and the man of letters was reemerging radiantly beside the penitent.

4
Divus litterarum princeps

PPRECIATION of Jerome's greatness as a scholar and man of letters became newly articulate in the work of early fifteenth-century Italian humanists: teachers, scholars, and men of letters passionately devoted to antiquity and to subjects that they variously described as literature (*studia litterarum*); the good, human, or liberal arts (*bonae artes, humanae artes, artes liberales*); or most expressively, the humanities (*studia humanitatis*), a cycle of studies comprising the Latin and Greek languages and literatures, history, and moral philosophy. Humanists included Jerome among the classical authors because they rightly viewed the Christian fathers as ancient men of letters who wrote before Roman eloquence was corrupted (as they believed) by Gothic barbarism and who often had been themselves orators, poets, historians, and philosophers.[1]

It should occasion no surprise, therefore, that humanists looked for patristic manuscripts in the older monastic libraries of Italy and the North as tirelessly as they hunted the pagan classics: from the beginning of the "revival of antiquity" enthusiasm for early Christian literature was inseparable from love of pagan literature. Ambrogio Traversari (1386–1439), a monk in the Camaldulensian monastery of S. Maria degli Angeli in Florence and member of a humanist circle that included Coluccio Salutati, Leonardo Bruni, Niccolò Niccoli, and Poggio Bracciolini had read Jerome's letters so often in his youth that he knew some of them by heart. His discovery of Jerome's translation of Origen's *Homilies on Luke* at S. Cecilia in Rome delighted him, he said, as much as finding the gold of Croesus.[2] Poggio, who thought Jerome an "extraordinary luminary of holiness and wisdom," was negotiating in 1430–1431 with the abbot of Monte Cassino for the loan of a manuscript "in Lombard characters" which he had heard contained 225 of Jerome's letters (he was having his own collection of the letters copied by a secretary, illuminated, and bound in two volumes).[3] Their self-congratulation at recovering patristic texts from "dust, filth, and neglect," as they put it with often misplaced exaggeration, or "rotting away in mouldy obscurity," or "among roaches and worms," was as eager as their delight in discovering a lost work of Plautus or Tacitus.

The admiration of Italian humanists for Jerome is thus a single instance of a larger cultural phenomenon, the rediscovery and reevaluation of Christian antiquity, itself an integral part of the rediscovery and reevaluation of ancient art and letters.

The grounds of their admiration were as various as their own needs and purposes, as many-sided as patristic literature itself. Everyone praised the eloquence of the fathers and emphasized that their own aspiration to write with elegance, grace, and style was modeled on patristic precedent.[4] Augustine's admiration for Cicero or Jerome's quotations and reminiscences of the poets—so extensive, remarked Coluccio Salutati (1331–1406), that the uninitiated might well mistake Jerome for a pagan professor—demonstrated the utility and legitimacy of the *studia humanitatis*. If Augustine had been ignorant of the poets, he would not have been able to defend Christianity so effectively against the attacks of the Gentiles. If Jerome had not studied with Donatus, he would not have been able to translate the Bible into correct Latin.[5] And did not Jerome himself say of the Greek fathers that all of them had "so nourished their books with the teachings and maxims of the philosophers, that one hardly knew what to admire more, their secular erudition or their knowledge of Scripture"?[6]

But what of the dream? And the fact that St. Jerome had been beaten by angels for reading Cicero and Plato?[7] And that he had sworn an oath: "Lord, if ever again I possess worldly books, if ever again I read them, I shall have denied you"?

Petrarch, who admired Jerome's learning, style, and genius, made the point, frequently repeated after him, that although Jerome had said he rejected all secular writers, his continued quotation of the poets and the imitative style of his later writings show that he actually approved them. The lesson Petrarch drew for himself was the continued possibility of a double loyalty. "Now my orators shall be Ambrose, Augustine, Jerome and Gregory; my philosopher Paul; my poet David. But although I put the Christian writers first, I do not reject the others."[8]

Pier Paolo Vergerio (1370–1444), doctor of arts, medicine, and both laws, professor of logic at the universities of Padua and Bologna, and author of an important treatise on education as well as lives of Seneca and

Petrarch and an invective against Carlo Malatesta for pulling down a statue in Mantua believed to be of Vergil and an antique, praised St. Jerome's eloquence for "flowing deliciously like a clear sparkling stream. And I do not hesitate to praise his style simply because he once heard himself condemned as a Ciceronian in an ecstatic vision (*visio extatica*). For the supreme judge did not condemn eloquence itself, but only its too exclusive cultivation. For without literary study we could hardly even read Scripture and certainly not with so much pleasure." The range of Jerome's biblical studies and the number of books he wrote on sacred subjects after the dream might suggest that he would have had no time left for the poets, even if he had wanted to read them, Vergerio continued; however, the knowledge of secular history and Gentile literature and philosophy displayed in those same works is so vast that one is almost forced to conclude that he read no authors *but* pagan ones.[9]

In the introduction to the fourth book of his *Elegancies of the Latin Language*, the best Renaissance manual on stylistics, Lorenzo Valla (1407–1457) lashed out at those who used Jerome's dream to attack students of Latin literature. He argued that the Judge had not condemned Cicero's eloquence but only Ciceronian philosophy. For Valla agreed with Jerome that philosophy is a seedbed of heresy and that the opinions of the philosophers are dangerous to faith. Eloquence, in contrast, is "the queen of knowledge and a perfect wisdom." All the Greek and Latin fathers clothed their divine discourse with the gold and silver of eloquence. Philological expertise is indispensable for understanding Scripture; rhetoric is indispensable for persuading men and women to accept the truth and to pursue the good and avoid evil. Eloquence embellishes the house of the Lord; its beauty and majesty raise the mind to God. Eloquence, indeed, is the only form of secular learning appropriately applied to theology. Rightly understood, therefore, the charge against Jerome was that he had lingered too long over Plato's and Cicero's philosophical works and had not devoted enough time to sacred literature. He answered the charge in a principled way, not by turning his back on humane letters, but by spending most of the rest of his life translating and commenting on the Bible.[10]

Angelo Poliziano (1454–1494) took yet a different tack. He defended Cicero and Jerome in the *Liber miscellaneorum* by citing the famous passage in Augustine's *Confessions* about Cicero's lost *Hortensius*, the book, Augustine said, that had "first kindled his longing for immortal wisdom and set him at last on the path to his salvation"; and then went on, "Oh how I wish that those who bring up Jerome's dream would read these words of Augustine's!"[11]

Scrupulous clerics nevertheless complained that reading the poets corrupted morals. A common rejoinder was to show, on the authority of Jerome, that even St. Paul had quoted the poets: "For when he wrote to Titus, 'Cretans are always liars, evil beasts, and lazy gluttons' [Tit. 1:12], he was using a verse of the poet Epimenides. In another letter, he cites a line of Menander: 'Bad company ruins good manners' "[12] [1 Cor. 15:33]. If Paul read the poets, how can lesser men prohibit them? Another way of disarming criticism was to agree that Terence, Persius, and Juvenal were sometimes obscene, but then to argue that they pictured lust only to castigate it. Properly understood, their purpose was to teach the young what to imitate and what to avoid. "Our Jerome," said the famous schoolmaster Guarino Veronese (1374–1460), "whose strict probity, divine holiness, capacious learning and eloquence sweeter than honey are beyond praise" often painted vice in lively colors for the same reason, shocking his readers with descriptions of illicit pleasures in order to make them hate immodesty the more.[13] A third argument, also derived from the fathers, was that pagan poets and philosophers could, and should, be read, but with discrimination. Leonardo Bruni translated St. Basil's *Ad adolescentes,* a homily on the proper place of classical studies in a Christian education, because, he said, "through the authority of such a man I wished to put an end to the ignorant perversity of those who attack the *studia humanitatis* and regard them as wholly abhorrent."[14] The little essay became one of the works most frequently copied and printed in fifteenth-century Italy.[15] Its theme is that pagan literature is beneficial if we select what is useful and avoid the rest. To the degree that a pagan poet or prose writer benefits character (and the degree is considerable, because Christian and pagan ethics agree on many points), read him. When he falls into error, reject the passage and move on. Jerome's letter to Flavius Magnus, official orator of the city of Rome, laid down the same principle to guide the reading of ancient authors and was as popular in the Renaissance and often quoted as Basil's *Ad adolescentes:* when reading the ancients, he advised, absorb what is wholesome and beautiful, leaving their idolatry, error, and lust to pass to its natural decay.[16]

Error, though, especially philosophical error, is not always easy to discern. The fathers are helpful here too: they identify the dangers and show us what to reject and why. Some of Aristotle's teachings had long been recognized as perilous. By the end of the fifteenth century, sensitive observers perceived threats from other ancient schools, their doctrines now more accurately known and widely circulated. Zanobi Acciaiuoli, Florentine poet, Dominican friar converted by Savonarola, and prefect of the Vatican Library under Pope Leo X, suggested a patristic remedy. Between 1500 and 1519 he translated from the Greek Eusebius of Caesarea's *Against Hierocles,* an attack on a provincial governor under Diocletian who had written a book showing that the Neo-Pythagorean wise man and magus Apollonius of Tyana, who had died aged almost one hundred during the reign of Nerva, was as great a sage, as remarkable a worker of miracles, and as potent an exorcist as Jesus Christ; and two works by Theodoret, bishop of Cyrrhus, near Antioch, from 423 to 466: a treatise *On Providence* and a work entitled *A Cure for Pagan Maladies or the Truth of the Gospels Proved from Greek Philosophy.* He selected these works for translation because he thought they would be useful antidotes to particular intellectual poisons. "A few years ago," he wrote in his preface to Theodoret's *Cure for Pagan Maladies,* "when the *Life of Apollonius of Tyana* by Philostratus was published in Latin, I decided to translate Eusebius's *Against Hierocles* . . . as an antidote to Philostratus's poison, in order that no one should be deluded by his legendary story and think like the Pythagorean Hierocles that Apollonius was the equal of Jesus Christ, but rather recognise him as the poisonous impostor he really was." Turning to Plato, he went on: "I now hear that the Greek text of Plato has appeared [Zanobi was referring to the edition of Marcus Musurus and Aldus, published in Venice in 1513, the *editio princeps* of Plato], a philosopher whose eloquence is incomparable but some of whose doctrines have always been perniciously harmful to the Christian church. In these circumstances I think it useful to translate this book of Theodoret into Latin, for he shows how contradictory are Plato's teachings and those of many other philosophers on the most important matters and how shameful their morals. From it our contemporaries may learn to avoid what is harmful in the philosophers and to devote themselves with renewed piety and ardor to reading sacred literature."[17]

Zanobi was using patristic authority and arguments to counter the errors of Hellenism. Through Theodoret's *Cure* he warned his contemporaries against Plato's community of wives and his foolish notion about the transmigration of souls and showed them that Socrates, whom all proclaimed "the best of the Greek philosophers," was in reality an irascible and libidinous old man who went to the gymnasium to look at handsome boys, got drunk with Aristophanes and Alcibiades, had two

wives at once, and frequented prostitutes as well.[18] He hoped that Eusebius's *Against Hierocles* would alert the attentive reader to the diabolical
traps hidden in contemporary as well as in ancient Neo-Pythagoreanism.
He considered Theodoret's *On Providence* an antidote to Epicurus and
Democritus, "who say that our lives are ruled by chance and fortune
rather than by providence," and to the Aristotelian teaching that God is
indifferent to what happens in the sublunar world, a doctrine commonly
discussed by the secular Aristotelians of the Italian universities of his own
day. In passing he approved the Stoics for their more acceptable teachings
about providence, but showed in the end how only the Hebrew and
Christian fathers knew and spoke the truth, the Hebrews through a glass
darkly, the Christians clearly and plainly.[19]

Heresy, most people believed, was more dangerous even than pagan
error; and since old heresies, like old philosophies, tend to reappear, the
arguments of the fathers against them remain useful. The interlocutors of
an anonymous dialogue prefacing a life of St. Jerome and a French
translation of the letters of Pseudo-Eusebius of Cremona, Pseudo-Augustine, and Pseudo-Cyril, prepared around 1510 for Anne de France, duchess of Bourbon, lament that the church and the faith are riddled with
divisions and heresies, among them the belief that men's souls perish like
those of animals and that there is no other life than this present corruptible one on earth; that man has no need to believe in anything but what he
sees in this world; that God is indifferent to the acts of men because his
mind, attuned only to the infinite, cannot stoop to a knowledge of
corruptible particulars; that we can acquire no merits by faith because all
merits come from operations of the will, not of the mind, whereas faith is
an intellectual operation; that men need only the law of nature and have
no need of Scripture or the law of grace; and that it is folly to believe what
reason tells us is impossible—the Trinity or the Incarnation, for example.
In order to keep evangelical doctrine pure and to stamp out heresy, God
sent mankind the four doctors of the Latin Church: St. Augustine to
refute errors about the Trinity; St. Ambrose to allay doubts about the
immortality of the soul and future rewards and punishment; and St.
Gregory to publish good ordinances, rules, statutes, and instructions for
living uprightly. The other great source of error comes from misreading
and misunderstanding Scripture, which leads to the "detestable heresy of
not confessing the divinity of our Lord Jesus and not believing him to be
truly God and truly man, consubstantial with the father, equal to him in
deity and coeternal by eternal generation." To eradicate this error God

sent St. Jerome "who, with great effort and continuous study, translated the truth of the two testaments into the Latin tongue and explained the high mysteries therein contained."[20]

The fathers' orthodoxy and moral seriousness, their purity of style and discriminating devotion to the classics, made them popular with schoolmasters. Morals and learning alike might well be improved by the judicious use of Gentile literature in education; or so most educators thought. Nevertheless, as the Franciscan Giovanni da Prato put it to Guarino, why continue to read lascivious poets when the works of Christian doctors are available? Cyprian, Augustine, and Jerome combine divine and human wisdom with eloquence, precisely that union of virtuous matter and good writing that is claimed for the best pagans. Why seek elsewhere for readings for the young?[21] The Italian grammaticus Lorenzo Astemio (c. 1435–c. 1506), best known for his translations into Latin of many of Aesop's *Fables* (and for composing fables of his own), answered the question by publishing a little book for his pupils containing Basil the Great's sermon on the solitary life, [Pseudo-]Hilary's life of St. Mary Magdalen, a poem by Petrarch in praise of St. Jerome, and Jerome's own lives of Malchus and Paul the first hermit. From each of them, he believed, young men would learn to tell good from bad in both life and literature. "Why should we teach such things from the books of the Gentiles when works like these are just as elegant and even more conducive to living well? Guarino of Verona, the best educator of his day, regularly used these eloquent treatises by St. Jerome in order to shape the tender minds of his pupils."[22] Astemio and Guarino were not exceptional: all humanistic reading programs and the curricula of every humanistic school included works by the fathers, grouped now with the classical writers rather than with the medieval theologians.

German pedagogues, hoping to coax the Muses north of the Alps, followed the Italian lead. Johannes Murmellius (1480–1517), schoolmaster and poet, famous among contemporaries for his *Elegiae morales,* and the poet laureate and itinerant professor of rhetoric Johannes Aesticampianus (1457–1520) wrote commentaries on several letters of St. Jerome in order to teach German youth eloquence (*copia dicendi*) and probity (*via honeste vivendi*). To this end, Murmellius asked his pupils to memorize brief sayings that he had drawn from Jerome's works: "Believe me, poison lurks beneath the honey"; "An old proverb says that man's life is as fragile as a bubble"; "Charity is the mother of all virtues"; "True friendship should not hide what it feels"; "Any man ignorant of his creator is a beast."[23] No medicine, asserted Aesticampianus, cures the maladies of the soul so well as Jerome's letters; they curb pride, root out avarice, bridle lust, and cleanse the heart of selfishness and ingratitude. The sweet and nourishing works of the fathers "marvellously join divine wisdom to human eloquence" and teach us how to lead a virtuous life.[24]

The fathers educated and appealed to Renaissance men and women in more sophisticated ways. Scholars found in many patristic works un-mined veins of information about ancient history, society, philosophy, and religion, both pagan and Christian, and a very large number of fragments of classical texts now lost. The *Divine Institutes* of Lactantius was an important source for Renaissance knowledge of Epicureanism. The historian Polydor Vergil, combing the pagan and Christian classics for information for his book on the inventors of things (1499), learned from Lactantius that Pythagoras was the first to call himself a philosopher or lover of wisdom; from Jerome that the Persians called the earliest thinkers magi, the Britons and Gauls called them Druids, and the Indians gymnosophists, the chief of whom was named Budda; and from Greek fathers that Cybele invented the shepherd's pipe or that the cithara of the Jews had twenty-four strings and was shaped like a triangle. In his *Cure for Pagan Maladies,* Theodoret of Cyrrhus quoted more than one hundred philosophers, poets, and historians in about 240 different passages. The *Preparation for the Gospel* of Eusebius of Caesarea, translated in 1448 by George Trebizond, enjoyed a great popularity (more than forty-five manuscripts survive, and there were seven printings between 1470 and 1501), among other reasons because in the course of explaining why Christians rejected the Greek tradition Eusebius had preserved an epi-gram by Callimachus, a fragment of Euripides' *Malanippe Captiva,* and passages in iambic verse from *Exodus,* a tragedy by the Jewish dramatist Ezekiel. Numenius the Neo-Pythagorean is known almost entirely from Eusebius. He quoted extensively from Porphyry's *On the Philosophy to be Derived from Oracles* and from the same Neo-Platonist's famous treatise *Against the Christians.*[25]

But the fathers, especially the Greeks, offered intellectuals more than scattered facts and new texts. Most humanists had fairly optimistic views of the dignity of man and the freedom of the will, preferences closely related to their professional duties and the central position of moral philosophy in the *studia humanitatis.* The Greek fathers allowed the human will a good deal more freedom than did the theological tradition of the Latin West. It is not surprising, therefore, to find Erasmus relying on the authority of Origen when he attacked Luther in 1524 in his *De libero arbitrio*.[26] Free choice, moreover, was fundamental to the idea of the dignity of man in its later fifteenth- and sixteenth-century formulation; namely, that man, a link between the physical and intellectual worlds, and between macrocosm and microcosm, is a largely autonomous moral agent, containing in his own nature the possibility of the most varied development, who can, by free choice, become akin to any being, become like a rock or plant or beast if he turn toward evil, like the angels if he turn toward good. This cluster of ideas had its immediate nourishing source in pages of Gregory of Nyssa and in Nemesius of Emesa's *De natura hominis* (c. 390). A remarkable encomium of man occurs at the end of the first chapter of Nemesius's treatise, a passage the direct source of which was Origen's *Commentary on Genesis* but which synthesizes themes from thinkers and works as various as Galen and Philo, Aristotle's *De anima*, and Posidonius's *Hymn to Man* (partially preserved in Cicero's *De natura deorum*) to forge an important link in a tradition that extends from Sophocles' *Antigone* to Pico della Mirandola's *Oration on the Dignity of Man*.

> Who can fittingly admire the dignity of man, who joins in himself the mortal and immortal, the rational and irrational; who bears in his own nature the image of the whole creation and for this reason is called a microcosm or little world; who is God's special care and for whose sake God made all things and himself became man. . . . Who can enumerate the excellence and ornaments of the nature of man. He crosses the seas, he penetrates the heavens with the eye of the mind, he understands the course of the stars and their intervals and sizes; . . . no science, art or doctrine escapes his penetration; . . . he foresees the future; he rules over all, he dominates all, enjoys all; speaks with angels and with God; commands at his pleasure all other creatures; subjugates the demons; learnedly investigates the natural world and the essence of God, becomes a house and a temple of God, and achieves all this by piety and virtue.[27]

Patristic works could of course be put to very different purposes: to assert the superiority of virginity to marriage (Jerome's *Ep.* 22 to Eustochium, "De virginitate servanda," was the most frequently copied of all his letters) or to promote ascetic sanctity and the solitary life (there are more early editions of Jerome's three saints' lives than of any other of his works). Churchmen used the fathers as authorities in theological controversies. When Cardinal Giuliano Cesarini began to prepare the Latin case before the meeting of the Council of Ferrara-Florence, called to negotiate the reunion of the Greek and Latin Churches, he asked Traversari to translate Basil's *Adversus Eunomium* because he believed it to support the Latin position on the procession of the Holy Spirit: he wished, that is, to refute the Greeks out of their own mouths. Reliance on the fathers for confessional advantage would become endemic after 1517. Serious Christians were sensitive to the relation of patristic example and reform of the church. By the end of the fourteenth century the apostolic and patristic church, the primitive and ancient church, had everywhere become a standard against which to measure the abuses of the present and a model for aspiration, imitation, and reform, while reform itself had come to be understood as the effort to restore the church to the image of its ancient holiness. And occasionally a father was used to salt a learned jest. The aging Poggio wrote a little dialogue celebrating his matrimonial felicity: *An seni sit uxor ducenda;* should an old man take a wife? He answered yes. The title echoed and the answer deliberately contradicted a characteristic piece of advice from Jerome: *Non est ergo uxor ducenda sapienti;* the wise man should not marry.[28]

But humanist intellectuals admired the fathers above all because they found in their works, or thought they had, a normative style of piety and religious sensibility, one distilled in the Petrarchan phrase *docta pietas* and in the formula used by many humanists to describe their religious program: the union of wisdom and piety with eloquence. This is why humanists used the fathers as polemical rods with which to beat the scholastics. For not only was the style of the theologians of the recent past said to be barbarous and therefore incapable of persuading men and women to love God and their neighbors, the *summae* were thought to be unnecessarily complex. When scholastic theologians raised knotty difficulties, opposed authorities *sic et non,* probed *quaestiones* in disputations and reconciled them by a subtle logic, they were pandering to their own dialectical pride rather than serving the faith; indeed they were contaminating theology with profane philosophy. To the theology of the schoolmen they opposed a *vetus ac vera theologia,* the piety of the fathers (which they conveniently claimed to have prefigured their own), and which they understood to be simpler, more pure, more personal and emotional, more humbly and accurately dependent on the divine text, directed less to the presumptuous and inevitably disputatious goal of trying to know God in his fullness than toward the more human and possible aim of ardently loving him, more persuasively concerned with moral teaching, closer to the source of the truth. The scholastics sought to make theology a science, a *scientia* in the Aristotelian sense, that is, to establish a systematically ordered body of true and certain knowledge derived from the certain but undemonstrable principles of revelation. This effort, too, humanists typically attacked as misguided, arrogant, and dangerous because it produced only sophistry, arid intellectualism, emotional poverty, and lack of charity. The learned and eloquent piety of the fathers, in contrast, was not a science but a positive wisdom, a holy rhetoric derived from the holy page of Scripture. The simple, evangelical, scriptural faith Renaissance humanists attributed to the fathers justified their own aversion to scholastic method, their insistence on a return to the sources in the original languages, the normally exegetical form of their own theological work, and the end they sought—an eloquent and warm personal piety joined to moral probity, an evangelical and scriptural faith consciously tailored to give spiritual and moral guidance to an educated laity.[29]

The fathers wrote no summas, therefore. As the most orthodox possible soldiers of Christian truth, they wrote polemics against the heretic or commentaries on Scripture, making the blinding illumination of the sacred text accessible to the fragile eyes of the human mind. We come to the fathers depressed with worldly cares; we leave them hungry and thirsty for the page of Scripture. The Christianity that compels men's hearts is the eloquently preached word of Scripture, not the subtle analysis of doctrine. Love is more important than knowledge, virtuous action than nicety of belief.

The fathers guarded the purity of the scriptural word with textual criticism. Origen and Jerome could read the Bible in its original tongues; they had developed the critical techniques necessary to maintain an uncontaminated transmission of the holy text, and both men prepared new translations and corrected older ones against the original. Such studies became models for the crowning part of the humanists' religious program: a return to the sources, the learning of Greek and Hebrew, the preparation of more reliable editions of the Greek and Hebrew texts, and the critical examination and correction of the Vulgate, studies associated with the name of St. Jerome throughout the Middle Ages and intermittently pursued with blinkered penetration by scholars like Nicolò Maniacoria and the biblical *correctores* of the thirteenth century (to medieval critics the *Hebraica veritas* normally meant Jerome's translation from the Hebrew, not the Hebrew text itself, while the relation of the Latin New

Testament to the *Graeca veritas* was barely understood even to raise a difficulty).

Giannozzo Manetti and Valla put biblical studies on a firmer philological ground. Manetti, especially, modeled himself on Jerome: Jerome's translation of the Bible, he wrote, has been so useful to Christians, especially Latin Christians, and so indispensable to the salvation of the human race, that "nothing to equal it has been produced by a single author from the creation of the world until the present time." Manetti translated the New Testament from the Greek. In 1442, he began to study Hebrew with Immanuel ben Abraham da San Miniato, a member of the Florentine Jewish community, and in 1454–55 he translated the Psalms from the Hebrew verity. The *Apology*[30] he wrote a year later to defend himself against the charge that he was needlessly presuming to do again what Jerome had already done superbly is as remarkable as Valla's *Collatio* of the New Testament.[31] But in Italy, in the fifteenth century, their pioneering achievements aroused little response. Manetti's work remained in manuscript; Valla's *Collatio* made its first historic impact on Erasmus. Only in the sixteenth century did European theologians come to recognize textual criticism of the Bible as permanently desirable, necessary, and fruitful.

A more focused picture of what fifteenth-century humanists admired in St. Jerome is provided by orations delivered in his praise on his feast day, 30 September. They have the added interest of showing how the cult of St. Jerome was reshaped in a humanist environment. A fair number of these orations survive, concentrated in date between the late fourteenth century and the early sixteenth. Among the orators were Pier Paolo Vergerio; Niccolò Bonavia of Lucca, a student at the University of Padua (he spoke at Mass in the church of S. Andrea on 30 September 1410);[32] Isotta Nogarola (1418–1466), a woman of broad humanistic interests whom the bishop and citizens of Verona about 1453 invited to deliver the annual oration in praise of Jerome; and the Sienese grammarian Agostino Dati (1420–1478).[33] Niccolò Bonavia and Agostino Dati have left the particularity of their "incredible love" and "singular veneration" for Jerome undefined. Vergerio and Nogarola reveal more about their personal feelings and the reasons for their devotion to him.

Vergerio was born in Capodistria, close to the presumed location of Jerome's birthplace at Stridon. Jerome was a local saint. But the family knew him to be its special *protector gloriosus* because of the "many benefits and graces" he had conferred on it. In particular, father and son believed that Jerome's miraculous intervention had saved them several times from the greatest perils, notably in 1380, when the Genoese burned Capodistria during the War of Chioggia. In gratitude Pier Paolo visited Jerome's tomb in S. Maria Maggiore and composed an office in his honor. Whenever father and son were apart on 30 September, the son wrote his father a letter in which he thanked their patron saint with "sincere devotion and pious joy" and prayed that with his intercession they might reach heaven after death. About 1390, when he was twenty, he vowed to give a yearly oration in praise of St. Jerome on his feast day. Ten of these orations survive. Two are dated, 1392 and 1408 respectively; the others probably fall between those dates.[34]

The devotion of Isotta Nogarola to Jerome helps us understand his appeal to educated women. Isotta was a member of a patrician family from Verona. She had a humanist tutor and before she was twenty was celebrated for her Latin eloquence. Then at the age of twenty-three, she turned from secular to sacred letters; refusing to marry, she pledged herself to perpetual virginity. She did not become a nun, but simply withdrew to her own property and lived in semi-eremitic retreat in a book-lined cell in one wing of her house, dividing her time between prayer and study.[35] She acquired a great contemporary reputation for learning and sanctity, and a host of distinguished men showered her with sexist compliments. Guarino Veronese urged her to "create a man within the woman."[36] Lauro Quirini congratulated her for overcoming her female nature and achieving the true virtue that usually only men possess.[37] Her difficulties come out vividly in her letters ("How often when I consider the position of women," she wrote to Guarino, "have I lamented my ill fortune in being born a woman, since men mock them both in words and practice")[38] and in her most interesting surviving work, a dialogue on the relative responsibility of Adam and Eve for the fall of mankind. Nogarola blamed Adam, but she based her defense of Eve on the acknowledged fact of female weakness. Since Eve was created imperfect by nature, she cannot be held primarily responsible for the fall: "For where there is less good sense and less constancy, there is less sin; and this is the case with Eve; therefore she sinned less."[39]

In spite of the perversity of his sexual ethic and his warning to priests and monks to be on guard even when visiting their mothers,[40] Jerome had a marked sympathy and admiration for women. His most cherished disciples were the female descendants of Camillus and Fabius, of the

Scipios and the Gracchi. He wrote almost daily to Paula and Eustochium. When contemporaries mocked him for discussing religion with women and for dedicating so many of his works to them, he replied that women had the knowledge and intellectual curiosity he would have liked to find in men.[41] What God values, he remarked, is not gender but the heart; and he supported his view by listing from secular and sacred history women distinguished for their virtue and learning. After his resurrection Jesus appeared first to women. These women became the apostles of the apostles: *apostolorum apostolae*.[42] So it is not surprising that Isotta found in him a congenial spiritual guide and that she chose to model her conduct on the devotional practices that Eustochium and her mother had established in their palaces on the Aventine before following Jerome to Bethlehem: retirement from the world in an isolated room ("May the privacy of your chamber protect you always," Jerome had written to Eustochium), virginity ("Preserve the virginity you were born with"), and study of the Bible ("Let sleep overtake you with the [holy] book in your hand").[43]

In form and decor the orations are markedly classical. The style is attempted Ciceronian; the genre the classical encomium or panegyric. Invariably the speakers begin by confessing that Jerome's virtues far outstrip the capacities of their eloquence. The events of his life evoke classical parallels. When his parents sent him to Rome to study with Donatus, the greatest scholar of the age, they were imitating Philip of Macedon, who had put small Alexander to school with Aristotle.[44] Jerome's travels remind Agostino Dati of Pythagoras, Plato, and Apollonius of Tyana, who had traveled to Egypt and elsewhere to learn the secrets of the sages, while his appetite for learning reminds Nogarola of Euclid. He is more eloquent than Isocrates, Cicero, or Quintilian. He is more prudent than Cato, Solon, or Socrates. Attilius Regulus, Paulus Aemilius, Scipio Africanus are praised for their virtues; but in comparison with Jerome's, theirs are only insubstantial reflections of virtue: *virtutis simulacra*.[45] Like Pythagoras, Jerome was a vegetarian. His speech on his deathbed was weightier and suaver than Socrates' "on the day he took poison in an Athenian prison."[46] Even his superiority as an ascetic is measured by comparing him to ascetic pagans; his austerities were more rigorous than those of Socrates Thebanus, Xenocrates, Diogenes the Cynic, or Anacharsis the Scythian (also reputed to have invented the wheel). Whole sections of the orations are structured on ancient philosophical definitions, distinctions, or arguments. To help him classify Jerome's virtues, Bonavia turned to Plotinus. Plotinus says that the

Platonists distinguish four kinds of virtue: political, purgative, the virtues of a pure, clean mind (*puri et detersi animi virtutes*), and exemplary virtues, the archetypal reasons in God's mind inaccessible to human beings. Jerome excelled in each of the first three virtues: the political through his active services to the church and his unremitting efforts to foster the salvation and welfare of his fellow citizens, namely, that all men and women be united in the Heavenly City under a single law and a single orthodox faith; the purgative through his penitential austerities in the desert; and the virtues of a pure and clean mind through preserving his virginity.[47] Wishing to characterize Jerome's wisdom, Bonavia cast the net of allusion even wider: "If wisdom and philosophy are a school of virtue, as certain Stoics say, or the desire for right reason and a disciplined intelligence, or, according to Plato, a preparation for death and the calming of the mind's perturbations, then no one, by Hercules, was wiser than Jerome, no one finer in this kind of philosophizing."[48]

If we now move behind the classicizing decor and ask which of Jerome's achievements or qualities these humanist orators especially admired, then it is clear that they emphasize first his eloquence, regularly termed divine; second, his knowledge of languages (though there is no hint yet that one should follow his example and wish to read the Old Testament in Hebrew and the New Testament in Greek, still less that knowledge of these tongues should be used to correct the Vulgate text); third, his knowledge of Graeco-Roman literature, classical mythology, and history, of the "good arts" or the humanities, and his exemplary practice of basing theological study on the foundation of the *studia humanitatis,* imitating Moses and Daniel, who mastered the learning of the Egyptians and Chaldeans before turning to sacred things;[49] fourth, his heroic virtue and his distinction as a moral philosopher, one, as P. P. Vergerio put it, who taught by example as well as words, who was as pure in his life as he was in his speech, who practiced what he preached, unlike contemporary preachers who urge virtue on their hearers but make no effort to live well themselves; fifth, the union itself in him of *ars bene dicendi* and *ars bene vivendi* and so his embodiment of the Roman ideal of the orator: *bonus vir dicendi peritus;* and finally, his knowledge of Scripture, his skill and usefulness as a biblical commentator, and his mastery of true theology.[50]

The orators do not fail to marvel at the "white martyrdom" of his mortifications, his contempt for "what was then most beautiful and distinguished in the world," namely the city of Rome, and his decision to exchange his fatherland for the desert, his home for a convent, his relatives and friends for the companionship of monks, and civic life (*vita civilis*) for the life of a hermit.[51] But what they admired most was his Christian scholarship. "He understood," said Isotta Nogarola, "that nothing is sweeter to a servant of God than studious leisure, than the study of letters through which we learn about the infinity of things and of nature, about the sky, earth, seas, and at last about God himself. He read so much we can hardly imagine how he found time to write; he wrote so much that it is difficult to believe he could have found time to read."[52]

A characteristically humanist pattern of exaggeration colors the orations. We learn that the Tiburtine Sibyl predicted Jerome's birth, career, and death;[53] that Aristotle wrote four hundred books, Epicurus three hundred, Chrysippus seven hundred, and Democritus and Zeno very many too, but that Jerome wrote more than any of them; or that what Averroës said of Aristotle should rather be said of him: "Not the smallest error is to be found in any of his works."[54] Bonavia therefore called him more than human (*fere supra hominem vir maximus Hieronymus*).[55] P. P. Vergerio claimed that he possessed every branch of learning and all the virtues in the rarest and most excellent degree. His life was a model of sanctity, his eloquence prodigious, his knowledge a miracle. "Is it not obvious then that there was something divine in this man?"[56]

A series of large-scale Jerome altarpieces, commissioned at intervals between 1420 and 1520 by Italian burgher patricians and elegantly painted in the new manners of the Quattrocento and high Renaissance, translated the Latin orations into a visual vernacular. About 1430, Rinieri di Luca di Piero Rinieri, one of the richest merchant-bankers in Florence, commissioned from Francesco d'Antonio a Virgin and Child with saints, probably for the Florentine community of the Gesuati, who from 1409 to 1438 occupied the church and nunnery of S. Trinitá Vecchia in Via Guelfa (fig. 29). On the Virgin's right is John the Baptist; on her left, Jerome as a doctor of the church, a book in one hand, a pen in the other. The predella illustrates the Ciceronian dream (see fig. 2), Jerome's vision of the Trinity and the legendary anecdote about how he lifted himself up in bed with a cord during his last illness (see fig. 11), and his death. The little figure on the left of the predella is Blessed Giovanni Colombini, that on the right a flagellant, a reminder that flagellation continued to be a central spiritual exercise in the congregations and confraternities dedicated to St. Jerome.

A generation later, the Medici presented a Jerome altarpiece by the Master of the Buckingham Palace Madonna, a follower of Fra Angelico,

Fig. 29.   Franceso d'Antonio, *The Rinieri Altarpiece*, c. 1430

possibly the miniaturist Zanobi Strozzi, to the Hermits of St. Jerome in
Fiesole (fig. 30). Not to be outdone, the Ruccelai donated to the Fiesole
Hieronymites for the same church a second Jerome altarpiece, by Francesco Botticini (see fig. 27). The altarpieces record Jerome's special devotion to the Virgin, his equality in sanctity to John the Baptist, the favor
shown him by Pope Damasus, his friendship with Paula and Eustochium,
and his penitential asceticism, while the predellas recall by now wholly

Fig. 30.   Master of the Buckingham Palace Madonna, *St. Jerome Altarpiece*, c. 1460.
The Virgin and Child flanked by St. Jerome with Saints Cosmas and Damian, on the
one side, and St. John the Baptist with Saints Francis and Lawrence, on the other. The
predella shows *The Dream of St. Jerome, The Death of St. Jerome, Christ Entombed, The
Apparition of St. Jerome to St. Augustine,* and *The Miraculous Punishment of the Heretic
Sabinianus,* another of the miracles invented by Ps.-Cyril of Jerusalem. The Medici arms
appear at each end of the predella.

familiar incidents from his life and legend as well as the miracles *post
mortem* invented by Ps.-Augustine and Ps.-Cyril.

Elsewhere in Tuscany, wealthy patrons were equally careful of their
salvation and prestige. In 1471, members of the Placidi family acquired
rights to the Chapel of St. Jerome in the church of S. Domenico in Siena
and, soon after, commissioned Matteo di Giovanni to paint an altarpiece
showing the Madonna Enthroned flanked by a penitent Jerome and a
kneeling John the Baptist. When Giovanni di Angelo Placidi made his
will in 1474, he instructed his younger brother and heir to bury him in the

family chapel and to go himself (or send another) on pilgrimage to "St. Jerome's body in Rome" and make an offering there on his behalf.[57] In Arezzo, Niccolò Gamurrini, a wealthy lawyer, paid half of the cost (50 *fiorini d'oro larghi*) of a Jerome altarpiece of similar type commissioned in 1519 from Luca Signorelli by the Compagnia di S. Girolamo of his native city. The main subject, now in the picture gallery at Arezzo, shows the Virgin and Child with Saints Jerome, Nicholas, Stephen, and Donatus, patron of Arezzo, accompanied by angels and the donor. Among the scenes on the predella were three of Jerome's apparitions: to Sulpicius Severus, St. Augustine, and Cyril of Jerusalem (see figs. 19 and 20). In a fatiguing act of piety, members of the Company carried the heavy altarpiece from Cortona, where Signorelli painted it, to Arezzo.[58]

Orations and altarpieces offered a classicizing version of Jerome's life and legend tailored to contemporary humanist taste. Its shape emerges clearly in a biography of the saint by an interesting minor figure, Laudivio Zacchia. Laudivio was born about 1435 at Vezzano Ligure, south of La Spezia, studied under Guarino at Ferrara, was in Rome during the pontificate of Nicholas V (1447–1455), and in 1465 dedicated to Duke Borso d'Este a Senecan tragedy about the death of the famous condottiere Giacomo conte Piccinino (murdered by order of Ferrante of Aragon in July of that same year). Soon after, he moved to Naples where he was a member of the circle around Pontano and Panormita. He wrote in Naples a brief exhortation in praise of wisdom and virtue (in it he refers to himself for the first time as a knight of the Order of St. John of Jerusalem); a curious book purporting to be a collection of letters from Muhammed II, the grand Turk, to divers kings, princes, signors, and republics; and, about 1470, a life of St. Jerome. In the summer of 1475 he was with the knights of St. John on the island of Rhodes. He returned to Italy with a library of Greek books. In 1478 he was in Hungary.[59]

Laudivio's *Vita beati Hieronymi*[60] is as stylized and tendentious in its way as the notice of Jerome in the *Golden Legend* or a work like Machiavelli's *Life of Castruccio Castracani of Lucca*. The key to it is supplied by the colophon of a manuscript copy in Heidelberg. It identifies Jerome as *divus litterarum princeps*. As Aristotle was *philosophorum princeps* and Averroës prince of commentators, or *the* commentator, so Jerome became in the fifteenth century prince of scholars and patron of schools, universities, and men of letters. Plutarch and Livy have eloquently recounted the deeds of the noble Greeks and Romans, whose glory was brief and mortal, writes Laudivio in his introduction; how much more properly we should praise the life, works, and saintly character of Jerome, whose glory is eternal. We read Plato and Aristotle every day, although they can teach us only about things human; from Jerome we learn about both human and divine things. In virtue he was superior to Aristides and Cato; in continence, to Socrates. He much surpassed in wisdom Pythagoras and Apollonius of Tyana and all the other wise men of antiquity. Demosthenes and Cicero were not more eloquent. So let us praise Jerome; better still, let us imitate his life and deeds![61]

Jerome's father, a patrician and a chief magistrate in Stridon, made sure that his son was properly trained in the humanities from his earliest childhood. As the handsome, wise, and diligent boy grew older, he became ever more passionately attached to literary studies. Stridon began to seem provincial to him. Aroused by the fame of the rhetoricians and philosophers of Rome, he decided at the age of sixteen to leave home and go there. Neither the tears of his parents nor the pleas of his friends could hold him back. With dry eyes he withdrew from their embraces, set sail (barely escaping shipwreck on the stormy Adriatic), and landed at Brindisi. From there he followed the Via Appia to Rome. Needless to say, much of this picturesque detail is imaginary.[62]

In Rome he studied Greek and Latin literature with Donatus and Victorinus, read Plato and Aristotle, and acquired "an incredible knowledge of all things" and contempt for the subtleties of the gymnosophists—Laudivio's crack at the scholastics.[63] Having been ordained a priest and appointed a cardinal presbyter, he repaid the favor shown him by Pope Damasus by defending the Christian commonwealth against the Arian heresy, exciting admiration as much for the uprightness of his life as for the orthodoxy of his doctrine and the gold of his eloquence. What especially marked him was his respect for Gentile literature, for he always cited both Scripture and the "reasons of the philosophers" and taught that reliance on the Bible did not mean abandoning what is useful in the pagans.[64] In spite of his goodness, wicked men conspired against him. Laudivio retells the story of how Jerome was tricked into wearing women's clothes to church, emphasizing though that he left the city voluntarily.

Looking now for the leisure and solitude he needed for literary and biblical study, he went to the East, first to Constantinople, then to Jerusalem. Laudivio is particularly inventive about Jerome's impressions of Jerusalem—where he went, what he saw, his happiness when he walked in the very places Jesus had walked, his tears on the Mount of

Olives and on Calvary, and his fruitful meditation on Christ's death.[65] The account of Jerome in the desert (the same desert where John the Baptist had lived as an anchorite) mirrors exactly the bloodier contemporary Florentine pictures of St. Jerome in penitence. "You would scarcely have taken him for a Roman citizen then. . . . O happy Jerome, no mortal can be compared to you. A hundred tongues, a hundred mouths, a voice of bronze would not suffice me to sing your praises!"[66] But at the pope's request he left the desert and began to translate the Bible for the common good. Settled in Bethlehem, he produced the corpus of work which very recently German printers have reproduced with "marvellous art and ingenuity," and that was so well edited that what had been corrupted by the passage of time and the carelessness of copyists can now be read with confidence and ease.[67] (Laudivio refers to the editions issued in Rome in 1468 by C. Sweynheym and A. Pannartz and by Sixtus Riessinger, each in two folio volumes.) Laudivio ends the life with three chapters describing Jerome's last days and death, an abridgment of the letter of Pseudo-Eusebius of Cremona.[68]

Laudivio had no notion of what a critical biography might be and not a clue to the method one would have to use to write one. But like the panegyrics humanist orators delivered on 30 September in Italian churches, monasteries, academic gatherings, princely courts, or public squares, his life was a warm, enthusiastic account, very different in style, tone, and emphasis (Laudivio and the orators gave only muted attention to Jerome's miracles) from anything written about the saint before 1400, a lively portrait of an orator, teacher, scholar, man of letters, and controversialist as well as a hermit, monk, and ascetic.

It is this image that contemporary artists captured and enriched in their portrayals of St. Jerome in his study, a second major new way of representing him invented in Italy during the Renaissance (fig. 31).[69]

The subject was not as popular as Jerome in penitence. A recent list of pictures of St. Jerome dating from about 1400 to 1600, excellent though not exhaustive, yields 558 examples of St. Jerome in penitence and 133 of Jerome in his study.[70] Nor was it as long-lived. Penitential Jeromes remained popular throughout the seventeenth century, and there are scattered examples from the eighteenth century and a handful from the nineteenth. The theme of Jerome in his study originated in northern Italy in the second half of the fourteenth century (the earliest surviving example about which there is general agreement dates from around 1360, a fresco by Tomaso da Modena in the church of S. Nicolò in Treviso,

Fig. 31. Matteo di Giovanni da Siena, *St. Jerome in His Study,* 1492. Jerome is translating the Bible.
Peeping out of open drawers in his *scrivania* are copies of *Ep.* 130, *ad Demetriadem virginem,* and the spurious *De assumptione Virginis,* beginning *Cogitis me (Ep. supp.* 9). The small crystal vase is another Marian reference. It symbolizes her purity and perpetual virginity, following *Ep.* 24:2 where Jerome compared a young virgin to "a brilliant crystal vase purer than any mirror."

though even here Jerome sits in a space that is more a niche than a believable three-dimensional room); it flourished both in Italy and in the North during the fifteenth and early sixteenth centuries, became increasingly rare after about 1530, and had virtually disappeared by 1600.[71] Nor was it as original. Pictures of St. Jerome in his study develop directly out of late medieval illuminated author portraits enclosed within an architectural frame; while these, in turn, go back to early medieval representations of evangelists and doctors showing them writing their books or translations and ultimately to the author portraits of late antiquity. And, of course, seating Jerome indoors at a desk was not the only way to convey visually that he was a biblical scholar and a man of letters as well as a hermit and ascetic. Artists could, and did, scatter books about an otherwise savage landscape, or picture him reading in the wilderness or writing letters or saying his prayers, rather than beating his breast with a stone. In a woodcut by Dürer, we discover him at work inside his cave, visibly supplied with all the books and writing materials he needs.[72] Finally, Jerome is not the only author Renaissance artists pictured in a room with a shelf full of books. A north Italian master, perhaps Altichiero of Verona (d. c. 1385), had painted a famous portrait of Petrarch at work in his study, a fresco that became the model for several early representations of Jerome. Other pagan, Jewish, and Christian authors— King David, the evangelists, Ovid, Seneca, Valerius Maximus, St. Augustine, St. Thomas Aquinas, St. Catherine—were shown similarly closeted.[73]

All that being said, an image like the Detroit *St. Jerome*, attributed to Jan van Eyck, is new and informative. This small picture much resembles the lost *St. Jerome* by Van Eyck admired by the humanist Bartolomeo Fazio for its illusionistic realism (''Jerome like a living being in a library done with rare art'') and is perhaps the very panel by Van Eyck inventoried in the Medici collections in 1492.[74] Jerome sits reading in a Gothic interior (fig. 32). An open book lies on the lectern before him, and his cheek rests against his left hand in the antique gesture of the seer or inspired poet. The tame lion crouches at his feet. He is dressed in red. Although the red hat had been part of a cardinal's insignia since the thirteenth century, the red clothing is more unusual: until the reign of Paul II (1464–1471) the *vestis rubea* was a papal prerogative, while cardinals customarily wore a violet or blue *cappa* over a white tunic or, if they were monks, over the habit of their order (see fig. 13). Individual cardinals wore red only by special permission of the pope or when they

Fig. 32. Attributed to Jan van Eyck, *St. Jerome in His Study*, 1435

represented him as overseas ambassadors (*legati trans mare*) or as legates *a latere,* deputies who exercised papal authority in its highest delegated form.[75] On the table are an hourglass, pens, an inkwell, a box of blotting sand, a straightedge, and other writing materials. The letter on the table is addressed "To the most reverend father and lord in Christ, Lord Jerome, cardinal priest of the title of Santa Croce in Gerusalemme."

The titular cardinal priest of the church of Santa Croce in Gerusalemme from 24 May 1426 until his death in 1443 was Nicolò Albergati.[76] Van Eyck has given Cardinal Albergati's features to St. Jerome, an early example of a kind of travesty portraiture that would become fairly common later on: St. Antonino, archbishop of Florence (d. 1459), Cardinal Nicholas of Cusa (d. 1464), the French humanist and philosopher Jacques Lefèvre d'Etaples (d. 1536), Cardinal Albrecht von Brandenburg (d. 1545), even Martin Luther, are other examples of churchmen and scholars portrayed as St. Jerome.[77] The practice was at once a flattering testimonial that the sitter possessed at least some of Jerome's titles and merits and an act of sympathetic magic by which the devotee declared his special veneration for Jerome and sought to secure his blessing and protection.

The tribute to Cardinal Albergati was not misplaced; he was one of the most distinguished churchmen and ecclesiastical statesmen of his time. The son of a patrician family from Bologna, he entered the Carthusian monastery of S. Girolamo di Casara, the convent that Giovanni d'Andrea had helped to found and caused to be dedicated to St. Jerome, and in due course became its prior. He was associated with a second center of the cult of St. Jerome, S. Maria Maggiore in Rome; he was Guillaume d'Estouteville's predecessor as archpriest of the basilica. In 1417 he was elected bishop of Bologna and in 1426 made a cardinal. In Bologna, he undertook an ambitious program of reform. His most original initiatives were the establishment of a seminary to train young priests, the first of its kind in Europe, and the foundation of a confraternity, the Compagnia di San Girolamo di Miramonte, the mission of which was to catechize the children of the city, one origin of the Sunday school. After Mass on Sundays and feast days, members of the company scattered to the various churches in Bologna where they taught small groups of children to recite and learn the meaning of the *Pater, Ave Maria,* and other prayers; the Ten Commandments and the seven sacraments; the cardinal and theological virtues and the seven capital sins; the Beatitudes and the seven works of mercy. At the age of fourteen, those who had learned their lessons were enrolled among the "maestri evangelici," became members of the confraternity, and in their turn instructed those younger than themselves.

Albergati led active and contemplative lives of equal intensity. His special devotions were to the cults of the Passion, the Eucharist, and the Madonna. "Every moment he could spare from his other activities," reports his first biographer, "he gave over to reading sacred books." The other activities, especially after his promotion to the cardinalate, included many diplomatic missions for the Holy See, a service that culminated in the presidency of the Congress of Arras, a meeting of the duke of Burgundy and representatives of the kings of France and England and the pope in the Benedictine abbey of Saint-Vaast in the summer of 1435 to negotiate an end to the Hundred Years' War. (The Congress was only a partial success: France and Burgundy made peace; England and France remained at war.) Protocol at diplomatic gatherings of this sort demanded exchanges of gifts, tokens of esteem that might become lubricating bribes. Van Eyck's portrait of Cardinal Albergati as St. Jerome was probably commissioned by Duke Philip the Good of Burgundy from his court painter for presentation to the papal legate *a latere* at the close of the Congress.

During the Congress, Albergati was quartered in one room of the apartment of the abbot of Saint-Vaast. The "study" in which we see him sitting, wearing the red of a cardinal legate, is perhaps a corner of that room. An astrolabe hangs from the top shelf of the cupboard recessed into the wall at his left. On its back face it has been possible to read a date, the fifth of the month, a reference to the formal opening of the Congress on 5 August 1435. On the shelves of the cupboard stand a variety of apparently ordinary objects. Their disguised symbolism defines the virtues, teachings, and devotions that Van Eyck's iconographical advisors wished to suggest Albergati shared with St. Jerome. At one level of meaning the books stand for Jerome's learning and theological insight; at another, they are the spiritual texts that Albergati, like every serious monk, read regularly as part of the ordinary monastic regime of prayer and meditation. Below the books, on the right, is a ceramic jar with an apple sitting on top and the word *Tyriaca* painted on its side. Theriaca was a medicament believed to cure the stings of serpents, scorpions, and spiders. The apple is Eve's apple. Theriaca denotes the Christian cure for sin, the medicine of Jesus Christ, the supreme physician. (Two objects absent in the Van Eyck but present in a work much influenced by it, Ghirlandaio's *St. Jerome in His Study* in the church of Ognissanti in Florence,[78] also

Fig. 33.   Albrecht Dürer, *St. Jerome in His Study*, 1514

contain Christian antidotes to sin: an apothecary jar bearing the monogram of Christ and a flat box made of thin strips of wood. The shingle wooden box is a pyx, a shrine containing Eucharistic wafers, the medicine of immortality.) The remaining objects are Marian symbols. The glass jar with the water in it at the opposite end of the shelf from the theriaca attempts a visual translation of phrases from the Song of Songs (Cant. 4:12, 15) customarily applied to the mother of the Savior: a fountain sealed (*fons signatus;* the jar has a paper cover), a well of living water, a stream flowing from Lebanon. The tall thin-necked glass carafe half filled with water and stoppered with a wad of paper represents the mystery of the Virgin Birth and Mary's perpetual virginity, a thesis vigorously defended by the historical Jerome. The beads hanging next to the crystal carafe signify the devotion of both cardinals to the blessed Virgin, for they would have used them to count the prayers into which each "decade" of the Rosary is divided: ten *Ave Marias* preceded by a *Pater noster* and followed by a *Gloria Patri*.[79]

The most eloquent of all representations of St. Jerome in his study is Albrecht Dürer's engraving of 1514 (fig. 33).[80] Jerome is writing rather than reading, perhaps answering one of the several letters tucked under a tape on the wall behind him (his lectern sits on the window sill to his right; his books are out of reach on the sill of the adjoining window and on the bench that runs under both windows). A little dog, an often pictured companion of Christian scholars since Altichiero gave Petrarch one when he painted him in Padua, is curled up asleep on the floor. His lion, sleeping with its eyes open, guards the entrance to the room. The room itself is warm and pleasant, and, because constructed according to an exact mathematical perspective, reassuringly solid, the simplicity of its furnishings relieved by an abundance of plump, soft cushions. Sunlight fills it. The old saint's bald head glows with inspiration. All here is radiant serenity, peace, and calm.

Or so it seems until the image begins to make felt its darker vibrations. Two emblems of transience—the candle and the hourglass—had appeared frequently in earlier representations of Jerome reading or writing in an interior, but this is the first time that a death's head had invaded the tranquillity of the study; while the presence of a large, freshly cut, pear-shaped gourd (*concurbita lagenaria*) hanging from the lintel over the entrance is wholly new and unique. It is the gourd of Jonah 4:6–10, the gourd that at God's command "came up in a night and withered in a night," like a skull, therefore, a reminder of the mortality and vanity of created things. Even the sandals are there to remind the spectator of the Old Testament verses where God ordered Moses (Exod. 3:5) and Joshua (Ios. 5:16) to put off their shoes before stepping onto holy ground. Jerome has slipped out of his before sitting down to work. A lion and a dog sleeping side by side recall those conjugal tombs on which a dog lies at the feet of the wife, a lion at the feet of the husband, the wife having died faithfully at home, the husband valorously in battle. In a niche on the wall between the two windows is a small metal pot with a brush stuck in it, an aspergillum containing holy water, used to ward off evil spirits and erotic temptations conjured up by the devil. On a shelf attached to the back wall are a hearth-brush (for sweeping up the ashes of mortality) and the familiar Marian symbols, stoppered carafe and rosary beads, and only half visible, next to the candle on the far right, the pyx containing hosts. Jerome's work table is bare except for an inkwell and a crucifix.

Dürer's juxtaposition of skull and crucifix insinuates into his *St. Jerome in His Study* the spiritual climate and attributes of a *St. Jerome in Penitence*. The skull is an emblem of transience, like the candle and hourglass; at the same time, it recalls Golgotha (*golgotha* is the Hebrew word for skull), the hill of Calvary (*calvaria* is the Latin word for skull), where the Cross, or so it was commonly believed, had been erected over the grave of Adam. Jerome was an early witness to this legend and to its meaning. "In this city, indeed on this very spot, as it then was," he wrote from Jerusalem to Marcella in Rome, "Adam is said to have lived and died. This is why the place where our Lord was crucified is called Calvary, because the skull of the first man was buried there. Thus it happened that the blood of the second Adam dripped from the Cross onto the first Adam, the father of the human race, who lay below, and washed away his sins, thus accomplishing the words of the Apostle: 'Awake O sleeper, and arise from the dead, and Christ shall give you light' " (Eph. 5:14).[81] Dürer underlined the point by the way he positioned skull and crucifix. When we look at the print we see the skull frontally, and it appears to have no meaningful relation to the crucifix. But if we imagine Jerome raising his eyes from his letter, we realize that he would see the skull in profile and directly in line with the crucifix, a visual comment on the drama of redemption. In the end, Dürer seems to suggest, *lectio divina* and sacred scholarship must lead, like penitential discipline, to an alert consciousness of mortality and meditation on the Passion. By studying God's word the Christian scholar may achieve some small understanding of that death which assures victory over death.

Renaissance pictures of St. Jerome in his study make visible a humanist vision of Christian antiquity and celebrate a Christocentric, evangelical, and learned piety nourished on study of the Bible. At the same time, it is important to recognize that the message they projected to contemporaries drew its power as much from traditional aspirations associated with the solitary life as from the values embodied in humanistic scholarship. The interior where the saint reads or writes is a scholar's study; just as plausibly it can be understood as a monk's cell. The books may denote learning, and sometimes they do: for example, when a spine bears the title of one of Jerome's commentaries, treatises, or letters or when he is shown translating from Hebrew or Greek. Just as plausibly they may suggest no more than the *legere et meditari* of the Benedictine Rule or the *lectio divina* Jerome used to recommend to his Roman protégées. In either case, the books are invariably Christian books, usually the Bible itself, and the scholarship is Christian scholarship. To be sure, the image of the saint has been secularized to some degree. He is not shown as a hieratic icon or an abstract doctor of the church, but as a living man engaged in expected activity in an appropriate setting; but that setting is a place of monkish peace, psychologically distant from the town and the marketplace, free of the obligations and pleasures of family, friends, and civic society.

Oppidum mihi carcer est, solitudo paradisus;
Pax est in cella, foris instant jurgia, bella.

The town is my prison, solitude my heaven.
Peace is in my cell, outside are war and strife.[82]

Nor did artists, any more than humanist orators, feel the need to distinguish respect for the scholar from veneration of the saint. The purpose of picture, oration, and saint's life, whatever its style, remained edification. Thanking Pisanello, a favorite painter of humanists of the first half of the fifteenth century, for the gift of a picture of St. Jerome, Guarino praised the "noble whiteness of his beard, the stern brows of his saintly countenance—simply to behold these is to have one's mind drawn to higher things."[83] We please the saints, wrote Vergerio, by leading a virtuous life and by trying to imitate them: "Whenever we read a saint's life, whenever we hear his merits praised, we should be provoked to imitation."[84] The view of the fathers at the Council of Nicaea in 787 had been no different. We praise the saints and picture them because we want

Fig. 34.   Francesco Bianchi Ferrari, *St. Jerome Altarpiece,* 1505. The Virgin enthroned, with Child; on her right, the penitent St. Jerome; on her left, St. Sebastian. The predella shows *The Dream of St. Jerome, St. Jerome in His Study,* scenes from the legendary anecdote about the lion, and *Eusebius of Cremona Resuscitates Three Dead Men by Laying Jerome's Cloak over Them* (see fig. 23).

to acquire their virtues by imitating them. We write their lives and represent them in images, not because they need to be commemorated by us, but because we need them as models on which to pattern our own lives.[85]

History and legend, finally, remained as compatible as scholarship and sanctity. Jerome was still a cardinal with a tamed lion. As late as the first decade of the sixteenth century, the predellas of altarpieces dedicated to him regularly included scenes from the fourteenth-century pseudographs (fig. 34; see fig. 19), and panegyrists invariably recounted miracles lifted from the same source. It is against this background of enthusiastic but uncritical admiration that the originality, scholarly principles, and genius of Erasmus of Rotterdam stand out in striking relief.

5
Hieronymus redivivus:
Erasmus and St. Jerome

RASMUS grew up in an environment of devotion to St. Jerome. The Latin school at Deventer he attended from 1478 to 1483 was named for Jerome. He may have lived there in a hostel run by the Brethren of the Common Life, a congregation of priests and laymen associated with a reformed branch of the Augustinian Order; it is certain that he spent two years (1485–1487) in the Brethren's hostel at 's-Hertogenbosch. So attached were the Brothers to Jerome that it became customary in the fifteenth century to call them *Hieronymiani* too; contemporary documents sometimes refer to them as the "order of St. Jerome"; and several of their houses were dedicated to Jerome. Clearly the saint's cult was lively among them.[1]

In 1487, Erasmus became an Augustinian canon at the monastery of Steyn. Here he discovered a personal, elective affinity for the saint who loved Cicero, the monk who was a scholar and man of letters, the doctor who cared so much for the Bible and so little for theological subtlety. He copied all of Jerome's letters with his own hand and defended reading the poets with the assertion that anyone who looks at the letters will understand that "lack of culture is not holiness, nor cleverness impiety."[2] In his first major treatise, the *Antibarbarians,* begun as early as 1488, he made comparative judgments that he was to repeat for the rest of his life. Imitate only what is best: "Take Peter and Jerome, one the first among the apostles, the other first among the doctors. In Peter there was the ardour of faith at its highest; in Jerome there was learning at its best. It is for you to imitate the spirit of the one and the scholarship of the other."[3]

Erasmus continued to study Jerome's letters in Paris in the late 1490s and by 1500 was "burning" to edit them, because, as he put it, although they deserve to be memorized by everyone, they are in fact read by few, respected by fewer still, and understood by fewest of all. Badly transcribed by careless copyists, garbled and corrupted by divines ignorant of antiquity and of Greek, disfigured by the interpolation of spurious texts, the corpus offered him, he believed, a magnificent challenge of restoration and explanation and the opportunity of contributing to the greater end of restoring true theology.[4] Justifying his project, a massive enterprise "never before attempted by anyone," he repeated with vigor and economy the humanist view of Jerome. He is eloquent: in "stylistic and rhetorical accomplishments . . . he not only far outstrips all Christian writers, but even seems to rival Cicero himself. For my part, at any rate, unless my affection for that saintly man is leading me astray, when I compare Jerome's prose with Cicero's, I seem to find something lacking in even the prince of prose writers." He is learned: on the one hand, master of Greek and Hebrew; on the other, vastly read and a storehouse of information about the ancient world. "Look at the classical learning, the Greek scholarship, the histories to be found in him"; he is "the only scholar in the church universal who had a perfect command of all learning both sacred and heathen." He is not only the best scholar and writer among the fathers, he is also the best theologian, "the supreme champion and expositor and ornament of our faith."[5]

Mastering Greek, work on other major projects like the *Adages*, preparation of a first draft of his Latin translation of the Greek New Testament, and an extended trip to Italy took up much of Erasmus's time between 1501 and 1511, when, settled peacefully at Queens' College, Cambridge, he resumed serious study of his favorite author, improving the text by collating the early printed editions with a "large number of ancient manuscripts" and writing a commentary in the form of philological and historical notes. "My mind is so excited at the thought of emending Jerome's text, with notes," he wrote in September 1513, "that I seem to myself inspired by some god."[6] The task was difficult. Collation is a tedious treadmill, he confessed.

> Often too I had to work with volumes which it was no easy business to read, the forms of the script being either obscured by decay and neglect, or half eaten away and mutilated by worm and beetle, or written in the fashion of Goths or Lombards, so that even to learn the letter-forms I had to go back to school; not to mention for the moment that the actual task of detecting, of smelling out as it were, anything that does not sound like a true and genuine reading requires a man in my opinion who is well informed, quick-witted, and alert. But on top of this far the most difficult thing is either to conjecture

from corruptions of different kinds what the author wrote, or to guess the original reading on the basis of such fragments and vestiges of the shapes of the script as may survive.[7]

The annotations, as well as the conjectural emendations, required a well-informed scholar. Erasmus identified persons and places, tracked down the classical and biblical citations that peppered the text, translated Greek words and phrases and defined unusual Latin ones, and explained, often in detail, Jerome's allusions to the history, institutions, practices, and manners of his time.

In the meantime, a team of scholars was independently at work in Basel preparing an edition of the complete works of Jerome for the publishing firm of Amerbach-Froben. Johann Amerbach had long wished to publish good editions of the *opera omnia* of all four principal doctors of the Latin church: Ambrose had appeared in 1492, Augustine in 1506. When he died in December 1513, his partner Johann Froben took over direction of the business and the preparations for an edition of Jerome. The active editors were Johann Amerbach's carefully educated sons, Bruno, Basilius, and Boniface, helped and advised by Beatus Rhenanus, a pupil of Jacques Lefèvre d'Etaples and Erasmus's future biographer, Gregor Reisch, author of the popular *Margarita philosophica,* the Dominican Greek scholar Johannes Cuno of Nuremberg, and the Hebraists Johann Reuchlin and Konrad Pellikan.[8]

It was the prospect of collaboration with a scholarly printer-publisher and with this congenial group of enthusiasts that in August 1514 attracted Erasmus to Basel. Joining the team of editors, he took over responsibility for the letters, while the Amerbach brothers and their associates concentrated on the biblical commentaries. In May 1515, he described these arrangements and the progress of the enterprise in proud and happy letters to Cardinals Raffaele Riario and Domenico Grimani and to the pope. St. Jerome, he wrote Leo X, is "chief among the theologians of the Latin world (*apud Latinos theologorum princeps*), and is in fact almost the only writer we have who deserves the name of theologian (not that I condemn the rest, but men who seem distinguished on their own are thrown into the shade by his brilliance when they are compared with him). . . . And yet the one man we possess who richly deserves to be read by all is the one author so much corrupted, so mixed with dirt and filth, that even scholars cannot understand him!" But now a great printing shop is in full activity. "St. Jerome is printing (or rather, being reborn) in most elegant type, at such an expense of money and of effort that it cost Jerome less to write his works than it has me to restore them. I at least have expended so much effort on this task that I came near to death myself while trying to give him new life. The whole work, if I mistake not, will run to ten volumes."[9] In fact, it came to nine, the first four of which, comprising Erasmus's edition of the letters and treatises, finished printing in April 1516 and the remaining five, the Amerbachs' edition of the commentaries, in September of the same year. On 5 September, Bruno Amerbach sent Erasmus seven copies of the complete set.[10]

The volumes were on sale in Antwerp by early October, in London before the end of the month. In Brussels, all copies were sold out by 9 November.[11] The reception was rapturous. So formidable a work, wrote François Deloynes from Paris at the end of November, would have been too much for the strength of "any but our modern Hercules whose name is Erasmus."[12] Guillaume Budé was equally enthusiastic: When I read "what he has done for St. Jerome's works (on whose interpretations almost alone rests our understanding of the divine law), with his immense labours of elucidation and explanation, of setting in order and renewing and virtually resurrecting, then I feel how fortunate is this age of ours, and our successors, to have that sacred body of doctrine, the source of our rule of living and of dying, rightly and duly ordered and indeed restored to us." Albert of Brandenburg, archbishop of Mainz, topped even that. Thanks to you, he wrote Erasmus, Jerome "has returned to the light of day and is as it were raised from the dead. Go forward, beloved Erasmus, glory of Germany! Thus do men scale the sky!"[13]

In what does the originality and historical significance of Erasmus's four volumes consist?

They are, to begin with, marginal to the single most important and original achievement of Renaissance patristic scholarship: the reappropriation by the Latin West of the Greek literature of the early church. The chronology of the reception of Greek pagan literature is well known. The central fact is that Homer, the lyric poets, the tragedians, Herodotus and Thucydides, Aristophanes, the mathematicians (with the exception of Euclid), the later medical authors (Oribasios, Paul of Aegina), the Dialogues of Plato (with the exception of the *Timaeus*), Aristotle's *Poetics,* and a variety of other works were read in Europe, first in Latin translation, then in the original, and by more than a handful of people, only after 1400. It is less widely known that the reception of Greek patristic literature followed much the same pattern. With the exception of those works already translated into Latin in antiquity (by St. Jerome, Rufinus, and others) and a very few works translated in the Middle Ages (most notably the Dionysian corpus), the bulk of Greek patristic literature was first made readily available to Western intellectuals by humanist scholars like Ambrogio Traversari, Cristoforo Persona, and Zanobi Acciaiuoli and by Greek emigrés like George Trebizond and Cardinal Bessarion, in Italy and in the fifteenth century. Erasmus was in due course to contribute handsomely to widening and deepening Western knowledge of the Greek fathers, by both translating and editing; but in 1516 he had not yet done so.

The characteristic contribution of Renaissance, and more specifically humanist, patristic scholarship to knowledge of the Latin fathers was not that they were read again after centuries of neglect—for they were available, read, and used, to a greater or lesser degree, throughout the Middle Ages—but that they were read with a more consistent historical and critical sense, judgment, and erudition. Before the middle of the sixteenth century, the permanent results were principally two: first, the identification and elimination of large numbers of suppositious works which over the centuries ignorance and pious fraud had attributed to the most respected and authoritative of the fathers; and, second, the subjection to skeptical scrutiny of the legendary episodes that had distorted their biographies. Progress in a third direction, the establishment of better texts, was less marked.

Erasmus's work on St. Jerome is a paradigmatic example of these achievements. But although his ambition—and in large measure his success—was to recover the historical Jerome, his project was not without scattered precedent. Earlier efforts to assemble the letters and treatises in a single collection, prepare *florilegia,* or make a list of all Jerome's surviving works had necessarily forced scholars to consider the problem of what was genuine and what was not. Already in the twelfth century, the Carthusian Guigue du Châtel had prefaced his collection with an intelligent note explaining why he had omitted texts traditionally accepted as authentic.[14] Part four of Giovanni d'Andrea's *Hieronymianus* is a bibliography of the letters and treatises arranged alphabetically according to the name of the person to whom the text was addressed. Each title is followed by one to twelve brief extracts from the work itself. Andrea listed every work that an indefatigable search for manuscripts turned up. He had received from the Paris Carthusians a copy of Guigue's letter, but, while noting its judgments, continued to excerpt the incriminated texts. He accepted even works of which he had seen no copies, quoting two of them from the *Golden Legend, De Ioachim et Anna (Ep. supp.* 48) and *The Fifteen Signs before the Last Judgment* (Lambert, 3B, nn. 652–55).[15] Despite its almost total lack of discrimination, his list remained a much-used tool for over a century, a point of departure for future editors, and a warning to beware.

Fifteenth-century editors offered marginally better solutions to the same problems of selection and arrangement. The first, and most important, was Teodoro de' Lelli, doctor of both laws, a papal diplomat, and bishop of Feltri (1462) and Treviso (1464), who prepared a two-volume collection of the letters and treatises before his death in 1466.[16] He was much concerned to order the material in a systematic way. He classified the letters and treatises in three parts: those teaching the Christian faith and defending it against heretics; those explaining Holy Scripture; and those instructing people of every rank, sex, and age how to live according to God's law, a wording reminiscent of Giovanni d'Andrea's *Hieronymianus*.[17] He subdivided each of the three parts into books or tractates, also arranged by subject matter. Part one, for example, consists of four sections, classified as works *de fide,* polemics against heretics and their calumnies, works exposing the pernicious errors of Origen, and works touching on the origin and destiny of the soul.

Problems of attribution concerned him less. He assembled 131 of the 154 surviving authentic letters, an admirable achievement; but, like Giovanni d'Andrea, he included among them a large number of spurious works. The first tractate of part one is typically inclusive. Lelli attributed everything in it to Jerome; in reality, it contains a commentary on the Apostles' Creed by Rufinus; an exposition of the faith by Pelagius; Pseudo-Jerome, *Expositio fidei Niceni concilii* and *De essentia divinitatis*; Pseudo-Augustine, *Contra quinque haereses*; Pseudo-Hilary, *Tractatus fidei credulitatis*;[18] and only two authentic works, *Epp.* 15 and 16, both addressed to Pope Damasus, which Lelli, a vigorous defender of papal primacy, had used in his treatises *pro sede Romana* to refute the conciliarist pretensions of the college of cardinals (in the next century Catholic apologists used the same letters to defend the see of Peter against Protestants). At the end of the second volume, he put Nicolò Maniacoria's *Vita Hieronymi* and the letters of Pseudo-Eusebius of Cremona, Pseudo-Augustine, and Pseudo-Cyril of Jerusalem on Jerome's death, *magnificentiae,* and miracles.

A manuscript of Lelli's two volumes was the principal source of the most influential early printed edition of Jerome's letters and treatises, that of Conrad Sweynheym and Arnold Pannartz (Rome, 13 December 1468), prepared by Giovanni Andrea de' Bussi (1417–1475), secretary to Cardinal Nicholas of Cusa, Vatican librarian under Sixtus IV, and bishop of Aleria, in Corsica. Bussi made a modest effort to emend the text. The learned Lelli, he reported to Pope Paul II in his letter of dedication, had collected and ordered Jerome's letters and treatises from a great variety of manuscripts, many of them corrupt; his own task, accomplished to the best of his ability, was to provide a text somewhat more correct (*emendatiusculus*), using many manuscripts and consulting Theodore Gaza for the Greek, in the hope that abler scholars would follow his example and continue the good work.[19] Later editions do in fact depend on Bussi's. His text is the vulgate of the letters and treatises. Later critics emended it in many places (often happily), but its general outline is clearly recognizable in the successive landmark editions of Erasmus, Mariano Vittori (Rome, 1565), the Benedictine Maurist Jean Martianay (Paris, 1693–1706), and Domenico Vallarsi (Venice, 1766–1772), the text of which is reproduced in Migne's *Patrologia Latina*. Only in the nineteenth century did stemmatic analysis of the manuscript transmission lead to a fundamental recasting and a nearer approach to a definitive text.[20]

Two years after the appearance of the Roman editions of 1468, the German printer and publisher Peter Schoeffer of Gandersheim issued the letters and treatises in Mainz. His work exhibits critical sense and credulity in roughly equal measure. He attacked the looseness of critical principle behind Giovanni d'Andrea's list of Jerome's writings:

> I want to warn the reader that Giovanni d'Andrea the learned canon and civil lawyer and devotee of blessed Jerome, despite his great diligence in searching out Jerome's letters and bringing together those he found in his *Hieronymianus*, as in a single body, burned so ardently to exalt his idol that he included among the genuine letters any text he came across attributed to him in the past, without making any effort to judge it by the quality and character of its style. What is more, he omitted all the letters written to Jerome, such as those from Pope Damasus, Augustine, Theophilus, and Rufinus. Conversely, he included about thirty-five of his introductions to the various books of Holy Scripture. He included, too, ludicrous apocryphal texts like the *De infantia salvatoris, De Ioachim et Anna* [*Epp. supp.* 48–49], *The Fifteen Signs before the Last Judgment,* and a sermon on Lent, beginning *Apostolica,* which should rather be ascribed to Pope Leo I (Migne, *PL* 54:281).

His statement of his own strategy is a remarkable early expression of the wish to recapture a historical individual from the past: "My intention in this volume is to show Jerome as a living man, dictating, writing, arguing, consoling and instructing."[21]

The results were mixed. He omitted Lope de Olmedo's *Regula monachorum* (which had never pretended to be other than what it was), but retained the popular *Regula monacharum* (Lambert, 3B, no. 560), a deliberate falsification. He omitted the dialogue between Jerome and Augustine on the origin of souls (*Ep. supp.* 37) on the authority of Guigue the Carthusian, while retaining, in spite of Guigue's testimony (and Augustine's), a spurious letter to Demetriades (*Ep. supp.* 1, in reality by Pelagius) because "its elegance of style and similarity of tone and content to Jerome's other letter to the same virgin, beginning *Inter omnes* [*Ep.* 130], leads me to believe that it is by Jerome," a defensible argument though a mistaken one. Yet having relied on the test of style in this and other decisions, he was in the end driven to confess that, since stylistic discrimination is as subjective as taste in wine, he would leave such judgments to others and retain in his own edition any work accepted by Giovanni d'Andrea which he could also find in old manuscripts (*exemplares perantiqui*).[22] Application of such criteria did eliminate a certain number of dubious works; it did not weed out the very large number of more plausible misattributions scattered throughout the volume: *De perfecto homine* (*Ep. supp.* 6), *De tribus virtutibus* (*Ep. supp.* 8), *De assumptione Mariae Virginis* (*Ep. supp.* 9), *De honorandis parentibus* (*Ep. supp.* 11), *De vera circumcisione* (*Ep. supp.* 19), *De observatione vigilarum* (*Ep. supp.* 31), *De vita clericorum* (*Ep. supp.* 42), to name only a few. And at the end of the volume he too printed, without comment, the letters of Pseudo-Eusebius of Cremona, Pseudo-Augustine, and Pseudo-Cyril of Jerusalem.

Interest in expunging the legendary fictions that continued to soil Jerome's biography was, before 1516, even rarer and less sustained than efforts to identify spurious works. The most probing early critique was by St. Antonino Pierozzi, archbishop of Florence. Like that of his fellow Tuscans, his regard for Jerome was high.[23] As he retold Jerome's life in his *Chronicon* (1458), he nevertheless paused cautiously from time to time to expose a legendary detail. When he came to the story of the *vestis muliebris*, he noted that it was probably fictitious (*sed hoc non est multum autenticum*).[24] Exceptionally, he made a strong case against the fourteenth-century pseudographs, singling out for explicit censure Pseudo-Cyril's account of the miracle of the three dead men resuscitated by Jerome's cloak: in the *Speculum historiale,* he argued, Vincent of Beauvais did not quote this or any of the other miracles liberally assigned to Jerome by those "doctors"; neither did Jacopo da Varrazze or any other early historian mention them or their works; had they been in circulation in the thirteenth century, he continued, admirers of St. Jerome would not have failed to use them. Antonino therefore rejected their narratives too as inauthentic.[25] Using only the argument of silence, Abbot Trithemius was perhaps more radical. In his biographical and bibliographical dictionary first published in 1494, he not only passed over the letters of Pseudo-Eusebius, Augustine, and Cyril and Giovanni d'Andrea's *Hieronymianus,* he failed even to entertain his readers with the story of the lion.[26]

The ground was thus not wholly unprepared for Erasmus's work of restoration. What distinguishes him from his predecessors is the scale, rigor, consistency, and brio of his attack. The amplitude of his achievement astonishes still. He produced a readable, if still very imperfect, text. He was the first to establish a reliable canon of Jerome's authentic letters and treatises. His philological and historical commentary is the earliest attempt to wrestle seriously with the many difficulties of the text and to ferret out its meaning. He was the first to construct a biography largely free of chronological confusion and legendary elaboration. The accolades of his friends were not unjustified.

The printed sources Erasmus used to establish his text were the folio volumes issued by Sweynheym and Pannartz, Peter Schoeffer, Nicholas Kessler (Basel, 1492 and 1497) and Jacobus Saccon (Lyons, 1508). His manuscript sources are unknown, though his letters make clear that he had been collating manuscripts and collecting variants for some years, most actively while he was in Cambridge. The actual book on the margins of which he entered his emendations and early notes was almost certainly a copy of the very clearly printed Lyons edition of 1508, itself based on Kessler's Basel editions, and behind these on Andrea de' Bussi's Roman edition. Most of the commentary, however, was put into publishable shape only after his arrival in Basel, between September 1514 and March 1516, during months of what must have been the most intense and concentrated labor: the surviving manuscript of the commentary, written in Basel, runs to some 1,400 pages.[27]

In his arrangement of the letters and treatises, he followed the three-fold grouping that had become standard since Teodoro de' Lelli's edition. He placed pieces containing moral instruction in volume one, "because what deals with the ordering of life deserves attention first"; the rest he classified as works of controversy and apologetics or texts explaining Holy Scripture. Erasmus's crucial innovation was to winnow out the works traditionally but mistakenly ascribed to Jerome and group them together in a separate volume (the second in the edition of 1516, the fourth in later editions). This material too he divided into three classes: "Certain things that show some degree of culture and are worth reading, but are falsely ascribed to Jerome" (here are most of the patristic and early medieval works circulating under Jerome's name but now assigned by Erasmus, and by modern scholars, to other authors); next, "things which are not his, but carry an author's name in their headings" (a class of miscellaneous writings, not properly spurious, addressed to Jerome, associated with him, or relevant to his career, letters from St. Augustine, for example, or Rufinus's introduction to his translation of Origen's *Peri archon* and his *Contra Hieronymum*); finally, he threw "the supremely worthless rubbish of some impostor" into the "cesspool" of part three.[28]

The body of work assigned by tradition to every major author, he pointed out in his preface to the second volume of the edition, contains spurious works. Orphic hymns and a poem called *The Battle of the Frogs and Mice* have been given to Homer; several Platonic dialogues are not by Plato; many dubious works carry the names of Aristotle and Plutarch; a number of poems claiming to be by Vergil are certainly not by him. Letters allegedly exchanged by Seneca and St. Paul, unworthy of either, circulate still. Many scholars doubt that the epistles to the Hebrews and Laodicians are authentically Pauline. It can cause no surprise, therefore, that many supposititious works have infiltrated the *opera* of Ambrose, Augustine, and Jerome. Such misattributions have several causes. One is a similarity of names: an author whose name is John gets assigned to him the writings of an entirely different John. Or when the subject of two treatises by different authors is the same, both works are ignorantly assigned to the better-known authority. This is the easier because many manuscripts have no titles or any indication of authorship. Thus whenever an ill-educated or hasty reader comes across anonymous *argumenta*, brief summaries introducing the different books of the Bible, he will tend to assign them to Jerome because the historical Jerome was known to have written similar *argumenta*. Finally, false attributions originate in fraud, in the attempt of lesser men to get their ideas into circulation by putting them under the protection of a greater name.[29]

Erasmus's discriminations were overwhelmingly stylistic, based on the sensitivity of his ear, the virtuosity of his Latin, the fineness of his response to the differing tone, rhythm, and diction of individual authors, and above all his comprehensive feeling for the distinguishing characteristics of Jerome's own prose. An author's particular genius stamps his likeness on what he writes in the same way that parents are reflected in their children: *totius animi simulachrum semel exhibet oratio.* As the trained musician can identify the composer of a piece from its harmonic pattern or a painter or sculptor the hand that produced a painting or statue, so the literary critic can often identify an author's style, manner, and temperament.[30]

Erasmus summarized his particular judgments in a *censura* placed before each text. He had this to say about a letter now assigned to Eutropius, a priest from Aquitaine who flourished about the year 400: "This letter has been carefully composed by a man of learning and eloquence, but his style is so different from Jerome's that neither he nor Jerome would have been able to imitate the other's manner even if he had wished to do so."[31] About a Latin translation from Origen entitled *De tribus virtutibus,* he commented: "Although the author of this letter was a man of piety and not unlearned, the text shows no trace whatever of Jerome's style and manner";[32] about a letter now given to Pelagius: "The style differs from Jerome's in every possible way";[33] about a text pieced together from the *Formulae spiritalis intelligentiae* of Eucherius, a fifth-century bishop of Lyons: "There is nothing here that savors of Jerome's language, learning, or temperament."[34]

Erasmus rarely tells us why such texts do not "savor" of Jerome; they simply offend experienced taste. Occasionally he offered no argument at all, just bald rejection: "Several creeds are found among Jerome's letters, none of which I consider to have been composed by him."[35] His commoner response to mistaken attributions, even of texts from as early as the fifth and sixth centuries, was mockery or indignation. "Whoever cannot distinguish this work from one of Jerome's," he said of *De vita clericorum,* a fifth-century work of Pelagian origin, "can't tell an ass from a horse."[36] Of an exchange of letters ostensibly between Jerome and Pope Damasus he remarked: "Dear God, what impudence to attribute these to Damasus, whose eloquence even in verse is praised by Jerome: . . . Can an eye, ear or mind be found so insensitive as to suppose that Jerome could have written such obvious rubbish?"[37] And when he censured actual forgeries, he deployed with relish the full range of classical rhetorical abuse: the prose of these drunk or feverish charlatans is awkward, tongue-tied, uneducated, badly arranged, dull and stupid, rambling, inept, insipid, uncultivated, sordid, filthy, and barbarous.

Erasmus was also alert to discrepancies other than those of style and diction. To be sure, the supposed author of the letter *Ad Oceanum de vita clericorum* wrote like an ass, but he brayed a second time when he called himself Sophronius Eusebius Hieronymus, not realizing that Jerome invariably used only the single name Hieronymus when he addressed his letters.[38] Erasmus noticed too that it was Jerome's habit to name his correspondent and praise him or her several times in the body of the text. Letters, therefore, which lacked headings or failed to mention by name the person to whom the letter was addressed were automatically suspect.[39] When Jerome had written at length about an important subject in one of his letters, it was again his custom to refer to that discussion elsewhere in his works. It followed that the *De septem ordinibus ecclesiae* (possibly by Pelagius) was not by Jerome, for (in addition to the facts that its diction did not savor of Jerome and that in some manuscripts it was addressed to Pope Damasus, in others to Rusticus, bishop of Narbonne, and in still others carried no address at all) if Jerome had really written as extensively as this about so important a matter, he would certainly have referred to the work elsewhere, "since it was his frequent practice to cite works of his own much shorter and less weighty than this one."[40]

Some inconsistencies were easy to spot. Erasmus rejected a letter on the celebration of Easter (perhaps by St. Columban) because the man who wrote it confessed more than once that he knew no Greek or Hebrew.[41] To detect less obvious implausibilities required a sharper historical sense and a wider learning. A letter allegedly from Pope Damasus addressed Jerome as *sacerdos* rather than *presbyter.* The falsifier was ignorant of the fact that only bishops were called *sacerdotes* in the fourth century.[42] Erasmus strengthened his case against another letter by noticing that the author, already censured on grounds of style, had cited works by Chrysostom which Jerome had never read. What is more, the impostor made Jerome request that the pope excommunicate certain laymen outside his jurisdiction as bishop of Rome, a double anachronism: the verb "excommunicate" was not yet in use, and the papal monarchy grew up only after Jerome's lifetime.[43] Unlike Peter Schoeffer, he rejected the spurious letter to Demetriades and on the same grounds that Guigue du Châtel had rejected it before him.[44] To demolish the genuineness of the famous letter to Paula and Eustochium on the assumption of the Virgin Mary, he pointed out that in the opening line Pseudo-Jerome remarks that he wants this time to write to them in Latin. The statement is absurd; the historical Jerome always wrote to them in Latin. In the next sentence the author disparaged his own style: he will write, he said, "without elegance, like a stammering child." Jerome had no false modesty in literary matters; it is inconceivable that he would have said such a thing. A Greek, however, inexperienced in writing Latin, might well have made both remarks. Erasmus conjectured that the real author of the letter was a Greek, possibly the Sophronius who had translated several of Jerome's works into Greek.[45] Erasmus was mistaken. The author was not a fourth-century Greek but a ninth-century Latin, Paschasius Radbertus.

Erasmus was usually more cautious. Only rarely did he suggest an alternative attribution to texts the authenticity of which he had rejected with confidence and authority ("the turn of phrase suggests St. Augustine," "the style is not inconsistent with Paulinus of Nola's," or "if I may be permitted a conjecture, I would assign this letter to Tertullian"). He recognized perfectly the hazards of the enterprise and admitted that "it would be out of place to pick an author from the vast crowd of writers active in that age and assign the work to him," for "some of them wrote in so similar a manner that it is the better part of wisdom to withhold judgment."[46] Yet so sound was Erasmus's connoisseurship that even today the identification of which letters were spurious, as well as their sequence, remains largely that first established by him.

One of the most popular of the Hieronymite *spuria* was the *Regula monacharum*, a rule for nuns in the form of a letter from Jerome to Eustochium and her nuns in Bethlehem, probably dating from the second half of the fourteenth century.[47] Like the fifteenth-century *Regula monachorum* of Lope de Olmedo, it is composed in large part of sentences from Jerome's own letters and treatises, but with fictional modifications. The twenty-sixth chapter, for example, describes the joys of contemplation and is based on the famous passage in *Ep.* 22 to Eustochium in which Jerome described his penitential austerities in the Syrian desert and, at the end, called on the Lord himself to witness that after many tears when he fixed his eyes on heaven he seemed to find himself among the angelic hosts (*videbar mihi interesse agminibus angelorum*).[48] The author of the *Regula monacharum* found this account disappointingly inconclusive. Following the rules of legendary elaboration, he embroidered it as follows: "I know of what I speak, dearest ones. So let me speak out in my foolishness. For although I am an abject homunculus, the lowest servant in the house of the Lord, and still imprisoned in a body, I have often been among the angelic choirs; for weeks at a time, feeling no corporeal sensation, I have seen with the sight of divine vision; after many days, foreknowing things to come, I returned to myself and wept. But how faultless was my happiness there! How unspeakable my delight! My witness is the Trinity itself, which I saw, I know not with what kind of sight."[49] The qualification "seemed" has disappeared. Jerome saw angels, a vision often singled out by his admirers as evidence of God's special favor toward him, as in these verses from a fifteenth-century liturgical hymn:[50]

> O sanctitatis speculum
>   et gloria doctorum,
> Consolator pauperum
>   pater monachorum,
> Qui interesse meruit
>   choris angelorum.

The historical Jerome called on the Lord to witness the truth of his angelic vision (*ut mihi testis est dominus*); Pseudo-Jerome called on the Trinity and reported to St. Eustochium that he had actually seen the Trinity (*testis est ipsa Trinitas quam cernebam, nescio quo intuitu*)(see figs. 8, 11).

Erasmus aimed his censure directly at this passage. "The remarkable impudence of the man amazes me. He speaks with such authority you would take him for one of the apostles. This impostor imagines himself more blessed than St. Paul himself.[51] . . . He holds week-long dialogues with the angels and even claims to have conversed with the Trinity. He returned to earth a prophet, able to foresee the future. What could be more impudent than this masquerade? What more lacking in piety?" The author is an ignorant scoundrel, whose impudence is rivaled only by the stink of a prose polluted by the sordid vocabulary of a barbarous age.[52]

The establishment of a reliable canon of authentic works made it possible for Erasmus to fulfill in practice the promise of his biographical method. The theoretical principle on which the method rested was hardly new; after all, Nicolò Maniacoria's had been the same: use only contemporary sources, compose the chronological narrative from the biographical data scattered throughout Jerome's own works (for "who can better know Jerome than Jerome himself?"), and supplement this material with relevant evidence drawn from the genuine works of Jerome's contemporaries—Prosper of Aquitaine, Sulpicius Severus, Augustine,

Orosius, and Rufinus (even though he was an enemy). In 1512, when Christianus Massaeus, a brother of the Common Life and *rector puerorum* in the Collège des Bons-Enfants at Cambrai, sat down to write yet another traditional, uncritical life of Jerome, he too promised his readers to seek the truth of history only in Jerome's own books. Erasmus, however, by disregarding the medieval lives, excluding the testimony of writings traditionally and falsely ascribed to Jerome, and rejecting the evidence of the narratives associated with the spread of Jerome's cult in the fourteenth century, gave the definition of a contemporary source an untraditional strictness. The life of Jerome with which he prefaced his edition is a saint's life written to an unprecedented standard of accuracy and critical skepticism and a turning point in Renaissance hagiography.[53]

Since Jerome's own *Life of Paul the First Hermit,* the purpose of the typical saint's life had been to glorify the saint and edify the reader. Like the classical panegyric, it was marked by a high degree of stylization and a pervasive indifference to documented fact, a biographical genre closer to fiction than to history. Erasmus's *Vita Hieronymi* is a work of history, not of fiction; for it was his intention and achievement to praise, edify, teach, and reform by telling the truth. He opened his biography with an attack on the venerable practice of lying to people for their own good, a practice made easier, he believed, by the ingrained tendency of men and women to prefer invention to reality. This penchant for the marvelous disfigures the biographies even of secular heroes, but the exploitation of the credulity of the common people by the authors of saints' lives is especially deplorable. Far from glorifying the saints, these tasteless, childish fictions diminish and dishonor them. Saints should be described as they actually were, without resort to sackcloth, hair shirts, scourges, prodigious fasts, and incredible vigils.[54] "Truth has a power of its own which no artifice can equal."[55] In this spirit he reviewed the biographical tradition, winnowing out accumulated error, denouncing legendary elaboration, and reordering the facts that remained in a plausible chronological order, while candidly admitting that "it is not always easy to determine exactly when each event took place."[56]

Devotees are inclined to attribute noble birth to a cherished saint. Jerome never tells us whether his father was a plebian or a patrician, rich or poor. Erasmus suggests that he came from a milieu of moderate substance. As a student in Rome, his teacher was Donatus only, not Victorinus; for although Jerome mentioned the great rhetorician several times, he never called him his teacher; what is more, he criticized him for writing like a dialectician.[57] The adolescent student had already lost his virginity; Jerome twice plainly says so in his letters, a good example of why truth is more useful than fiction; for nothing is more edifying than progress from youthful disorder to piety; and if we admire only virgins, how can we continue to admire the patriarchs and the apostles?[58]

It was in Rome, too, that Jerome "put on the robe of Christ." By this he meant that he was baptized, not that he was ordained a priest, "for in baptism a white garment used to be given as a symbol of innocence and those baptized were ordered to keep the whiteness of their garments unsullied." He was ordained only later, in Antioch.[59] Jerome was not a cardinal. Nowhere in his works does he call himself a cardinal; none of his correspondents address him by that title. In his day, not even the word cardinal existed, to say nothing of the dignity itself.[60] Jerome did not spend a prolonged youth in Rome, then move permanently to the East. He was twice in Rome, first as a student, and again—after four years in the Syrian desert—as Pope Damasus's secretary; only then did he settle in Bethlehem for good. Nor did he leave Rome after the death of Pope Damasus because he was tricked into wearing a woman's dress. Jerome was not accustomed to sparing his enemies. In several letters he complains bitterly about his treatment during those last months before his final departure from Rome. His complaints do not include being trapped into wearing female clothes to Matins.[61]

No miracles are recorded of him. Like Trithemius, Erasmus silently suppressed the lion, reserving his polemical invective for an acid attack on the anonymous author of the fourteenth-century pseudographs. Like a mime, this person (who truly deserves to be stoned) assumes varying disguises, pretending now to be Eusebius of Cremona, now Augustine, now Cyril of Jerusalem. Whatever role he plays, the impostor shows his ignorance and barbarous style. He is an impudent liar, so stupid he makes even the truth sound fictional. The miracles and other ridiculous stories he has introduced into Jerome's life are false. Fables of this kind should be rejected by every Christian.[62] "But if there is still someone who requires extravagant miracles as well, let him read Jerome's own books; there he will find as many miracles as sentences."[63] If he requires relics, let him read the same books. We carefully preserve a saint's shoe, pieces of his shirt, or his dirty handkerchief in gilded reliquaries, while the "books into which they put so much work, and in which we have the best part of them still living and breathing, we abandon to be gnawed at will by bug, worm, and cockroach." In the writings he has left us, Jerome lives again, teaching, consoling, encouraging, kindling our piety from the fire of his own heart. These are his true, most sacred, most powerful and efficacious relics.[64]

Soon after Johann Reuchlin's death in June 1522, Erasmus wrote the colloquy entitled "The Apotheosis of that Incomparable Worthy Johann Reuchlin." He playfully patterned his encomium of the great Hebrew scholar on the popular and frequently pictured apparitions of St. Jerome to Pseudo-Augustine and Pseudo-Cyril, casting Jerome in the role of Christ and Reuchlin in that of Jerome. At the very moment Reuchlin died, Erasmus reports, a holy Franciscan at Tübingen dreamed that he saw St. Jerome come to meet Reuchlin's soul as it ascended to glory. The two embraced affectionately. Then the sky opened and a dazzling pillar of fire descended and lifted the two of them to heaven, accompanied by a wonderful fragrance and the ravishing music of angelic choirs. "Tell me," asks one of the interlocutors, "just what did Jerome look like? How was he dressed? Was he as old as they paint him, or was he wearing a cowl, or the hat or mantle of a cardinal, or did he have his lion with him?" "Nothing of the sort," replied the other, "his appearance was pleasant; it showed his age, yet he didn't look run-down but quite dignified. And what need had he there of the lion those painters have added as his companion?" In point of fact, he wore a crystalline garment decorated with tongues painted in three different colors, bronze, emerald, and sapphire, symbols of his mastery of the three languages of the Christian scholar, an interpretation confirmed by inscriptions in Hebrew, Greek, and Latin, each in a different color, on the fringes of the robe. The interlocutors agreed that all students of languages and literature, especially sacred literature, should place golden images of Reuchlin in their chapels and libraries and inscribe his name on the calendar of saints. For true veneration is not that commanded by official papal canonization but that "freely paid to the heaven-deserving merits of the dead, merits whose good effects are felt forever."[65]

The colloquy alerts us to another side of the *Vita Hieronymi*. It is a witty polemical tract unabashedly relevant to contemporary concerns. It inculcates admired values, builds a model for imitation, and uses the past to shame the present. Erasmus does show his subject "as a living man, dictating, writing, arguing, consoling and instructing"; at the same time, his portrait of Jerome is a self-portrait, that of a Christian scholar attractively but disconcertingly Erasmian in attitude and personality. This can hardly surprise us. We revive a figure from the past because he meets a present need, suggests a present strategy, can be used to beat a present enemy and further a present cause, makes legitimate a present call for change and reform. The author of the fourteenth-century pseudographs had emphasized Jerome's devotion to poverty in order to attack contemporary trimmers, his austerities to press for radical monastic reform, his evangelical piety and pastoral concern to show up the wickedness and irresponsibility of contemporary theologians and prelates. What Erasmus admired was not always the same; his tactic was.

That Jerome had become a monk and his sister a nun mildly embarrassed Erasmus, as did his extravagant praise of monastic and eremitical life: "Monks and virgins," Jerome had typically written to Marcella, "are the flowers and most precious jewels among the ornaments of the church";[66] while Erasmus, as early as 1501, had already summed up his different view in a lapidary formula: "Monachatus non est pietas."[67] He was especially irritated by religious who claimed that Jerome had founded their order or was the author of their rule. He therefore took pains to contrast the monastic life of his own day with an idealized picture of monasticism in Jerome's. "In those days, the profession of a monk consisted in no more than the practice of the original, free, purely Christian life." Monks then were men who wished only to live with willing friends in liberty of spirit close to the teachings of the Gospel. Their lives were sweetly leisured. No ceremonies or man-made regulations fettered them. No single dress was prescribed. No deference was paid to total abstinence. They studied, fasted, and sang psalms as the spirit moved them. They took no vows.[68] Becoming a nun meant something equally different. Today, in an age of corrupted piety, virgins are imprisoned against their will behind stone walls and iron gates, despite the fact that Christ accepts a monastic profession only when it is freely offered; in the primitive church, freedom and leisure for study were the marks of the religious life for women as well as men. This was the kind of life Jerome chose when he rejected riches, the obligations of public service and office, marriage (the "shipwreck of liberty"), the growing tyranny of bureaucrats and bishops, in short, a world that still savored too much of its ancient paganism.[69]

Every consideration of personal interest, instinct of temperament, and intellectual and spiritual commitment conditioned Erasmus to picture Jerome as preeminently the Christian scholar and only incidentally as a monk and an ascetic. Even in the desert, he lived for both Christ and his books. He reread all the books in his library, pagan, heretical, and Christian, taking what was good in each and rejecting what was poisonous. He studied Hebrew, Aramaic, and Syriac. He wrote his first Old Testament commentary, on Obadiah, now lost. Above all, he meditated on the Gospels and St. Paul's letters and from them "drank the philosophy of Christ as from the purest fountain."[70] Study was his vocation, psalmody and penitential prayer his relaxations. It follows that those who quote the Ciceronian dream to prove that he abandoned philosophy and the humanities when he chose to devote himself wholly to sacred studies abuse the text. In his book against Rufinus, written in his maturity, Jerome stated that his experience was not a true vision but simply a dream, as empty and without significance as another dream in which he had seen himself flying over the sea with Daedalus. The youthful account in the letter to Eustochium, as he had already explained in the *De copia*,[71] should be understood as a rhetorical anecdote designed to strengthen the vocation of a young maiden, an example of the common ancient practice of narrating dreams as genuine visions in order to encourage virtue and deter vice. "Finally, if it is a crime to own secular books and if anyone who reads them has denied Christ, why was only Jerome whipped? Why is Aristotle more honored today in our theological schools than Peter or Paul? But enough of this puerile ridiculous subject. For myself, I would rather be flogged with Jerome than fêted in the company of those who are so frightened by Jerome's dream that they scrupulously avoid good literature, while in the meantime they make no effort to avoid the vices of the pagan authors whose works they are afraid to read."[72]

Commentary on the dream led him even farther afield. Theodore Gaza, to the reported merriment of Cardinal Bessarion and Gemisthos Plethon, had once jested that Jerome was unjustly beaten as a Ciceronian because he was not Ciceronian enough; that is, he lacked truly Roman eloquence. Erasmus seized the opportunity to attack the Ciceronians of his own day and to offer a sophisticated statement on the historicity of style. Naturally Jerome did not write like Cicero. Style reflects period, place, and individual temperament. Jerome was a Christian, a monk, and a theologian, he lived in a different period and another world: *alia religio, alia cultus, diversi auctores, novata omnia.* It is one thing to ape Cicero, quite another to write splendidly about important matters with the usage and diction of one's own time. The true Ciceronian is the author who writes well, even if he writes differently. Besides, it is Jerome who was the more eloquent: "Cicero speaks; Jerome thunders and flashes like lightning. We admire the tongue of the one, but of the other the heart as well."[73]

The main enemy remained the scholastics. Like his Italian humanist predecessors, Erasmus compared them to Jerome in order to blacken their reputations and undermine their authority. Jerome approached the majesty of theology after long years of study and with an appropriate elevation of style. Today, doctors ignorant of languages and the humanities rashly teach theology equipped with nothing but a few sophisms and a bit of undigested Aristotelian philosophy. They even have the effrontery to say that Jerome is a poet and orator and not a theologian because he does not split hairs like the Dominicans Durand de Saint-Pourçain (d. 1334) or Johannes Capreolus (d. 1444) or spend time on frivolous *quaestiunculae* and empty disputations like Alexander Hales, Egidio Colonna, and Duns Scotus. In better days, before Aristotle was taught in the schools, there was only divine theology; now, prattling sophists purvey Thomist theology, Scotist theology, Occamist theology, new kinds of theology unknown to the ancients, all examples of the same trivializing of religious thought condemned by Paul as subversive of piety. The true theologian will be a modern imitator of Jerome. Among Christian authors some are weak in knowledge of secular literature; some lack linguistic competence, some purity of faith, some integrity of life. "Jerome, and Jerome only, excels in all."[74]

Such partiality led to uncharitable verdicts on Jerome's enemies (Rufinus was a poisonous intriguer, never a true friend; Bishop John of Jerusalem was a sycophant, cunning, lubricious, violent, and tyrannical); to an exaggeration of Jerome's knowledge of classical literature and philosophical culture (although Erasmus was the first correctly to read "Plautus" instead of "Plato" in the passage on the Ciceronian dream);[75] and to a sentimental sweetening of Jerome's personality: he was courteous and urbane, a lover of peace and tranquillity, modest and kind, gentle in controversy (he wrote intemperately only about heretics, who deserve it), disinterested and open-minded.[76] Yet Erasmus was not blindly partial. There are hundreds of places in Jerome's writings open to objection, he warned. From time to time in his commentary, in special *scholia* called "antidotes," he noted some of these apparent deviations from orthodoxy, usually arguing that when Jerome wrote "more vehemently" than he should have done—in praise of Origen, for example, or preaching absolute poverty to monks, priests, and bishops, or denigrating marriage—his imprudence must be understood in the context of his time. Contemporary clerics were mad for lucre; marriage was not yet one of the seven sacraments; Origen was in disrepute, yet many besides Jerome continued to read his scriptural commentaries with profit.[77] And when in later years Erasmus himself was sometimes charged with heresy, he generalized the point. Not only Jerome erred, so, on occasion, did Cyprian, Hilary, Ambrose, and Augustine. These are human faults that equity pardons in consideration of other merits.[78]

"Who will deny," Maniacoria had asked in the twelfth century, "that Jerome was rather an angel than a man?" And in the fifteenth, Pier Paolo Vergerio had echoed him: "Is it not obvious that there was something divine in this man?" Erasmus's final judgments measure the change he had effected. Jerome should be studied as an author, not an authority. He was not a dogmatist; we read him, as he read Origen, in order to learn his opinions, accepting what is useful. He could have defined his task as Erasmus did his own: "I write explanatory notes, not dogmas."[79] Jerome was a "pious and learned man, but after all only a man."[80]

6
Between Protestants
and Catholics

popular literary genre in the Renaissance was
the comparison (*comparatio*). Intellectuals com-
pared the relative merits of medicine and law,
poetry and painting, Homer and Vergil, Plato
and Aristotle, Cicero and Quintilian, St.
Augustine and St. Jerome. The humanist comparison of Augustine and Jerome goes back to
Petrarch. Writing to a friend who preferred Jerome, Petrarch contrasted
"my Augustine" with "your Jerome," expressed his own preference for
Augustine, especially the Augustine of the *Confessions,* and called Augustine, because he was first in Christian doctrine, the supreme doctor of the
church (*doctor doctorum*).[1] About 1343, he sharply attacked Giovanni
d'Andrea for extravagantly praising Jerome in what he called a *disputatio
longissima,* a disparaging reference to the *Hieronymianus.*[2] Francesco Filelfo (1398–1481) echoed Petrarch's preference for Augustine in the
fifteenth century: Jerome is superior in eloquence, but Augustine is
superior in dialectic.[3] In a letter to Erasmus of February 1518, the German
Dominican Johann Maier von Eck broadened the distinction by understanding Filelfo's "dialectic" to mean "philosophy": "Augustine is
more penetrating, subtle and discriminating in everything that concerns
philosophy; Jerome is superior in eloquence rather than doctrine."[4]

Erasmus continued to champion Jerome. Rebutting Filelfo and Eck,
he pointed out that Jerome was born almost in Italy and educated in
Rome; Augustine was born in Africa where literary study was little
practiced. Jerome was born a Christian and drank the philosophy of
Christ with his mother's milk; Augustine only began to read St. Paul
when he was thirty. Jerome spent thirty-five years studying the Bible;
Augustine became a bishop almost as soon as he became a Christian and
was at once obliged to teach what he had not yet properly learned himself.
Jerome knew Hebrew and Greek at a time when, in Erasmus's opinion,
"all philosophy and all theology belonged to the Greeks." Augustine

knew no Hebrew and almost no Greek. He was ignorant of Aristotle and had barely read any other Greek philosopher, while there was "not a single book in the whole library of Greek literature that Jerome had not mastered." Filelfo was mistaken when he said that Augustine surpassed Jerome in dialectic. In Jerome's polemical works against heretics, there is not a single place where one can point to a lack of dialectical skill. Eck's claim that all the learned accord to Augustine the superiority in theology that Filelfo accorded him in philosophy is equally mistaken. Jerome was superior to Augustine not only in eloquence but as a philosopher and theologian as well.[5]

The comparison of Jerome and Augustine acquired a new and weightier historical significance when Martin Luther entered the lists against Erasmus. Luther's opinion of Jerome—and of Erasmus—was not high. "I am reading our Erasmus," he wrote in March 1517,

> but I dislike him more every day, though it pleases me that he is constantly yet learnedly exposing and condemning monks and priests for their deep-rooted and sleepy ignorance. I am afraid, however, that he does not advance the cause of Christ and the grace of God sufficiently. . . . Human things weigh more with him than divine. . . . We live in dangerous times, and I see that not everyone is a truly wise Christian just because he knows Greek and Hebrew. St. Jerome with his five languages cannot be compared with Augustine, who knew only one language. Erasmus, however, is of an absolutely different opinion on this. But the discernment of one who attributed weight to man's will is different from that of him who knows of nothing else but grace.[6]

Luther preferred Augustine to Jerome because Augustine, in his view, was more often right than wrong about the difference between faith and works, the law and the Gospel. Augustine, at least by the time of his controversy with the Pelagians, was a "strong and faithful defender of grace," that is to say, he denied the freedom of the will and man's ability to cooperate in his own salvation, plainly asserting that only God saves and that man is therefore justified by faith alone without the works of the law, while faith itself is a gift of God's grace. Jerome, in contrast, because his understanding of Paul was defective, was more often wrong than right. In the lectures on the Epistle to the Galatians that he gave in 1535, Luther referred regularly to Jerome's commentary on the same epistle, always pejoratively. Paul, he says, did not mean here what Jerome "supposes"; Augustine "has considered this issue more carefully than

Jerome"; Jerome "speakes foolishly" here; he "rushes into Paul without any judgment"; he "miserably lacerates this passage"; he "labors here but says nothing that matters." Jerome's root error was his perverse conviction that human beings are saved by faith and works together, a delusion that made him misunderstand Galatians and think that when Paul opposed faith to works he had in mind only the works of the Ceremonial Law and not the Ten Commandments and the moral teachings of the New Testament as well. "Origen and Jerome were the originators of this error. They were extremely dangerous teachers on this point; all the scholastics followed them, and in our day Erasmus approves and confirms their error."[7]

The full measure of Luther's dislike shows up in the unbuttoned informality of the "table talk." Jerome was no theologian. He can help us with the literal meaning of the Old Testament, but he has nothing at all to say about faith and the teaching of true religion. There is more learning in Aesop than in all of Jerome. He has probably been saved somehow by his faith in Christ, and for this he should be reverenced; but his teaching has done much harm. He should not be numbered among the doctors of the church. "I know no writer whom I hate as much as I do Jerome. All he writes about is fasting and virginity."[8]

Luther attacked Jerome so violently, in part, because Erasmus admired him so much. The fact of the matter, though, is that there was little in Jerome that could appeal to a sixteenth-century Protestant. His greatest scholarly achievement was the Vulgate Bible; Protestants preferred the Greek and Hebrew originals, new Latin versions alleged to be more accurate than the Vulgate, or a good vernacular translation—though it is true that a few scholars, Catholic as well as Protestant, advanced the erroneous opinion, made current by Flavio Biondo in his *Italia illustrata* (1453), that Jerome had translated the Bible into "Dalmatian," and so cited him as an authority for reading Scripture in the vernacular.[9] Jerome was the most important early theorist of the monastic life and ideal in the Latin West. Protestant theologians attacked monastic vows as impious, displeasing to God, absent in the Gospel, and unknown to the primitive church; Protestant princes secularized monasteries. Jerome exalted the excellence of virginity and proved the superiority of celibacy to marriage; Protestants praised marriage and abandoned sacerdotal celibacy. Jerome defended the cult of relics and veneration of saints. His visits to the holy places of Palestine and to the anchorites of the Egyptian desert were testimonials in favor of pilgrimages. Protestants frowned on all these devotional practices. Jerome founded Western Mariology; Protestants deprecated the veneration of the Virgin. More insistently, perhaps, than any other father of the Latin church, Jerome had magnified the dignity and primacy of the Roman see; Protestants called the bishop of Rome an antichrist. The fundamental doctrine of classical Protestantism is justification by faith alone without the works of the Law. Jerome's asceticism was a glorification of works; and although he repudiated Pelagius and emphasized the role of grace in the economy of salvation, he taught also that God has given men and women free choice, the liberty to do what they will, whether for good or evil, in order to earn the recompense of heaven or deserve the punishment of hell.[10] Jerome, finally, was intermittently a visionary; classical Protestantism was deeply hostile to the assumptions of mysticism and to any claim by fallen man that he had been privileged to see the divine Persons.

The dissatisfaction of Protestants with St. Jerome was not entirely untypical of their attitude toward Christian antiquity in general. Although the fathers were much to be preferred to the modern sophists, Protestant theologians necessarily had reservations about even the best of them. For in their view Scripture was the sole authority in doctrinal matters—*sola scriptura*. They rejected as latently unreliable every human interpretation of Scripture, because, they said, quoting St. Paul, all men lie (*omnis homo mendax*), preferring to believe, against overwhelming evidence to the contrary, that the meaning of the Bible is simple and unambiguous and that the Word of God teaches its own truth.[11] Since, moreover, their aim was a restoration of biblical Christianity and not a revival of patristic piety, the best that they could do in the circumstances was to cite the patristic texts that supported their own positions, while minimizing or rejecting the authority of the rest as nonscriptural and purely human. So Luther banned Origen; had no use for Chrysostom, "for he is only a gossip"; and wouldn't give a penny for Basil ("he was a monk after all"). Ambrose, in contrast, is good because he "sometimes treats excellently of the forgiveness of sins, which is the chief article, namely, that the divine majesty pardons by grace."[12] His respect even for Augustine was wholly relative: "Ever since I came to an understanding of Paul, I have not been able to think well of any doctor [of the church]. They have become of little value to me. At first I devoured, not merely read, Augustine. But when the door was opened for me in Paul, so that I understood what justification by faith is, it was all over with Augustine."[13]

Zwingli included the fathers (when he disagreed with them) among the "crowd of carnal divines" (*die huf der fleischlich geistlichen*) and argued, as had Luther, that right understanding of Scripture is from the Holy Spirit, unmediated by doctors, fathers, bishops, popes, or councils, given directly to the believer without the intervention of anything human. When a father agrees with evangelical truth, it may be useful to cite him in support. Thus, although his view of Jerome was little higher than Luther's (Faber reports that during the first Zurich disputation Zwingli said that even "if he were only half a man, stood on one leg and closed one eye, he would nevertheless not yield to Jerome"),[14] he did not fail to cite him against Luther (and the Catholics) on the correct interpretation of "This is my body" (Matt. 26:26), namely, that what Jesus taught when he instituted the Supper was a spiritual rather than a corporeal eating and that we must understand the words of institution in a figurative and not in a literal sense: "But note with what clarity Jerome describes the bread as simply a sign or sacrament of the Pascal Lamb, that is, Christ. He sees clearly that it is the intention of Christ to signify or represent his very body and blood. Hence Jerome takes the words of Christ, 'This is my body,' to mean: The bread represents my body, the very body which I have given for you."[15] After giving his own definition of true faith, he again added patristic testimony, while minimizing the need to do so: "And this is not merely my view, but St. Hilary was of the same opinion, though we do not need his help: Christ and Peter and Paul and John were all of this opinion."[16] Patristic opinion is never necessary or decisive. Only God can teach us the truth with such certainty that all doubts are removed.

Like Zwingli, Melanchthon, followed by later Lutherans, considered some fathers acceptable, some not. Within the theology of a single father, some things are well said and provide heavenly doctrine; others are badly said; still others are wicked and pernicious. Everything the fathers say must be filtered through the sieve of Scripture. Teachings that fail the scriptual test (*iudicium scripturae*) are to be rejected; those that pass it become positive witnesses to the absolute truth. Anyone who denies that Jerome's translation of the Old Testament has been most useful to the church is either unlearned or ungrateful. His commentaries on the prophets explain well the historical meaning of those books. He possessed many virtues that deserve imitation; he did, however, wrongly slander women and the divine institution of marriage. In his book against Jovinian, he lent the weight of his authority to superstitious opinions and human traditions. He wrote "ridiculously" about many other topics. His devotion to ascetic works was misguided; and in some places he attributed too much to free will. Yet in *Adversus Pelagianos* he argued rightly when he said that our *renovatio* is due not to the strength of free will but to the help of the Holy Spirit. He spoke well when he denied that saints are without sin. And he has left us a memorable maxim: "We are just when we confess ourselves sinners. Our justice comes to us from no merit of our own, but from God's mercy." On balance, though, Melanchthon found him wanting: "It is evident," he concluded, "that there are many serious errors in Jerome's works."[17]

Calvin distinguished the ancient fathers from the "sounder schoolmen" (among whom he sometimes included St. Bernard and Peter Lombard) and from the "more recent Sophists," less sound as "they are farther removed from antiquity." He had read most of patristic literature and admired some of it, especially the works of Augustine: "As for St. Augustine," he wrote, "he agrees so well with us in everything and everywhere, that if I had to write a confession upon this matter [his subject is predestination], it would be enough for me to compose it from evidences drawn from his books." But even the ancient fathers were too anxious to please the wise men of this world by trying to harmonize the doctrine of Scripture with the beliefs of the philosophers, and so mixed the earthly with the heavenly, a hateful thing. Thus led astray by the common judgments of the flesh and of human understanding, they disagreed among themselves, contradicted themselves, and sometimes fell into serious error, notably by allowing some natural virtue and freedom to human beings. "Even though the Greeks above the rest—and Chrysostom especially among them—extol the ability of the human will, yet all the ancients, save Augustine, so differ, waver, or speak confusedly on this subject, that almost nothing certain can be derived from their writings."[18] Jerome was sound on the Supper, for he carefully guarded against the fiction of a corporeal eating of the body and blood of Christ. He is helpful on ecclesiology: he shows, for example, that in the primitive church the office, function, and name of bishop and pastor were one and synonymous, thus proving that the modern elevation of bishops over ordinary clergy is "a human custom and rests on no scriptural authority." But on other important issues Jerome's judgment was lamentable; for although "that famous man was endowed with outstanding virtues," in debate he was often carried away by excessive zeal and so was not always concerned about sticking to the truth. This was especially the case whenever he wrote about virginity and marriage. Blinded then by "a zeal which defies description," he rushed headlong into false and childish views, putting marriage in a bad light and spreading abroad all sorts of puerile fallacies. On the most important issue of all, justification by faith alone and what Paul meant by "works of the law," he erred fundamentally. Like Origen and Chrysostom and "all the Papists," he interpreted the works of the law as mere ceremonies, stubbornly blind to the truth that Paul was discussing the free righteousness given us by Christ.[19]

In view of the Anglican predilection for the middle way, it is not surprising that it was one of Queen Elizabeth's bishops who defined with the most precise balance the Protestant attitude toward the fathers. "But what say we of the fathers, Augustine, Ambrose, Hierome, Cyprian, etc.? What shall we think of them, or what account may we make of them?" asked Bishop John Jewel in *A Treatise of the Holy Scriptures* (1570). It is worth quoting his answer in full.

> They be interpreters of the word of God. They were learned men, and learned fathers; the instruments of the mercy of God, and vessels full of grace. We despise them not, we read them, we reverence them, and give thanks unto God for them. They were witnesses unto the truth, they were worthy pillars and ornaments in the church of God. Yet may they not be compared with the word of God. We may not build upon them: we may not make them the foundation and warrant of our conscience: we may not put our trust in them. Our trust is in the name of the Lord. . . . Some things I believe, and some things which they write I cannot believe. I weigh them not as holy and canonical scriptures. Cyprian was a doctor of the church, yet he was deceived: Augustine was a doctor of the church, yet he wrote a book of Retractations; he acknowledged that he was deceived. . . . They are our fathers, but not fathers unto God; they are the stars, fair, and beautiful, and bright; yet they are not the sun: they bear witness of the light, they are not the light. Christ is the Sun of righteousness, Christ is the Light which lighteneth every man that cometh into this world. His word is the word of truth.[20]

Catholics rapidly occupied the patristic bulwarks that Protestants were beginning to leave so weakly guarded. Choosing to illustrate beliefs and practices rejected by Protestants as false or superstitious, Catholic iconographers made Pope Gregory the Great a witness to purgatory, a place and doctrine invented by the medieval Western church and denied by Protestants, or pictured St. Augustine washing the feet of a pilgrim whom he discovers to be Jesus Christ, a celebration of meritorious works of charity and an affirmation that Christians are saved by faith and works together, not by faith alone.[21] Frescoed on pendentives, Gregory, Jerome, Augustine, and Ambrose had long supported the domes of churches. Now, in an altarpiece of Jacob Jordaens, a Calvinist who did not scruple to accept commissions from the Catholic authorities of Antwerp, the four doctors of the Latin church and other saints were shown adoring an allegorical figure of the church triumphant seated on a lion.[22] Zurbarán painted St. Thomas Aquinas in glory adored by the same four fathers.[23] Two Greek and two Latin fathers hold up Bernini's *Cathedra Petri* in St. Peter's in Rome.[24]

Pictures of St. Jerome taught more specific lessons. A painting by the Florentine artist Domenico Passignano commissioned about 1599 to decorate a chapel dedicated to Jerome in the church of S. Giovanni dei Fiorentini in Rome shows him supervising the construction of the monasteries in Bethlehem.[25] In an early work by Guercino (c. 1617), Jerome, in his cave in the Syrian desert, fixes his seal to a letter, very probably the one to Pope Damasus in which he called him "sun of justice," "light of the world," "salt of the earth," and "vase of gold and silver" and said that the bishop of Rome alone occupies the seat of Peter (*cathedra Petri*) and conserves uncorrupted the inheritance of the apostles (*fides apostolica*). What the Roman church teaches, he, Jerome, will teach; what it believes, he will believe.[26] The last communion of St. Jerome had been a subject occasionally represented in the fifteenth and early sixteenth centuries on the small scale of the predella panel, domestic devotional picture, and manuscript illumination (figs. 35 and 36); in the late sixteenth century it was revived and enlarged to the dignity and scale of the major altarpiece. Agostino Carracci's influential version was commissioned about 1590 by the Carthusians of the convent of S. Girolamo di Casara at Bologna; that of Domenichino was painted between 1612 and 1614 for the Roman church of S. Girolamo della Carità, believed to have been erected on the site of St. Paula's palace. The renewed and novel emphasis given a legendary episode first imagined by the author of the fourteenth-century pseudographs made Jerome a witness to the Real Presence of the body and blood of Christ in the Eucharistic elements, thus rebutting Zwinglian and Calvinist interpretations of authentic texts, and, indirectly, to Transubstantiation and the Mass, condemned by all Protestants as a form of sacrificial magic.[27] Jerome's penance in the wilderness remained a subject of undiminished popularity, newly relevant (along with

Fig. 35.   Sandro Botticelli, *The Last Communion of St. Jerome*, c. 1494–1495

images of the tearfully repentant St. Peter and Mary Magdalen) in an age when, as St. Peter Canisius lamented, so many people (namely Protestants) held the very word penance in horror and even expunged it from German translations of the Bible.[28]

Material needed to enlist Jerome in the defense of the cult of Mary was already available before the Lutheran revolt. It was widely known that he had been especially devoted to the infant Jesus and his mother, that he had written a tract affirming her perpetual virginity, that he had been buried

Fig. 36.   Circle of Jean Bourdichon, *The Last Communion and Death of St. Jerome*, c. 1510

near the grotto where Jesus was born and reinterred next to the Chapel of the Presepio in S. Maria Maggiore. It is therefore unsurprising to find him so often among the two, four, or six saints flanking the Madonna and Child in altarpieces and devotional pictures. Less obvious is why Renaissance artists regularly connected him not only with Mary's perpetual virginity but with her Assumption and Immaculate Conception as well. In a *St. Jerome in His Study* signed by the Sienese master Matteo di Giovanni and dated 1492, a strip of paper hanging out of a drawer under Jerome's desk bears the title *De Assumptione Virginis* (see fig. 31). The Boucicaut Master, in an elegant miniature painting of the same subject, decorated Jerome's study with a pitcher containing a spray of *lilium candidum,* the white madonna lily that symbolizes Mary's purity and freedom from original sin in so many pictures of the Annunciation.[29] Colantonio's *St. Jerome in His Study* (Naples, Capodimonte) and Joos van Cleve's (Busch-Reisinger Museum, Harvard University) (fig. 37) make Jerome a witness to the Immaculate Conception by hanging a spotless white towel on the wall of his study. The authority for these anachronisms was a text universally believed before the sixteenth century to be by Jerome, the spurious letter *De assumptione Mariae* beginning *Cogitis me (Ep. supp. 9,* by Paschasius Radbertus). The letter not only defends the proposition of the Virgin's Assumption, it also contains a passage that even today remains part of the Office of the Immaculate Conception in the Roman Breviary: "Not unfittingly, therefore, is she bidden to come from Lebanon, for Lebanon means a radiant whiteness. For she was dazzlingly white with her many virtues and merits, and by the gifts of the Holy Spirit she was cleansed whiter than snow; showing in all things the simplicity of a dove; for all in her was purity and simplicity, truth and grace; all mercy and justice, which has looked down from heaven [Ps. 84:12] and for this reason was she immaculate, because corruption was not found in her."[30]

Erasmus censured *Cogitis me* as spurious; but when Lutherans and Zwinglians ridiculed it, Catholic controversialists defended its authenticity.[31] Catholic iconographers came to their support by encouraging artists to illustrate Jerome's devotion to the Virgin and his testimony to her Immaculate Conception and Assumption by showing him rapt in Marian visions. The visions need not be taken literally. They rest on no textual base: *Cogitis me* did not assert that Jerome, in an ecstasy, had actually seen the Virgin. Nor did painters necessarily mean to suggest that he had registered the Immaculata or her Assumption on more than his inner eye.

Fig. 37.   Joos van Cleve, *St. Jerome in His Study,* c. 1525. A picture rich in references to the Blessed Virgin Mary and to the Passion as well as to life's end.

Fig. 38.   Agostino Carracci, after Tintoretto, *St. Jerome's Vision of the Assumption of the Virgin,* 1588

Their purpose was to confirm that he had adored her and to make him a witness to contested doctrines. Tintoretto's influential *St. Jerome's Vision of the Assumption of the Virgin,* painted c. 1582 for the Venetian Scuola di San Gerolamo presso San Fantin and popularized in an engraving by Agostino Carracci (fig. 38), is a straightforward reminiscence of *Cogitis me.*[32] Parmigianino's *Madonna and Child with Saints John the Baptist and Jerome* (fig. 39) teaches a more complicated doctrine. Madonna and Child

Fig. 39. Parmigianino, *The Madonna and Child with Saints John the Baptist and Jerome*, 1527

sit on the crescent moon. John the Baptist, a leopard skin draped over his knee, points to the Child to announce the coming of the Messiah; Jerome, who according to Pseudo-Augustine was a white or spiritual martyr but in sanctity of life and glory after death fully equal to John the Baptist, lies stretched out on the ground holding a crucifix and martyr's palm. He is asleep. His dream pictures the Virgin Immaculate and is a testimonial that in Mary "all was purity and simplicity, truth and grace, ... for this reason was she immaculate, because corruption was not found in her."[33]

On 30 September 1574 Angelo da Bergamo, a Carmelite monk, professor of theology and rector of the University of Bologna, delivered a commemorative oration in praise of wisdom and of St. Jerome. His purpose was the same as the iconographers': to show the living connection of the patristic past with the contemporary Roman church. Jerome's importance, he emphasized, apart from the fact that he is the protector and patron of the theological faculty of the University of Bologna and a model for every member of the "Catholic and orthodox church," is that he can tell us what Scripture means. The heretics refuse to understand this. The Wyclifs, Luthers, Carlstadts, Oecolampadiuses, and Melanchthons think they have penetrated the meaning of the Bible and understand the mysteries of holy theology and sacred doctrine. They are mistaken. They and we, all of us, are simple *idiotae*. The Bible is obscure and full of mystery, opaque and difficult, locked and sealed with seven seals, inaccessible without the key of David. Understanding it requires a kind of supranatural cognition, a form of vision akin to the beatific, in which we learn to know the Word (the Wisdom of the Father) in the scriptural word. It is impossible to gain such knowledge without the grace of Christ and the illumination of the Holy Spirit, a light easily but not promiscuously available: for God has primarily localized the interpretive clairvoyance of the Holy Spirit in the fathers; the fathers mediate that light to us.[34]

Echoing the symbolic pairings of the Middle Ages and the language of Boniface VIII's decretal ordering the feasts of the four doctors of the Latin church to be celebrated with special solemnity, Angelo compared Jerome, Augustine, Ambrose, and Gregory to four fountains of wisdom and four rivers that have their origins in paradise. They water the whole world with their life-giving teachings. Every age has admired Augustine's penetration, Ambrose's prudence, Gregory's affability, and Jerome's wisdom. Jerome especially should be our guide. His eloquence, asceticism, and knowledge of Scripture make him a star in the "firmament of the church militant whose light illumines the world." He teaches us the shining truth in so many letters, treatises, dialogues, sermons, and orations; he has solved so many difficult questions, confuted so many heretics, and explained so many scriptural texts; he has translated so many books and preserved so many sayings of the early fathers, it seems not too much to say that it was he who laid the foundations of the whole Western church. No wonder our ancestors made Jerome the special patron of this university. All theologians should model themselves on him. The pope rightly recognized his wisdom and piety by making him a cardinal.[35]

Jerome has illuminated the church in every age; but sixteenth-century Catholics recognized that his support was even more necessary in a period like their own when the words of Jeremiah (5:30–31) seemed to have come true: "An appalling and horrible thing has happened in the land: the prophets prophesy falsely, and the priests rule at their direction; my people love to have it so, but what will you do when the end comes?" Laymen disobey their bishops and subjects disobey their rulers. Everyone twists Scripture to his own purposes. Heresies condemned for centuries circulate again among the credulous pleb.[36] In 1529, a Paris theologian found the root of infection in the doctrine of *sola scriptura*. By teaching people that they are not required to accept any doctrine, ordonnance, or institute of the Christian religion as necessary for their salvation unless it is explicitly spelled out in Scripture, the Lutherans seek to destroy the authority of the church and the power of the pope, reverence for priests, the sacraments, observance of fasts, Canon Law, monastic vows, the virginity of nuns, veneration of saints, purgatory, and the honor of the holy Mother of God.[37] Observing the European world from Augsburg in 1565, St. Peter Canisius was distressed by the same symptoms of disintegration: ancient piety mocked, the sacraments abused, altars and churches profaned, traditional ceremonies denounced as pharisaical and abandoned.[38] Twenty years later a French priest traumatized by religious war asserted baldly that satanic furies were loose in the world and that their ministers were Protestant pastors.[39]

Who could better refute these errors than St. Jerome, hammer of heretics? Nobody; or such was the view, and the chief motive, of the publishers, editors, and translators who offered the public selections from Jerome's letters and treatises after 1517. They regularly stressed the consonance of Jerome's doctrinal views with contemporary Catholic orthodoxy. "I want the readers of this book to be sure of one thing," wrote Juan de Molina in a note at the end of his Spanish translation of the letters; "in the whole of this work there is not a single heretical sentence, nor a scandalous one, nor one of doubtful orthodoxy or offensive to pious Catholic ears."[40] Jerome combats heresy the more effectively because he joins eloquence to his impeccable orthodoxy and possesses all the qualities of Cicero's orator: knowledge, upright life, and the ability to sway men's minds to truth and virtuous purposes. Moreover, God endowed him with universal appeal and the ability to touch and speak to men and women of every age, condition, and class. He teaches all, consoles all, and is loved by all.[41]

While he lived, Jerome refuted the heretics of his own day; his pure doctrine remains a powerful antidote to the seditions and impieties of the present age. To defend the Blessed Virgin, the Strasbourg humanist Hieronymus Gebwiler republished *Adversus Helvidium*, and to defend the cult of saints and the veneration of relics the *Adversus Vigilantium*. Canisius published selected letters in a convenient cheap format in the expectation that exposure to Jerome's true, health-giving doctrine would help dispel Protestant errors. Every right-minded person agreed that the best tactic of all was to distrust one's individual opinion and align one's views on those of the doctors of the church, especially Jerome.

The post-Erasmian lives of St. Jerome show a similar confessional bias and apologetic purpose. In 1528 Loys Laserre, a canon of Tours and member of the Collège de Navarre of the University of Paris, dedicated his vernacular life to Françoise de Tonnerre, prioress of the convent of Notre-Dame de Relay, a dependency of the reformed abbey of Fontevrault. Virginity and chastity, monasticism and monastic reform, contemplative and visionary piety, charitable and penitential works, the value of tradition and the authority of the theological faculty of the University of Paris—Laserre defended them all on the example of St. Jerome. Where Erasmus had emphasized the scholar, Laserre reemphasized the monk, the celibate, the solitary contemplative, the ascetic penitent, reminding his readers that Jerome was best painted as a thin, wasted man in a hair shirt, on his knees before a crucifix, beating his chest with a stone and weeping, an image that usefully incites the spectator to repentance and imitation.[42]

Not only does Laserre present Jerome as the spiritual father of a multitude of monks and nuns and a model of the monastic virtues, he goes on to push back the origins of monasticism to the very beginning of Christianity (insinuating that St. Mark founded monasteries in Egypt and that St. Matthew consecrated to God a virgin daughter of the King of Ethiopia) and to urge the religious of his own day to reform their lives and orders by imitating Jerome. If they do this, they will live not merely physically separated from the world, shut up in their convents, but in a truly spiritual solitude, horrified by the pleasures of the flesh, fleeing all occasions of sin, and burning with love of God. They will then enjoy the sweetest fruit of solitude, the tranquil contemplation of divine things and, like Jerome, possess a spiritual ladder, one end resting on earth, the other pushing into heaven, which they will mount when they meditate on heavenly things and climb down to succor human nature and their neighbors, a traditional mystical image as well as a moving reminiscence of a passage from Pico della Mirandola's *Oration on the Dignity of Man*.[43]

Equally characteristic of Laserre was his tender regard for many of the legendary details mocked by Erasmus. The obvious relish with which Erasmus had gone about his job of demystification offended his respect for tradition and all things edifying. He himself included even speeches and miracles from the fourteenth-century pseudographs. Things like these may seem difficult to believe, he confessed, but they were written down by men of substance and honor, and such men would not lie. In any case, we see every day more remarkable things, "works of God the creator (for whom nothing is impossible) which manifest themselves in nature in divers marvellous ways incomprehensible to the understanding and inexpressible in words." Given all this, Jerome might very well have tamed a lion, for example, even if he was too modest to mention the exploit himself.[44]

A sharper, and an entirely more sophisticated, answer to Erasmus came not from Paris but from Rome. In 1561 Cardinal Girolamo Seripando, on behalf of Pius IV, invited Paulus Manutius, son of the great printer Aldus, to move his press from Venice to Rome and serve the church by printing accurate and scholarly editions of the Vulgate Bible and the ancient fathers of the church. Paulus set up his printing office on the Campidoglio and in the next year issued several patristic works in praise of virginity, in 1563 the works of Cyprian (edited to show that he had not been hostile to the bishop of Rome, as Protestants alleged), in 1564 the *Canons and Decrees of the Council of Trent* and the Roman Breviary, and in 1565 the first three volumes of a superb nine-volume edition of the complete works of St. Jerome. The editor was Mariano Vittori, a distinguished scholar and linguist (he wrote a grammar of the Ethiopian language) who had been in the service, successively, of Cardinals Marcello Cervini (who became

Pope Marcellus II), Reginald Pole (whom he followed to England when he returned as legate under Queen Mary), and Giovanni Morone. Cardinal Morone took him into his household about 1559, assigned him a generous pension, encouraged his plan to reedit St. Jerome, and helped him substantially in this enterprise by putting monks in his orbit of influence to work in Florence, Bologna, Brescia, the Vatican Library, the abbey of Monte Cassino, and the Dominican convent in Naples collating twenty manuscripts of Jerome's letters and treatises with the text of Erasmus's edition of 1516.[45]

Vittori begins by attacking Erasmus and his edition. The worst kind of heretic is the one who pretends to be an orthodox member of the family. Erasmus is like this: he hands out poison calling it an antidote, offers bread with one hand and throws a rock with the other. Several scholars, he continues, have already pointed out the heresies in Erasmus's works, but he is the first, he thinks, to show how shoddy Erasmus's editions of the fathers actually are. Vittori claims (with some justice: Erasmus was both an inspired editor and, like Jerome, a hasty and often careless worker) that he has been able to correct or improve Erasmus's text in over 1,500 places, while at the same time refuting the many errors in his notes.[46] He prefaced his edition with another life of Jerome, dedicated to Cardinal Carlo Borromeo.[47] It too marks an advance. To be sure, it lacks the freshness, originality, and sparkle of Erasmus's *Life*. But his principles are the same: he will admit as sources only Jerome's own authentic works and the works of Jerome's contemporaries, and his story is more detailed and more accurate. He improves Erasmus's chronology. He is more objective, less present-minded, and, alas, duller. Instructed by Erasmus, and by the fathers at Trent, he too pruned his narrative of every legendary tendril: no lion appears; Jerome knows only Latin, Greek and Hebrew; he is neither a cardinal nor a virgin; he is not forced to leave Rome because his ecclesiastical enemies tricked him into wearing a woman's dress to church; and although he cites the authority of the Roman Breviary for the statement that miracles occurred before and after the saint's death, he is reticent about their frequency and character. He agrees, of course, that Jerome is now buried in Rome next to the Chapel of the Presepio in S. Maria Maggiore, and reminds his readers that Pope Pius II had promised a plenary indulgence to whomever visited the tomb on 9 May, the feast of Jerome's translation. No better life would be written before the eighteenth-century one of Joannes Stilting in the Bollandist *Acta Sanctorum*.

Mariano Vittori's emphases naturally reflect his time and purpose, as Erasmus's had reflected his. He hardly mentions the dream; but there is a great deal about Jerome's respect for the Roman pontiff and his wish to be ever guided by him in order that he may always believe what the Roman church believes. He provides a wealth of detail on Jerome's fights against heresy, the Origenist controversy, and his polemics against Rufinus. And since Protestants constantly urged the superiority of Augustine, Vittori inevitably felt obliged to compare the two fathers and to prefer Jerome. The church, he concluded, has produced many learned and famous men, but none more learned than Jerome. "Augustine himself confesses that he doesn't have or ever could have Jerome's knowledge of Holy Scripture."[48]

Vittori spelled out his confessional purposes with disarming candor. His edition of Jerome will be "hugely useful to the church." One: the work will demonstrate the legitimacy of the Index of Prohibited Books. The Protestant heretics say that malice and pressure from interested persons get books put on the Index. This edition of Jerome will show that Erasmus is on the Index for the good and objective reason that his works are full of errors and false doctrine. Second: to those who say that the Roman church is good at destroying books but not at restoring them, he answers that the great editorial project of which this edition of Jerome is a part is, with the decrees and canons of the Council of Trent, the firmest foundation of the Catholic faith and the Roman church. Third: the edition shows that the Roman church is the only true church, which cannot be led astray from the Word of Christ, and by which the other straying churches should be taught the truth and confirmed in faith, and that this true church is not less active in restoring the books of the holy fathers than the heretics are in corrupting them and twisting their meaning.[49]

Cardinal Baronius built on the foundations laid by Erasmus and Vittori. Cesare Baronio (1538–1607) was a man of encyclopedic culture whose scholarly interests centered on the early history of the church. Begun in the early 1560s, the first volume of his massive *Annales Ecclesiastici* appeared in 1588. It was largely through his narrative that the best sixteenth-century work on Jerome was mediated to the seventeenth and eighteenth centuries. His purpose too was of course confessional: to defend the church by careful historical and archeological research, to demonstrate the continuity between the practices of the earliest church and those of his own day, and to document most scrupulously and accurately the lives of the saints and martyrs in the expectation that a simple statement of the facts would demonstrate the authenticity of the Roman church and its claims. The reality combines impartiality and unbridled bias. The sections in the *Annales* on Jerome are examples of the first and help make good his claim that "ecclesiastical candor and the modesty of Christian simplicity abhor everything spurious and reject anything forged, just as truth (*sincera fides*) always hates and reviles every falsehood and its author." He is as harsh on the fourteenth-century pseudographs as Erasmus. They are a "cesspool of lies," filled with ludicrous errors and anachronisms. He dismisses the story of the lion as the work of an *indiscretus laudator* of Jerome, a "simple soul" who believed the story to be true because he heard that it was confirmed by inhabitants of Bethlehem. Either he did not rightly understand what he heard, or the person who told him was misinformed. The incident itself may possibly be true. But it happened to St. Gerasimus, not to Jerome. The miracle of the one has been mistakenly credited to the other because of a similarity of names. His positive principle was the by now familiar one: he would write Jerome's life "ex suis ipsius scriptis." The result was a brief account resting solidly at every point on Jerome's authentic works.[50]

The last Renaissance biography of St. Jerome is that of Fray José de Sigüenza. José Martinez de Espinosa was born in Sigüenza (his father was a cleric and he was illegitimate) in 1544. He received the B.A. in 1563 after two years' study in the faculty of arts of the Universidad de Portaceli de Sigüenza. He joined the Hieronymite Order in 1566 and continued his theological training at the convent of Santa María de Párraces in Segovia. He was ordained in 1572. During the next decade and a half he taught arts and theology in several houses of the order before moving permanently to San Lorenzo el Real de el Escorial in 1587 as preacher, teacher, librarian, archivist, and keeper of relics (among them St. Jerome's head). In 1592 he fell victim to the jealous intrigues of several of his colleagues and was tried (and acquitted) by the Inquisition. He began his history of the Hieronymite Order in 1594 and published the first part, his massive life of Jerome, in Madrid in 1595. Sigüenza made intelligent use of the earlier lives by Erasmus and Vittori and of Baronius's *Annales*. He had read and digested all of Jerome's works, and clearly distinguished authentic letters and treatises from spurious ones. He is immensely long-winded, but so sinewy and savory is his prose that he is not tediously so.[51]

A few examples will sufficiently convey the central characteristic of his book: the balanced tension between a sophisticated historical sense, on the one hand, and on the other, a reverence for tradition and a sharply polemical purpose.

One way that Erasmus, Calvin, and other heretics attack the ecclesiastical hierarchy and disturb the harmony of the mystical body of the church, says Sigüenza, is to deny that Jerome was a cardinal. In order to diminish the office's antiquity and authority, they claim that it is of recent invention and that to imagine that Jerome had ever occupied it is therefore anachronistic; and so they laugh at the habit of painting him in cardinal's dress and identifying him by a red hat. Such persons are malicious and ignorant of ecclesiastical history. Sigüenza admits that it is anachronistic to paint Jerome wearing the clothes cardinals wear nowadays, because Innocent IV granted them the red hat only at the Council of Lyons 1254, Boniface VIII the red soutane in 1294, and Paul II the rest of their costume in 1464. But clothes are one thing, the office and dignity another. The word cardinal, he rightly goes on, is very old and was applied from an early date to priests attached to the Roman *tituli* or parish churches. We know that Jerome was a presbyter; we know that he worked closely with Pope Damasus; what is most likely than that he was a cardinal presbyter? The difficulty that Sigüenza too conveniently fails to mention is that these early "cardinals" were very different in rank and function from the cardinals of the fifteenth and sixteenth centuries. And the question he fails to ask is when in fact these early cardinals first appeared. Were there any in the fourth century? On the continued propriety of painting Jerome in the dress of a modern cardinal, Sigüenza takes a sensible line. The practice is venerable and useful. How else will the illiterate identify the saint? How would those who can read only pictures identify St. Peter as pope unless he is shown with a tiara, even though the tiara did not exist in his time? It is permissible then to show Jerome dressed anachronistically in order that the faithful may recognize him for the cardinal he in fact was, even though the cardinals of his day did not wear red hats.[52]

He is very good on the lion. He is obviously fond of the story, so he tells it in detail. He lashes out at those who ridicule such stories; they are the sort of people who would have us reject entirely "every miracle and sign God has given us in confirmation and approval of his evangelical doctrine." Then, with careful reluctance, he shows, following Baronius, that the story properly belongs to St. Gerasimus, who lived on the banks of the Jordan a century and a half later, and that the similarity of names accounts for its attribution to Jerome; that Jerome never mentioned the lion in his own writings, nor did his contemporaries; and that, according to the geographers, there are no lions in the environs of Bethlehem, but there are on the banks of the Jordan.[53]

His discussion of Jerome's virginity is less persuasive. Until Erasmus, Sigüenza asserted, everyone who had written about Jerome said that he died a virgin. (This is a deliberate misstatement; Sigüenza knew very well that Jacopo da Varazze had long ago quoted Jerome's own statement that he was not a virgin.) Erasmus, a "modern author whom everyone knows was arrogant and lacking in piety when writing about the saints," explained the lapse by saying that Jerome after all was only a man and therefore weak. Unlike Erasmus, Mariano Vittori was modest, pious, and learned. He proposed and solved the following paradox: It is true that Jerome was a virgin; it is also true that he was not. The clue to remember is that Jerome was twice born: first naturally, then reborn a second time in baptism. Jerome lost the flower of virginity while he was a young student in Rome; in baptism he was reborn a virgin and chastely remained so. (Fray José fails to mention that it was Erasmus himself who had first suggested that Jerome lost his virginity before he was baptized, but remained chaste thereafter.) The rest of his argument explains why we should reject Jerome's own testimony. We all know that the saints castigate themselves for a peccadillo as though it were murder and are so humble about their virtues that they often confess to sins they really didn't commit. This is what Jerome did. "We can therefore affirm that although Jerome *says* that he was not a virgin in the flesh or in the spirit . . . , we are not bound to believe him."[54]

A campaign to clean up the images of the saints paralleled the effort to free their biographies of legend and their bibliographies of *spuria*. A decree of the twenty-fifth session of the Council of Trent defined the legitimate uses of sacred images (December 1563). Since religious pictures teach the articles of faith, show the miracles God has performed by means of his saints, and set before the faithful examples by which they may order their own lives and manners in imitation of the saints, they should not teach false doctrine or lead the uneducated into error. Their subjects must be authentic and purged of superstition, and no figure in them should be painted with a beauty that excites lust.[55] Interpreters of the decree demanded sobriety and decorum; clarity and simplicity; a popular, useful art intelligible to everyone. Pictures should instruct, edify, and move, but within the limits of historical accuracy; artists must avoid distracting detail, legendary events, spurious sources, and subjects that might expose Catholic devotions to the ridicule of heretics. Religious painters are mute orators (*taciti predicatori del popolo*) whose role is to instruct the faithful and persuade them to be good.[56]

What these principles could mean for the iconography of St. Jerome was partly spelled out by Jan Vermeulen (Molanus), a theologian and hagiographer at the University of Louvain, in a book on the use and abuse of images of the saints, first published in 1570 and again, revised and enlarged, in 1594. Molanus approved pictures of Jerome in penitence because they were based on a famous letter of undisputed authenticity, though, with a literal-minded respect for documented fact, he pointed out that "the stone with which he beats his breast has been added by the painters themselves." He noted that painters often put a candle on Jerome's work table when they showed him in his study. He allowed it no symbolic meaning. It refers to a passage from the preface to his *Commentary on Ezekiel* where he complained in his old age that his sight was so dim that he could no longer read his Hebrew books by candlelight. Including a skull and crucifix in pictures of Jerome does not distort the truth "because [Jerome] often meditated on the cross and on death and the Last Judgment." But why is Jerome still painted as a cardinal with a lion, since Mariano Vittori did not mention either one in his *Life?* Molanus replied that these are benign errors; what we must do is change the meaning (*significatio*) of familiar attributes like these. Dressing Jerome as a cardinal signifies only that he performed many of the same functions for Pope Damasus that modern cardinals perform for their papal masters; the lion signifies the wilderness and is shown with Jerome in order to remind us of the four years he spent there in study, meditation, and mortification of the flesh.[57]

Later sixteenth- and seventeenth-century artists commissioned to paint Jerome shared the intentions of the Counter-Reformation theorists. They almost never illustrated his miracles, all of them by now recognized as dubious by responsible judges. While retaining the attributes needed to identify him, they suppressed the legendary episodes connected with them. We no longer see him being ordained a cardinal or removing a thorn from the lion's paw, or, as in earlier works, discern an ass, camels, and turbaned Orientals through his study window (see fig. 43). A certain number of spurious texts, often no longer consciously recognized or remembered, continued to influence Hieronymite iconography, but explicit desire was for authenticity, historical truth, and simplicity, for a striking image teaching an important lesson understandable at a glance. Such an image is that of St. Jerome hearing the trumpet of the Last Judgment. The process by which Jerome became the chief patristic witness to the Last Judgment summarizes visually his transformation from a Renaissance to a Counter-Reformation saint.

The historical Jerome had had the Last Judgment much on his mind, both in fear and in complacent expectation. "Behold, the trumpet sounds from the sky, behold the armored general advances over the clouds to wage war on the world. Behold, the two-edged sword which springs from the king's mouth is ready to cut down everything in his way." Or again: "The day will come, yea it will come, when this corruptible and mortal flesh will put on incorruption and immortality. Blessed the servant whom his lord finds alert and ready on that day. Then the voice of the trumpet will terrify the earth and its peoples, but he will rejoice."[58]

It was not an authentic text, however, that was to make Jerome an important witness to the Last Judgment. As early as the tenth century he was credited with the discovery "in the annals of the Hebrews" of a short eschatological work entitled "The Fifteen Signs before Doomsday." Heralding the end, the sea will rise forty feet and then sink back nearly out of sight; earth, water, and sky will burn, trees bleed, buildings fall down, rocks crack, earth quake, the stars move from their courses and lose their light, the sun darken, and the moon turn to blood. Men and women will run about mad with fear. When the graves have opened, four angels will blow trumpets and Christ will arrive in his earthly body. Then there will be a new earth and a new heaven. The good will go to paradise glorious in new bodies and souls too; the wicked will go to all the torments of hell. The legend, in its several versions, in Latin and in the vernaculars, was extremely popular.[59] The incorporation of the little text in the *Golden Legend* guaranteed it an even wider diffusion.[60]

In the early fourteenth century, the moral of the "Fifteen Signs" was condensed into a single statement and it too attributed to Jerome.

> Sanctus Iheronimus
> Sive bibam sive comedam sive dormam
> Sive aliquid aliud faciam, semper videtur
> Michi illa vox terribilis sonare in auribus meis:
> Surgite mortui venite ad iudicium.

"Whether I am drinking or eating or sleeping or doing anything else at all, I seem to hear that terrifying voice resound in my ears, saying, Arise ye dead and come to judgment."[61] There exist several variants. The first line sometimes adds "waking" to "sleeping": "Sive bibo, sive comedo, sive dormio, sive vigilo: Whether I drink, whether I eat, whether I sleep or wake"; and in line three, *tuba* often replaces *vox:* "I seem to hear that terrifying trumpet resound in my ears."[62] All representations of St. Jerome hearing the trumpet of the Last Judgment rest directly or indirectly on this text.

Like "St. Jerome in Penitence" and "St. Jerome in His Study," the subject was invented in Italy, probably no earlier than 1400. The earliest surviving examples are two wall paintings. In the first, an early fifteenth-century fresco from the church of the former Vallombrosan nunnery of Santa Marta in Siena, Jerome stands full length in the middle of a macabre landscape. He holds a scroll in his right hand; with his left he points downward at the skeletons, bones, decaying corpses, worms, and serpents that surround him. In the top left of the fresco flies an angel who blows a trumpet into his right ear (fig. 40).[63] The second example is a fresco of the Last Judgment by an unidentified central Italian master in the chapel of Gregory the Great in the Benedictine monastery at Subiaco (fig. 41). It is in three sections. At the top, Jesus Christ, the supreme judge of the apocalypse, sits in glory on a rainbow, flanked by angels carrying the instruments of the passion; a lily and a sword leap from his head. The panel on the left below shows St. Jerome in penitence, wearing sackcloth, on his knees before a large crucifix, a bloody stone in his right hand. At his feet are his lion and his cardinal's hat. In the lower right panel, an angel blows the trumpet of the Last Judgment and the dead crawl out of their graves. From the angel's trumpet issues a scroll with the words *Surgite mortui, venite ad iudicium.* A scroll flowing out of Jerome's mouth bears a variant of the entire inscription, *Sive bibam, sive comedam,* much defaced. At the junction of the three sections of the fresco, a fictive piece of paper is tacked up. On it is written the beginning of the *Dies irae* and the date: 1466.

The subject then disappeared from the visual arts for over a hundred years. The idea itself of Jerome as a witness to the Last Judgment, however, powerfully survived, and different visual expressions of it multiplied in the later fifteenth and sixteenth centuries. In the cemetery of S. Secondo in Gubbio there is a small chapel dedicated to St. Sebastian, through whose intercession in 1458, according to an inscription, God freed the city from plague. The four doctors of the Latin church appear in

Fig. 40.   Tuscan school, *St. Jerome Hears the Trumpet of the Last Judgment,* c. 1400

the pendentives. St. Jerome is standing, a dignified, bearded old man. He holds a book in his hand, open to a passage beginning *Sive bibo, sive comedo.*[64] In a French miniature of about 1480, St. Jerome stands before an altarlike table pointing to a copy of the Book of Life lying open before him. Recorded there are the deeds by which we will be judged on the last day. On the wall behind the table hangs a painting of the Christ of the Last Judgment (fig. 42).[65] A German devotional woodcut of St. Jerome in penitence of about 1490 has inscribed at the top, *Sancte Jeronime ora pro nobis.* Lettered on a scroll coming out of his mouth is the text about hearing the terrible sound of the trumpet.[66] Its presence gives the subject of St. Jerome in penitence the added meaning of a meditation on death and the Last Judgment, thus making explicit what was latent in images of the penitent Jerome from the beginning, the close connection between repentance, man's death, and Christ's death; the coming of the Kingdom; and the judgment that will precede it.

In the sixteenth century, the perception of St. Jerome as a witness to the Last Judgment profoundly modified the iconography of St. Jerome in

Fig. 41.   Tuscan school, *St. Jerome Hears the Trumpet of the Last Judgment*, 1466

his study. By bringing a skull into the study in his engraving of 1514, Dürer had already begun to shift the meaning of the image from a celebration of Christian scholarship to a meditation on death and the vanity of worldly things. Even more influential was the gloomy *St. Jerome* he presented in March 1521 to Rodrigo Fernandez d'Almada, Portuguese consul in Antwerp, in which the saint is shown in half length, seated at his desk, resting his head on his right hand and touching a large skull with the index finger of his left.[67] For fifty years after Dürer's visit to the Netherlands, artists like Lucas van Leyden, Quentin Metsys and his son Jan, Joos van Cleve, Marinus van Reymerswaele, Pieter Coeck van Aelst, Jan Gossaert, and a tribe of pupils and imitators produced scores of pictures of St. Jerome in his study much indebted to Dürer's painting.[68] In these pictures, the study window can open out on an anecdotal land-scape; books abound, sometimes identifiable as the Greek and Hebrew Testaments, or Jerome's biblical commentaries, or, once, the works of Plato; Marian symbols and references to the Passion remain common, as do the customary symbols of transience, a guttered candle and an hour-glass. But the most striking object is invariably a skull, the most striking gesture the saint's long, bony finger touching it (fig. 43; see fig. 37). A rich crop of inscriptions reinforces the minatory gesture: *Homo bulla*, Man is a bubble; *Respice finem*, Look to life's end (see fig. 37); *Cogita mori*, Think about your death (see fig. 43); *Memorare novissima tua et in aeternum non peccabis*, Keep in mind your last day and you will not sin in eternity; *Facile contemnit omnia qui se semper cogitat moriturum*, He who is conscious always that he will die shows an easy contempt for worldly things; *Putasne mortuus homo rursum vivat?* Do you believe a dead man will live again? (Job 14:14).[69]

Meditatio mortis was commonly allied to thoughts about the Last Judg-ment and the future life (*meditatio vitae futurae*), whether in heaven or in hell, becoming thus a meditation on the four last things: death, heaven, hell, and the Last Judgment. Artists of the Antwerp workshops and their imitators encouraged this more comprehensive meditation by conflating the identifying motifs of a St. Jerome in his study and a St. Jerome in penitence and adding an explicit reference to the Last Judgment. In a much-copied composition of Joos van Cleve, he sits at his desk in his study; but his breast is bare and in his hand is a stone streaked with blood. On his desk is a half sheet of paper. The words on it are easily legible: "Whether I drink, whether I eat, whether I sleep or wake, that voice seems always to ring in my ears, saying: arise ye dead and come to

Fig. 42. French school, *St. Jerome Meditates on the Last Judgment*, c. 1480. The accompanying text (from Jean de Vignay's French translation of the *Golden Legend*) gives three reasons why sentences meted out at the Last Judgment are irrevocable and without appeal. The little picture illustrates the passage in column 2, lines 20–24 of the text, where Jerome is reported to have said that on Judgment Day all our deeds will be made known as clearly as if they were written down and recorded on a tablet.

Fig. 43. Attributed to Pieter Coeck van Aelst, *St. Jerome in His Study Meditates on the Four Last Things,* before 1550

judgment" (fig. 44).[70] Joos van Cleve, Marinus van Reymerswaele, Coeck van Aelst, and other artists visualized the same lesson in another way. On Jerome's lectern a folio Bible lies open to a full-page miniature of the Last Judgment modeled on a woodcut from Dürer's *Little Passion* (B52) (see fig. 43). On the facing page in some versions, or in a second open book in others, are texts from the twenty-fourth and twenty-fifth chapters of the Gospel of Matthew in which Christ foretells the wars, famines, earthquakes, persecutions, treachery, apostasy, and unprecedented distress that will happen before the great trumpet announces the Second Coming: "But when the Son of Man shall come in his glory, and all the angels with him, then he shall sit upon the throne of his glory. And there shall be gathered before him all the nations: and he shall separate them from one another as the shepherd separates the sheep from the goats" (Matt. 25:31–32) (see fig. 44).

The presence in the Church of the Escorial of a contemporary painting by an Italian artist of St. Jerome actually hearing the *tuba terribilis* of the Last Judgment, attested by José de Sigüenza in 1595,[71] and the publica-

Fig. 44. Circle of Joos van Cleve, *The Penitent St. Jerome in His Study,* c. 1530–1540. A popular composition of which many versions and copies survive.

tion in 1590 of an engraving by Antonio Tempesta showing Jerome and the trumpeting angel, with, in the background, the dead rising from their graves,[72] mark the reappearance of the subject in the visual arts. A quarter of a century later, in 1621, Ribera, by then working in Naples, executed an etching of the subject (fig. 45), quickly following it with

Fig. 45. Jusepe de Ribera, *St. Jerome Hears the Trumpet of the Last Judgment,* 1621

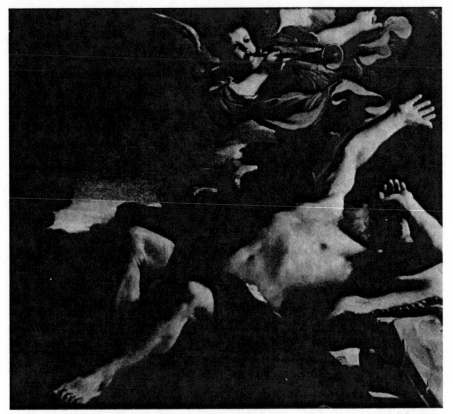

Fig. 46. Guercino, *St. Jerome Hears the Trumpet of the Last Judgment*, c. 1620

another etching and several paintings.[73] At about the same time, Guercino, in Bologna, painted the *St. Jerome Hears the Trumpet of the Last Judgment* now in the Louvre (fig. 46).[74] Artists and patrons all over Catholic Europe soon followed their lead. The many pictures are of three main types. In the first, Jerome has been busily at work out of doors in the wilderness when the trumpet's blast interrupts him writing, reading, even sharpening his pen. He turns toward the sound, flinging out an arm in an ample gesture of astonishment. Ribera's etching is characteristic of the type. Pictures of the second type are violent nocturnal scenes. Jerome has been asleep. Awakened by the trumpet call of an angel swooping down on him in a whirl of drapery and feathered wings, he starts up, his face and gesture vividly expressing his fear and horror. Guercino's picture is typical. The third (rare) type rests on the didactic second-person version

Fig. 47. Francisco de Zurbarán, *St. Jerome Hears the Trumpet of the Last Judgment,* 1640

of the source: "Whether you drink, whether you eat, whether you wake, whether you sleep, may the fearful trumpet always sound in your ears." A painting by Zurbarán illustrates it exactly: Jerome, dressed as the founder of the Spanish Hieronymites in the white habit and brown apron of the order, points to the trumpet in the sky calling humanity to the Last Judgment. He stares directly out at the spectator, sternly advising him to be ready at all times to meet his maker and judge (fig. 47).[75]

Jerome's witness to the Last Judgment dominates the seventeenth-century iconography of the saint. Under its apparent unity and simplicity, it is an encyclopedia of reminiscences from the past, conflating with skill and economy in a single dramatic, easily readable image his identifying attributes, the emblems of his Christian scholarship, his penitential mortifications in the wilderness, and his moralistic meditation on the four last things. Its meaning is explained with luminous brevity by Cornelius van der Steen in a commentary on the Pauline epistles published in Antwerp in 1614.[76] He quotes the text behind the pictures. He speculates about what the *tuba* is made of, perhaps of a sonorous material unknown to humankind, and emphasizes that the sound it will make is not immaterial but the maximum clangor endurable by the senses. The trumpet blows in order to arouse the dead and summon them to judgment, to call the elect to the joy of eternal happiness, and to terrify the reprobate and cast them into Gehenna. It is the instrument through which Jesus Christ will operate the resurrection in the same way that the words of consecration are the instruments of transubstantiation. Seeing the great scholar, orthodox doctor, penitent, and saint shattered by the trumpet's blast reminds good Catholics to take nothing for granted, to live today as though they will die tomorrow. It teaches bad Catholics fear, repentance, and mending of life. It promises heretics and schismatics eternal punishment.

7
The Translator of the Vulgate Bible:
A Sixteenth-Century Controversy

 beautiful picture by Guido Reni from the early 1630s (fig. 48) shows Jerome in his cave at work translating the Bible. As he writes, he turns and looks up attentively at an angel hovering near him. The angel makes the traditional gesture of teaching, gracefully holding the middle finger of his left hand between the thumb and index finger of his right, as though showing a small child how to count. The subject is "The Inspiration of St. Jerome." Its meaning is that Jerome was the author of the Latin Bible by then universally known as the Vulgate and that divine inspiration guarantees the faithfulness, authenticity, and authority of his translation.[1]

Behind this unambiguous message lies a history of uncertainty and debate reaching back to the high Middle Ages. Before the sixteenth century the standard view had been that the "Latin translation commonly used in our churches" (*ea tralatio qua nostrae ecclesiae passim utuntur*), or what contemporaries more simply referred to as "our translation" (*nostra tralatio*), was Jerome's greatest gift to the church. "After much labor," wrote Nicolò Maniacoria, "Jerome mastered all the books of the Old and New Testaments in Hebrew and Greek. . . . He translated into Latin all the books of the Old Testament, first from Greek, and then more accurately from Hebrew. He revised the New Testament from the original Greek."[2] A century later Vincent of Beauvais testified to Jerome's authorship in almost the same words: "Jerome, skilled in the three languages, revised the New Testament from the original Greek and translated the Old Testament from the original Hebrew."[3] Abbot Trithemius repeated the common wisdom in his biographical and bibliographical dictionary, published in 1494: "Among all the doctors none benefited the church more than Jerome; for in addition to his innumerable writings he translated the Old Testament from Hebrew into Latin, corrected the

Fig. 48. Guido Reni, *The Inspiration of St. Jerome*, 1631–1635

New Testament from the Greek original, and offered them both to the church for its faithful reading."[4]

Yet according to Roger Bacon in 1267, some of his contemporaries were already suggesting that the "translation in common use" was defective and very likely not by Jerome. Scholars who knew Hebrew, like the biblical commentator Nicholas of Lyra or the Dominican friar Raymundus Martinus (1220–1285), an accomplished orientalist and author of the *Pugio fidei adversus Mauros et Iudaeos*, pointed out the many places where "our translation" failed to reflect the *Hebraeica veritas*, while even scholars without Hebrew noticed that the Latin of their Old Testament was not always the same as the Latin translation used by Jerome in his own biblical commentaries and other works.[5] Roger Bacon explained the discrepancy by supposing that Jerome had made two translations of the Old Testament, of which "our translation" was the earlier. In this first version, he accepted the readings of the *vetus translatio* or *vetus Latina,* the Latin Bible of the early church, except where the old translation was manifestly in error, in order to keep peace in the church and to protect himself from defenders of the old translation, who were calling him a heretic and false coiner for presuming to touch the traditional text at all. He based his second version entirely on the Greek and Hebrew verities, but he kept it secret from the vulgar, using it only in his commentaries for the instruction of serious scholars.[6] In the next century, the Oxford-trained theologian Richard Fitzralph, archbishop of Armagh (d. 1360), concluded from the same evidence that the Latins possessed three whole or partial translations of the Old Testament: one made from the Greek Septuagint (the Old Latin version); Jerome's translation, believed to survive (apart from the *Psalterium iuxta Hebraeos*) only in the quotations from it that he used in his commentaries; and the translation in common use (*illa translatio quam vocamus communis*), asserted to be anonymous, of uncertain origin, and possibly translated, at least in part, from a language other than Hebrew or Greek.[7]

Humanist critics were more sharply outspoken. Collating the Latin text of the New Testament against the Greek original and judging its language by the classicizing standards of the *studium humanitatis,* they were dismayed by its solecisms and barbarisms, its ambiguities and obscurities, its departures from the Greek, and as shocked by a Latin so unclassical as the young Jerome had been by the crudity of the prophets. "Careless translation," "barbarous word," "crudely translated" are some of Lorenzo Valla's criticisms of the man he referred to simply as the *interpres Latinus.*[8] By 1506, Reuchlin, who had learned Hebrew and Greek under the influence of St. Jerome in order to read the Scriptures in the languages "in which they are believed to have been originally composed under the inspiration of God," had rejected both the Septuagint and the Vulgate, remarking that "although I revere St. Jerome as an angel and honor Lyra as a teacher, I worship only truth as I worship God." In his *De rudimentis Hebraeicis* he corrected the Vulgate in over 200 places.[9] Erasmus found more mistakes: "The translator has added something of his own here"; "This passage is ridiculously translated"; "The translator, whoever he may be, has nodded here, or wandered in his mind."[10] How could Jerome, universally acclaimed for his eloquence, learning, and mastery of the three languages, be this translator?

It was Jacques Lefèvre d'Etaples, however, the great French humanist, Aristotelian philosopher, and biblical critic, who first tried to save Jerome's scholarly reputation by proving in some detail that he was not the author of "our translation" of the New Testament. In 1512 he published commentaries on the Pauline epistles, accompanied by a new Latin translation. In order to defend himself against possible charges that he was insolently tampering with Jerome's translation, he prefaced his version with an *Apologia* in which he showed that the "old translation of Paul's epistles everywhere read today" was by a man who had lived much earlier than Jerome and that it was identical with the translation Jerome called the *vulgata editio.*[11] (Lefèvre was using the word "vulgate" exactly as Jerome had done, to mean either the Septuagint Greek or the Old Latin versions of the Greek Old and New Testaments. Only gradually after about 1520 did biblical critics begin to call "our translation" the *vulgata editio,* thus usurping for it the name of the version it had long since displaced, and not until after 1546, when the Council of Trent described the "translation in common use" as *haec vetus et vulgata editio,* did the new usage become common. The title of the official bibles issued by Popes Sixtus V and Clement VIII in the early 1590s, *Biblia sacra vulgatae editionis,* made the name universal.)[12]

Lefèvre found his evidence in Jerome's own commentaries on Paul's epistles to the Galatians, Ephesians, Titus, and Philemon. He pointed out that Jerome called the author of the Latin text he was explaining the *Latinus interpres,* regularly cited him as someone other than himself, censured his ignorance, and corrected his errors. He invited his readers to compare the text of "our translation" with the improved readings Jerome offered in his commentaries. They would find in the translation "everywhere read today" the same errors Jerome had censured and none of his corrections. "Who but a fool will now say that our translation is Jerome's translation and that he criticized himself for ineptly mistranslating into Latin a correct Greek text?" No one doubts, of course, that Jerome did indeed revise the Old Latin text of the New Testament at the request of Pope Damasus, for at the end of *Famous Men* he tells us that he did: "I corrected the New Testament from the Greek and translated the Old Testament from Hebrew." What is at issue is whether "our translation" is the one Jerome corrected. It is not. "Our translation" is the one Jerome criticized, an uncorrected text that still swarms with infelicities and errors. Defenders of "our translation" sometimes try to explain its relation to Jerome's Pauline commentaries by supposing that he wrote the commentaries before he revised the New Testament. But this hardly explains why he failed to remember his earlier suggestions for improvements when he was revising the New Testament. Moreover, the redating accuses that most holy and learned father, or so Lefèvre thought, of presuming to explain a text before he could properly read it, arrogance inconceivable in so holy a man, "nay more, a hero and more than a man." Yet others have asked why so defective a translation was received by the church instead of Jerome's corrected one. The fault, answered Lefèvre (it is his weakest argument), lay with those in Rome who envied him and forced him into exile. Lefèvre concluded that Jerome's recension, not just of the Pauline epistles, but of the whole New Testament, the labor he had undertaken for the common good at Pope Damasus's request, had perished.[13]

Independently of Lefèvre and at almost the same time, Paul of Middleburg, a graduate of the University of Louvain, professor of mathematics and astronomy at Padua, and since 1494 bishop of Fossembrone in the duchy of Urbino, came to the same conclusion, not only about the "common" translation of the New Testament, but about that of the Old Testament as well. In a treatise dense with miscellaneous learning, published in 1513 and principally devoted to establishing the precise date of the crucifixion, he digressed to discuss the authorship of the translation of the Bible commonly used in the church. Citing many of the same examples from Jerome's Pauline commentaries already used by Lefèvre, as well as others from the *Commentary on Matthew,* he showed that the translator of the New Testament was an unknown man whom Jerome often criticized and disparaged.[14]

He used similar arguments to question Jerome's authorship of the *usitata editio* of the Old Testament. In his *Hebraeicae quaestiones,* Jerome proposed improved renderings of many words and phrases in the book of Genesis; his suggested improvements cannot be found in *nostra usitata editio.* Jerome based his *Commentary on Ecclesiastes* on a text he explicitly described as his own translation from the Hebrew; it does not correspond with the text of Ecclesiastes in "our translation." And it is well known, continued the bishop of Frossembrone, that Jerome's translation of the Psalms from the Hebrew, the *Psalterium iuxta Hebraeos,* is not the version included in our bibles. "From all of this it is plain that Jerome's translation was not accepted by the church." We know that Jerome translated the canonical books of the Old Testament from the Hebrew. We know too that he corrected the Old Latin translation from the Septuagint Greek, indicating his revisions by asterisks and obelisks. Neither of these versions is the text of our present-day bibles. "Enough has been said to prove that the common translation of the Bible is not by Jerome, even though his little prefaces appear before some of its books."[15]

As he prepared his edition of the Greek New Testament and revised to go with it the new Latin translation he had made for John Colet in 1506–1507, Erasmus read Lefèvre and Paul of Middleburg and agreed with their conclusions. The translator of "the edition that we have in common use" (*qua vulgo utimur*) was often careless, clumsy, and inattentive to the Greek. Although his version has often been attributed to St. Jerome, "it is known to be neither Cyprian's nor Hilary's nor Ambrose's nor Augustine's nor Jerome's, for [Jerome] has different readings; much less is it the version which he tells us he has corrected, for things are found in it which he condemns, in respect not only of the wording but of the sense." No council, no official decision of the Roman church has formally approved it. In the age of the fathers, it was only one of many Latin translations in circulation. Ambrose cited one of these, Augustine another, Hilary and Jerome still others. In time, by virtue of being used, it gradually gained strength and authority, by custom as it were. Eventual acceptance, however, does not make Jerome its author. The scholarly consensus is that Jerome was not the translator.[16]

Doubts about Jerome's authorship or competence were especially strong among Hebrew scholars who were themselves offering new translations of the Old Testament to the public in the 1520s and 1530s. The Dominican Sanctes Pagnini of Lucca (d. 1536), the first modern scholar to translate the whole Bible from the original languages, did not deny that the translation *quae passim legitur* was by Jerome, but he emphasized that the text of it available to him and his contemporaries was not reliable (*germana, genuina*), but so corrupted by time, careless copyists and type-setters, and the emendations of the ignorant that what Jerome said of the Old Latin New Testament of his day could be said of it: there are as many versions as codices. But even a pure text would be found to be full of errors. Jerome was holy and learned; we venerate and adore him; but he was a man, and erred as all men do. Indeed, he often confessed that he worked too fast, and in his commentaries frankly acknowledged his mistakes and retracted and corrected them.[17] In a brief excursus prefacing his translation of the Hebrew Bible entitled *An Hieronymus vulgatae aeditionis fuerit auctor* (a good example of the use of "Vulgate" in the modern sense), Sebastian Münster (1489–1552), a professor at the University of Basel, using arguments by then traditional, repeated that Jerome translated the Old Testament from the Hebrew but that our *vulgata editio* is not that translation.[18] Joannes Campensis, professor of Hebrew at the Trilingual College at Louvain and author of a Latin paraphrase of the Hebrew Psalms first published in Nuremberg in 1532, was brief but firm: "The identity of the author of the translation used in the church does not greatly concern me; what I do insist on is that the translation is unworthy of St. Jerome."[19]

So much for the critics. Supporters of the traditional version were not wanting. Before the Council of Trent, the most influential treatises defending Jerome's authorship of the translation gradually becoming known as the *vulgata editio* were the *Annotations against Lefèvre d'Etaples* (1519) by Diego López de Zúñiga (Stunica), one of the team of scholars assembled at Alcalá by Cardinal Ximénez to prepare the Complutensian Polyglot;[20] the *Five Treatises on Paul's Epistle to the Romans* (1529) by the Observant Franciscan Franz Titelmans, praelector in Holy Scripture at the University of Louvain, who prefaced the volume with a *Prologus apologeticus pro veteri et ecclesiastica novi Testamenti Latina interpretatione,* directed principally against Lefèvre and Erasmus;[21] an exceptionally important and influential work by another professor from Louvain, *De sacris scripturis et dogmatibus* by Johannes Driedo (1533);[22] and, finally, the brief but dense *An vulgata editio sit divi Hieronymi* (1535) by Agostino Steuco, an Augustinian Canon Regular, bishop of Gubbio, prefect of the Vatican Library, and a distinguished Hebrew scholar.[23] Their common conclusions were that the Vulgate was eloquent, accurate, authoritative, and almost entirely, since he revised and translated it, the work of St. Jerome. Their views on the character and extent of the divine inspiration Jerome had been vouchsafed to help him were positive but not without nuance. From these shaping works emerged the orthodoxies defined at Trent and in the papal prefaces to the editions of the Sisto-Clementine Bible.

To those who said that the Vulgate was rude and barbarous, full of solecisms, ambiguities, and places difficult to understand, they replied by distinguishing secular eloquence, often magnificent and sublime, from Christian eloquence, the simple, tender language in which Jesus spoke to his disciples. This is the eloquence captured by the Greek original and faithfully reproduced in *nostra tralatio*. The number of solecisms has in any case been much exaggerated. The old translator did make a few grammatical mistakes, but they were minor ones, and not more numerous nor more serious than the errors of the evangelists and apostles themselves, though whether *they* committed them in order to shame the delicate ears of the wise men of this world, or to underline their own humility, or because they were carried away by the impetuosity of their message, or simply because they were ignorant, is unclear. What is plain is that we cannot criticize in the translation what we accept in the evangelical original. As for barbarisms, we recognize them as such only because our taste has been educated to the new standard of the *humanitatis studium.* Humanists say that the Latin of the New Testament is barbarous because it is not the Latin of Cicero, Livy, and Vergil. But each period and each author possesses an individual peculiarity of style. That of the *vetus interpres* was appropriate to his purpose, time, and place. It may be rude and humble, but such is its *energia* that its heavenly heat penetrates the innermost chamber of the human heart.[24]

Does the Vulgate contain more serious errors, departures from the meaning of the Hebrew and Greek originals? Everyone agreed that the translation contained errors. Two explanations were offered. The mistakes were the fault of copyists and printers, not the translator. The remedy for these was not a new Latin translation but a critical edition of the one in common use, to expunge the corruptions of transmission and restore the text to its pristine purity. The second explanation concerned only the New Testament. We must remember that *nostra tralatio* is a revision of the Vetus Latina, not an original translation. We must remember and understand how Jerome revised this old translation: unwilling to offend tradition and custom by tampering too much with a familiar and much-loved text, he corrected only those places where the meaning did not agree with the Greek, leaving the rest intact. Minor errors and verbal infelicities that did not affect the meaning, he left untouched, even though he discussed them at length in his commentaries and suggested better readings there. In sum: the errors of the Vulgate are trivial, and it contains no mistranslations that distort the meaning of the inspired originals.[25]

The essential point, most clearly formulated by Johannes Driedo, who, unlike the more enthusiastic of his colleagues, felt no need to minimize the weaknesses of what he called the *interpretatio Latina seu communis editio vulgata qua ecclesia nunc utitur,* was that it accurately reproduced the Greek and Hebrew originals in everything touching faith and morals. The Vulgate's solecisms and stylistic lapses have spawned no heresies, led to no deviant behavior. Despite its many small mistranslations, despite its obscurities and ambiguities, every "mystery of faith," every "evangelical precept" shines out with straightforward clarity.[26] In this respect the Vulgate is similar to the Septuagint. Although it too departed in many places from the Hebrew, Christ and the apostles respected and quoted it. Augustine, Ambrose, and Jerome honored the Old Latin version, even though they were aware of the places where it differed from the oldest Hebrew and Greek texts. We should honor "our translation" in the same way; for the fact that it has been universally accepted for over a thousand years authenticates its freedom from doctrinal error and confirms that it was a providential gift of God to the Latin church to serve as its foundation of truth and unity.[27]

It was a further common view of apologists for the Vulgate that a special providence of the Holy Spirit had acted directly on the translator to guarantee his trustworthiness. The point was recognized to be a delicate one, and there was a good deal less agreement about what it might mean to call a translation inspired. Some commentators, believing that the Latin church would be proved fallible if even a single error could be found in its Latin Bible, took the line that the Holy Spirit had made "our translation" through St. Jerome precisely as it had made the Greek and Hebrew verities through the prophets and apostles. Titelmans considered the problem in some detail, and with greater subtlety. He knew that there were those, like Paul of Middleburg, who argued that a translation is authoritative (*autentica*) only to the extent that it agrees with the original and not because it has been used by the church for a long time. The truth of the Gospel is one and eternal; translations are many, time-bound and relative, subject to change and repudiation by the ecclesiastical authorities; only the Greek and Hebrew originals remain the same.[28] He remembered too that Jerome, after ridiculing the legend of the seventy translators in their separate cells, had said that "it is one thing to be a prophet, another to be a translator; in the one case, the Spirit predicts things to come; in the other, the translator uses learning and literary skill to reproduce in another language his understanding of the text." It was Titlemans's opinion that Jerome had not meant to deny that the translator of the Bible needs the inspiration of the Spirit as well as knowledge of languages and rhetorical training. For at the end of the same letter, the preface in which he dedicated the first part of his translation of the Old Testament to his friend Desiderius, Jerome prayed that the same Spirit that had written the Pentateuch would help him translate it.[29] He asked for help because he knew that secular erudition is incapable of reaching the hidden meanings of Scripture. Only with the inspiration of the Holy Spirit, as he emphasized in his *Commentary on Galatians,* can the commentator move from the words of Scripture to their meaning, from surface to marrow, from rhetorical superficialities to the root of understanding.[30] To translate Cicero does not require divine help. But texts originally dictated by the Spirit must be read, understood, and translated under the inspiration of the Spirit. Only in this context does the argument from age acquire its true weight. For the Vulgate does not possess public authority (*publica authoritas*) simply because it is old. Other translations are as old or older, but they are not "authentic" for all that. The *ecclesiastica translatio* is authentic, official, and public because for over a thousand years the church has registered its approval by using it in its public worship and teaching and in its definition and defense of orthodoxy. The church's choice is a reliable guarantee that "our translation" can be trusted in everything that pertains to faith and morals because the Holy Spirit, which permanently inhabits the church, has enabled it to recognize the same inspiration in the translation and its author. Any translation made without the Spirit is purely human; and any doctrine or teaching based on it, without authority.[31]

Driedo faced squarely the further difficulty of explaining how a translation of the Bible could be at once admittedly defective and divinely inspired. He may have got the germ of his solution from Erasmus. Pointing out that the presence of mistakes in the New Testament's Greek need not shake the credit of the whole of Scripture, Erasmus had suggested that "perhaps it is not for us to dictate how the Holy Spirit shall tune the instrument that he makes of his disciples; however he may have done this, he has done it in the way that he knew to be most conducive to the salvation of the human race. He was present in them so far as pertained to the business of the Gospel, but with this limitation, that in other respects he allowed them to be human none the less." Inspiration does not guarantee correct grammar. The Greek of the apostles, clumsy, not to say barbarous, was no gift from heaven. Jerome often said that Paul's writing was uncouth. "So it is not necessary that whatever was in the apostles should at once be attributed to a miracle. Christ allowed his chosen to make mistakes even after they had received the Paraclete, but not to the extent of imperilling the faith, as today we admit that the church can err, but short of any risk to faith and religion."[32]

What Erasmus had said about the Greek verity could be applied even more appropriately to the translation. Driedo emphasized that Jerome never considered his translation divine or something that reflected perfectly the originals in every particular. Quite the reverse; time after time, he offered his readers alternate renderings, forcing them in this way to use their own judgment. He was keenly aware that no translator can avoid ambiguities and obscurities and that it is impossible to reproduce fully and precisely in one language the meaning and style of a passage in another. This is why it is legitimate and necessary for modern scholars to return constantly to the originals from which Jerome was working. And this too is why it is foolish to assume that Jerome had received a mystical intelligence of the text. He was helped by the Spirit, but the Spirit works in different ways: there is a Spirit of wisdom, a Spirit that operates miracles and deeds of heroic virtue, a Spirit that brings with it the gift of tongues, a Spirit of faith and charity, and, finally, a *spiritus propheticus.* Jerome was a translator, not a prophet. He was human and made mistakes. Since, however, he amply possessed the *spiritus fidei et caritatis,* his translation was not a purely human work. The Spirit did not illumine him to the degree that he understood the meaning of the prophetic books as fully as the prophet himself, dictating in Hebrew in the radiance of prophetic vision. He did not always reproduce the *Hebraeica veritas* of the Old Testament. Nor has the church approved every word of his revision of the New Testament just because Pope Damasus commissioned him to make it. But the Spirit of faith and charity prevented him from mistranslating things that matter; his translation never deviated from the truth of faith or the rules of Christian living. Jerome was not a prophet nor an evangelist; but he was, in the precise sense that he was incapable of error about faith and morals, an inspired translator.[33]

Driedo's views on the authorship of the Vulgate were not as straightforward as his discussion of Jerome's inspiration might lead one to suppose. Other scholars trying to rebut Valla, Lefèvre and Erasmus, Paul of Middleburg, Sanctes Pagnini, and Joannes Campensis, liked to argue that no one but Jerome *could* have produced the Vulgate. Who but Jerome among the Latins possessed the necessary command of Hebrew and Greek? Augustine hardly knew Greek. And had not Jerome's version displaced the Old Latin in spite of St. Augustine's opposition? They cited the evidence of the prefaces attached to the various books of the Old Testament Vulgate. In them Jerome himself had affirmed that he was responsible for what followed. It is inconceivable that the church should have been so misguided as to put Jerome's prefaces in front of someone else's translation.[34] The chronological argument appeared repeatedly. Agostino Steuco supposed that Jerome had translated the Old Testament after, not before, writing his commentaries on the major and minor prophets. It is the Vulgate, therefore, that reflects his mature opinion and learning. Where there are disagreements, its readings are better than those proposed in the commentaries.[35] Stunica had said the same. Jerome wrote his commentaries on Paul before he revised the New Testament at the request of Damasus. When he wrote the commentaries his youthful head was swollen with pride at his rhetorical skill and command of Greek, and he railed unnecessarily at the supposed errors of the Old Latin. By the time Damasus commissioned him to revise the New Testament, he was a wiser and better biblical scholar; he left unchanged words and expressions he had earlier incriminated because his method required him to leave the wording reverently untouched except where he found it seriously un-faithful to the meaning of the Greek.[36] Driedo explained more inge-niously the frequent failure of commentaries and translations to harmo-nize. The Vulgate, as we have it now, is a mixed text. It is not wholly Jerome's translation, nor is it wholly the earlier Old Latin version; it is a conflation of the two. Driedo does not make clear how this came about. What he seems to have believed is that Jerome's translation replaced the Old Latin very gradually and that during the several centuries when both translations were in competitive use Jerome's version became heavily contaminated by the Old Latin. This is why some of the renderings, corrections, and emendations that Jerome testifies he made do not appear in the Vulgate, while others do.[37]

Although ordinary scholars may have been ill informed about such textual arcana, they were well aware, from Jerome's own testimony, of the heterogeneous authorship of their Latin Bible. Jerome had not consid-ered books like the Wisdom of Solomon and Ecclesiasticus canonical, one of his few judgments cited with approval by Martin Luther; they appear in the Vulgate in unrevised Old Latin versions. Jerome did translate Tobit and Judith from Aramaic, though he considered them apocryphal too; that is, uncanonical but suitable for the edification of the faithful. Since his Aramaic was weak, he engaged a learned Jew to help him. As the Jew translated the Aramaic orally into Hebrew, Jerome dictated a Latin version to his secretary. He alleges that he translated Tobit in a single day and Judith in a single night.[38] Of his three versions of the Psalms, it was the *Psalterium Gallicanum,* his critical revision of the Old Latin according to the Septuagint column of Origen's Hexapla, and not the *Psalterium iuxta Hebraeos,* his translation direct from the Hebrew, that found a place in the Vulgate.[39] The further conclusion toward which his sixteenth-century apologists were gradually moving was that the Vulgate translation of the remaining books of the Hebrew canon was the work of St. Jerome (an opinion ratified by modern scholarship) and that the Vulgate of the entire New Testament was the translation of an anonymous *interpres Latinus,* made long before Jerome but so thoroughly revised by him that it faithfully reproduced the meaning of the Greek original in all matters concerning faith and morals. In sum, the opinion was regaining ground that Jerome was the principal author (*primarius auctor*) of the *vulgata editio.*[40]

The Council of Trent dealt with the problems concerning sacred Scripture in March and April 1546. The decree on the Vulgate is dated April 8:

> The same holy synod considering that no small advantage may accrue to the Church of God, if out of all the Latin translations of the sacred books in circulation it made known which is to be held as authoritative (*authentica*): determines and declares that this ancient vulgate translation (*haec ipsa vetus et vulgata editio*) which is recommended by the long use of so many centuries in the church, be regarded as authoritative in public lectures, disputations, sermons, and expository discourses, and that no one may make bold or presume to reject it on any pretext.[41]

The scope, meaning, and implications of this decree have been much debated. What seems certain is that the Tridentine fathers attributed to the Vulgate supreme authority in the Latin West on the grounds that the church, made infallible in faith and morals by the Holy Spirit, had used it for so long. It follows that the Council also asserted, by implication, that the Vulgate does not err in doctrine or ethical teaching, that it is in all necessary matters in conformity with originals directly inspired by God. Nevertheless, the Council did not say that the Vulgate was in perfect conformity with its Hebrew and Greek originals, still less that it was superior either to them or to other Greek and Oriental versions. It was the work of a man, and so contained errors and infelicities; but since the translator was to some degree inspired by the Holy Spirit, none of his lapses touched faith or morals. Nor, it should be emphasized, did the Council, even in its own journals and minutes, identify the translator as St. Jerome. In a letter of 26 April to Cardinal Farnese, the legates told him that some of those present thought that the Vulgate was the work of Jerome, but that many others—learned Dominicans, Franciscans, and other religious from France, Spain, and Italy (*periti*, not prelates)—disagreed and referred to the Vulgate as the work of an unknown author.[42]

Protestants were outraged at what they took (mistakenly) to be the real meaning of the decree: that the Vulgate was the only authoritative translation of the Bible, superior to vernacular translations and even to the Greek and Hebrew originals. If we were to accept that judgment, wrote Melanchthon, we would have to agree that "the Vulgate has been revealed to us by the Holy Spirit." But how can this be, when Valla's *Annotationes,* Erasmus, Sebastian Münster, and even Agostino Steucho have shown that it departs constantly from the Hebrew and Greek sources? Nicholas of Lyra, Paul of Burgos, and Johann Reuchlin have proved the same. If even the most modestly endowed linguist will compare the Vulgate with a good recent translation, he will soon see that it is not the support and rule of truth that the Council claims it is.[43] The Council's defense of the Vulgate goaded Calvin to blind vituperation. The clerics at Trent are trying to make us adore this hopelessly corrupt translation as though it has come down from heaven. There is not a single page that contains three lines in a row unsoiled by a major error. Have they no shame pretending that the Vulgate of the New Testament is "authentic" when works by Valla, Lefèvre, and Erasmus listing its innumerable errors and corruptions are in every hand?[44] Martin Chemnitz's *Examination of the Council of Trent* moderately repeated some of the objections that had been accumulating for over half a century. "Jerome himself in matters of the Hebrew renders and interprets many things differently than we now read in the Vulgate edition. We have Jerome's version of the Psalter and of Ecclesiastes; but in the Vulgate we have far other versions of these books. Jerome confesses that he had emended the four Evangelists by a comparison of the Greek codices, and yet when he translates Matthew, he criticizes certain things in the Vulgate, as he also does in the epistles of Paul." Actually, the translation is not bad, Chemnitz concluded, though of course one must go back to the originals when the translator "appears to have rendered something incorrectly, or not adequately or appropriately."[45]

Catholic scholars writing after the Council of Trent continued to express a wide range of opinion about the authorship, quality, and inspiration of the Vulgate. Some assigned the whole Vulgate to Jerome; some referred cautiously to "the translator, whoever he may be"; some gave the Old Testament to Jerome, while assigning the revision of the New Testament, with the possible exception of the Gospels, to an anonymous fifth-century cleric. On the quality of the translation most commentators followed Driedo. The translator, whether Jerome or another, was a man; he made mistakes. The translation does not always accurately reproduce the Hebraeica and Graeca veritas; and of course it is soiled by scribal errors. What matters, as Cardinal Bellarmine authoritatively repeated, is that "there is no error in this translation in matters pertaining to faith and morals."[46]

Judgments about the accuracy of the Vulgate remained closely tied to the question of its inspiration. In response to Protestant attacks on the Vulgate and on the decree of the Council of Trent confirming its authority, the tendency was to assert plainly that the Vulgate was "written under the inspiration of the Holy Spirit" or that the "translator was wonderfully adorned with the gifts of the Holy Spirit." Nevertheless, other scholars still preferred to say only that "a singular providence had guarded the translator from error" or that the Spirit had not inspired him to infallibility but that he possessed a spirit close enough to the prophetic to guard him from error in matters pertaining to faith and morals. The rest denied that the Vulgate had fallen from the sky and was "inspired from above" (divinitus inspirata), while firmly maintaining that it was faithful to the substance of its divinely inspired original.[47]

The papal prefaces to the Sistine (1589) and Clementine (1592) editions of the Vulgate Bible concentrated minds and opinions. Here at last was the critical edition recommended by the Council of Trent to correct a text corrupted by the ravages of time, the carelessness of copyists and printers, reckless emendations, and the audacity of recent translators. Returned now to its pristine purity, its excellence and authority were said to be so great that it far surpassed all other Latin translations. The popes carefully described its contents, authorship, and inspiration. Our Bible, they wrote, consists in major part of books translated or revised by St. Jerome, in minor part of books in the earlier translation that Jerome called *vulgata,* Augustine the *Itala,* and Gregory the Great the *vetus translatio.* St. Jerome was the principal translator of the Vulgate, and his dignity, learning, and holiness should make us honor it the more; for Jerome is unsurpassed in eloquence, linguistic skill, and knowledge of Scripture. As an exegete he has no rivals. From his own day to this, the luminaries of the church— Gregory the Great, Isidore of Seville, the Venerable Bede, Alcuin, Rhabanus Maurus, St. Anselm, Peter Damian, St. Bernard, Richard and Hugh of St. Victor, Peter Lombard, Alexander Hales, Albertus Magnus, Thomas Aquinas, and Bonaventura—have admired the *versio Hieronymi* and used it in all their commentaries, sermons, treatises, and disputations. "This is why the Catholic church rightly celebrates St. Jerome as *doctor maximus,* moved as he was from on high to translate Holy Scripture, and why it condemns those who withhold their assent to the work of so outstanding a doctor and presume to equal it or even to do better."[48] The wording is careful. Jerome was divinely inspired to translate Holy Scripture, moved to it from on high: *ad Scripturas sacras interpretandas divinitus excitatus.* Interpreted narrowly, there is no claim here that his translation was itself inspired. At the same time, the phrase had an inspirational resonance that tempted commentators to give it the wider, more specific meaning that Jerome translated the Vulgate Bible under the direct (but not necessarily verbal) inspiration of the Holy Spirit.

The distinction between form and substance, superficial detail and passages of doctrinal significance, retained its force. A "special inspiration of the Holy Spirit" (*specialis Spiritus Sancti afflatus*) guided Jerome as he translated Holy Scripture. But he enjoyed its help only in reproducing perfectly the doctrinal and moral teachings of the Bible, not in translating single words: he could, and did, make errors in translating the names of plants and animals, for example. "In everything pertaining to faith and morals and to other matters of like weight," wrote the Procurator General of the Friars Minor in France, "Jerome had the help of the Holy Spirit in making his translation; but in places of less moment the Holy Spirit left him to himself and to his human learning." A professor at the Jesuit University of Ingolstadt seemed to go even further when he wrote that "God so directed the hand and pen of the translator that he nowhere missed the meaning of the Holy Spirit"; at once, though, he made it clear that the Holy Spirit guaranteed only the accuracy of passages touching faith and morals and not necessarily the exact rendering of everything in Hebrew and Greek.[49]

Painters, however, instructed by ecclesiastical advisers anxious to reassure an audience more heterogeneous than learned and baffled in any case by the difficulty of representing pictorially so abstract a distinction as that between the verbal and substantive inspiration of a text, supported without reservation or qualification the claim that God had guided the hand and pen of the translator of the Bible by showing Jerome taking dictation of the Vulgate from the Holy Spirit in the shape of an angel. Lodovico Carracci,[50] Domenichino,[51] Albani,[52] Rubens,[53] van Dyck (fig. 49),[54] Simon Vouet,[55] and Johann Liss[56] are some of the painters besides Guido Reni who honored Jerome and the Vulgate in this way.

The representation of Christian inspiration in a pictorial motif is very old. Early medieval manuscript illuminations regularly show the evangelists and fathers of the church inspired by the Holy Spirit in the shape of a dove. In miniatures in a ninth-century manuscript from Saint-Denis and an eleventh-century manuscript from Canterbury (fig. 50), Jerome sits on a throne translating the Bible; the dove of the Holy Spirit whispers the words into his right ear.[57] The subject of the elegant early fifteenth-century pen and ink drawing of St. Jerome in his study now bound at the front of a *Bible moralisée* in the Bibliothèque Nationale in Paris (MS. fr. 166) is the same: a dove dictates the text of Jerome's translation as divine illumination irradiates his mind from above.[58] A picture by Lodovico Cardi, known as Cigoli, painted in 1599 for the church of S. Giovanni dei Fiorentini in Rome, shows Jerome at work in his study translating the Old Testament, the Hebrew text propped up against a skull and open before him (fig. 51). Divine inspiration, symbolized here by three allegorical figures representing Faith, Prudence, and Eloquence, guarantees the truth and beauty of his translation. From an archetypal book of the Word drop down the flowers and pearls of rhetoric, while religion and prudence make certain that he does not mistranslate anything pertaining to faith and morals.[59] Cigoli's picture catches a critical moment of transition: not only is it an early instance of the revived interest in showing Jerome translating the Bible under divine inspiration, it is the last Italian St. Jerome in his study as well as a precocious example of another revival, the illustration of Jerome's penitential lament that he seemed always to hear the fearful voice of the trumpet of the Last Judgment—for on the wall behind him is a painting of the Last Judgment on which can be discerned a

Fig. 49. Van Dyck, *The Inspiration of St. Jerome*, c. 1620.

Fig. 50. English school, *The Inspiration of St. Jerome,* c. 1070. This miniature illustrates a manuscript of Jerome's *Life of Paul the First Hermit.*

Fig. 51.   Cigoli, *The Inspiration of St. Jerome*, 1599

trumpeting angel, a skeleton climbing out of its grave, and two words of an inscription: *con tremisco,* with fear and trembling.

To embody Jerome's inspiration in a beautiful angel, however, was a recent conceit, no earlier than the end of the sixteenth century. But for this too models were conveniently at hand. In antiquity, authors composing their works were depicted accompanied by their Muse. A nearer and more important visual source was the symbol of St. Matthew, a winged man, usually understood to be an angel, shown, from at least the tenth century, gently instructing the untutored simplicity of the senior evangelist. Representations of the inspiration of St. Matthew, of which Caravaggio's (Rome, S. Luigi dei Francesi), Guercino's (Rome, Capitoline Museum) and Rembrandt's (Paris, Louvre) are late but celebrated examples, are the direct prototypes of the seventeenth-century inspirations of St. Jerome,[60] a borrowing encouraged by familiar parallels between the two saints. Both were believed to be buried in S. Maria Maggiore. Matthew owed his symbolic angel to Jerome, assigned to him in the preface of Jerome's *Commentary on Matthew,* a text that established as well the primacy of Matthew's gospel over the other three. When the four doctors of the church were paired with the four evangelists, Jerome was often paired with Matthew.[61]

But the nearer literary source of the notion that the Holy Spirit inspired Jerome through an angel, like several other texts that shaped Jerome's image in the visual arts, lurks among the *spuria.* It is an abbreviated Psalter, probably no older than the fourteenth century, made up of some one hundred verses from different psalms and beginning with the verse from Ps. 5, *Verba mea auribus precipe Domine.* The tiny Psalter (fig. 52) was designed for the use of the sick, for travelers, soldiers, hermits, for men and women submerged by their work or weak from fasting, in short, for all who lacked the time and strength to recite the whole Psalter. "He who wishes the merciful God to save his soul, let him assiduously recite the abbreviated Psalter and he will possess the kingdom of God." Many fifteenth- and early sixteenth-century handwritten Breviaries, Books of Hours, and Books of Prayers conclude with the little Psalter. It had a great success in print as well, in Latin and in the vernaculars: Marsiglio Ficino translated it into Italian for Clarice de' Medici, wife of the Magnificent Lorenzo. The anonymous compiler begins his brief preface with the following sentence: *"Sanctus Ieronimus in hoc modo disposuit hoc psalterium, sicut angelus Domini docuit eum per Spiritum Sanctum:* St.

Fig. 52. English school, *St. Jerome Writing the Psalterium abbreviatum*, 1420–1430. The text on the rotulus is from the *Abbreviated Psalter*, included in a Book of Hours: "O Lord, rebuke me not in thy anger, nor chasten me in thy wrath. Be gracious to me, O Lord, for I am languishing; O Lord, heal me, for my bones are troubled" (Ps. 6:1–2).

Jerome abbreviated the Psalter in this way as an angel of the Lord taught him to do through the Holy Spirit."[62]

Embodying the idea of inspiration in an angel instead of in a dove or abstractly as a ray of light was particularly appropriate. It allowed the artist to express through a variety of gestures the verbal inspiration of the text that Jerome was pictured writing, while the presence of a dictating angel at once made clear that the text he was inspiring was the Bible; for although any number of texts have been thought to be divinely inspired, only the Bible was dictated, word by word, "into the pen" of its authors. We see the angel ticking off his instructions on his fingers, handing the saint his pen, sharpening his quill, guiding his writing hand, reading to him from a heavenly book held open by a putto or another angel, holding up a book from which the saint copies, pointing to a particular word on the page, or dictating the text softly into his ear. Jerome listens and writes. Theological *periti* may have wished that the painters had distinguished more carefully a doctor from an evangelist or a prophet and the "spirit of faith and charity" from the "spirit of prophecy." The interest of these images is precisely that they blur those distinctions in order to make an unambiguous statement about the church's Latin Bible and its author: Jerome wrote it instructed by the same Spirit that had dictated the original to the prophets and evangelists.

Early seventeenth-century representations of Jerome hearing the trumpet of the Last Judgment or writing down the Vulgate "as an angel of the Lord taught him to do through the Holy Spirit" are the last Hieronymite images of power, invention, and more than local influence. They mark the end of the extraordinarily creative period in the history of Jerome's *fortuna* that had begun late in the thirteenth century with the translation of his remains from Bethlehem to Rome.

Possibilities for approved devotion to St. Jerome had been contracting for some time. Protestants were most radically affected. Luther reports that when he was a young man he imagined that a saint was someone who lived in the desert and subsisted on roots and cold water. Later, the Bible taught him that saints were not monks or hermits who performed superstitious and unnatural works, tortured the body by fasting, wore hair shirts, renounced marriage, and hid away in caves—for these extravagances are works of the flesh—but simply men and women who have declared that Christ alone is their wisdom, righteousness, sanctification, and redemption. Zwingli pointed out that the correct translation of *hagioi* and *sancti* is "pious ones" or "pure ones" and that the phrase "communion of saints" in the Apostles' Creed means no more than "the community of pious people." The saints, repeated Calvin, are the elect, past, present, and future, "all those who, by the kindness of God the Father, through the working of the Holy Spirit, have entered into fellowship with Christ, [and] are set apart as God's property and personal possession." In sum, every man, woman, or child, called by the Gospel, baptized, and justified by his faith alone, is a saint. Just as all true Christians are priests and monks (*religiosi*), so all true Christians are saints.

Protestant divines most sharply attacked the traditional piety of ordinary people when they branded the cult of saints as a kind of spiritual witchcraft blinding men's eyes and minds and seducing them from the path of holiness. The veneration of saints is unscriptural and superstitious. It transfers to the holy dead what properly belongs to God and Jesus Christ (or to one's needy neighbor). The dead, however holy, are creatures. In heaven, they glorify God and are wholly isolated from us. They do not hear our prayers; they cannot pray for either the living or the dead; they do not intercede for us with God. Especially pernicious is the belief that the saints have stored up a surplus of merits by their own godly works on which their devotees can draw to redeem their own sins, a doctrine annulled by the truth of justification by faith alone. Jesus Christ is the sole and single mediator between God and humanity, since he alone paid the ransom and deposit for us all. To invoke any other advocate is sacrilege and insults Jesus Christ. Venerating a saint makes void the Cross. The "Romish" doctrine of the saints, concluded the twenty-second article of the Church of England's Thirty-Nine Articles, is "a fond thing vainly invented."

Equally deplored, especially among Zwinglians and Calvinists, was Catholic teaching about religious images. Pictures and statues of the saints, like their relics, lead inevitably to idolatry; for people always end by putting their hope and trust in these carved or painted idols, praying to them, swearing oaths by them, sacrificing to them, giving them offerings, asking for their blessing, even superstitiously imagining that they speak or bleed in order to reveal future events. God and the Holy Scriptures have forbidden images. The only picture a believer needs is the one of Jesus in the Gospels and in his own heart. Images of Jesus' life are not the "Bible of the poor"; preaching is the proper way to teach the simple who cannot read. In 1524, the Council of Zurich ordered the removal of all paintings and statues from the city's churches, an example largely followed by other "reformed" churches, sometimes in orderly cooperation with the secular authorities, at other times imposed by violent iconoclastic riots.

As Europe split permanently into Protestant and Catholic territories on the principle of *cuius regio eius religio,* Jerome's cult and image, like those of other saints, gradually disappeared from Protestant lands. Why his cult lost much of its earlier luxuriance even among Catholics is less obvious.

In part, of course, it was because Catholic bishops shared some Protestant, and earlier, medieval, reservations about the cult of saints. Episcopal reformers drew with increasing vehemence the line between popular piety and superstition. Let the people be taught that God is Alpha and Omega, that God only must be loved and worshipped, that in themselves the saints are nothing, that we venerate them only to the extent that they lead us to worship the one true God. The cult of saints must be orderly; seemly; uncorrupted by avarice, legend, and enthusiasm. In the fourteenth and fifteenth centuries, Jerome's cult had rested on a translation of relics, miracles, successful intercession, and answered prayers. After about 1520, he worked no recorded miracles and his old ones were, by many of the devout, disbelieved or forgotten. Erasmus had done his work well: the evidence for every traditional miracle, for every appealing legendary anecdote, had been proved spurious. Cardinal Baronius much disliked Erasmus, but he ratified his judgment in this. Before the end of the sixteenth century, Jerome's tomb in S. Maria Maggiore was built over, his remains misplaced, and his monument dismantled; devotees no longer earned plenary indulgences by visiting him on the anniversary of his translation, nor could they hope that he might introduce them, as he had St. Cajetan of Thiene, to the Virgin and Child when they prayed at the Chapel of the Presepio. We cannot suppose that such events necessarily scandalized learned piety in Rome.

Popular veneration for Jerome cooled also because the three important currents in European religious and intellectual life that had between 1300 and 1600 principally propelled his reputation had lost by the seventeenth century their original urgency and character. In the earlier Renaissance, his writings, life, and personality had aroused a vivid imitative response among penitential ascetics, hermits, and monastic reformers. Men and women struggling to reform the church by returning it to the evangelical poverty, simplicity, and abnegation of its beginnings found in Jerome a lucid, radical supporter. They gratefully promoted him to parity with John the Baptist and dedicated their houses and congregations to his name. By 1600, the eremitical impulse at the heart of Hieronymite spirituality had evaporated. The Italian congregations, so important a locus of devotion to him, gradually diminished in ardor, number, membership, and prestige. The Spanish Hieronymites, by every worldly standard, flourished still; but contemporaries admired them more for the liturgical splendor than for the austerity of their devotions. The seventeenth century was typically the age of the Jesuit and the Oratorian, of activist teachers, preachers, and performers of the seven acts of mercy, not solitary ascetics; while by the early eighteenth century frivolity in such matters had reached the point where a great European garden could hardly be considered complete without a picturesque grotto with a hermit in it. Monks still cited Jerome when they needed to defend celibacy and the religious life. But even Catholic reformers found him less attractive once Protestants learned to tease them by quoting his mordant criticisms of fourth-century monks and priests.

In the fifteenth and early sixteenth centuries, Jerome's reputation had been magnified by a second constituency: humanist literati who found in him a justification for their admiration of the classics and a model of how to reconcile their study of pagan literature and philosophy with Christian piety and commitment. He taught them biblical criticism and offered them a positive, evangelical, affective, eloquent piety as an alternative to the systematic and (as they thought) rebarbative theology of the scholastics. By the seventeenth century success had blunted need, and this constituency too was much diminished. The long battle was won; the humanists had captured the castle of learning. Now everyone admitted the propriety and desirability of uniting wisdom and piety with eloquence. The *studia humanitatis* constituted the core curriculum of every Protestant secondary school and Jesuit college. Every teacher was a humanist now, just as every professor of theology was weaned on Cicero. No one had an urgent motive to cite Jerome in favor of an educational and cultural program that had triumphed everywhere in Europe.

After 1517, in response to the Protestant Revolution, a third group propagated Jerome's example and teachings. Adopted by the militants of the Counter-Reformation as Augustine had been coopted by Luther and Calvin, Jerome became the most frequently cited of the fathers in defenses of the traditional faith and in counterattacks against the innovators. Repeatedly he supplied the clinching authority for doctrines like the intercession of saints, the veneration of relics, papal power, monasticism, sacerdotal celibacy, Mariology, ascetic and meritorious works, the sacrament of penance—all those and more could be, and were, defended from Jerome. Success again blunted need. By the middle of the seventeenth century, the church had permanently recovered from the low point of its fortunes in the 1560s. Reformation, Counter-Reformation, and the religious wars were over. Jerome played a significant role in the reconquest, but his relevance to Catholic militants diminished with the end of the heroic age and the acceptance by both sides of religious diversity within fixed frontiers.

Much remained, of course. The papacy had confirmed his authorship of the Vulgate Bible; the Council of Trent established it as the authentic expression of the word of God for all public use in the liturgy and in sermons, lectures, and disputations. He continued to be venerated as one of the four principal doctors of the church and, in paintings, to remind attentive observers of their mortality. Clerics of literary bent savored his style. Biblical scholars relied on his commentaries. Historians reedited his works and rewrote his life. But after he lost his monastic, humanist, and militant constituencies, he no longer spoke directly to contemporary controversies and issues. The change of status is recorded in a change of titles. In the centuries when he was a culture hero his most common title was *doctor gloriosus,* bestowed on him by the author of the fourteenth-century pseudographs. In the prefaces to the Sisto-Clementine Bible, the popes, silently quoting Alcuin, called him *doctor maximus,* a most respectful tribute to his linguistic expertise and knowledge of the Bible.

By the mid-seventeenth century, *doctor maximus* had
usurped his former glorious title. Henceforth
he was a subject for research rather than
an object of awe and devotion.

Abbreviations

A.B.   *Analecta Bollandiana.*

Acta SS.   *Acta Sanctorum.*

Allen   *Opus epistolarum Des. Erasmi Roterodami,* ed. P. S. Allen, H. M. Allen, and H. W. Garrod. 12 vols. Oxford, 1906–58.

Altaner-Stuiber   B. Altaner and A. Stuiber, *Patrologie.* 8th ed. Freiburg-im-Breisgau, 1978.

B.H.L.   *Bibliotheca Hagiographica Latina antiquae et mediae aetatis.* 3 vols. Brussels, 1898–1911.

B.S.   *Bibliotheca Sanctorum.*

Cavallera   F. Cavallera, *Saint Jérôme, sa vie et son oeuvre.* 2 vols. Louvain, 1922.

C.C.L.   *Corpus Christianorum, series Latina.* Turnhout, 1954 ff.

C.I.C.   Codex Iuris Canonici.

C.L.   *Collection Latomus.*

Clavis   *Clavis Patrum Latinorum,* 2d ed. (*Sacris Erudiri,* 3). Steenbrugis, in abbatia Sancti Petri, 1961.

C.R.   *Corpus Reformatorum.* Halle, 1834 ff.

C.S.E.L.   Corpus scriptorum ecclesiasticorum Latinorum. Vienna, 1886 ff.

C.W.E.   *The Collected Works of Erasmus.* Toronto, 1974 ff.

Ep. (Epistula)   St. Jérôme. Lettres, ed. Jérôme Labourt. 8 vols. Paris, 1949–63.

G.C.S.   Die griechischen christlichen Schriftsteller der ersten drei Jahrhunderte. Berlin, 1902 ff.

G.W.   *Gesamtkatalog der Wiegendrucke.* Leipzig, 1925 ff.

Heimbucher   Max Heimbucher, *Die Orden und Kongregationen der katholischen Kirche.* 3d ed. 3 vols. Paderborn, 1933–34.

Hieronymianus   Giovanni d'Andrea, *Hieronimianus diui Hieronimi vite mortis prodigiorum doctorum ac scriptorum exflorationes perstringens (ut sequens indicat prologus) principaliter quattuor in partes diuisus. per Decretorum famosissimum doctorem D. Johannem Andree studiosissime compilatus.* Basel, A. Petrus de Langendorff for Leonhardus Alentseius et Luc Fratres, June 1514.

Hody   Humphrey Hody, *De Bibliorum textibus originalibus, versionibus Graecis, et Latina Vulgata.* Oxford, 1705.

Jungblut   Renate Jungblut, *Hieronymus. Darstellung und Verehrung eines Kirchenvaters.* Tübingen, 1967.

Kelly   J. N. D. Kelly, *Jerome: His Life, Writings, and Controversies.* London, 1975.

Klapper   *Schriften Johannes von Neumarkt, 2 Teil. Hieronymus. Die unechten Briefe des Eusebius, Augustinus, Cyrill zum Lobe des Heiligen (Vom Mittelater zur Reformation, 6),* ed. Joseph Klapper. Berlin, 1932.

Lambert   Bernard Lambert, *Bibliotheca Hieronymiana manuscripta. La tradition manuscrite des oeuvres de saint Jérôme.* 4 vols. in 6. Steenbrugis, in abbatia S. Petri, 1970.

Legenda aurea   *Legenda aurea,* ed. Th. Graesse. Vratislava, 1890.

L.W.   *Luther's Works,* ed. Jaroslav Pelikan and H. T. Lehmann, St. Louis, Mo., 1955 ff.

M.G.H.   *Monumenta Germaniae Historica. Societas aperiendis fontibus rerum Germanicarum medii aevi.* Berlin, 1877 ff.

Mombritius   Boninus Mombritius, *Sanctuarium seu vitae sanctorum,* ed. Benedictines of Solesmes. 2 vols. Paris, 1910.

Opera   *Divi Eusebii Hieronymi Stridonensis opera omnia,* ed. Erasmus of Rotterdam, Boniface Amerbach, et al. 9 vols. Basel, Johannes Froben, 1516.

PL   Jacques Paul Migne, *Patrologiae cursus completus . . . omnium SS. patrum. Series Latina.* 221 vols. Paris, 1844–64.

Pöllmann   A. Pöllmann, "Von der Entwicklung des Hieronymus-Typus in der älteren Kunst," *Benedictinische Monatschrift* 2 (1920): 438–522.

S.C.   *Sources Chrétiennes.*

W.A.   *D. Martin Luthers Werke.* Weimar, 1883 ff.

Notes

1: THE HISTORICAL JEROME

1. The important modern biographies are G. Grützmacher, *Hieronymus: Eine biographische Studie*, 3 vols. (Berlin, 1901); F. Cavallera, *Saint Jérôme, sa vie et son oeuvre*, 2 vols. (Louvain, 1922); and the readable, balanced, and amply documented study by J. N. D. Kelly, *Jerome: His Life, Writings, and Controversies* (London, 1975), to which this chapter owes much. C. Favez has sketched a lively portrait of Jerome by assembling passages from his 111 prefaces, *Saint Jérôme peint par lui-même* (C.L. 33) (Brussels, 1958). For the abundant monographic literature, see the bibliographies in *S. Hieronymi Presbyteri Opera*, pt. 1, 1 (C.C.L. 72: ix–lii) and Altaner-Stuiber, 394–404.

2. The date of Jerome's birth is still the subject of complex debate. The conflicting evidence is fairly set forth by Kelly, 337–39, who concludes that Jerome was "almost certainly" born in 331 and died in 420 at the age of ninety. I am still persuaded by the older view that he was born in the mid-340s and died in 420 at the age of about seventy-five, a chronology that seems to me to fit with less strain the particular events and general contour of Jerome's life. A single example must suffice: Jerome reports (*Ep.* 52, 1) that when he lived as a hermit in the Syrian desert he was a young man (*adulescens*), indeed almost a boy (*immo paene puer*). By Kelly's chronology (46), he would then have been in his early forties, not too old to describe himself as *iuvenis*, but careless surely of the usual meaning of *adulescens* (a young man of thirty-three or less), and certainly too long in the tooth to be "almost a boy" still struggling to curb his earliest sexual impulses (*primos impetus lasciuientis aetatis heremi duritia refrenarem*). Supposing him to have been in his late twenties makes better sense of this and analogous passages. Cf. P. Jay, "Sur la date de naissance de Saint Jérôme," *Revue des études latines* 52 (1973): 262–80, and Cardinal Baronius, *Annales Ecclesiastici*, ad an. 372, lix–lxi (Lucca, 1739), 5: 377, col. 1–378, col. 2, who, after a perceptive weighing of the evidence, concluded that Jerome was born in 342 or 343 and died in 420 at the age of seventy-eight or seventy-nine.

3. In *Ep.* 8 he contrasts the *cruda rusticitas* of uncivilized people with the *humanitas* of those polished by the liberal arts. All references to Jerome's letters are to the edition of J. Labourt.

4. For Jerome's education and his knowledge of the classics, see P. Courcelle, *Les Lettres grecques en Occident de Macrobe à Cassiodore* (Paris, 1943), 37–115, and H. Hagendahl, *Latin Fathers and the Classics* (Göteborg, 1958), 89–328.

Cf. H.-I. Marrou, *Saint Augustin et la fin de la culture antique* (Paris, 1938), 1–104, and P. Brown, *Augustine of Hippo* (London, 1967), 35–39, for Augustine's education.

5. *Comm. in Hiezechielem*, XII, 40, 5–13 (*C.C.L.* 75:556–57). The passage has been inscribed over the door leading to the catacombs under the church of S. Sebastiano in Rome.

6. *Epp.* 15, 1; 16, 2. For the date, see Kelly, 23.

7. The "Aquileienses clerici quasi chorum beatorum," as he affectionately recalled them later: Eusebius Pamphilius, *Chronici Canones*, ed. J. K. Fatheringham (London, 1923), 329, 19. See Giuseppe Cuscito, *Cristianesimo antico ad Aquileia e in Istria (Fonti e studi per la storia della Venezia Giulia, 3)* (Trieste, 1977), 155–238.

8. *Ep.* 5, 2. In Trier he copied two works of Hilary of Poitiers (c. 315–367), the *Commentaries on the Psalms* and *De synodis contra Arrianos.*

9. *Ep.* 15, 3.

10. *Ep.* 10, 1.

11. *Ep.* 4, 2; 7, 3–4.

12. *Ep.* 50, 1.

13. *Ep.* 22, 30. The large literature on the dream is conveniently reviewed by P. Antin, "Autour du songe de S. Jérôme," in *Recueil sur saint Jérôme (C.L. 95)* (Brussels, 1968), 71–100. For the location and date of the dream I follow Kelly. Rufinus (*Apol. contra Hieronymum*, II, 7–8, *C.C.L.* 20:88–89) was the first to identify the bystanders as angels. Cf. Gregory of Tours (*Praef. in gloria martyrum, M.G.H., Scr. Merov.* 1:487): "Hieronymus presbyter et post apostolum Paulum bonus doctor Ecclesiae, refert se ductum ante tribunal aeterni iudicis et extensum in supplicia graviter caesum eo quod Ciceronis uel Vergilii fallacias saepius lectitaret, confessus se *coram angelis sanctis* ipsi Dominatori omnium numquam se deinceps haec lecturum neque ultra tractaturum, nisi ea quae Deo digna et ad Ecclesiae aedificationem opportuna iudicarentur." Later generations of writers and artists agreed that it was also angels who whipped him: for example, Otto of Vercelli (d. 961), *De pressuris ecclesiasticis* (*PL* 134:75B): "Legimus quoque de beato Hieronymo, quoniam cum librum legeret Ciceronis, ab angelo correptus sit, quod vir Christianus paganorum intenderet figmentis"; Jean Gerson, *Collatio in festo S. Michaelis archangeli, Oeuvres complètes,* ed. Mgr. Glorieux (Paris, 1963), 5:321; and *Aeneae Silvii de liberorum educatione,* ed. J. S. Nelson (Washington, D.C., 1940), 174; and figs. 2 and 3. A life of St. Jerome by the Gesuate monk Matteo da Ferrara prefacing his Italian translation of the *Epistolae* (Ferrara, Lorenzo de' Rossi da Valenza, 12 October 1497) contains an unusual variation. His version of the story is accurate and straightforward; but the title he gave the chapter about the dream is "Come Hieronymo fo battuto da demonii," and an accompanying woodcut shows two horned and winged demons beating Jerome as he sits at his book-laden desk, while in the top right of the illustration he is pictured kneeling before Christ and two angels (unnumb. leaf 2r).

14. 2 Cor. 6:14–15.

15. *De praescr. haer.* 7, 9 (*C.C.L.* 1: 193).
16. *Ep.* 22, 29; *Adv. Pelag.* I, 14 (*PL* 23:506D); *Ep.* 14, 11.
17. *Apol. contra Hier.* II, 7 (*C.C.L.* 20:88). The passage Rufinus had in mind is *Ep.* 84, 6: "Sed fac me errasse in adulescentia, et Philosophorum, id est, gentilium studiis eruditum, in principio fidei ignorasse dogmata Christiana, et hoc putasse in apostolis, quod in Pythagora et Platone et Empedocle legeram." Jerome excused his blunder by saying that he meant only the doctrines of Pythagoras, Plato, and the rest (which he had learned about from Cicero and Seneca), not their books.
18. *Ep.* 70, 2. Jerome's use of the text about the "lovely captive" is modeled directly on Origen, *In Leviticum homilia,* VII, 6 (G.C.S. 29:390–91). Cf. *Ep.* 66, 8 and *Ep.* 21, 13: "Itaque et nos hoc facere solemus, quando philosophos legimus, quando in manus nostras libri ueniunt sapientiae saecularis: si quid in eis utile repperimus, ad nostrum dogma conuertimus, si quid vero superfluum, de idolis, de amore, de cura saecularium rerum, haec radimus, his caluitium indicimus, haec in unguium morem ferro acutissimo desecamus."
19. *Ep.* 22, 7.
20. *Ep.* 22, 6.
21. *Ep.* 125, 13. For achieving chastity by the knife, see H. Chadwick, *The Sentences of Sextus* (Cambridge, 1959), 110–11.
22. *Ep.* 14, 2.
23. *Ep.* 14, 6. Cf. *Epp.* 2; 3, 4; 14, 10.
24. A. J. Festugière, *Antioch paienne et chrétienne. Libanius, Chrysostome et les moines de Syrie* (Paris, 1959), 291–310, 415–18.
25. *Ep.* 5, 2.
26. *Ep.* 125, 12; *Praef. in Dan.* (*PL* 28; 1292B). Cf. E. F. Sutcliffe, "St. Jerome's Pronunciation of Hebrew," *Biblica* 29 (1948): 116–17. One of Jerome's odder titles to admiration in the fifteenth century was that he had ground down his irregular teeth with an iron file in order to be able to pronounce Hebrew correctly, a legendary detail noted by Matteo Bosso, *De instituendo sapientia animo* (Bologna, Plato de Benedictis, 1495), sig. P, i: "An non virorum iste ita mirabilis atque sanctissimus preliatus est cum difficultate potentiaque naturae? cum recte pronunciandi Hebraicam linguam, quam discebat, contentione dentes impeditiores quibus non satis poterat anhelantia perfracta inculcataque verba illa proferre (res inaudita) ferro aequandos sectori concessit et tradidit?"
27. *Epp.* 50, 1; 52, 8; 84, 3; *De viris inlustribus,* 117 (ed. E. C. Richardson, 51).
28. *Comm. in Hier.* III, Praef., 2 (*C.C.L.* 74: 119).
29. Jerome's preface to his translation of Origen's *Homilies on Ezekiel* (G.C.S. 33: 318).
30. *Praef. in quatuor evangelia,* in *Nouum Testamentum,* ed. J. Wordsworth and H. White (Oxford, 1889–98), 1: 1–2: "Nouum opus facere me cogis ex ueteri, ut post exemplaria scripturarum toto orbe dispersa quasi quidam arbiter sedeam et, quia inter se uariant, quae sint illa quae cum Graeca consentiant ueritate decernam. . . . De nouo nunc loquor testamentum,

205

quod Graecum esse non dubium est, excepto apostolo Mattheo, quo primus in Iudaea euangelium Christi Hebraeis litteris edidit. Hoc certe cum in nostro sermone discordat et diuersos riuulorum tramites ducit, uno de fonte quaerendum est." Cf. *Ep.* 27, 1.

31. *Praef. in quatuor evangelia,* 2. The Old Latin MSS can offer as many as twenty-seven variant readings in a single verse (for example, Luke 24:4–5).

32. *Ep.* 27, 1. See B. M. Metzger, *The Early Versions of the New Testament* (Oxford, 1977), 352–62.

33. R. Lorenz, "Die Anfänge des abendländischen Mönchtum im 4. Jahrhundert," *Zeitschrift für Kirchengeschichte* 76 (1966): 1–61; D. Gorce, *La lectio divina des origines du cénobitisme à St. Benoît et Cassiodore,* I. *St. Jérôme et la lecture sacrée dans le milieu ascétique romain* (Paris, 1925).

34. *Ep.* 45, 2–3: "Omnium paene iudicio dignis summo sacerdotio decernebar; beatae memoriae Damasi os meus sermo erat; licebar sanctus, dicebar humilis et disertus." Cf. *Ep.* 127, 7.

35. *Ep.* 108, 6. Cf. Horace *Odes* 1.13.18. The scene of Paula's departure was fancifully reconstructed c. 1639 by Claude in one of the paintings commissioned by King Philip IV of Spain for the Landscape Gallery of the Buen Retiro, his new pleasure palace on the outskirts of Madrid: *The Port of Ostia with the Embarkation of St. Paula* (Madrid, Prado). See H. Diane Russell, *Claude Lorrain, 1600–1682* (Exh. cat., National Gallery of Art, Washington) (Washington, D.C., 1982), no. 27, 140–41.

36. *Ep.* 108, 8–13 describes their itinerary.

37. In Bethlehem, in 385, Paula had been vouchsafed a vision. She saw, with "the eyes of faith," the baby wrapped in swaddling clothes crying in his crib, the magi adoring God, the star shining overhead, the virgin mother, the caring father, the shepherds come by night to see the word made flesh. "And so I, a miserable sinner, have been judged worthy to kiss the crib in which our Lord lay as a baby and to pray in the very grotto where the virgin mother gave birth to the infant God" (*Ep.* 108, 10). Jerome, too, was devoted to the infant Jesus in the manger (*Ep.* 64, 8). Given the important role this humble crib would play later in Jerome's legend and cult, it is worth noting that he believed that the original manger was made of clay, but that before his own arrival in Bethlehem it had been replaced by one made of silver: "O, how I wish I could have seen the crib in which our Lord lay! Today we have removed the old crib because it was made of clay and replaced it by a silver one, as though by doing this we honor Christ. But I think the old one was the more precious. Gold and silver are good enough for pagans; the Christian faith deserves a crib made of clay. For he who was born in a manger despised gold and silver" (*Sancti Hieronymi Presbyteri tractatus sive homilia,* ed. G. Morin, *Anecdota Maredsolana* [1897], 3(2): 393).

38. *Ep.* 51, 1.

39. *Ep.* 22, 35; A. Boon, *Pachomiana Latina* (Louvain, 1932); P. Antin, *Recueil sur saint Jérôme,* 108 ff.; Kelly, 129–40.

40. *Praef. in Pentateuchum (PL* 28: 150–51). The source of the legend is the *Letter of Aristeas,* in reality the work of a Hellenized Jew of Alexandria

about 130 B.C. but purporting to be an account of the translation of the Hebrew Pentateuch into Greek under the sponsorship of Ptolemy I Philadelphus (285-247 B.C.) by a contemporary pagan Greek official in Ptolemy's court (ed. and tr. Moses Hadas [New York, 1951] and André Pelletier [Paris, 1962]).

41. *Ep.* 102, 2.

42. Of this revision of the Old Testament from Origen's text of the Septuagint in the *Hexapla* only Psalms, Job, and the Song of Songs survive. Jerome himself says that he corrected the whole of the Old Testament in this way, a statement supported by what seems to have been the presence of a copy of it in Cassiodorus's library at Vivarium in the sixth century (*Inst.* I, 14, 2-3, ed. Roger Mynors, 40: "in codice grandiore littera conscripto . . . in quo septuaginta interpretum translatio veteris testamenti . . . continetur"). This version of the Psalter, widely diffused in Gaul (hence its name, *Psalterium Gallicanum*), acquired preeminent authority in the West; liturgical conservatism ensured that Jerome's later translation from the Hebrew (the *Psalterium iuxta Hebraeos*) never superseded it. It is the version of the Psalms of the Vulgate Bible and the Roman Breviary.

43. *Praef. in Pentateuchum* (*PL* 28: 151A): "Aliud est enim vatem, aliud esse interpretem. Ibi Spiritus ventura praedicit: hic eruditio et verborum copia, ea quae intelligit, transfert. Nisi forte putandus est Tullius Oeconomicum Xenophontis, et Platonis Protagoram, et Demosthenis pro Ctesiphonte, afflatus rhetorico spiritu transtulisse."

44. *Ep.* 106, 3.

45. *Ep.* 48, 4.

46. *Ep.* 57, 5.

47. *Ep.* 112, 19. Cf. *Epp.* 21, 42; 57, 10; 106, 29; and W. Schwarz, "The Meaning of *Fidus interpres* in Medieval Translation," *Journal of Theological Studies* 45 (1944-45): 73-78; W. H. Semple, "St. Jerome as a Biblical Translator," *Bulletin of the John Rylands Library* 48 (1965): 227-43; G. Q. A. Meershoek, *Le Latin biblique d'après saint Jérôme. Aspects linguistiques de la rencontre entre la Bible et le monde classique* (*Latinitas Christianorum Primaeva*, 20) (Utrecht, 1966), 4-30; and G. J. M. Bartelink, *Hieronymus. Liber de optimo genere interpretandi* (*Epistula 57*). *Ein Kommentar* (*Mnemosyne*, Suppl., 61) (Leiden, 1980), esp. 46-47.

48. *Praef. in Lib. Sam. et Malachim* (*PL* 28: 558A); *Praef. in Lib. Isaiae* (*PL* 28: 772B); *Praef. in Ps. iuxta Hebraeos* (*PL* 28: 1126A); *Heb. Quaest. in geneseos Praef.* (*C.C.L.* 72: 1). For Augustine's view, *De ciuitate Dei*, XVIII, 43 (*C.C.L.* 48: 639).

49. Raphael Loewe, "The Medieval History of the Latin Vulgate," in *The Cambridge History of the Bible* (Cambridge, 1969), 2: 102-54.

50. *Epp.* 37, 3; 36, 14.

51. *Apol. adv. Rufinum*, I, 16 (*PL* 23: 409-10).

52. *Ep.* 121, Praef.: The Old Testament "involves so many obscurities and types of future things that all of it demands explanation."

53. *Comm. in Hiezech.* XIII, 42, 13 (*C.C.L.* 75: 615-16.)

54. *Comm. in Eph.* I, Prol. (*PL* 26: 440B).
55. *Ep.* 84, 3.
56. *Praef. in Psalterium iuxta Hebraeos* (*PL* 28: 1125).
57. *Comm. in Hier.* VI, 2 (*C.C.L.* 74: 289–90). The passage continues: "Nor is there any difference between Jews and Christians except this, that although both they and we believe that Christ, the son of God, has been promised, they hold that the things foretold of the Messianic age have yet to come to pass, we that they have already been fulfilled." For Jerome's relation to the Rabbinic tradition, see Jay Braverman, *Jerome's Commentary on Daniel: A Study of Comparative Jewish and Christian Interpretations of the Hebrew Bible* (Washington, D.C., 1978).
58. *Comm. in Eph.* II, Prol. (*PL* 26: 477A); *Comm. in Zachariam,* Prol. (*C.C.L.* 76A: 748). See E. Arns, *La technique du livre d'après saint Jérôme* (Paris, 1953), and, for a general appreciation of Jerome's commentaries, A. Penna, *Principi e carattere dell'esegessi di S. Gerolamo* (Rome, 1952), 37–81, and E. Bonnard, ed. and tr., *Saint Jérôme. Commentaire sur S. Matthieu* (*S.C.* 242) (Paris, 1977), 1: 27–50.
59. I. Opelt, *Hieronymus' Streitschriften* (Heidelberg, 1973).
60. *Epp.* 136 and 137. The identification of the raiders as supporters of Pelagius was made by Augustine, *De gestis Pelagii,* 35, 66.
61. *Epp.* 138 and 154, 2.
62. *Comm. in Hiezech.,* Prol. (*C.C.L.* 75: 3–4). See also J. R. Palanque, "St. Jerome and the Barbarians," in *Monument to St. Jerome,* ed. F. X. Murphy (New York, 1952), 173–99.
63. *Ep.* 126, 2.
64. *Ep.* 123, 15–16; 128, 5.
65. *Comm. in Hiezech.* VII (*C.C.L.* 75: 277–78).
66. *Ep.* 84, 3.
67. *Epitoma chronicon* 1274 (*M.G.H. Auct. ant.,* 9: 469): "Hieronymus presbyter moritur anno aetatis suae XCI, pridie kal. Octobris."

2: FROM HISTORY TO LEGEND

1. *PL* 22 (1864): 175–84. *B.H.L.* 3869; *Clavis,* no. 623, 142; A. Vaccari, "Le antiche vite di S. Girolamo," *Scritti di erudizione e di filologia* (Rome, 1958), 2: 31–51 (revised version of an article first published in 1920); Cavallera, 1(2): 137–40. Lambert, 3B, no. 901, lists 81 manuscripts. Three ninth-century manuscripts are earlier than any listed by Lambert: Sangallensis 552 (E. A. Lowe, *Codices latini antiquiores,* no. 942) and Par. lat. 11.635 and 10.863 (G. Philippart, in *A.B.* 90 [1972]: 188). The *Life* is anonymous in all of them. We know that it was written before c. 850 because Ado of Vienne used it in his *Martyrologium* (*PL* 123: 370–72).
2. The *Life* exists in two recensions: (1) the authentic text (Mombritius, 2: 31–36; *B.H.L.* 3871) and (2) a text contaminated by many awkward interpolations from *Hieronymus noster* (*PL* 22: 201–14; *B.H.L.* 3870). See *Clavis,* no. 622, 141. A possible attribution to Sebastianus, a disciple of St.

Benedict at Monte Cassino (suggested by Cavallera, 1(2): 141–43), rests on
Paul the Deacon's (d. c. 800) notice of Sebastianus in his *De viris illustribus
Casinensibus* (*PL* 173: 1013A): "Sebastianus B. Benedicti monachus,
Hieronymi doctoris egregii Vitam describens, legendam Ecclesiis tradidit:
in qua, quae ei a puero institutio, quale in juventute studium, quae in
senectute ei scientia fuerit, lucidissime satis demonstrat." Lambert, 3B, no.
900, lists 123 manuscripts. The earliest date from the late ninth or early
tenth century (for example, Arras, Bibl. mun. 1079 [235], fols. 97v–105v
from Saint-Vaast), evidence that tends to confirm Vaccari, "Antiche vite,"
45–46, and "Un prossimo centenario o la morte di S. Girolamo," *Civiltà
Cattolica* (1918), 2: 204–14, who puts the author in the ninth century and
discounts the attribution to Sebastianus. Three pieces of evidence suggest
the province of Rome as the place of origin: it is the first life to describe the
miracle of taming the lion, a story probably latinized and attached to
Jerome in the environment of the Greek monasteries in Rome; it is the first
to call Jerome a "cardinal presbyter," a phrase used to describe the senior
priests of the Roman *tituli* after the middle of the eighth century; and it
alone quotes extensively from the *Acta* of the Roman martyrs Nereus and
Achilleus. The life of Jerome that Paul the Deacon attributed to Sebastianus
of Monte Cassino may well have been one source of *Plerosque nimirum*.

3. *PL* 22: 183–202; *B.H.L.* 3873; Vaccari, "Antiche vite," 46–51, who made
    the brilliant attribution of this text to Maniacoria; Cavallera, 1(2): 143–44;
    Lambert, 3B, no. 904. Inspired by the example of St. Jerome, Nicolò
    Maniacoria, deacon of S. Lorenzo in Damaso and a monk in the Cistercian
    abbey of S. Anastasio "ad Aquas Salvias" in the Roman Campania during
    the pontificate of Lucius II (1144–1145), wrote a penetrating essay on the
    textual criticism of the Bible and a work on the Psalms in which he
    compared the *Psalterium Romanum* and the translations of the Psalms used
    by Augustine and Ambrose in their commentaries with Jerome's *Psalterium
    iuxta Hebraeos*. Having learned some Hebrew from a Jewish scholar, he
    found that even the *Psalterium iuxta Hebraeos* sometimes missed the *He-
    braeica veritas*. See V. Peri, "Nicola Maniacutia: un testimone della filologia
    romana del XII secolo," *Aevum* 41 (1967): 67–90, and for a detailed survey
    of the earlier literature the same author's "Notizia su Nicola Maniacutia,
    autore ecclesiastico romano del XII secolo," *Aevum* 36 (1962): 534, n. 2.

4. *De vita et actibus sancti Hieronymi presbyteri et gestis eiusdem*, in *Speculum
    Historiale Vincentii* (Venice, Hermanus Liechtenstein Coloniensis, 5 Sep-
    tember 1494), bk. XVI, chaps. 18–88, 92–93, fols. 198–207v.

5. *Legenda aurea*, 653–58. Jean de Mailly, O.P., *Abrégé des gestes et miracles des
    saints*, tr. A. Dondaine (*Bibliothèque d'histoire dominicaine*, 1) (Paris, 1947) is
    an earlier (c. 1240) example of the same genre. The chapter on Jerome (no.
    152, 431–34) is one source of the notice in the *Golden Legend*. Cf. Don-
    daine, "Le Dominicain français Jean de Mailly et la *Légende dorée*," *Archives
    d'histoire dominicaine* (1946), 1: 53–102.

6. *De viris inlustribus*, 135 (ed. E. C. Richardson, 55).

7. *Hieronymus noster* (*PL* 22: 180).

8. *Itinerarium,* 29 (ed. P. Geyer, C.S.E.L. 39 [1898], 178).

9. These testimonials have been carefully identified by Vaccari, "Antiche vite," 42–46. Cf. F. Lanzoni, "La leggenda di S. Girolamo," *Miscellanea Geronimiana. Scritti varii pubblicati nel XV centenario dalla morte di San Girolamo* (Rome, 1920), 30–36, and M. L. W. Laistner, "St. Jerome in the Early Middle Ages," in *A Monument to St. Jerome,* ed. F. X. Murphy (New York, 1952), 235–56.

10. *Plerosque nimirum* (Mombritius, 2: 31, lines 26–31).

11. *Legenda aurea,* 653. The translation is based on that of G. Ryan and H. Ripperger (New York, 1941), 2: 587. For the etymology of personal and place names, see I. Opelt, "Etymologie," in *Reallexikon für Antike und Christentum* (1966), 6: 797–844, and F. Lanzoni, *Genesi, svolgimento e tramonto delle leggende storiche* (*Studi e testi,* 43) (Rome, 1925), 32–33.

12. *Chronicon,* ad an. 392 (ed. Th. Mommsen, *M.G.H., Auct. ant.,* 11: 63).

13. *Epp.* 15, 1; 16, 2; *Contra Joannem,* 41 (*PL* 23: 392–93); Kelly, 58. For the white baptismal garment of the later fourth century, see Ambrose, *De mysteriis,* V, 34–35 (*PL* 16 [1845]: 399–400, and Augustine, *Sermones,* 120, 3 (*PL* 38: 677) and 223, 1 (*PL* 38: 1092).

14. *Ep.* 45, 2.

15. Paris, BN., MS. lat. 1, fol. 3v; Rome, S. Paolo fuori le mura, Bible, fol. 3v. W. Köhler, *Die karolingischen Miniaturen. Die Schule von Tours,* 4 vols. (Berlin, 1930–71), 1(2): 50–53, 214–17; H. Schade, "Studien zu der karolingischen Bilderbibel aus St. Paul vor den Mauern in Rom," *Wallraf-Richartz-Jahrbuch* 21 (1959): 9–40; 22 (1960): 13–48; P. E. Schramm and Florentine Mütherich, *Denkmäler der deutschen Könige und Kaiser,* 2 vols. (Munich, 1962–78), 1: 129–30, no. 42; J. E. Gaehde, "The Turonian Sources of the Bible of San Paolo Fuori le Mura in Rome," *Frühmittelalterliche Studien* 5 (1971): 361–65; and Herbert Kessler, *The Illustrated Bibles from Tours* (*Studies in Manuscript Illumination,* 7) (Princeton, 1977), 84–95 and pls. 130–31.

16. *Hieronymus noster* (*PL* 22: 177). Cf. *Comm. in Gal.* I, Praef. (*PL* 26: 308B): "Non quod ignorem Caium Marium Victorinum qui Romae, me puero, rhetoricam docuit edidisse Commentarios in Apostolum." Some scribes, misunderstanding the sentence in the same way, emended *qui Romae, me puero, rhetoricam docuit* to read *qui Romae me puerum rhetoricam docuit.*

17. *Ep.* 45, 1; Cf. above, n. 14 and p. 206, n. 34.

18. *Hieronymus noster* (*PL* 22: 178).

19. Mombritius, 2: 32, lines 9–14. Cf. *Liber pontificalis,* 37, *Vita Liberii* (ed. L. Duchesne [Paris, 1886–92], 1: 207).

20. *Summa de ecclesiasticis officiis,* 157i (ed. H. Douteil, *C.C.L. Con. med.* 41A: 301).

21. *Vita Hieronymi* (*PL* 22: 186).

22. *Legenda aurea,* 654.

23. *Hieronymus noster* (*PL* 22: 183); Maniacoria, *Vita Hieronymi* (*PL* 22: 200). In Botticelli's *St. Augustine* (Florence, Ognissanti, 1480), an Italian twenty-four-hour clock suspended behind Augustine's head points to the

twenty-fourth hour, the hour of sunset, further evidence that the true subject and better title of the fresco is *The Apparition of St. Jerome to St. Augustine,* a vision vouchsafed him immediately after Jerome's death (see above, pp. 51–52). Cf. Ronald Lightbown, *Sandro Botticelli,* 2 vols. (London, 1978), 2: 38–40, cat. no. B25.

24. Jerome, addressing a letter to Augustine, a bishop, wrote: *Domino uere sancto et beatissimo papae Augustino;* while Augustine replied to Jerome, a monk and priest: *Sancto fratri et conpresbytero Hieronymo (Epp.* 103 and 104). In his hagiographic works, Jerome avoided the epithet, preferring *beatus Paulus* and *beatus Hilarion;* however, he often used it to describe pious women: *sancta Marcella* or *sancta et beata Paula (Epp.* 54, 18; 108, 34).

25. Virgins, argued Methodius of Olympus (c. 260–290) suffer a lifelong martyrdom *(Symposium,* VII, 3, ed. H. Musurillo, *S.C.,* [1963], 95: 186–87). "Your mother has been crowned after a long martyrdom," wrote Jerome to Eustochium after Paula's death. "For it is not only the effusion of blood that makes a true witness, but the spotless service rendered by a devout soul is a daily martyrdom. . . . God awards the same recompense to the victors, whether they have won it in peace or war" *(Ep.* 108, 31).

26. H. Delehaye, *Sanctus, essai sur le culte des saints dans l'antiquité* (Brussels, 1927), 1–161. See also the same author's *Les Origines du culte des martyrs (Subsidia hagiographica,* 20) (Brussels, 1933); E. W. Kemp, *Canonization and Authority in the Western Church* (Oxford, 1948); and Peter Brown, *The Cult of the Saints* (Chicago, 1981).

27. Ed. H. Quentin and H. Delehaye, in *Acta SS. Nov.* (1931), 2(2): 534. On the *Martyrologium Hieronymianum,* see René Aigrain, *L'hagiographie. Ses sources, ses méthodes, son histoire* (Paris, 1953), 32–50, and the literature cited by R. Bryan, in *New Catholic Encyclopedia* (1967), 9: 318–19, and Altaner-Stuiber, 235–36.

28. Bede (d. 735), *Martyrologia (PL* 94: 1058B); Wandalbert (848) (ed. E. Dummler, *M.G.H., Poetae latini medii aevi,* 2: 595, lines 605–7); Ado (850–860) *(PL* 123: 370–72); Rhabanus Maurus (d. 856) (ed. J. McCulloh, *C.C.L. Con. med.* 44: 99–100); Usuard (c. 875) (ed. J. Dubois, *Subsidia Hagiographica,* 40 [Brussels, 1965], 312). On the martyrologies and Jerome's place in them see Henri Quentin, *Les martyrologes historiques du Moyen Age* (Paris, 1908); Anselm Manser, "Vom heiligen Rufe des Hieronymus und seine frühe Ehrung im Martyrologium vorab des abendländischen Mönchtums," *Benediktinische Monatschrift* 2 (1920): 363–80; and Aigrain, *L'hagiographie,* 51–68.

29. José Madoz, *Liciano de Caragena y sus cartas (Estudios Onienses,* I, 4) [Madrid, 1948], 86.

30. Johannes Monachus, *Liber de miraculis,* Prolog. (ed. Michael Huber [Heidelberg, 1913], 1). See also Carl Weyman, "Les docteurs de L'Eglise," *Revue d'histoire et de littérature religieuses* 3 (1898): 562–63; Otto Bardenhewer, *Geschichte der altkirchlichen Literatur,* 2d ed., 4 vols. (Freiburg-im-Breisgau, 1913–24), 1: 46–49; and J. de Ghellinck, *Le mouvement théologique du XIIe siècle,* 2d ed. (Bruges, 1948), 514–17.

31. *Corpus Iuris Canonici, Lib. VI Decretalium,* III, tit. xxii, cap. 1. For the text see below, chap. 3, n. 1.

32. Leningrad State Library, MS. Q.v. I. Nr. 13, fol. 3v. See E. H. Zimmermann, *Vorkarolingische Miniaturen* (Berlin, 1916), 2: 65–67, 187; 1, pls. 88, 92; O. Dobiaš-Rozdestvenskaïa, *Histoire de l' atelier graphique de Corbie de 651 à 830* (Leningrad, 1934), 115–16; Lambert, 4A, pl. I (a colored reproduction of good quality); Peter Bloch and Hermann Schnitzler, *Die ottonische Kölner Malerschule,* 2 vols. (Düsseldorf, 1967–1970), 2: figs. 656 and 657 (illustrating the dependence of this representation of Jerome on a late classical model); and W. Braunfels, *Die Welt der Karolinger und ihre Kunst* (Munich, 1968), 49, fig. 21.

33. Vienna, Staatsbibliothek, Cod. lat. 1332, fol. 1v. W. Neumüller and K. Holter, *Der Codex Millenarius (Forschungen zur Geschichte Oberösterreichs,* 6) [Linz, 1959], 158 and fig. 58; Lambert, 4A, pl. II; and Bloch and Schnitzler, 2: 145 and fig. 630.

34. Paris, BN., MS. lat. 1152, fol. 4. See V. Leroquais, *Les Psautiers manuscrits latins des bibliothèques publiques de France,* 2 vols. (Macon, 1940–41), 2: 67, no. 314; Köhler, *Die karolingischen Minaturen,* 2: 106–7; Schramm and Mütherich, *Denkmäler der deutschen Könige,* 1: 131, no. 44; Bloch and Schnitzler, 2: 145 and fig. 636.

35. Mombritius, 31, lines 31–36; Maniacoria, *Vita Hieronymi (PL* 22: 185); Beleth, *De eccl. officiis,* 157i *(C.C.L. Con. med.* 41A: 301: "Iheronimus sub septem pontificibus Rome fuit et cardinalis in ecclesia beati Laurentii."

36. Stephan Kuttner, "Cardinalis: The History of a Canonical Concept," *Traditio* 3 (1945): 129–214, but esp. 138–52.

37. Ibid., 129–32, 145–46, 172–77; Peter Damianus, *Contra philargyriam,* 7 *(PL* 145: 540B); *Ep. I Leonis papae IX ad Michaelem Constantinopol. patriarcham,* 32 (ed. J. D. Mansi, *Sacrorum conciliorum nova collectio,* 19: 653B); *Die Kanonensammlung des Kardinals Deusdedit,* ed. V. Wolf von Glanvell (Paderborn, 1905), 268, all quoted by Kuttner.

38. *Plerosque nimirum* (Mombritius, p. 34, lines 14–26). The author began his account with the words "unum autem miraculum." See also Pöllmann, 471–75; Grete Ring, "St. Jerome Extracting the Thorn from the Lion's Foot," *Art Bulletin* 27 (1945): 188–96; the article on the iconography of St. Jerome by Maria Letizia Casanova in *B.S.* 6 (1965): 1132–38; Jungblut, 22–35; Herbert Friedmann, *A Bestiary for Saint Jerome. Animal Symbolism in European Religious Art* (Washington, D.C., 1980), 19–22, 229–68; and, for the literature on lions, L. Réau, *Iconographie de l'art chrétien* (Paris, 1955–59), 1: 92–94, and H. Van de Waal, *Iconoclass. An Iconographic Classification System,* 2–3. *Bibliography* (Amsterdam, 1973), 60–63.

39. *Fabulae,* III, 1 (story 231); *Caxton's Aesop,* ed. R. T. Lenaghan (Cambridge, Mass., 1967), 103–5; Jacques de Vitry, *Exempla,* ed. T. F. Crane (New York, 1890; reprint, 1971), no. 185, 78, follows Aesop and points the following moral: "Non igitur agrestes sitis aut rustici sed liberales et benivoli." In the Buddhist Jātaka (bk. II, no. 156), carpenters tame an elephant by removing a splinter of acacia wood from its infected foot: "So

ever after that, he used to pull up trees for them, or when they were chopping he would roll up the logs; or bring them their adzes and any tools they might want, holding everything in his trunk like grim death" (E. B. Cowell, ed., *The Jātaka or Stories of the Buddha's Former Births*, 6 vols. [Cambridge, 1895–1913], 2: 14). The story is very likely a reworking of the Aesopian fable and reached India from Greece. Similar tales circulated in China.

40. Seneca, *De beneficiis*, I, 19, 1; Aulus Gellius, V, 14 (quoting Apion, *Aegyptiaca*); and Aelian, *De natura animalium*, VII, 48. Cf. Pliny, *Hist. nat.* VIII, 21, 56–57, and John of Salisbury, *Policraticus*, V, 17 (ed. C. C. I. Webb [Oxford, 1909], 1: 361–62). Apion ended the story like this: "Afterwards, we used to see Androclus with the lion, attached to a slender leash, making the rounds of the shops throughout the city; Androclus was given money, the lion was sprinkled with flowers, and everyone who met them anywhere exclaimed: 'This is the lion that was a man's friend, this is the man who was physician to a lion' " (tr. J. C. Rolfe). George Bernard Shaw called the slave Androcles and made him a Christian.

41. Cyril of Scythopolis, *Vita sancti patris nostri Sabae*, 49 (Ed. Schwartz, *Texte und Untersuchungen zur Geschichte der altchristlichen Literatur*, [1939], 49(2): 138; tr. A.-J. Festugière, in *Les moines d'Orient* [Paris, 1962], 3(2): 65). On Sabas and Cyril, see also Altaner-Stuiber, 241 and A. Amore, in *B.S.* 11 (1968): 533–35; and for the monastery of S. Saba in Rome, Guy Ferrari, *Early Roman Monasteries* (Vatican City, 1957), 181–90.

42. Johannes Moschus, *Pratum spirituale*, 107 (*PL* 74: 172D–174B; *PG* 87(3): 2965C–2970B; ed. D.-C. Hesseling, in *Morceaux choisis du Pré spirituel de Jean Moschos* [Paris, 1931], 84–86; tr. M.-J. Rouët de Journel, in *S.C.* [Paris, 1946], 12: 154–55).

43. Mirella Levi d'Ancona, *The Garden of the Renaissance. Botanical Symbolism in Italian Painting* (Florence, 1977), 377–81, assembles texts identifying thorns with sin and quotes Petrus Berchorius, *Morale reductorium super totam Bibliam* (Venice, heirs of Hieronymus Scotus, 1583), fol. 564, col. 1: "Spina pungens significat peccatum originale, quod pungit per carnis stimulum peccatores." For more details, see William S. Heckscher, "Dornauszieher," *Reallexikon zur deutschen Kunstgeschichte*, (1958), 4: cols. 289–99.

44. *Gesta Romanorum*, 104 (ed. Hermann Oesterley [Berlin, 1872], 434–35).

45. Wera von Blankenburg, *Heilige und dämonische Tiere. Die Symbolsprache der deutschen Ornamentik im frühen Mittelalter* (Leipzig, 1943), 214–24.

46. Edgar Hennecke, *New Testament Apocrypha*, ed. W. Schneemelcher, tr. R. M. Wilson et al., 2 vols. (Philadelphia, 1963–65), 2: 388–89. The Ephesus episode of the *Acta Pauli* has been reconstructed from eleven fragmentary pages of a Greek papyrus codex of c. 300 (Schmidt, with W. Schubart, *Acta Pauli, nach dem Papyrus der Hamburger Staats-und Universitäts-Bibliothek* [Glückstadt, 1936], 38–40, 85–98) and, for the baptism of the lion, from a fragmentary fourth-century Coptic papyrus in the Bodmer collection in Geneva (R. Kasser, "Acta Pauli 1959," *Revue d'histoire et de philosophie*

religieuses 40 [1960]: 45–57, but esp. 51, n. 61). Cf. Edgar J. Goodspeed, *The Epistle of Pelagia* (Chicago, 1931), 12.

47. Hennecke, 2: 372–73. See Hippolytus, *Com. in Dan.* III, 29 (*S.C.* [Paris, 1947], 14: 254), written c. 204: "If we believe that when Paul was condemned to the circus the lion which was set upon him lay down at his feet and licked him, why should we not also believe what happened in the case of Daniel?" Cf. W. Deonna, "Daniel, le 'maître des fauves': A propos d'une lampe chrétienne du Musée de Genève," *Artibus Asiae* 12 (1949): 119–40, 347–74. Also Jerome, *De vir. illus.* 7, who branded the Acts of Paul and Thecla "and the whole fable of the baptized lion" as apocryphal. Bruce M. Metzger, "St. Paul and the Baptized Lion," *Princeton Seminary Bulletin* 39(2) (November 1945): 11–21, includes a translation into English of the section of the Hamburg papyrus on Paul and the wild beasts.

48. *Plerosque nimirum* (Mombritius, 34, line 26–35, line 55).

49. *The Hieroglyphics of Horapollo*, I, 19 (tr. George Boas [New York, 1949], 70); Aelian, V, 39; *Physiologus Latinus*,. ed. Francis J. Carmody (Paris, 1939), 11: "Secunda natura leonis: cum dormierit, oculi eius uigilant, aperti enim sunt; sicut in Canticis Canticorum testatur sponsus, dicens: Ego dormio, et cor meum uigilat [Cant. 5:2]. Etenim corporaliter dominus meus obdormiens in cruce et sepultas, deitas eius uigilabat: Ecce non dormitabit neque dormiet qui custodit Israel" [Ps. 120:4].

50. R. A. Jairazbhoy, "Lions as Guardians and Bearers," *Oriental Influences in Western Art* (Bombay, 1965), 267–87. For Alexander, Diodorus Siculus, 18, 27. Four superb lions crouch at each corner of the lid of the so-called Alexander Sarcophagus in the Archeological Museum, Istanbul.

51. Marcellinus Comes, *Chronicon,* ad an. 392 (ed. Mommsen, *M.G.H. Auct. antiquiss.*, 11: 63): "Porro ad Bethleem oppidum iuvenis advenit, ubi prudens animal ad praesepe Domini se mox obtulit permansurum." Cf. *Plerosque nimirum* (Mombritius, 34): "Omni ergo belluina feritatis deposita rabie, coepit inter eos citro citroque quasi domesticum et tranquillum animal pariter commorari"; or *Legenda aurea*, 654: "leo . . . omni feritate deposita inter eos quasi domesticum animal habitavit."

52. Cf. Cardinal Baronius, *Annales ecclesiastici,* ad an. 420, XLIX (Lucca, Leonardus Venturinus, 1741, 7: 231, col. 1): "Id vero rerum ignaro de Hieronymo asserendi occasionem tribuisse videtur, quod ejusdem S. Hieronymi imago una cum leonis effigie antiquitus consueverit in Ecclesia pingi, utpote hieroglyphicum ejus in haereticis insectandis infracti roboris, et vehementis in eos, instar leonis rugitus, clamoris."

53. Petrus Berchorius, *Reductorium morale* (Venice, 1583), fol. 402, cols. 1–2.

54. K. Ziegler, "Orpheus und das Christentum," in Pauly-Wissowa, *Real-Encyclopädie* (1939), 18(1): 1313–16.

55. *Vita S. Pauli primi eremitae,* 16 (*PL* 23, 27C).

56. *Passio sancti Mammetis,* 20 (ed. H. Delehaye, *A.B.* 58: [1940], 140). Soldiers sent to fetch Mammas were instead captured by the lion. St. Mammas said to them: " 'Ecce leones ferocissimi mitiores sunt vobis; vos autem nec in tantis signis cognoscitis Christum?' Tunc illi clamabant dicentes: 'Libera

nos et credimus Christum Deum tuum esse verum Deum.'" For St.
Mammas see *Acta SS. Aug.* (Paris, 1867), 3: 4233–46; Anne Hadjinicolaou-
Morava, *Ho hagios Mamas* (Athens, 1953); and B. Cignitti, in *B.S.* 8
(1966): 592–612. The anecdote is a reminiscence of a story in Apuleius *Met.*
8, 22.

57. François Halkin, "Un émule d'Orphée. La légende grecque inédite de saint
Zosime, martyr d'Anazarbe en Cilicie," *A.B.* 70 (1952): 249–61, and K.
Kunze, *B.S.* 12 (1969): 1497–98.

58. *Plerosque nimirum* (Mombritius, 34, lines 11–14 and 35, lines 55–56):
"Unum autem miraculum eius monasterii quoddam priscorum simile:
quod per succedentium relationem memoriae nondum religio abstulit: et a
religionis uiris qui caelestis amore patriae Bethleem fuere huc est delatum:
huic compendioso necto sermoni. . . . Haec autem Bethleem acta: et ab
incolis loci illius ita fuisse narrantur."

59. A further episode in the legend of St. Sabas is only an apparent exception.
St. Sabas had a disciple named Flavius, who owned an ass. When Sabas sent
him off on distant business, Flavius entrusted the ass to the care of the lion.
Holding the halter in his mouth, the lion watched over the ass while he
drank and pastured. So far the narratives are similar enough. But the rest is
completely different. For while he was away, Flavius neglected his salvation, gave way to temptation and fornicated. On that same day, the lion
devoured the ass. The cause of this, Flavius realized, was his own sin. No
longer daring to show himself before St. Sabas, he remained in his garden
lamenting his sin (Cyril of Scythopolis, *Vita Sabae*, 49, ed. Schwartz, 139;
Festugière, *Les moines d'Orient*, 3(2): 65–66.

60. Moschus, *Pratum spirituale*, 107 (*PL* 74: 172-D-174B: *PG* 87(3): 2965C–
2970B; Hesseling, 87–91). When Gerasimus died, the lion was inconsol-
able. He lay down on the grave, striking his head on the ground and
roaring, and remained there until he died on the grave of the old man. The
moral: "This did not happen because the lion had a rational soul, but
because God wanted to glorify those who glorify Him, not only during
their lifetimes, but also after their deaths, and to show us in what manner
animals were subject to Adam before he disobeyed the commandment and
was expelled from the paradise of delights."

61. On Moschus, see H. Usener, *Der heilige Tychon* (Leipzig, 1907), 86–100;
E. Mioni, "Il Pratum spirituale di Giovanni Mosco," *Orientalia Christiana
Periodica* 17 (1951): 61–94; N. H. Baynes, "The Pratum spirituale,"
Orientalia Christ. Per. 13 (1947): 404–14; and Altaner-Stuiber, 241–42.

62. Richard Krautheimer, *Rome, Profile of a City, 312–1308* (Princeton, 1980),
89–91.

63. Ambrogio Traversari translated the *Pratum* in 1423–1424 and dedicated it
to Pope Eugenius IV in 1431. See E. Mioni, "Le 'Vitae patrum' nella
traduzione di Ambrogio Traversari," *Aevum* 24 (1950): 319–31, and
Charles L. Stinger, *Humanism and the Church Fathers. Ambrogio Traversari
(1386–1439) and Christian Antiquity in the Italian Renaissance* (Albany, N.Y.,
1977), 127. A number of lives from the *Pratum* had been translated earlier

under the title *Liber de miraculis* (ed. Michael Huber [Heidelberg, 1913]) by Johannes Monachus, who belonged to a monastery in Amalfi and lived between 950 and 1050. He did not translate the story of Gerasimus and the lion. Traversari's Latin version was turned into Italian in 1443 by the poet Feo Belcari (1410–1484).

64. He is identified as "Geronimus" in a miniature on the Boethius Diptych (c. 650) in the Museo Civico Cristiano, Brescia, where he appears with St. Augustine and Gregory the Great. This is the earliest surviving representation of Jerome. Reproduced in Pöllmann, pl. facing p. 353, and M. Salmi and G. Muzzioli, *Mostra storica nazionale della miniatura* (Rome, 1953), pl. 10. See also R. Delbrück, *Die Consulardiptychen* (*Studien zur spätantiken Kunstgeschichte*, 2, [1929]), cat. no. 7, pp. 103–6, and Gaetano Panazza, *La Pinacoteca e i musei di Brescia* (Bergamo, 1968), 58–59, with full bibliography on 216–17. Cf. *Acta SS. Sept.* (Antwerp, 1762), 8: 661–62; Vaccari, "Le antiche vite," 44–45; and Cavallera, 1(2): 141–42.

65. Cassiodorus, *Institutiones*, I, 8, 1, (ed. R. A. B. Mynors, [Oxford, 1937], 28).

66. For the *spuria* attributed to Jerome, see *PL* 23: 1329–1402; 26: 821–1270; 30, in its entirety; F. Lanzoni, "La leggenda di S. Girolamo," pp. 19–29; *Clavis*, 142–48, nn. 623a–642; P. Glorieux, *Pour revaloriser Migne* (Lille, 1952), 17–22; *PL Supplementum*, ed. A. Hamman (Paris, 1960), 2: 264–328; B. Fischer, *Vetus Latina*, I(1). *Verzeichnis der Sigel für Kirchenschriftsteller*, 2d ed. (Freiburg-im-Breisgau, 1963), 307–12; Lambert, 3A–B, nn. 301–807, who gives an almost exhaustive listing, with incipits, explicits, lists of manuscripts, and secondary literature; R. E. Reynolds, "The pseudo-Hieronymian De Septem ordinibus ecclesiae," *Revue Bénédictine* 80 (1970): 238–52; and Avrom Saltman, ed., *Pseudo Jerome. Quaestiones on the Book of Samuel* (*Studia Post-Biblica*, 26) (Leiden, 1975).

67. *Ep.* 22, 7.

68. *Regula monacharum*, 26 (*PL* 30: 414C).

69. *Liber de ortu beatae Mariae et infantia salvatoris, a beato Matthaeo evangelista Hebraice scriptus et a beato Ieronimo presbytero in Latinum translatus* = *Pseudo-Matthaei evangelium* (ed. C. von Tischendorf, *Evangelia apocrypha*, 2d ed. [Leipzig, 1876], xx–xxi, 51–112; E. Amann, *Le Protoévangile de Jacques et ses remaniements latins* (Paris, 1910), 272–339). Written before the middle of the ninth century and prefaced by Pseudo-Jerome, *Epp.* 48 and 49 (*Clavis*, no. 633, p. 146, and Lambert, 3A, nos. 348–49). See also M. R. James, *The Apocryphal New Testament* (Oxford, 1955; 1st ed. 1924), 70–79; ibid., *Latin Infancy Gospels: A New Text* (Oxford, 1927); Hennecke, *New Testament Apocrypha*, 1: 406–7; E. de Strycher, *La Forme la plus ancienne du Protoévangile de Jacques* (*Subsidia Hagiographica*, 33) (Brussels, 1961), 41–43; and Jan Gijsel, *Die unmittelbare Textüberlieferung des sog. Pseudo-Matthaeus* (Brussels, 1981).

70. Pseudo-Jerome, *Ep.* 50, "De nativitate Mariae" (*PL* 30: 297–305). Written by Paschasius Radbertus, abbot of Corbie (d. 865). *Clavis*, no. 633, p. 146; Lambert, 3A, no. 350.

71. Pseudo-Jerome, *Ep.* 9 (ed. Albert Ripberger, *Der Pseudo-Hieronymus-Brief IX "Cogitis me." Ein erster marianischer Traktat des Mittelalters von Paschasius Radbert, Spicilegium Friburgense,* 9, [Freiburg-Schweiz, 1962], 57–113). Lambert, 3A, no. 309, lists 324 manuscripts. See T. A. Agius, "On Pseudo-Jerome, Epistle IX," *Journal of Theological Studies* 24 (1922–23): 176–83; C. Lambot, "L'homélie du Pseudo-Jérôme sur l'Assomption et l'Evangile de la Nativité de Marie d'après une lettre inédite d'Hincmar," *Revue Bénédictine* 46 (1934): 265–82; G. Quadrio, *Il trattato "De assumptione Beatae Mariae Virginis" dello Pseudo-Agostino e il suo influsso nella theologia assunzionistica latina (Analecta Gregoriana,* 52) (Rome, 1951), 86–90, 175–180; and H. Barre, "La lettre du Pseudo-Jérôme sur l'Assomption est-elle antérieure à Paschase Radbert?" *Revue Bénédictine* 68 (1958); 203–25 (the answer is no).

72. Pseudo-Jerome, *Liber Comitis* (*PL* 30: 487–532). *Clavis,* 444, no. 1960; Lambert, 3A, no. 372. See also Berno of Reichenau, *De officio Missae* (*PL* 142: 1057D); Honorius of Autun, *Gemma animae,* II, 17 and IV, 1 (*PL* 172: 621A and 689C); Johannes Beleth, *Summa de eccl. officiis,* 19c–d (*C.C.L. Con. med.* 41A: 41–42). Cf. W. H. Frere, *Studies in Early Roman Liturgy, 3. The Roman Epistle-Lectionary* (Oxford, 1935), 73–79, and Gerhard Kunze, *Die gottesdienstliche Schriftslesung* (Göttingen, 1947), 1: 52–53.

73. *Ep.* 64, 8. Cf. *Ep.* 60, 19.

74. W. W. Heist, *The Fifteen Signs before Doomsday* (East Lansing, Mich., 1952), and ibid., "The Fifteen Signs before Judgement. Further Remarks," *Medieval Studies* 22 (1960): 192. Lambert, 3B, nn. 652–60.

75. Fully documented in the lists of manuscripts assembled by Lambert. The surviving manuscripts of the *Epistulae* by century are as follows, a count that confirms Jerome's special popularity in the ninth, twelfth, and fifteenth centuries: VI, 5; VII, 5; VIII, 28; IX, 122; X, 99; XI, 141; XII, 364; XIII, 175; XIV, 155; XV, 604; XVI, 35; XVII, 2.

76. *Comment. in Joan.,* Praef. (*PL* 100: 740A). Cf. *PL* 101: 279C; 742B; and 774A.

77. *PL* 125: 246C.

78. *Policraticus,* ii, 22; vii, 10 (ed. Webb, 1: 131; 2: 134). Cf. ibid., 1: xxxvi.

79. J. Uttenweiler, "Zur Stellung des hl. Hieronymus im Mittelalter," *Benediktinische Monatschrift* 2 (1920): 522–41; Laistner, "The Study of St. Jerome in the Early Middle Ages," 235–256; Henri de Lubac, *Exégèse médiévale. Les quatres sens de l'Ecriture,* 2 vols. in 3 (Paris, 1959–64), 2(1): 199–285; Augustine, *Contra Julianum,* I, vii, 34 (*PL* 44: 665, n. 2): "instar lampadis resplenduit" (although the phrase does not occur in the early manuscripts); Cassian, *Contra Nestorium,* VII, 26 (C.S.E.L. 17: 384): "Hieronymus, catholicorum magister, cuius scripta per uniuersum mundum quasi diuinae lampades rutilant."

80. *Guigonis maioris Cartusiae prioris quinti ad fratres Durbonenses De supositiis B. Hieronymi epistolis* (*PL* 30: 307–8; 153: 593–94). See also U. Chevalier, *Répertoire des sources historiques du Moyen Age. Bio-Bibliographie* (Paris,

1883), 945, and Lambert, 3A, no. 353 (only two MSS.). The letter was first published by Mabillon.
81. *Legenda aurea*, 655, citing *Ep*. 49, 20.
82. I. Opelt, "Das Bienenwunder in der Ambrosius-Biographie des Paulinus von Mailand," *Vigiliae Christianae* 22 (1968): 38–44.
83. Pierre Courcelle, *Recherches sur saint Ambroise. "Vies" anciennes, culture, iconographie* (Paris, 1973).
84. *PL* 22: 199.

3: THE CULT

1. *Epistola beati Eusebii de morte gloriosissmi Hieronymi doctoris eximii; Epistola sancti Augustini Hipponensis episcopi ad Cyrillum Jerosolymitanum episcopum de magnificentiis beati Hieronymi; Epistola sancti Cyrilli de miraculis beati Hieronymi ad sanctum Augustinum* (*PL* 22: 239–326; ed. Joseph Klapper, *Schriften Johannes von Neumarkt*, 2. Teil. *Hieronymus. Die unechten Briefe des Eusebius, Augustinus, Cyrill zum Lobe des Heiligen, Vom Mittelalter zur Reformation*, 6 [Berlin, 1932]). *BHL*. 3866, 3867, and 3868.

Cavallera, 1(2): 144, distinguished Pseudo-Eusebius from the author of the other two letters and argued that he wrote in the twelfth century. In my opinion all three letters are the work of a single author writing between 1295 and 1334, probably in the first decade of the fourteenth century.

The *terminus post* of the first letter is 1295 because Pseudo-Eusebius quotes indirectly a passage from the decretal of Boniface VIII (20 September 1295) ordering the feasts of the doctors of the church to be celebrated *sub duplici solemnitate* (see above, p. 33):

Deinde pertransiens usque ad fines terre, sanando oppressos ab hereticorum iaculis, illuminando mentes hominum, *scripturarum enigmata reserando, soluendo nodos, obscura dilucidando, dubia exponendo*, confutando et corrigendo falsitates, verissima ex linguis quam plurimis adunando, ut nobis faceret uias uitae et nos adimpleret gaudio, letitia et exultacione. Templum domini corroborauit et eius aditum *ad instar lucerne non sub modio, sed supra candelabrum in domini aula posite*, dominico *irrigante* rore plenissime *fecundate*, posteris omnibus suaui verborum pre ceteris *elegancia singulari*, excellentia omnibus aliis patefecit. (*Ep. Ps.-Eusebii*, 2; *PL* 22: 240–41; Klapper, 13–15)

Compare C.I.C., *Lib. VI Decretalium*, III, tit. xxii, cap. 1:

Egregios quoque ipsius Doctores ecclesiae, beatos Gregorium, qui meritis inclytis sedis apostolicae curam gessit, Augustinum et Ambrosium, venerandos antistites, ac Hieronymum, sacerdotii praeditum titulo, eximios confessores summis attollere vocibus, laudibus personare praecipuis et specialibus disponit honoribus venerari. Horum quippe doctorum perlucida et salutaria documenta praedictam illustrarunt ecclesiam, decorarunt virtutibus, et moribus informarunt. Per ipsos praeterea, *quasi* luminosas ardentesque *lucernas super candelabrum in domo Domini positas*, errorum tenebris profugatis, totius corporis ecclesiae tanquam sidus irradiat matutinum. Eorum etiam *foecunda* facundia, coelestis *irrigui* gratia influente, *scripturarum aenigmata reserat, solvit nodos, obscura dilucidat, dubiaque declarat;* profundis quoque ac decoris illorum sermonibus ampla ipsius ecclesiae fabrica, velut gemmis vernantibus, rutilat, et verborum *elegantia singulari* gloriosius sublimata coruscat.

The list of manuscripts assembled by Lambert (3B, no. 903) strongly suggests that the other two letters also date after 1295: no manuscript of any of the letters can be dated incontestably before 1300.

All three letters were in circulation before 1334 when Giovanni d'Andrea began to use them in his *Hieronymianus*. Andrea recalls that he became especially devoted to Jerome twenty-five years earlier. If the reason for his conversion was a first reading of the apocryphal letters, as I suspect it was, the *terminus ante* may be as early as c. 1310.

The letters were probably published as a unit; for although individual letters circulated separately, they much more commonly appear together in the manuscripts. The same evidence suggests single authorship, a hypothesis given added weight by cross references among the three letters and by consistency of purpose and theme. Lambert tentatively identified the author as Johann von Neumarkt, bishop of Olmütz and chancellor of the emperor Charles IV, who translated the three letters into German around 1370, an attribution sufficiently disproved by chronology. García Jimenez de Cisneros, *Obras completas*, ed. Cipriano Barauta, 2 vols. (Montserrat, 1965), 2: 722, no. 2, has incomprehensibly suggested Lope de Olmedo (d. 1433). The author was certainly Italian and remains anonymous.

2. Lambert, 3B, no. 903, lists nearly 400 manuscripts, the bulk of them copied in the fifteenth century. Thirty-six printed editions appeared before 1501 (*G.W.* 3048, 9446–9481). See also D. Dodge, "An Apocryphal Letter of St. Augustine to Cyril and a Life of Jerome, Translated into Danish," *PMLA* 8(1893): 381–407; Matta Jaatinen, *Die mittelniederdeutsche Uebersetzung der sogenanten Hieronymus-Briefe* (Helsinki, 1944); J. Klapper, *Johann von Neumarkt, Bischof und Hofkanzler. Religiöse Frührenaissance in Böhmen zur Zeit Kaiser Karls IV* (Leipzig, 1964), 29–38; and Costanzo Di Girolamo, ed., *Libru di lu transitu et vita di Misser Sanctu Iheronimu (Collezione di testi siciliani dei secoli XIV e XV,* 15) (Palermo, 1982), with a valuable introduction.

3. Biblioteca Vaticana, MS. Barb. lat. 714, fols. 321–39. Cf. A. Poncelet, "Le Légendier de Pierre Calo," *A.B.* 24 (1910): 5–116.

4. *Catalogus sanctorum et gestorum eorum ex diversis et multis voluminibus collectus,* VIII, 132, Strasbourg ed. (1514), sig. E, vii–viii. Pietro de'Natali (Natalis, de Natalibus) finished the *Catalogus* on 26 May 1372, according to the colophon of a manuscript of the work copied in 1408 (Bibl. Vaticana, MS. Ottob. lat. 225, fol. 363, col. 2).

5. For works of art whose subjects come from these letters, see Helen I. Roberts, "St. Augustine in 'St. Jerome's Study.' Carpaccio's Painting and Its Legendary Source," *Art Bulletin* 41 (1959): 285–303 (full citation of

earlier literature); Jungblut, 35–40; George Kaftal, *Saints in Italian Art.*
Iconography of the Saints in Tuscan Painting (Florence, 1952), 523–35; *Iconography of the Saints in Central and South Italian Schools of Painting* (Florence, 1965), 593–98; *Iconography of the Saints in the Painting of North East Italy* (Florence, 1978), 478–506; Jeanne Courcelle and P. Courcelle, *Iconographie de St. Augustin. Les cycles du XIVe siècle* (Paris, 1965), 96–97 and pl. 96; *Les cycles du XVe siècle* (Paris, 1969), 104–5, 149–50, and pls. 64 and 109; P. Antin, "L'apparition de S. Jérôme et S. Jean Baptiste à S. Augustin par Mino de Fiesole," in *Recueil sur saint Jérôme (C.L. 95)* (Brussels, 1968), 24–26; Martin Davies, *National Gallery Catalogues. The Earlier Italian Schools,* 2d ed. (London, 1961), 486–89; and Erica Trimpi, " 'Iohannem Baptistam Hieronymo aequalem et non maiorem': A Predella for Matteo di Giovanni's Placidi Altar-Piece," *Burlington Magazine* 125 (1983): 457–66.

6. *Pro Milone,* 97.
7. *Ep. Ps.-Augustini (PL* 22: 281, 283; Klapper, 246, 248) and frequently elsewhere in the letters. For the changing and various meanings of *gloria,* see art. "Gloire," in *Dict. de théologie catholique* (1913), 6: 1386–1432, and A. J. Vermeulen, *The Semantic Development of Gloria in Early-Christian Latin (Latinitas Christianorum Primaeva,* 12) (Nijmegen, 1956).
8. *Ep. Ps.-Augustini (PL* 22: 281, 283; Klapper, 246, 248); *Ep. Ps.-Eusebii,* 1, 10 *(PL* 22: 240, 244; Klapper, 12, 18–19, 34–35); *Ep. Ps.-Cyrilli,* 25 *(PL* 22: 324; Klapper, 498–99).
9. *Ep. Ps.-Eusebii,* 7, 12 *(PL* 22: 242–43, 245; Klapper, 25–28, 44–45); *Ep. Ps.-Augustini (PL* 22: 282; Klapper, 249–51).
10. *Ep. Ps.-Eusebii,* 52 *(PL* 22: 274–75; Klapper, 209–13). See also below, chap. 7, n. 11.
11. *Ep. Ps.-Augustini (PL* 22: 283–85; Klapper, 255–66). The Augustinian Hermits of San Gimignano commissioned a fresco representing St. Augustine's first vision of St. Jerome from Benozzo Gozzoli in 1465. The program was devised by Domenico Strambi, a former student at the University of Paris who taught theology at the convent. The fresco has the following inscription:—*Quemadmodum Hieronimus paulo ante beatus / Augustinum de celesti gloria informavit.* See Courcelle and Courcelle, *Iconographie de St. Augustin* (Paris, 1969), 104–5 and pl. 64.
12. *Ep. Ps.-Augustini (PL* 22: 286–87; Klapper, 267–72).
13. *Ep. Ps.-Eusebii,* 53 *(PL* 22: 275–76; Klapper, 214–17).
14. *Ep. Ps.-Augustini (PL* 22: 287–88; Klapper, 274–81). Cyril of Jerusalem (!) had a similar vision in which John the Baptist reemphasized the fact that Jerome was equal to him in glory and sanctity: *Ep. Ps.-Cyrilli,* 25 *(PL* 22: 323–24; Klapper, 493–503). Cf. *Ep. Ps.-Eusebii,* 4 *(PL* 22: 242; Klapper, 22–25).
15. *Ep. Ps.-Augustini (PL* 22: 288–89; Klapper, 283–86).
16. *Ep. Ps.-Cyrilli,* 27 *(PL* 22: 326; Klapper, 510–11).
17. *PL* 22: 237–40; *Acta SS. Sept.* (1762), 8: 636, nn. 1090–93; Paris, Bibliothèque Nationale, MS. lat. 5588, fol. 43v: "Quomodo translatum fuit corpus beati hieronimi Romam." *B.H.L.* 3878; Lambert, 3B, no. 909. No

mention of Jerome's translation appears in the *Legenda aurea* (c. 1260), while Giovanni d'Andrea was able in 1334 to give a condensed account of it, found, he says, "in quadam legenda de Roma" (*Hieronymianus*, Basel ed. [1514], fol. 35). Other evidence allows a nearer dating. There survives in S. Maria Maggiore a mosaic picturing Jerome with the Madonna, executed for a monument to Cardinal Consalvo (d. 1299), with the legend *Recubo presepis ad antrum* (Carlo Cecchelli, *I mosaici della Basilica di S. Maria Maggiore* [Turin, 1956], fig. 85, p. 299). Francesco Pipino, O.P., writing in the early fourteenth century and recording the death of Pope Nicholas IV (whose name in religion was Fra Girolamo) on 4 April 1292, notes that he was buried "in Ecclesia Sanctae Mariae Majoris juxta sepulcrum Beati Hieronymi" (*Chronicon* IV, 23, ed. Muratori, *Rerum Italicarum Scriptores* [1726], 9: 728A). By 1292, then, Jerome was believed to lie in S. Maria Maggiore. The *Translatio beati Hieronymi* was thus probably composed sometime during the last decade of the thirteenth century, after the alleged reburial of Jerome's remains in Rome and before Ps.-Cyril finished his letter to Ps.-Augustine.

18. *PL* 22: 237–40. Cf. *Acta SS. Sept.* (1762), 8: 635, nn. 1086 and 1088, and Pietro de' Natali, *Catalogus sanctorum*, IV, 145, Strasbourg ed. (1514), sig. o, i, v. By the middle of the fourteenth century many people believed that the iron slab carried the following epitaph:

> Hic dux doctorum iacet et flos presbiterorum
> Sanctus Jeronimus, sed ei locus est nimis ymus.
> Hic tu discrete catholice sive facete
> Dic veniens: Ave! desuper ire cave.

The verses appear first in Giovanni d'Andrea's *Hieronymianus* (Cologne ed. [1482], sig. d, 6v), then independently in many manuscripts. Par. lat. 5588, fol. 44, reads *tumulus* instead of *nimis* in line 2. See J. Klapper, "Aus der Frühzeit des Humanismus. Dichtungen zu Ehren des heiligen Hieronymus," *Bausteine. Festschrift Max Koch zum 70. Geburtstage dargebracht,* ed. Ernst Boehlich and Hans Heckel (Breslau, 1926), 263; Lambert, 3B, nn. 928–29; and G. Biasiotti, "La riproduzione della Grotta della Natività di Betlemme nella basilica di Santa Maria Maggiore in Roma," *Dissertazioni della Pontificia Accademia Romana di Archeologia* 15 (1921): 95–110. In the early fourteenth century the patriarchal basilica was served by seventeen secular canons and eighteen beneficed chaplains (G. Falco, "Il catalogo di Torino delle chiese, degli ospedali, dei monasteri di Roma nel secolo XIV," *Archivio della R. Società Romana di Storia Patria* 32 [1909]: 431).

19. G. Ferri, "Le carte dell'archivio Liberiano dal secolo X al XV," *Archivio della R. Società Romana di Storia Patria* 30 (1907): 153–64; Biasiotti, "Le memorie di S. Girolamo in Santa Maria Maggiore di Roma," *Miscellanea Geronimiana*, 239.

20. Charles Seymour, Jr., *Sculpture in Italy 1400 to 1500* (Baltimore, 1966), 156–57 and 244, n. 7; Gianni Carlo Sciolla, *La scultura di Mino da Fiesole*

(Turin, 1970), 23–26. The subjects represented were Jerome in penitence; seated on a throne reading and explaining scripture to his monks; extracting the thorn from the lion's paw; the vindicated lion returning the stolen ass; and St. Augustine's vision of Jerome and John the Baptist. The panels are in Palazzo Venezia. Reproduced by Biasiotti, "Memorie di S. Girolamo," pl. 3, facing p. 243; Sciolla (one panel only), fig. 19; and Herbert Friedmann, *A Bestiary for St. Jerome* (Washington, D.C., 1980), 71, fig. 49 (one panel). Cardinal d'Estouteville's Roman patronage was generous. In addition to his benefactions to S. Maria Maggiore, he created Piazza Navona on the site of the ancient circus of Severus, restored the church of S. Agostino, and repaired the fortifications of Ostia and Frascati.

21. *Acta SS. Sept.* (1762), 8: 641–49, nn. 1114–51; Pastor, 22: 282–85; Armellini, *Le chiese di Roma dal secolo IV al XIX,* 2d ed., 2 vols. (Rome, 1942), 1: 292–93; Giorgio Koska, *S. Girolamo degli Schiavoni* (Rome, 1971), 69.

22. *PL* 22: 238.

23. *Acta SS. Sept.* (1762), 8:637B, no. 1095.

24. The monks of Cluny possessed Jerome's head too. They kept it in an ivory casket and claimed to have owned it since 1304. The cathedral church of Nepi also owned a head alleged to be Jerome's. The episcopal authorities said that it had been given to the church by three brothers, citizens of the town, who had stolen it from S. Maria Maggiore in 1527 during the sack of Rome. Gregory XIII, searching for a relic of each of the four doctors of the church, thought well enough of this claim to ask Alexius Stradella, bishop of Nepi (1575–1580) to send him a piece (letter dated 28 April 1580). See *Acta SS. Sept.* (1762), 8: 649–56, nn. 1152–89; José de Sigüenza, *Fundación del monasterio de el Escorial* (Madrid, 1963), 371; A. Benet, "Le trésor de l'abbaye de Cluny," *Revue de l'art chrétien* 6 (1888): 197; X. Barbier de Montault, "Le culte des Docteurs de l'Eglise à Rome," *Revue de l'art chrétien* 43 (1893): 106; and D. Bethell, "The Lives of St. Osyth of Essex and St. Osyth of Aylesbury," *A.B.* 88 (1970): 97, n. 5.

25. *Ep. Ps.-Eusebii,* 54 (*PL* 22: 276–77; Klapper, 221–24).

26. *Ep. Ps.-Cyrilli,* 2–3 (*PL* 22: 290–92; Klapper, 299–301). Prayers for the dead sometimes referred to this miracle: "Largitor gratiarum deus, qui pro defensione fidei per beatum Hieronimum tres simul mortuos suscitasti, nostros et omnes in vera fide defunctos a delictorum quae lugent laqueis et latebris liberatos tuae lucis facias esse consortes" (Paris, Bibliothèque Nationale, MS. lat. 1865, fol. 3r).

27. *Ep. Ps.-Cyrilli,* 7 (*PL* 22: 304–6; Klapper, 381–89). Cf. B. de Gaiffier, "Un thème hagiographique, le pendu miraculeusement sauvé," *Revue Belge d'archéologie et d'histoire de l'art* 13 (1943): 123–48, and Kaftal, *Iconography of the Saints in Central and South Italian Schools of Painting* (Florence, 1965), 598, fig. 693.

28. *Ep. Ps.-Cyrilli,* 11 and 13 (*PL* 22: 308, 310; Klapper, 404–7, 415–16).

29. Plutarch, *Theseus,* 36; *Cimon,* 8, 5–7. See Friedrich Pfister, *Der Reliquienkult im Altertum,* 2 vols. (Giesen, 1909–12), 1: 198–204; H. Delehaye, *Les légendes hagiographiques,* 4th ed. (Brussels, 1955), 153–54; and Patrick J.

Geary, *Furta sacra. Thefts of Relics in the Central Middle Ages* (Princeton, 1978).

30. The story was first recorded by Pietro Giorgi Tolomei about 1472 but is best known in the narrative by the poet Giovanni Battista Spagnoli of Mantua after he visited the sanctuary in 1489. See Luca da Monterado, *Storia della devozione e dei pellegrinaggi a Loreto (sec. XIV–XV)* (Bahia, 1954); Floriano Grimaldi, *Il libro lauretano. Edizioni e illustrazioni (1489–1599)* (Macerata, 1973); and Kathleen Weil-Garris, *The Santa Casa di Loreto. Problems in Cinquecento Sculpture,* 2 vols. (New York, 1977), 1:1–11.

31. *Vita Hieronymi (PL* 22: 185).

32. How closely related are the *Translatio corporis beati Hieronymi* and the three apocryphal letters remains uncertain. Jerome's devotion to the Virgin Mary is emphasized only in the *Translatio,* but this may be due to the importance Mary would naturally have in a narrative mainly concerned with Jerome's reburial in a church dedicated to her. Nevertheless, the *Translatio* and the letters share several motifs (the appearance of Jerome in dreams *in visione terna,* for example, and the regular accompaniment of apparitions by brilliant light, sweet singing, and ineffable fragrances); and reputable judges, among them Erasmus, have noted a sufficient similarity of tone and language to suggest a single author (Lanzoni, "Leggenda di San Girolamo," *Miscellanea Geronimiana,* 39, and Cavallera, 1 (2):144). The hypothesis is plausible, attractive, and unconfirmed.

The further hypothesis of Dominican authorship rests in part on the special stress the letters lay on preaching (for example, *PL* 22: 247–48; Klapper, 58–62), in part on the author's understanding of *gloria* and *beatitudo.* For Aquinas possession of the highest good was an intellectual operation, a vision of the divine essence. Duns Scotus taught that an operation of the will was fundamental to glory and beatitude and that man's highest happiness was a form of love. A third group of scholastic theologians argued that beatitude did not consist solely in vision or solely in love but in both love and vision. Of these solutions Ps.-Cyril chose the Thomist: "Visio est cognitio divina, in qua tota consistit beatitudo sanctorum," and again, "in patria etiam beatorum omnes animae gloriosae divinam contemplantur speciem, in qua omnis consistit gloria" (*PL* 22: 290, 294; Klapper, 296–97, 319). Cf. *Summa theologiae,* IaIIae, quaest.4, art.5: "Unde manifestum est quod animae Sanctorum separatae a corporibus, ambulant per speciem, Dei essentiam videntes, in quo est vera beatitudo," and *Summa contra gentiles,* IV, 91: "Statim igitur cum anima sancta a corpore separatur, Deum per speciem videt: quod est ultima beatitudo."

A related problem concerns the timing of the beatific vision. When do the souls of the just first see God face to face? Immediately is the right answer. Many Greeks, though, taught that souls will not enjoy the happiness of heaven (or suffer the pains of hell) until they are reunited with their bodies after the Last Judgment, a proposition regularly refuted by Dominicans attacking the errors of the Eastern church (*Tractatus contra errores Graecorum,* produced in 1253 by Dominicans in Constantinople [*PG* 140:

511]; Aquinas, *Summa contra gentiles*, IV, 91: "Quod animae statim post separationem a corpore poenam vel praemium consequuntur. . . . Per hoc autem excluditur error quorundam Graecorum, qui purgatorium negant, et dicunt animas ante corporum resurrectionem neque ad caelum ascendere, neque in infernum demergi"; Manuel Caleca, Dominican patriarch of Constantinople in the mid-fourteenth century, *Adversus Graecos*, 4, *De dormientibus (PG* 52:225). Ps.-Cyril thus attributed a Dominican teaching to St. Jerome and invented a miracle to prove it and refute the error of the Greeks (cf. above, p. 59).

33. *Acta SS. Sept.* (1762), 8:637A-B, nn. 1094–95; Ferri, "Le carte dell'archivio Liberiano," 163–64; and Biasiotti, "Memorie di S. Girolamo in Santa Maria Maggiore," 238–39. For the text of Pope Pius's letter, which the canons caused to be inscribed on a marble plaque, see Barbier de Montault, "Le culte des Docteurs de l'Eglise à Rome," 107; and for Cajetan's vision, Paul Hallett, *Catholic Reform: A Life of St. Cajetan of Thiene* (Westminster, Md., 1959), 45–47, called to my attention by Father Kenneth Jorgensen S.J.

34. *B.H.L.* 3876. There are three editions: the first, Cologne, [Konrad] Winters, 9 August 1482 (Hain, 1082, and *G.W.* 1727); a second, Paris, Johannes Petit, Johannes Frellon, and Jehan Barbier, 1511 (Rome, Biblioteca Nazionale, a rare volume called to my attention by Ms. Catherine Carbelleira); and Basel, A. Petrus de Langendorff for Leonhardus Alentseus et Luc. fratres, June 1514, which reproduces the Paris edition of 1511. For partial lists of the manuscripts, see Lambert, no. 907, as well as R. Sabbadini, *Le scoperte dei codici latini e greci ne' secoli XIV e XV. Nuove ricerche* (Florence, 1914), 156–63, and G. Pozzi, "Postille autografice di Bonsignore de' Bonsignori canonista a Praga," *Italia mediovale e umanistica*, (1958), 1: 347–50. Although Andreae himself says that he wrote the book in 1334 (*In Sextum Decretalium librum Novella commentaria*, De decimis, cap. 2, ed. P. Vendramaenus [Venice, Franciscus Franciscus, 1581], fol. 121, col. 2), there is evidence that he continued to work on the text until 1346/47: he mentions the death of Bishop Superanzio di Cervia (he died in 1337), while 1346 is the date of publication supplied by a manuscript in the Collegio di Spagna in Bologna (MS. 278, c. 1348, it too called to my attention by Catherine Carbelleira), as well as the colophon of the edition of 1482: "Extitit autem publicatum hoc opus anno domini .M.ccc.xlvi. paulo ante obitum Johannis Andree, qui obiit anno domini .M.ccc. xlviij. vij die Julij." Finally, he reports in pt. 4 of the *Hieronymianus* itself (Cologne ed. [1482], sig. 1, ii, v, col. 1) that he has just found a book he had been looking for, and gives the date: "Novissime autem sive currentis anni quadragesimi sexti die penult."

35. F. C. von Savigny, *Geschichte des römischen Rechts im Mittelalter* (Hamburg, 1831), 6: 87–111; J. F. von Schulte, *Die Geschichte der Quellen und Literatur des canonischen Rechts von Gratian bis auf die Gegenwart* (Stuttgart, 1877), 2: 208–10; A. Palmieri, "Un episodio nella vita di Giovanni d'Andrea ed una vecchia questione di diritto," *Atti e Memorie della R. Deputazione di Storia*

patria per le province di Romagna, ser. 3 (1907), 25: 1–15; J. Klapper, "Aus der Frühzeit des Humanismus," 255–62; Guido Rossi, "Contributi alla biografia del canonista Giovanni d'Andrea," *Rivista trimestrale di diritto e procedura civile* (1957), 11: 1451–1501; S. Stelling-Michaud, in *Dictionnaire de droit canonique* (1957), 6: 89–92; G. Le Bras et al., *Histoire du droit et des institutions de l'Eglise en Occident, 7. L'age classique, 1140–1378* (Paris, 1965), 327–28; and Costanzo Di Girolamo, op. cit., xii–xiv.

36. *Hieronymianus* (Basel ed. [1514]), fols. 16v–17.
37. Ibid., fol. 16v.
38. Jungblut, 29–31, 269–70.
39. Jean Porcher, *Les Belles Heures de Jean de France, duc de Berry* (Paris, 1953), pls. 122–33; Millard Meiss, *French Painting in the Time of Jean de Berry. The Limbourgs and Their Contemporaries,* 2 vols. (New York, 1974), 1: 127–28. The entire cycle is attractively reproduced in color in M. Meiss and Elizabeth Beatson, *The Belles Heures of Jean, Duke of Berry* (New York, 1974).
40. *Hieronymianus,* fol. 53; Klapper, "Aus der Frühzeit des Humanismus," 265–66:

> Ecclesiae doctor, Ciceronis codice flagrans,
> Cum tibi Stridoni dederat tria famina Roma,
> Verbera sancta luis. Promotus cardine sacro
> Corrigis errores. Falso tibi crimina vestis
> Addidit. Hinc aemulus Bethleem petis. Ardua fundas
> Multis claustra viris. Sacros, Hieronyme, libros
> Transfers et condis politi spectacula regni.
> Tunc leo mitescit, iussis obtemperat almis:
> Ligna tulit, raptumque gemit, laetusque reducit.
> Alta doces moriens, presepe conderis antro.
> Te nunc Roma tenet: te templo Virginis orat.
> Glorificus miris pictoris ordine clares.

The verses (by one Franciscus Thebaldus) are based on a hymn (*Hieronymianus,* fol. 54v; Klapper, "Frühzeit," 263–64), popularized by Andrea. Its stanzas also may be a literary source of the Jerome cycle in the *Belles Heures.* The first five miniatures, for example, show Jerome at school in Rome listening to a lecture on Plato, the Ciceronian dream, Jerome's elevation to the cardinalate, his arrival in church in female dress, and his departure from Rome. Compare the second and third stanzas of the hymn:

> Lege sub trina modulatus ora,
> Tullii lingua vagusque Platonis,
> Iussus est caedi gravibus flagellis
>   Judice celso.

> Post quod sacrorum studiis inherens
> Romae sacratus roseo galero
> Bethleem pergens emulata linquit
>   Vestis iniquae.

Later verses recall his penitence in the desert, the miracle of the lion, his translation of the Bible, the foundation of the Bethlehem monastery, his death (dependent on Pseudo-Eusebius), and the translation of his body to Rome. To the manuscripts listed by Klapper may be added Par. lat. 1428, fols. 17r–v and 5588, fol. 43v.

41. *Hieronymianus*, fols. 17–18.
42. Ibid., fols. 46v–49. Johannes Andreae commissioned Petrus de Viterbo, an Augustinian Hermit, to compose an office for the Dominicans of Troia; it was widely used later in the convents of the Hieronymite congregations (text in Klapper, "Frühzeit," 273–78).
43. Lope de Olmedo, *Laudatio Hieronymi* (*B.H.L.* 3876b; Lambert, 3B, no. 913); Vat. lat. 2666, fols. 356–60v; José de Sigüenza, *Historia de la Orden de San Jerónimo* (*Nueva Biblioteca de Autores Españoles*), 2 vols. (Madrid, 1907–9), 1: 2a–5b.
44. John Moorman, *A History of the Franciscan Order from Its Origins to the Year 1517* (Oxford, 1968), 334.
45. Pia Cividali, *Il beato Giovanni dalle Celle* (*Memorie della R. Accademia dei Lincei*, ser. 5, 12, fasc. 5 [Rome, 1907]), 354–477; John Henderson, "The Flagellant Movement and Flagellant Confraternities in Central Italy, 1260–1400," *Studies in Church History* 15 (Oxford, 1978), 147–60. For recent surveys of the Italian church and religious life in this period, see Brian Pullan, *A History of Early Renaissance Italy* (London, 1973), 60–80; Denys Hay, *The Church in Italy in the Fifteenth Century* (Cambridge, 1977), with a rich bibliography; and John Larner, *Italy in the Age of Dante and Petrarch, 1216–1380* (London, 1980), 228–55.
46. *Acta SS. Iulii* (Antwerp, 1731), 7: 333–408; Georg Dufner, *Geschichte der Jesuaten* (Rome, 1975), passim, but especially 3–55 (on Giovanni Colombini).
47. Dufner, *Jesuaten*, 183, quoting the *Tractatus sive alligationes pro ordine Iesuatorum* of Antonio Bettini da Siena, who in 1461 became bishop of Foligno.
48. M. Faloci-Pulignani, *Delle profezie del beato Tommasuccio-Saggio bibliografico* (Foligno, 1881); "Le arti e le lettere alla corte dei Trinci," *Giornale Storico della Letteratura Italiana* 1 (1883): 211–24; *Le profezie del beato Tommasuccio da Foligno* (Foligno, 1887); "La leggenda del beato Tommasuccio," *Miscellanea Francescana di Storia, di Lettere, di Arti*, N.S. 31 (1931): 149–51, 244–251; Carlo Frati, *I codici danteschi della Biblioteca Universitaria di Bologna* (Florence, 1923), app. 4 ("Profezia inedita di fra Tommasuccio da Foligno"), 154–74; Niccolò Del Re, in *B.S.* 12 (1969): 614–16.
49. Lope de Olmedo, *Laudatio Hieronymi* (Vat. lat. 2666, fols. 360–360v); Sigüenza, *Orden de San Jerónimo*, 1: 6a–8b; Heimbucher, 1: 592–94; Ignacio de Madrid, "La Orden de San Jerónimo en España. Primeros pasos para una historia critica," *Studia Monastica* 3 (1961): 409–27; Albert Sicroff, "The Jeronymite Monastery of Guadalupe in 14th- and 15th-Century Spain," in *Collected Studies in Honor of Américo Castro's Eightieth Year* (Oxford, 1965), 397–422; C. F. Fraker, "Gonçalo Martínez de Medina,

the *Jerónimos* and the *Devotio moderna,*" *Hispanic Review* 34 (1966): 197–217; Odette d'Allerit, "Hiéronymites," *Dictionnaire de spiritualité* (1969), 7: 451–62; *Studia Hieronymiana. VI Centenario de la orden de San Jerónimo,* 2 vols. (Madrid, 1973); J. Revuelta, *Los Jerónimos, fundación y primera expansión (1373–1414)* (Guadalajara, 1982); and J. R. L. Highfield, "The Jeronimites in Spain, Their Patrons and Success, 1373–1516," *Journal of Ecclesiastical History* 34 (1983): 513–33.

50. Pierre Hélyot, *Dictionnaire des ordres religieux* (Paris, 1848), 2: 602–7; *Bullarum diplomatum et previlegiorum sanctorum Romanorum Pontificum* (1859), 4: 643–54; D. Brunori, *L'Eremo di S. Girolamo a Fiesole* (Fiesole, 1920); Heimbucher, 1:596; G. Respini, in *B.S.* 3 (1963): 797–99; Bernard Ridderbos, *Saint and Symbol. Images of Saint Jerome in Early Italian Art* (Groningen, 1984), 73–88, contains a valuable account of the Compagnia di San Girolamo.

51. *Acta SS. Iunii* (Antwerp, 1701), 3: 531–49; Hélyot, 2: 588–602; Heimbucher, 1: 594–95; G. Battista Sajanello, *Historica Monumenta Ordinis S. Hieronymi Congregationis B. Petri de Pisis,* 2d ed. (Venice, 1759); L. Holstenius and M. Brockie, *Codex regularum monasticarum et canonicarum,* 6 vols. (Vienna, 1759), 6: 88–128 (the "constitutiones" and "regulae" of the congregation); P. Ferrara, *Luci ed ombre nella christianità del secolo XIV. Il beato Pietro Gambacorta da Pisa e la sua Congregazione (1380–1933)* (Vatican City, 1964), 59–255.

52. Lope de Olmedo, *Laudatio Hieronymi* (Vat. lat. 2666, fol. 360); *Responsio ad obtrectatores,* in Pius Rubeus, *Flores sancti patris Hieronymi* (Como, Io. Angelus Turatus, 1621), 313–52, Lope's defense of the *Regula monachorum; Codex regularum,* 6: 2. For the text of the Rule and the manuscripts, see *PL* 30: 319–86 and Lambert, 3B, no. 552.

53. Pius Rubeus, *Vita D. Lupi de Olmeto,* in *Flores,* 353–425; Sigüenza, *Orden de San Jerónimo,* 1: 315b–318b; Hélyot, 2: 607–14; *Codex regularum,* 3: 43–83; Heimbucher, 1: 595–96; Sicroff, "Guadalupe," 23–25.

54. Antonmaria Biscioni, ed., *Lettere di santi e beati fiorentini* (Florence, 1736), 93–95.

55. *Preparantia Christi Iesu habitationem et mansionem ineffabilem et divinam in nostris,* ed. Ronald G. Musto, in *Archivium Franciscanum Historicum* 73 (1980): 85–89; Nicola Mattioli, *Il beato Simone Fidati da Cascia dell'ordine romitano di S. Agostino e i suoi scritti editi ed inediti* (Rome, 1898), 467–71. For Angelo Clareno, see Gordon Leff, *Heresy in the Later Middle Ages,* 2 vols. (Manchester, 1967), 1: 168–75, 230–34, and Musto, "*The Letters of Angelo Clareno*" (Ph.D. diss., Columbia University, 1977), Introduction.

56. Adolfo Bartoli, ed., *Le lettere del B. Gio. Colombini da Siena* (Lucca, 1856), ep. 95, p. 228. For Paoluccio de' Trinci see D. Nimmo, "Poverty and Politics: The Motivation of Fourteenth-Century Franciscan Reform in Italy," *Studies in Church History* 15 (1978): 161–78.

57. *Ep.* 14, 1; *Comm. in Michaeam,* II, 6 (*C.C.L.* 76: 502).

58. *Ep. Ps.-Eusebii,* 17 (*PL* 22: 248; Klapper, 65).

59. Bartoli, *Lettere del Colombini,* ep. 1, p. 2.

60. *Lettere di santi e beati fiorentini,* pp. 87–88.
61. Bartoli, *Lettere del Colombini,* ep. 13, p. 52. Cf. *Epp.* 53, 3 and 62, 2 (*pia rusticitas*); not that Jerome really approved of rusticity, even that "which some people consider holy, arguing that they are disciples of fishermen, as though they were just precisely because they are ignorant" (*Ep.* 27, 1).
62. Pius Rubeus, *Vita Lupi,* in *Flores,* 391–400; *Contra Vigilantium,* 15 (*PL* 23: 351).
63. M. Laclotte and Elizabeth Mognetti, *Avignon. Musée du Petit Palais. Peinture italienne* (*Inventaire des collections publiques françaises,* 21), 2d ed. (Paris, 1977), nos. 69 and 139; Richard Spear, "Domenichino's Early Frescoes at S. Onofrio," *Arte Antica e Moderna* (1966): 223–31; F. Bisogni, "Contributo per un problema ferrarese," *Paragone* 23 (1972): 69–79 and fig. 44; Mina Gregori and T. Frati, *L'opera completa di Zurbarán* (Milan, 1973), no. 283 and pl. 56; Jonathan Brown, *Images and Ideas in Seventeenth-century Spanish Painting* (Princeton, 1978), 111–27; J. Hernandez Diaz, "Juan de Valdés Leal y los Jerónimos de Buenavista," *Studia Hieronymiana,* 2: 222–23.
64. Pius Rubeus, *Vita Lupi,* in *Flores,* 400–401; *Codex regularum,* 6: 104.
65. *Acta SS. Iunii* (1701), 3: 535–37; *Codex regularum,* 6: 89–90; Ferrara, *Gambacorta, 59–60.*
66. There was no "Penitent St. Jerome in the Wilderness" on Giovanni d'Andrea's house façade, nor is there one among the miniatures in the *Belles Heures.* No example before 1400 is listed in the Index of Christian Art, although the multiplication of hermit saints in penitence in the fifteenth century (John the Baptist, Mary Magdalene, St. Mary the Egyptian, and St. Anthony, as well as St. Jerome) was prefigured in a fresco of about 1350 in the Campo Santo of Pisa showing hermit saints in the Egyptian Thebaid. On the iconography of the penitent Jerome, see Pöllmann, 475–83; Jungblut, 137–246; Rudolf Wittkower, "Desiderio da Settignano's *St. Jerome in the Desert," U.S. National Gallery of Art. Studies in the History of Art* (1971–72), 7–37; Millard Meiss, "Scholarship and Penitence in the Early Renaissance: The Image of St. Jerome," *Pantheon* 32 (2) (1974): 134–40; Herbert Friedmann, *A Bestiary for Saint Jerome,* 48–100, marvelously illustrated; and Ridderbos, *Saint and Symbol,* 63–88.
67. Marvin Eisenberg, "*The Penitent St. Jerome* by Giovanni Toscani," *Burlington Magazine* 118 (1976): 275–83.
68. Cesare Brandi, *La Regia Pinacoteca di Siena* (Rome, 1933), 257–59; Brandi, *Quattrocentisti senesi* (Milan, 1949), 256, pls. 92, 107–12; Piero Torriti, *La Pinacoteca Nazionale di Siena. I dipinti dal XII al XV secolo* (Genoa, 1977), 254–57. In the center of the altarpiece are the Madonna and Child adored by Blessed Giovanni Colombini and flanked by Saints Dominic, Jerome, Augustine, and Francis. Augustine holds an open book on which we read, "Sanctus Ieronymus presbiter greco latino et hebraico eloquio eruditus, cuius nobis eloquium ab oriente usque in occidentem instar solis lampas resplenduit" (Augustine, *Contra Iulianum,* I, vii, 34; *PL* 44: 665).
69. Luc. 18:13. "The tax collector, standing far off, would not even lift up his eyes to heaven, but beat his breast, saying, 'God, be merciful to me a

sinner!'" Cf. Jerome, *Adv. Pelagianos,* I, 17 (*PL* 23: 511): "Publicanus in Evangelio, qui percutiebat pectus, quasi thesaurum cogitationum pessimarum. . . ."

70. Martin Davies, *National Gallery Catalogues. The Earlier Italian Schools,* 2d ed. (London, 1961), 119–22; Philip Foster, "Donatello Notices in Medici Letters," *Art Bulletin* 62 (1980): 148–49.

71. *Ep.* 22, 7.

72. *Legenda aurea,* 653. See above, p. 24.

73. *Revelationes Stae. Birgittae,* 2 vols. (Rome, Ludovicus Grignanus, 1628), 1: 414; 2: 215–17. After her death fifteen prayers on the Passion were attributed to Birgitta and were extremely popular. She was believed to have recited them in Rome before an image of Christ crucified. In a vision the image of Christ spoke to her, promising her that "who so saith this a whole year he shall deliver .xv. soules oute of purgatory of his next kindred: and converte other .xv. sinners to good life: and other .xv. righteous men of his kindred shall persevere in good life. And what he desireth of God he shall have it if it be to the salvation of his soul" (*The Revelations of Saint Birgitta,* ed. W. P. Cumming, *Early English Text Society,* 178, [London, 1929], xxxvii, n. 2; *Quindecim orationes,* Rome, Stephan Plannck, c. 1495 [*G.W.* 4368], fols. 1–1v).

74. E. D. Theseider, *Epistolario di Santa Caterina da Siena (Fonti per la Storia d'Italia,* 82) (Rome, 1940), 31, 353.

75. L. Jacobilli, *Vite dei santi e beati dell'Umbria* (Foligno, 1647), 1: 22; Bartoli, *Lettere del Colombini,* ep. 15, p. 59.

76. S. Kuretsky, "Rembrandt's Tree Stump: An Iconographic Attribute of St. Jerome," *Art Bulletin* 56 (1974): 571–80.

77. *Lettere di santi e beati fiorentini,* 80; Florence, Biblioteca Nazionale Centrale, MS. Cl. XXXIX, 75, fols. 99–99v (the letters of Angelo Clareno, read in the ed. of Ronald Musto); Theseider, *Epistolario di Santa Caterina,* 64–65, 150–51, 246–47; best of all, perhaps, a letter of Blessed Simone Fidati da Cascia (d. 1348) to the *frati eremitani* of S. Maria del S. Sepolchro, whose way of life helped shape the spirituality of both the Spanish Hieronymites and Gambacorta's Girolamini:

> O quam felix qui gregem animalitatum in secreta deserti provexit et remotionem quesivit a turbis, sibi soli vacans dum in rubo caritatis ignem in penitentia et incommunicabilitate sui ipsius ad mundum veritatem et Christum in cruce pro nobis pendentem aspexit, qui omnis anime corporisque virtutes actu et intellectu actrahit ad seipsum, ut affectibus discalciatis ab operibus mortuis, appropinquari possit ad rubi videlicet crucis asperitatem. Que mundo inepta solum Christum a terra subvexit. De qua pro ignorantibus non pro malignis orat, et segregato a mundo per crucem tradidit paradisum. Et solum virgines mente et corpore consolatur, qui in mundo erant, sed de mundo non erant. Et cum crucifiggentibus atque deridentibus turbis erant mente nec non et corpore, licet diversimode cruciformes. (Mattioli, *Il beato Simone Fidati da Cascia,* 369–70)

78. Oxford, Bodleian, MS. Canon. Misc. 268, fols. 158b–169, esp. 158b–158c, v and 168–69. A prayer by Angelo Clareno captures perfectly the nuances of tenderness, masochism, and morbidity so characteristic of the spirituality expressed in pictures of Jerome in penitence: "O dulcissime Jhesu filii dei vivi, inclinare digneris aurem ad preces meas, et pretioso tuo sanguine, quem pro humano genere fudisti, dele multitudinem peccatorum meorum. Sudor tuus sanguineus faciat me sudare lacrimas compunctionis. Clavis et lancea quibus fuisti vulneratus, vulnera cor meum in amore tuo. Omnia vitia carnis remove a me. Dyabolum et omnes insidias eius a me expelle. Qui vivis et regnas cum deo patre et spiritu sancto in secula seculorum. Amen" (Mattioli, *Simone Fidati da Cascia*, 471).

79. Guido Maria Dreves, *Analecta Hymnica medii aevi*, 26. *Liturgische Reimoffi-cien des Mittelalters* (Leipzig, 1897), 98. The many volumes of the *Analecta Hymnica* contain dozens of hymns dedicated to Jerome, the vast majority dating from the fourteenth and fifteenth centuries.

80. Cambridge, Fitzwilliam Museum, MS. 116, fols. 140v–141 (*Horae, French, ca. 1500; M. R. James, A Descriptive Catalogue of the Manuscripts in the Fitzwilliam Museum* [Cambridge, 1895], 266–68). More prayers in Oxford, Bodleian, MS. Canon. Pat. lat. 70, fols. 90–91.

81. University of Texas at Austin, Ms. file (Cath. Ch.) Misc. Hours 7, penulti-mate unnumbered leaf (s. 15); Charles Sterling, *The Master of Claude, Queen of France. A Newly Defined Miniaturist* (New York, 1975), 64, fig. 93 (= fol. 40 of a Book of Prayers copied and illuminated for Claude de France between 1511 and 1514), contains the same prayer.

82. Par. lat. 1865, fol. 3; Par. lat. 1904, fols. 334–334v; Klapper, "Frühzeit," 270–71. The prayers are by Giovanni d'Andrea.

83. Loys Laserre, *Vie de monseigneur S. Hierosme* (Paris, ed. [1541], fol. 395, r–v): Or doncques, mes freres Chrestiens et bonnes soeurs en Iesus Christ, prions le glorieux sainct Hierosme à ce que son bon plaisir soit, estre intercesseur pour nous envers dieu, pour obtenir de luy les vertuz d'humilité, ferme foy et bonne esperance, fondees en charité, avecques chasteté, et vraye intelligence de ce qui nous est necessair sçavoir pour accomplier sa volunté. Et qu'il nous donne la grace de ensuyvre les bons examples et saincte vie dudict sainct Hierosme et accomplir les bons enseignemens et saincte doctrine de luy, affin que puissons parvenir à la gloire des bien heureux, où il est de present. Laquelle nous vueille donner la benoiste trinité et une mesme essence: le pere, le filz, et le benoist sainct esperit. Amen.

84. Ronald F. E. Weissman, *Ritual Brotherhood in Renaissance Florence* (New York, 1982), 46–49.

4: *DIVUS LITTERARUM PRINCEPS*

1. For orientation in the literature on humanist patristic scholarship in Italy and the humanist idea of Christian antiquity see E. Garin, "La *dignitas*

hominis e la letteratura patristica," *La Rinascita* 1(4) (1938): 102–46; P. O. Kristeller, "Augustine and the Early Renaissance," in *Studies in Renaissance Thought and Letters* (Rome, 1956), 355–72; Hanna H. Gray, "Valla's *Encomium of St. Thomas Aquinas* and the Humanist Conception of Christian Antiquity," in *Essays in History and Literature Presented by Fellows of the Newberry Library to Stanley Pargellis,* ed. Heinz Bluhm (Chicago, 1965), 37–51; Riccardo Fubini, "Intendimenti umanistici e riferimenti patristici dal Petrarca al Valla," *Giornale storico della letteratura italiana* 151 (1974): 520–78; Charles L. Stinger, *Humanism and the Church Fathers: Ambrogio Traversari (1386–1439) and Christian Antiquity in the Italian Renaissance* (Albany, N.Y., 1976); and Max Schär, *Das Nachleben des Origenes im Zeitalter des Humanisimus (Beiträge zur Geschichtswissenschaft,* 140) (Basel, 1979).

2. Stinger, 81 and 83; Schär, 91–92.

3. Phyllis W. G. Gordan, *Two Renaissance Book Hunters. The Letters of Poggius Bracciolini to Nicolaus de Niccolis* (New York, 1974), 32, 165, 174.

4. Hans Baron, *Leonardo Bruni Aretino. Humanistisch-philosophische Schriften* (Leipzig, 1928), 6–7, 19.

5. Francesco Novati, *Epistolario di Coluccio Salutati,* 4 vols. (*Fonti per la storia d'Italia,* 15–18) (Rome, 1891–1911), 1: 301, 304–5; 4: 184–85; B. L. Ullman, *The Humanism of Coluccio Salutati* (Padua, 1963), 54–61. Cf. Guarino's similar argument, in R. Sabbadini, *Epistolario di Guarino Veronese,* 3 vols. (*Miscellanea di Storia Veneta,* 3d ser., 8, 11, 14) (Venice, 1915–19), 11: ep. 823, pp. 525–28.

6. *Ep.* 70, 4.

7. What Jerome actually reported to Eustochium (*Ep.* 22, 30) was that after fasting he read Cicero and, after a night of tearful vigil, Plautus: "Itaque miser ego lecturus Tullium ieiunabam. Post noctium crebras uigilias, post lacrimas, quas mihi praeteritorum recordatio peccatorum ex imis uisceribus eruebat, Plautus sumebatus in manibus." However, several of the early manuscripts listed in Hilberg's apparatus (Monacensis lat. 6299 dates from the late eighth or early ninth century; see C.S.E.L. 54: 189), all the medieval lives of St. Jerome, and all commentators on this passage before Erasmus read *Plato* instead of *Plautus.* The original error was no doubt made by an early medieval copyist who had never heard of Plautus and who therefore emended the text to read *Plato,* of whom he *had* heard. The error contributed to Jerome's exaggerated reputation for breadth of philosophical culture.

8. *Fam.* XXII, 10 (ed. Vittorio Rossi and Umberto Bosco, 4 vols. [Florence, 1933–42], 4: 127). Cf. *Fam.* II, 9, 9 (ed. Rossi, 1: 92).

9. *De divo Hieronymo oratio (PL* 22: 235); *De laudibus S. Hieronymi oratio* (Padua, Museo Civico, Cod. B.P. 1203, fol. 217): "Posthac [after the dream] autem, ut ipse asserit, codices gentilium legit, sed tanto studio divina tractavit, quod illa non modo legerat verum aut totum aut certe partem maximam suorum librorum postquam id evenerat edidit, in quibus tamen tam est peregrinae historiae, tantum gentilium fabularum externaeque disciplinae, omnia ad fidei usum accomodata, ut nihil aliud dies ac

noctes egisse quam ut illa conquerat videri possit. Sed et de fide tot tantaque praescripsit, ut nusquam ei vacasse libros gentilium legere facile credi queat."

10. *In quartum librum Elegantiarum praefatio* (Eugenio Garin, ed., *Prosatori latini del Quattrocento* [Milan, 1952], 612–22).

11. *Opera Omnia*, 2 vols. (Basel, 1553), 1: 225–26.

12. *Ep.* 70, 2. Aeneas Sylvius, *De liberorum educatione*, ed. J. S. Nelson (Washington, D.C., 1940), 176–77, made good use of this text.

13. Sabbadini, *Epistolario*, 11: ep. 666, pp. 212–13.

14. Baron, *Bruni Schriften*, 99–100.

15. Luzi Schucan, *Das Nachleben von Basilius Magnus "ad adolescentes." Ein Beitrag zur Geschichte des christlichen Humanismus* (Geneva, 1973).

16. *Ep.* 70, 2.

17. *Theodoriti Cyrensis episcopi de curatione Graecarum affectionum libri duodecim Zenobio Acciaolo interprete* (Paris, Henri Estienne, 1519), sig. a, ij, v; Bibl. Apostolica Vaticana, Ottob. lat. 1404, fols. lv-2.

18. Theodoret, *Curatio*, bk. I, 26–31; bk. XII, 58–69 (ed. and tr. Pierre Canivet, *S.C.* [Paris, 1958], 57(1): 110–12, and 57(2): 436–38).

19. *De providentia*, preface (Ottob. lat. 1404, fols. 155v–156).

20. Paris, Bibliothèque Nationale, MS. fr. 418, fols. 3v–10v. The splendid flower borders are closely related to those in the *Grandes Heures* of Anne de Bretagne (Par. lat. 9474, c. 1508), and the miniatures are in the style of Jean Bourdichon, information given me by Dr. Myra D. Orth, one of whose specialties is early sixteenth-century French manuscript illumination (see her "Progressive Tendencies in French Manuscript Illumination: 1515–1530. Godefroy de Batave and the 1520's Hours Workshop," Ph.D. diss., New York University, Institute of Fine Arts, 1976), who very kindly examined the manuscript for me. The catalogue of heresies was compiled by an author still ignorant of Luther, the *Life of Jerome* by one still ignorant of Erasmus's *Life*. A date well before 1516, Dr. Orth tells me, is perfectly compatible with the style of decoration and the manuscript's original ownership by Anne de France, whose coat of arms appears on fol. 1. See also Léopold Delisle, *Le Cabinet des Manuscrits de la Bibliothèque Impériale* (Paris, 1868), 1: 171.

21. Sabbadini, *Epistolario*, 11: ep. 824, p. 534.

22. *Francissi* [sic] *Petrarchae carmen in laudem Hieronymi. Hieronymus de monacho captivo. Idem de Paulo primo eremita. Hilarius de Maria Magdalena. Basilius Magnus de vita solitaria* (Fano, Girolamo Soncino, 23 July 1504), pref. ep. For Astemio, see Cosenza, 1: 5–6 and C. Mutini, in *Dizionario biografico degli Italiani* (1962), 4: 460–641.

23. *In epistolam divi Hieronymi ad Niciam Aquilegiensis ecclesie hypodiaconum Commentarioli duo Joannis Murmellij in quibus pleraque traduntur scribendis eleganter epistolis idonea. Ex epistolis eiusdem divi Hieronymi fideliter selecte Orationes* (Cologne, Henricus Quentell, 1505), sig. C iiij. For the quotations from St. Jerome, see *Epp.* 15, 4; 60, 4; 81, 1; 82, 11.

24. *Septem divi Hieronymi epistole ad vitam mortalium instituendam accommodatis-*

sime, cum Johanni Aesticampiani Rhetoris ac poete Laureati et Epistola et Sapphico carmine, aliorumque eruditissimorum virorum Epigrammatibus (Leipzig, Melchior Lotter, 1508), sig. a, ii–a, v, v.

25. *De rerum inventoribus libri octo* (Basel, 1545), 50–54; *Evangelicae praeparationis libri XV,* ed. E. H. Gifford, 4 vols. in 5 (Oxford, 1903), 3(1): xxv–xxx; and John Monfasani, *George of Trebizond. A Biography and a Study of His Rhetoric and Logic* (*Columbia Studies in the Classical Tradition,* 1) (Leiden, 1976), 71–73, 78.

26. *De libero arbitrio, passim,* but esp. 3a, 2–3, (ed. J. von Walter [Leipzig, 1910], 47–48). Important parts of Erasmus's argument rest on Origen, *Peri archon,* III, 1, 1–24, "De arbitrii libertate" (ed. H. Gorgemanns and H. Karpp [Darmstadt, 1976], 462–560). For details, see Schär, 273–80.

27. *PG* 40: 532C–533B. See also E. Garin, "La *dignitas hominis* e la letteratura patristica," 112–13; A. Horowitz and K. Hartfelder, *Das Briefwechsel des Beatus Rhenanus* (Leipzig, 1886), 43–44; David Amand, *Fatalisme et liberté dans l'antiquité grecque* (Louvain, 1945), 549–69; E. F. Rice, "The Humanist Idea of Christian Antiquity," 137–39, 148–49; Charles Trinkaus, *In His Own Image and Likeness,* 2 vols. (Chicago, 1970), 1: 186–87.

28. Joseph Gill, *The Council of Florence* (Cambridge, 1959), 195–204; Stinger, *Traversari,* 170–202, 215–17; and *Adv. Jovinianum,* 1: 47 (*PL* 23: 276C), quoted by R. Fubini, "Intendimenti umanistici e riferimenti patristici dal Petrarca al Valla," 521.

29. Rice, "The Humanist Idea of Christian Antiquity," 131–36; ibid., "The Impact of Greek Patristic Work on Sixteenth-century Thought," in R. R. Bolgar, ed., *Classical Influences on European Culture, A.D. 1500–1700* (Cambridge, 1976), 199–203.

30. Manetti's Latin New Testament is contained in Vatican MSS. Pal. lat. 45 and Urb. lat. 6; his translation of the Psalms, in Pal. lat. 40, 41 and Urb. lat. 5. The latter are triple Psalters, containing in parallel columns Jerome's translation from the Septuagint, Jerome's translation from the Hebrew, and Manetti's version. For details, see the introduction to Alfonso De Petris's edition of the *Apologeticus* (*Temi e testi,* 29) (Rome, 1981) and the important discussion of Manetti's biblical work in Trinkaus, 2: 581–601. For Manetti's worshipful view of Jerome's life, mores, and biblical scholarship, see *Apologeticus,* 47–49.

31. Valla's *Collatio Novi Testamenti* was first published by Erasmus (Paris, Badius and Jean Petit, 13 April 1505) in a version completed in 1449–1450. An earlier redaction from 1442–1443 has been edited by Alessandro Perosa (Florence, 1970). In addition to Perosa's introduction, see S. Garofalo, "Gli umanisti italiani del secolo XV e la Bibbia," in *La Bibbia e il Concilio di Trento* (*Scripta Pontificii Instituti Biblici,* 96) (Rome, 1947), 38–75, and Trinkaus, 2: 572–77.

32. A note at the end of the Vatican Library's copy of the oration describes the circumstances of its delivery and names the more distinguished auditors (Vat. lat. 5994, fol. 7v); "Recensita intra delubrum Andree dedicatum Patavii inter missarum solennia pridie Kal. Octobrias a Christi natalitiis

annum nobis agentibus millenum et quatercenum decimum coram deo amabilibus episcopis domino Petro Marcello, Patavine urbis antistite, domino Francisco Tabarello Florentino episcopo, dominisque reverendissimis archiepiscopis Patracensi et Corfusiensi, coramve viris preceptoribus meis peritissimis Rapphahele Fulgosio Placentino, Rapphahele Raimundo Cumano, Signorino Homodeo Mediolanensi et universo scolasticorum cetu. Deo gratias.'' Two other manuscripts of the orations are in, respectively, the Ambrosiana (Kristeller, *Iter*, 1: 309) and the Bodleian (MS. Canon. Pat. lat. 27, fols. 219–36). MS. Vat. lat. 5223, fols. 154–62, contains an earlier oration in praise of logic delivered at Siena in 1406. There is a fragment of a third oration, beginning ''Cum mihi per egregiam huius loci auctoritatem,'' in the Laurenziana (C. Paoli, *I codici Ashburnhamiani della R. Biblioteca Med\u2010Laurenziana. Indici e cataloge* [Rome, 1887], 8: 334). The paucity of surviving facts about Bonavia suggests that he died young.

33.　On Agostino Dati, see E. Garin, ''Testi minori sull'anima nella cultura del 400 in Toscana,'' *Archivio di Filosofia* (1951), 16–18; Cosenza, 2: 1184–87. The oration was delivered in Siena on a 30 September before February 1447, the date of a letter prefacing it in MS. Vat. lat. 13738, fols. 2–30v (Kristeller, *Iter*, 2: 388); it is printed in *Augustini Dati Senensis opera*, ed. Hieronymus Dathus (Siena, S. Nicolai Nardi, 27 October 1503), fols. 56v–58v.

34.　Leonard Smith, ed., *Epistolario di Pier Paolo Vergerio* (Rome, 1934), xvii, 91–93, 139–40, 184–87, 214, and 476–77. The *Officium divi Hieronymi editum per sp. iuris utriusque consultum dominum Petrum Paulum Vergerium Iustinopolitanum* is in Venice, Biblioteca Marciana, MS. Lat. cl. XIV, 254, fols. 38–42v. One oration (*Inc.*, ''Sanctissimum doctorem fidei nostre Hieronymum'') was published by Giovanni Andrea de' Bussi with his edition of the epistles and treatises (Rome [C. Sweynheym and A. Pannartz], 13 December 1468), 1: unnum. fols. 301–2, and reprinted by Migne, *PL* 22: 231–37. A second oration (*Inc.*, ''Hodie mihi, fratres carissimi'') and fragments of two others were published in the eighteenth century by Salmaso from Marciana MS. Lat. cl. XI, 56 (*Petri Pauli Vergerii Senioris De D. Hieronymo Opuscula nunc primum edidit e MSS. Dominicus Maurus Salmaso, adjecta sua de ejusdem D. Hieronymi studiis oratione* [Padua, 1767], 4–24). The others are unpublished. Smith, xxxvi–xlviii, described four manuscripts. To these may be added Padua, Museo Civico, MS. B.P. 1203, pp. 204–25, a copy and edition of B.P. 1287 that contains the same orations. The orations in Oxford, Bodleian, MS. Canon. Misc. Lat. 166 beginning ''Quotiens, reverendissimi patres fratresque carissimi, dies adventi'' (fols. 149–152v, dated Siena 1408) and ''Veni ad vos'' (incomplete, fols. 157v–158v) do not appear in the other manuscripts. These, plus the eight listed by Smith, bring the total to ten. I have used the Oxford manuscript and Padua, Museo Civico, B.P. 1203, called to my attention by Professor John W. O'Malley, S.J., who generously allowed me to borrow his microfilm of it as well. For other details, see David Robey, ''P. P. Vergerio the Elder: Republicanism and Civic Values in the Work of an

Early Humanist," *Past and Present*, no. 58 (1973): 3–37, esp. 27–31, 36–37, and John M. McManamon, "Innovation in Early Humanist Rhetoric: The Oratory of Pier Paolo Vergerio the Elder," *Rinascimento* 22 (1982): 3–32.

35. Eugenius Abel, *Isotae Nogarolae Veronensis opera quae supersunt omnia, accedunt Angelae et Zeneverae Nogarolae epistolae et carmina*, 2 vols. (Vienna, 1886); Abel, "Isota Nogarola," *Vierteljahrschrift für Kultur und Literatur der Renaissance* 1 (1886): 323–55, 440–73; and Margaret L. King, "The Religious Retreat of Isotta Nogarola (1418–1466)," *Signs* 3 (1978): 807–22 and "Book-lined Cells: Women and Humanism in the Early Italian Renaissance," in Patricia Labalme, ed., *Beyond Their Sex. Learned Women of the European Past* (New York, 1980), 66–90.

36. Sabbadini, *Epistolario*, 11: ep. 705, p. 307, line 21; Nogarola, *Opera*, 1: 85.

37. *Opera*, 2: 12.

38. *Opera*, 1: 79; Sabbadini, *Epistolario*, 11: ep. 704, p. 305.

39. *Opera*, 2: 188.

40. *Ep.* 125, 7 and 11.

41. *Ep.* 65, 1. Cf. *Ep.* 54, 2.

42. *Comm. in Sophoniam prophetam*, I, prol. (*C.C.L.* 76A: 655). See also M. Turcan, "Saint Jérôme et les femmes," *Bulletin de l'Association Guillaume Budé* (1968): 259–72. In bk. III of the *Courtier*, Castiglione compared the relative merits of men and women. A defender of women cites Jerome, "who celebrated certain women of his time with such marvelous praise that it would indeed suffice for the holiest man on earth" (Charles Singleton, tr. [New York, 1959], 221).

43. *Ep.* 22, 17, 19, and 25.

44. Nogarola, *Opera*, 2: 279. For the influence of classical epideictic rhetoric on orations and sermons of this sort, see John W. O'Malley, *Praise and Blame in Renaissance Rome: Rhetoric, Doctrine, and Reform in the Sacred Orators of the Papal Court, c. 1450–1521 (Duke Monographs in Medieval and Renaissance Studies, 3)* (Durham, N.C., 1979), esp. 85–87.

45. Dati, *Opera*, fols. 57–57v; Nogarola, *Opera*, 2: 282.

46. Nicolaus Bonavia, *De Hieronymi laudibus oratio* (Biblioteca Vaticana, MS. Vat. lat. 5994, fol. 5v; Oxford Bodleian, MS. Canon. Pat. lat. 27, fol. 228v).

47. Ibid., Vat. lat. 5994, fols. 4–5v; Canon. Pat. lat. 27, fols. 224–28.

48. Ibid., Vat. lat. 5994, fol. 4; Canon. Pat. lat. 27, fols. 223–223v.

[Hieronymus] vere sapiens fuit vereque philosophus. Si sapientia, cuius amor et professio philosophia dicitur, humanarum et divinarum rerum scientia sit, ut a philosophis traditur, nihil enim vel ex humanis vel ex divinis rebus quae nota esse hominibus liceat Ieronimum latuit. Sin vero sapienta et philosophia, ut a quibusdam Stoicis diffinitur, virtutis gignasium sit, vel studium corrigende mentis, vel recte rationis appetitus, vel secundum Platonis sententiam studium et sollicitudo mortis, omnium quoque mentis perturbationum interritus, nemo hercule Ieronimo sapientior, nemo hoc philosophandi genere sanctior. Nihil quippe videbitur ad Ieronimum comparatus Cato Ciceronis, quem vel sapientem putat si quisquam unquam sapiens fuit. Nihil Tales, Solon aut Phitias et hii qui sophi Athenis apellati sunt. Nihil itidem Apollo, nihil Socrates aut Cinnicus Diogenes.

49. Nogarola, *Opera*, 2: 281.

50. Smith, *Epistolario di P. P. Vergerio*, 184–85: Vergerio, *Orationes de laudibus divi Hieronymi* (Oxford, Bodleian, MS. Canon., Misc. lat. 166, fol. 148v; Padua, Museo Civico, MS. B.P. 1203, fols. 205–6): "De peritia vero literarum, quae et ipsa laus hominis sancti est, quid dicam? cum maxime in scripturis sacris ita doctum fuisse constat, ut in proverbium deductum sit, Nullum hominem scivisse quod Hieronymus ignoravit. Nec fuit, ut in plerisque, otiosa in hoc homine tanta doctrina. Multa enim et per se scripsit et aliorum multa interpretatus est. Trium linguarum eruditissimus, Hebraicae, Graecae, et Latinae. Obscura quoque sacrae scripturae permulta ac magna volumina commentatus est, ut non modo variis nationibus sed rudibus quoque ingeniis fundamenta fidei innotescere possent."

51. Vergerio, *Orationes* (Canon, Misc. lat. 166, fol. 145; B.P. 1203, fol. 219): "Nihil igitur apud eum aut amor patriae aut attinentium charitas, domusve aut vitae prioris consuetudo valuit, quia pro heremo patriam, pro monasterio domum, pro monachis attinentes et notos, vitamque civilem pristinam pro austerissima heremo commutaret." Ibid., Canon, Misc. lat. 166, fols. 156v–157; B.P. 1203, fol. 210: "Fugit urbes, fugit homines, fugit se, fugit denique omnia, quae esse chara hominibus solent, et ea quae sibi cara essent consequeretur. Domuit carnem, maceravit, afflixit, ne spiritus rebellis esset, utque docta senectute rationis imperium facilius servet."

52. Nogarola, *Opera*, 2: 283–84.

53. Ibid., 2: 283–84.

54. Dati, *Opera*, fols. 58–58v.

55. Vat. lat. 5994, fol. 4; Canon. Pat. lat. 27, fol. 223.

56. *Orationes* (PL 22: 233; Paris, Bibliothèque Nationale, MS. lat. 1890, fol. 438). Cf. Dati, *Opera*, fol. 57v. "Erat in Hieronymo religio Abel, Abrahae fides, patientia Isaac, laborum perpessio quanta in Iacob non fuit, continentia Ioseph, Iob sinceritas, misericordia Moysi, probitas qualis in Iesu Nave fuit, ac Samuele, David, Heliae ac Ioannis vehemens charitas, Salomonis sapientia, Tobiae integritas, Danielis iudicium. Ex quibus omnibus virtus eiusmodi conflata est, ut ad summum laudum cumulum nihil omnino addi possit."

57. Erica Trimpi, "Iohannem Baptistam Hieronymo aequalem et non maiorem: a Predella for Matteo di Giovanni's Placidi Altar-piece," *Burlington Magazine* 125 (1983): 457–67.

58. Martin Davies, *National Gallery Catalogues. The Earlier Italian Schools*, 2d ed. (London, 1961), 486–89; Vasari, *Vite* (ed. Milanesi, 3: 692–93); Exh. cat., *Mostra di Luca Signorelli*, ed. Margherita Moriondo (Florence, 1953), 116–17.

59. Franz Babinger, *Laudivius Zacchia, Erdicter der "Epistolae Magni Turci,"* *Sitzungsberichte der Bayer. Akad. d. Wissenschaften*, Philos.-hist. Kl., Jahrg.

1960, Heft 13 (Munich, 1960). Laudivio's presence in Hungary is documented by the publication there in 1478/79 of his *Vita beati Hieronymi*. See the facsimile reprint prepared by Elizabeth Soltesz (Budapest, 1975). There is a copy of the facsimile in the Morgan Library.

60. *B.H.L.* 3877; Lambert, 3B, no. 908, p. 672; Hain, 9943-45; and Hain-Copinger, 9946. I am aware of two manuscripts: Heidelberg, Univ. Bibl., cod. Salem 9, 71 and Oxford, Bodleian, MS. Canon. Pat. lat. 223, fols. 272-280v. Zacchia dedicated the work to Count Francí Beltran of Barcelona.

61. *De vita beati Hieronymi* (Naples, Sixtus Riessinger, 4 June 1473), unnumbered fols. 1-1v:

> Nam si Plutarchus Grecorum historias simul ac Romanorum oratione complexus est, et Livius summos ducere belli rebus a se gestis illustres eloquentia tamen ornaverit, quorum brevis inter mortales gloria censeatur, quanto sane rectius existimarim Hieronymi laudes, vitam, studia ac morum sanctitatem perscribere. Platonem enim et Aristotelem quottidie legimus, qui nil tamen nisi humanum aut ipsi didicerant aut alios instituere. Hieronymus vero omnium pene gencium ac linguarum interpres divina simul atque humana consecutus est studia. Catonis quoque et Aristidis virtutem et Socratis continentiam idem incredibili studio superavit. Iure etiam Pyctagorae, Appollonio, ceterisque sapientibus anteponendus, quos nil nisi ad pervestigandas naturae causas secretaque rerum in longinqua maris spatia ac terrarum orbem pervagatos accepimus. At is vero novos non solum adiisse populos remotissimasque gentes aut loca perlustrasse memoria proditum est, sed divinarum etiam rerum studio ad veram homines sapientiam instituit. Quando nec in Cicerone vis maior unquam dicendi seu in Demosthene copia emanavit, quin tot etiam Phoenicum, Graecorum, Arabum et Caldeorum. Hebraycas interpretationes aut nostras fecit aut meliores reddit. Et qui suo consilio Christianam rem publicam fide, doctrina, et auctoritate diu labentem confirmavit.

62. Ibid., fols. 1v-2.

63. Ibid., fol. 2v. "Hinc ad legendos Platonis libros in primis, atque Aristotelis analetica se contulit, ut in omni studiorum genere perfectus etiam in philosophia reliquos anteiret. Sed tamen arguta nimis gymnosophistarum theoromata contempsit, nec sibi antiquius quicquam ducebat quam ea omnia quae scire homini Christiano fas esset cognoscere."

64. Ibid., fols. 3-3v. "Adeo multa ex vetere novoque testamento interorandum proferebat, ut nihil tamen omittendum putaret quod ex libris quoque gentilium maxime conduceret."

65. Ibid., fol. 4v.

66. Ibid., fols. 5-5v.

67. Ibid., fol. 6. Laudivio would have listed all of Jerome's works "nisi bibliopolae Germani impressores suis queque in locis relata temporibus fideliter ad duo volumina digessissent, qui mira quadam arte eneoque in

singulos caracteres opificio multa cum admiratione omnium effinxere, ut que partim culpa temporum partim etiam librariorum vitio depravata erant, nostris aliquando hominibus quam emendatissime legi possent."

68. Ibid., 7v–8v. "Ossa vero eius postea Romam translata sunt et in ede virginis ad levam templi recondita, quae divinis illic honoribus summaque religione omnium servantur; signa vero, ac porro miracula, que vivo ei ac mortuo testimonio sanctitatis accessere hoc in loco referrem, nisi Cyrillus, Eusebius Cremonensis, et Augustinus summa apud nostros auctoritate viri duobus pene eulogiis singula explicassent."

69. On the iconography of St. Jerome in his study, see A. Venturi, *L'arte a San Girolamo* (Milan, 1924), passim; A. Strümpell, "Hieronymus im Gehäuse," *Marburger Jahrbuch für Kunstwissenschaft* 2 (1925–26): 173–252; O. Pächt, "Zur Entstehung des 'Hieronymus im Gehaus,' " *Pantheon* 21 (1963): 131–42; M. Meiss, "French and Italian Variations on an Early Fifteenth-Century Theme: St. Jerome and His Study," *Gazette des Beaux-Arts*, 105, 2 (1963): 147–70; Jungblut, 41–136; Friedmann, *A Bestiary for St. Jerome*, 29–47; P. H. Jolly, "Antonello da Messina's *Saint Jerome in His Study*: An Iconographic Analysis," *Art Bulletin* 65 (1983): 238–53; and Ridderbos, 15–40.

70. Friedmann, *A Bestiary for St. Jerome*, 313–48.

71. The last Italian examples known to me are paintings by Palma Giovane (Venice, Accademia, c. 1590) and Cigoli (Rome, S. Giovanni dei Fiorentini, dated 1599; see above, p. 189 and fig. 51). In the North, there is a seventeenth-century example by Hendrik van Steenwyck the Younger dated 1624. It is deliberately archaic: based on an engraving by Theodor de Bry (d. 1598), which is itself after a drawing in the Albertina ascribed to Ludwig Krug (d. 1532). See Exhibition Catalogue, Courtauld Institute Galleries, *Princess Gate Collection* (London, 1981), p. 64, no. 90. The other example known to me is a Rembrandt etching of 1642, though Rembrandt, Jan Lievens, Dou, and their followers produced many pictures of unidentified scholars and students in their studios, secularized versions of the earlier St. Jeromes (H. van de Waal, "Rembrandt's Faust Etching, a Socinian Document, and the Iconography of the Inspired Scholar," *Oud Holland* 79 [1964]: 7–48, esp. 26, fig. 19). For the fresco in S. Nicolò in Treviso, see Luigi Coletti, *Tomaso da Modena*, 2d ed. (Venice, 1963), 28, 121–22; figs. 50–52 and color pl. 6.

72. *St. Jerome in His Cave* (1512), B. 113; E. Panofsky, *Albrecht Dürer*, 2 vols., 2d ed. (Princeton, 1945), 2: 40, no. 333.

73. The fresco survives, but it was severely damaged by fire at the end of the fifteenth century and much repainted in the sixteenth and seventeenth. A miniature copy of the fresco in its original state exists in Darmstadt, Hessische Landesbibliotek, MS. 101, fol. 1v. See Theodor E. Mommsen, "Petrarch and the Decoration of the Sala Virorum Illustrium in Padua," *Art Bulletin* 34 (1952): 95–116, esp. 99–107 and figs. 3 and 5. See also R. Weiss, "Some Van Eyckian Illuminations from Italy," *Journal of the Warburg and Courtauld Institutes* 18 (1955): 319–21.

74. On the Detroit Van Eyck see E. Panofsky, "A Letter to St. Jerome: A Note on the Relationship between Petrus Christus and Jan van Eyck," *Studies in Art and Literature for Belle da Costa Greene* (Princeton, 1954), 102–8; Exh. cat., *Flanders in the Fifteenth Century: Art and Civilization* (Detroit, 1960), 69–72; Edwin Hall, "Cardinal Albergati, St. Jerome, and the Detroit Van Eyck," *Art Quarterly* 31 (1968): 2–24; ibid., "More about the Detroit Van Eyck: The Astrolabe, the Congress of Arras, and Cardinal Albergati," *Art Quarterly* 34 (1971): 181–201, to whom my account owes much. For the Medici inventory, E. Münz, *Les collections de Médicis au XVe siècle* (Paris, 1888), 78; for the remark of Bartolomeo Fazio, from the chapter on painters in his *De viris illustribus* (1456), Michael Baxandall, *Giotto and the Orators* (Oxford, 1971), 106 and 165. The attribution of this picture to Van Eyck is doubted by many specialists.

75. Pöllmann, 465–71; Hall, "Cardinal Albergati," 15.

76. The most detailed account is Paolo de Töth, *Il beato cardinale Nicolò Albergati e i suoi tempi, 1375–1444*, 2 vols. (Acquapendente, 1934).

77. E. Wind, "Studies in Allegorical Portraiture, I–II. Albrecht von Brandenburg as St. Erasmus," *Journal of the Warburg and Courtauld Institutes* 1 (1937–38): 142–62; F. Oswald, "Die Darstellungen des Hl. Hieronymus beim Meister des Bartholomäusaltares," *Wallraf-Richartz-Jahrbuch* 23 (1961): 342–46; E. Fahy, "A Portrait of a Renaissance Cardinal as St. Jerome," *Minneapolis Institute of Arts Bulletin* 59 (1970): 1–19; Exh. cat. Berlin, 1967. *Von der freyheyt eynes Christen menschen. Kunstwerke und Dokumente aus dem Jahrhundert der Reformation* (Berlin, 1967), no. 152 and fig. at p. 162; J. Hourlier, "Josse Clichtove et Jacques Lefèvre d'Etaples à Solesmes," *Revue historique et archéologique du Maine* 99 (1969): 71–95; P. H. Jolly, "Antonello da Messina's 'St. Jerome in His Study': A disguised portrait?" *Burlington Magazine* 124 (1982): 27–29; and Ridderbos, 41–62. There are woodcuts by Cranach showing Luther as St. Matthew and Melanchthon as St. Luke (H. van de Waal, "Rembrandt's Faust Etching," 12).

78. Jan Lauts, *Domenico Ghirlandajo* (Vienna, 1943), 14–15 and pl. 19.

79. E. Panofsky, *Early Netherlandish Painting*, 2 vols. (Cambridge, Mass., 1964), 1: 141–44; I. Bergström, "Disguised Symbolism in Madonna Pictures and Still Life," *Burlington Magazine* 27 (1955): 303–8, 340–49; ibid., "Medicina, Fons et Scrinium: A Study in Van Eyckean Symbolism and Its Influence in Italian Art," *Konshistorisk Tidskrift* 26 (1957): 1–20. The pyx was a Marian symbol also: the box containing the Eucharistic wafer was by analogy Mary's womb containing the body of Christ (M. Lavin, "The Altar of Corpus Domini in Urbino: Paolo Ucello, Joos van Ghent, Piero della Francesca," *Art Bulletin* 49 [1967]: 18).

80. On Dürer's print, see Panofsky, 1: 154–56; Jungblut, 84–90; P. Reuterswärd, "Sinn und Nebensinn bei Dürer: Randbemerkungen zur 'Melancolia I,' " in *Gestalt und Wirklichkeit. Festgabe für Ferdinand Weinhandl* (Berlin, 1967), 424–25; and Peter W. Parshall, "Albrecht Dürer's *St. Jerome in His Study*: A Philological Reference," *Art Bulletin* 53 (1971): 303–5. Reuterswärd has suggested an alternative meaning for the

brush. It is made of roots able to tolerate heat and fire, and its function is not to sweep up ashes but to manipulate the hot coals. "So wäre der kleine Besen dann genau so wie der brennende und vor dem Feuer dennoch nicht verzehrte Baum des Moses ein Reinheits-oder Marien-Symbol. Im Hieronymus-Stitch wurde er somit ähnlich wie der Rosenkranz nebenan fungieren" (424, n. 43).

81. *Ep.* 46, 3. Although the letter is addressed to Marcella from Paula and Eustochium, most authorities agree that Jerome wrote it himself. Elsewhere, however, he called the legend that Adam was buried on Calvary a popular superstition: "Favorabilis interpretatio et mulcens aurem populi nec tamen uera" (*Comm. in Matth.*, IV, 27, 33; C.C.L. 77: 270). See G. Bardy, "Saint Jérôme et ses maîtres hébreux," *Revue Bénédictine* 45 (1934): 162–63.

82. *Ep.* 125, 8, quoted in this form (the second line is not by Jerome) in the title under a miniature in the *Belles Heures,* fol. 97v. See Millard Meiss, *French Painting in the Time of Jean de Berry. The Limbourgs and Their Contemporaries,* 2 vols. (New York, 1974), 1: 126–27 and 2: fig. 472.

83. Sabbadini, *Epistolario,* 8: ep. 386, p. 556, lines 48–53, quoted by Baxandall, *Giotto and the Orators,* 92.

84. *Orationes* (Oxford, Bodleian, Canon. Misc. lat. 166, fol. 146; Padua, Museo Civico, B.P. 1203, fol. 220).

85. J. D. Mansi, *Sacrorum conciliorum nova collectio* (Florence, 1767), 13: cols. 302–3.

5: *HIERONYMUS REDIVIVUS:* ERASMUS AND ST. JEROME

1. Heimbucher, 2: 552; R. R. Post, *The Modern Devotion (Studies in Medieval and Reformation Thought,* 3) (Leiden, 1968), 658–76. Whatever may have been Erasmus's opinion of the *devotio moderna* in his youth, his later judgment was hostile. In a letter of 1517 (Allen, 3: ep. 665, p. 91), he remarked that the Brethren in no way resemble Jerome, although they bear his name.

2. Ep. 22 (Allen, 1:103; C.W.E. 1: 35).

3. *The Antibarbarians,* tr. Margaret Mann Phillips (C.W.E. 23:113). In his defense of the humanities, Erasmus especially relied on Jerome's "noble letter addressed to Magnus the Orator" and his explanation there of the meaning of the *mulier captiva* of Deut. 21:10–13 (Jerome, *Ep.* 70, 2) and on Augustine's interpretation of Exod. 3:22 and 12:35–36 on "spoiling the Egyptians" in *De doctrina Christiana,* II, 40, 60–61 (C.S.E.L. 80:75–76). See Charles Béné, *Erasme et Saint Augustin ou influence de Saint Augustin sur l'humanisme d'Erasme (Travaux d'Humanisme et Renaissance,* 103) (Geneva, 1969), 44 ff.

4. Epp. 67, 138 and 139 (Allen, 1:195, 321, 326, 328–29; C.W.E. 1:143, 295, 305).

5. Epp. 141 and 149 (Allen, 1:332, 353; C.W.E. 1:308–9 and 2:26–27).

6. Ep. 273 (Allen, 1:531; C.W.E. 2:253). Beginning in October 1511, Erasmus taught Greek at Cambridge and lectured on Jerome's letters and the

apology against Rufinus. See D. F. S. Thomson and H. C. Porter, *Erasmus and Cambridge* (Toronto, 1963), 38-43 and ep. 296 (Allen, 1: 570; *C.W.E.* 2:300).

7. Ep. 396 (Allen, 2:216; *C.W.E.* 3:260-61).

8. The preparations can be followed in detail in the *Amerbachkorrespondenz*, ed. Alfred Hartmann and B. R. Jenny (Basel, 1942-), vols. 1 and 2, passim, but esp. 1:315-16, 357-58, 382-83, 409, 417-18, 437, 462-63; 2:11, 13, 65. See also Allen, 2:50, 88, 210-11; *C.W.E.* 3:252-55; Fritz Husner, "Die Handschrift der Scholien des Erasmus von Rotterdam zu den Hieronymusbriefen," *Festschrift Gustav Binz* (Basel, 1935), 132-46; and John C. Olin, "Erasmus and Saint Jerome" *Thought* 54 (September 1979): 313-21.

9. Epp. 333, 334, and 335 (Allen, 2:71, 76-78, 86-89; *C.W.E.* 3:89-90, 96-98, 106-9).

10. Ep. 464 (Allen, 2:344; *C.W.E.* 4:75). *Divi Eusebii Hieronymi Stridonensis Opera omnia*, 9 vols. (Basel, Johannes Froben, 1516). During Erasmus's lifetime, subsequent editions appeared in 1524-1526 (Froben, Basel), 1533-1534 (Chevallon, Paris), and 1536-1537 (Froben, Basel). There were two later reprints in 1553 and 1565 (both Froben, Basel).

11. Epp. 474, 475, 478, and 483 (Allen, 2:354, 356, 360, 375; *C.W.E.* 4: 93-94, 101, 120).

12. Ep. 494 (Allen, 2:406; *C.W.E.* 4:155).

13. Ep. 583 (Allen, 2:566; *C.W.E.* 4:358); Ep. 661 (Allen, 3:85; *C.W.E.* 5:118-19).

14. Migne, *PL* 30:307-8; 153:593-94.

15. *Hieronymianus*, Cologne ed. (1482), sig. g, v, col. 1: "De historia Ioachim et Anne. Hanc ad contextum non vidi. Posuit tamen eam frater Iacobus in legenda c. xxvi. que est de nativitate virginis. Curiosus ibi videat et inveniet verbum angeli ad Ioachim quod peccati non nature deus est ultor." For the *De quindecim signis iudicii*, see sig. i, vii, cols. 1-2.

16. Biblioteca Apostolica Vaticana, MSS. Vat. lat. 343-44 (M. Vattasso and P. Franchi de' Cavalieri, *Codices vaticani latini* [Rome, 1902], 1:247-54); Paris, Bibliothèque Nationale, MSS. lat. 1890-91, copied in Florence in 1483-84 for Cardinal Georges d'Amboise (*Bibliothèque Nationale. Catalogue général des manuscrits latins* [Paris, 1940], 2:222-23). For Teodoro de' Lelli, see J. B. Sagmüller, *Ein Traktat des Bischofs von Feltre und Treviso Teodoro de' Lelli über das Verhältniss von Primat und Kardinalat.*, *Römische Quartalschrift für christl. Alterthumskunde und für Kirchengeschichte*, 2. Supplement Heft (Rome, 1893) and Rodolfo Dell'Osta, *Un teologo del potere papale e suoi rapporti col cardinalato nel secolo XV, ossio Teodoro de' Lelli* (Belluno, 1948).

17. Vat. lat. 343 (unnum. fol. 1); Par. lat. 1890, fol. 1: *Theodori de Leliis in tabulam epistolarum Hieronymi prefatiuncula*. Cf. *Hieronymianus*, Basel ed., (1514), fol. 16v; chap. 3, p. 65 above and fig. 25.

18. *PL* 42: 1101-16; Lambert, 3A, nn. 314, 316, 317; 3B, nn. 514, 515.

19. [*Tractatus et epistolae*], 2 vols. (Rome, Sweynheym and Pannartz, 1468) (HC. 8551; BMC. 4:5; Luigi de Gregori, *La stampa a Roma nel secolo XV*

[Rome, 1933], 10–11, 35–36), 1: fol. 1; 2: fol. lv. The two volumes contain 281 tracts and letters. The printers issued 275 copies. A second printing (1470) sold for five ducats per volume. Two other editions appeared at almost the same time: Rome, Sixtus Riessinger, 1468 (HC. 8550; BMC. 4:27; Gregori, 49) and Strasbourg, Johann Mentelin, [not after 1469] (BMC. 1:53). Riessinger prefaced his edition with Mattia Palmieri's translation of the *Letter of Aristeas* about the seventy translators of the Hebrew Pentateuch into Greek and a warm tribute to Teodoro de' Lelli for his devotion and services to St. Jerome. Unlike the two Roman editions, Mentelin's Strasbourg edition, which may be the *editio princeps,* is independent of Lelli. For Bussi, see M. Miglio, in *Diz. Bio. degli Italiani* (1972), 15:565–72.

20. Husner, "Die Handschrift der Scholien," 141–44.

21. [*Epistolae*], 2 vols. (Mainz, Peter Schoeffer, 7 September 1470) (H. 8554; BMC. 1:26–27), 1 (unnum. fol. 1, cols. 1–2): "Nos vero alia quadam ratione usi in hoc nostro volumine, virum hunc tanquam viventem, dictantem, scribentem, redarguentem, consolantem, instruentem facimus. Ob hanc causam aliorum epistolas ad vel contra ipsum scriptas apponimus . . . ; ceterum prologos quosque suis libris relinquentes, anilia apographa et dubia pertransimus." Like the Strasbourg edition, Schoeffer's is independent of Lelli and so stands apart from the main avenue of textual transmission.

22. Ibid. (unnum. leaf 1, col. 2): "Demum ne venerabilis patris Guidonis Carthusiensis videamur ignari, qui suis scriptis Iohannem Andream carpit[!], quod nonnullas epistolas litteris Hieronymi inseruerit non suas et stili discrepantia reiiciendas, nos concedentes unicuique cum apostolo [Rom. 14:5], ut in suo sensu abundet, stilique iudicium illis relinquentes qui soliti sunt, sicut de vino ita et de ingeniis disputare, eas epistolas quas Jo. Andreas immiscuit concordantibus exemplaribus perantiquis censuimus huic etiam nostro volumini adijciendas."

23. Antoninus Florentinus, *Chronicon,* 3 vols. (Nuremberg, Anton Koberger, 31 July 1484), 2: fol. 20, cols. 1–2.

Quasi arcus refulgens inter nebulas glorie, id est, gloriosus inter nebulas obscuras delinquentium et errantium positus irradiavit ecclesiam, scripturam sacram obnubilatam, falsitatibus Hebreorum et Grecorum et Latinorum male interpretantium verissima et tenacissima interpretatione, ex Hebreo quoad vetus testamentum et ex Greco quoad novum, exceptis paucis, transferens in Latinum fidelibus tradidit, plures eius libros commentando, multos hereticos sua doctrina confutando. Cui ecclesia tantum auctoritatis propter clarum lumen sapientiae eius tribuit, ut quas sententias vel libros scribentium ipse reprobavit reprobate habeantur et quae ipse scripsit firma teneantur.

24. Ibid., fol. 20, col. 2.

25. Ibid., fol. 21, col. 2: "Legitur in quibusdam opusculis que intitulantur Augustino, et alia Cirillo vel aliis de multis miraculis facti post mortem Hieronymi ad invocationem eius. Et praecipue de tribus mortuis suscitatis

posita tunica sua super eos, qui retulerunt penas et gloriam eis ostensa in alia vita. Sed quia non est autenticum tales doctores illa scripsisse, unde nec Vincentius in Speculo historiali, nec Jacobus de Voragine, nec alli hystoriographi de illis faciunt mentionem, ideo illa referre omittimus." Early in the next century, the grammarian Pietro Crinito (1475–1507) reported that "plerique affirmunt hunc ipsum librum [ie. the letter of Ps.-Augustine] minime Augustino adscribendum" (De honesta disciplina, VI, 6, ed. Carlo Angeleri [Rome, 1955], 167).

26. De scriptoribus ecclesiasticis (Paris, Bertholdus Rembolt, 1512), fols. 25–27.
27. Husner, "Die Handschrift der Scholien," 143–44.
28. Ep. 396 (Allen, 2:219; C.W.E. 3:264).
29. Opera (1516), 2: fols. 2v–3.
30. Ibid., fol. 3v.
31. Ep. supp. 6, ad amicum egrotum de viro perfecto. Inc.: Ecce iterum ad te scribo. Censura: "Eloquentis quidem et eruditi hominis fuit haec epistola ac diligenter elaborata, sed ita discrepans a phrasi Hieronymiana, ut nec hic illius dictionem potuerit imitari si voluisset, nec huius ille." And he continued: "Quod si divinare licet, nulli potius tribuerim quam Tertulliano. In plerisque codicibus nullum praeferebat nomen, in quibusdam Ctesiphontis erat additum. Nec in ipsa epistola sit ulla mentio euis ad quem scripta est" (Opera, 2: fol. 23).
32. Ep. supp. 8. Inc.: Tres quodammodo virtutes. Censura: "Ne pilum quidem Hieronymianae dictionis habet haec epistola, nec ullum vestigium pectoris illius, quamquam videtur hominis esse pii, nec indiserti. Forsitan Augustini aut Bernardi. Certe cuiuscuius est, Hieronymi non esse clamat ipsa" (Opera, 2: fol. 35v).
33. Opera, 2: fol. 32. See note 37 below.
34. Ep. supp. 14, De essentia divinitatis. Inc.: Omnipotens Deus Pater. Censura: "Nihil est in hoc opusculo nec sermonis, nec eruditionis, nec pectoris quod Hieronymum resipiat" (Opera, 2: fol. 53v).
35. Epp. supp. 15, 16, 17; Opera, 2: fol. 56.
36. Opera, 2: fol. 194v. See note 38 below.
37. Ep. supp. 46, Damasus ad Hieronymum. Inc.: Dum multa corpora librorum. Censura: "Clarius est quam ut admoneri debeat hanc epistolam eiusdem esse artificis cuius est ea quae proxime sequitur, et eadem febri laborantis. Deum immortalem, quae fuit impudentia hoc tribuere Damaso, cuius elegantiam etiam in scribendis versibus approbat Hieronymus; et extant alia quaedam eiusdem e quibus character hominis deprehendi possit. . . . Non saltem illud cavit, ne sacerdotem vocaret, qui non esset episcopus, cum eo saeculo non vocarentur sacerdotes nisi episcopi. Demiror cur non eadem opera vocarit cardinalem, cum hoc vocabulum illis temporibus adhuc fuerit inauditum." Ep. supp. 47, ad Damasum. Inc.: Legi litteras apostolatus tui. Censura: "Nihil vereor quantumvis sancte deerrare, non caruisse febri quisquis hanc scripsit epistolam. At primum demiror, ullum fuisse tam stupidum aut certe philauton qui sperarit futurum, ut haec epistola qua nihil fingi potuit, nec insulsius, nec indoctius, nec infantius, a

quoquam pro Hieronymiano legeretur. Sed nihil est tam absurdum in rebus mortalium quod non reperiat approbatorem. Quid non audeant histriones isti posteaquam viderint huic etiam impudentiae non defuisse successum. Inventi sunt tam nullis auribus, tam nullis oculis, imo tam nulla mente, ut has nugacissimas nugas ab Hieronymo scriptas putarent?'' (*Opera*, 2:195v).

38. *Ep. supp.* 42, ad Oceanum de vita clericorum. *Inc.*: Deprecatus es. *Censura:* "Quis non rideat hunc simium? In ipsa statim salutatione addidit Hieronymo patris nomen. Nec hoc contentus, Sophronium adiecit, tritavi opinor, ne non haberet tria nomina, cum ipse Hieronymus nusquam se nisi simplici nomine notet; in Catalogo proper historiae fidem presbyteri tantum titulum addens, nonnumquam modestiae causa peccatoris. Patris nomen et patriam indicavit dumtaxat non usurpat. . . . Quis non statim sentiat hunc scriptorem, ut libere quod sentio dicam, aut temulentum fuisse aut febri laborasse? Atque huius elegantiae totus est sermo reliquus, infans, incompositus, insulsus, diffluens, sordidissimis verborum portentis scatens, quod genus sunt illa, meliorare, secretaliter. . . . Adde his, quod tam reverenter citat Sulpicium, qui divi Martini vitam conscripsit. Atque is vidit quidem divum Hieronymum, sed senem iuvenis. Nec huius ullam facit mentionem in Catalogo, nec is Hieronymo mos recentiores scriptores praesertim Latinos tanta cum reverentia citare. Sed qui opus argumentis? Quisquis hunc sermonis characterem non potest ab Hieronymiano secernere, is nec asinum ab equo distinguet" (*Opera*, 2:194–194v).

39. *Ep. supp.* 7, ad Thesiphontem de divina lege. *Inc.*: Praesumptionem meam excusare conarer. *Censura:* "Praeterquam quod totus sermonis habitus modis omnibus dissidet a dictione Hieronymiana, vel hinc deprehendi poterat ab alio scriptam fuisse, quod in plerisque codicibus non erat asscriptum nomen eius ad quem fuerit scripta, quod divus Hieronymus nunquam solitus est omittere, nisi cum est argumentum odiosius, velut ad matrem et filiam de suspecto convictu, praesertim quoties versatur in argumento declamatorio, in quo studuit exemplum proponere magis quam rem narrare gestam. In ceteris non solum asscribit vocabulum, verum aliquid laudis admiscet epistolae. In quibusdam asscriptum erat ad Ctesiphontem" (*Opera*, 2: fol. 32).

40. *Ep. supp.* 12. *Inc.*: Sufficere quidem fidei tuae. *Censura:* "Et hanc sermonis discrepantia satis arguit ab Hieronymo non fuisse scriptam, quod quidem et hinc colligi poterat quod in exemplaribus variat titulus. In nonnullis ad Damasum inscripta est, in aliis ad Rusticum episcopum Narbonensem, in quibusdam nullius habet nomen. Deinde in aliis codicibus habetur integra, in aliis mutila. Postremo non est verisimile, divum Hieronymum si de re tanta tantum scripsisset librum, non alicubi citaturum fuisse, cum multo breviores et leviores argumenti tam frequenter citet" (*Opera*, 2: fol. 45).

41. Lambert, 1B, no. 149. *Inc.*: Lectis litteris tuis. *Censura:* "Hanc epistolam non esse Hieronymi, etiam si parum argueret stilus, ex hoc certe poterat intelligi, quod is qui scripsit non semel testatur sese Graeci et Hebraei sermonis ignarum. Extat autem inter epistolas Augustini, suo titulo

praenotata. Stilus quoque cum titulo consentit" (*Opera*, 2: fol. 76).

42. *Opera*, 2:195v. See note 37 above.

43. *Ep. supp.* 43, ad Damasum de oblationibus. *Inc.*: Noverit sancta auctoritas tua. *Censura:* "Et hic quisquis fuit conatus est suas nugas Hieronymiani nominis umbra praetexere. Quam apte vero conferit authorum nomina, e quibus tamen nihil adducit, quia nihil illorum legerat. Chrysostomi commentarios nominatim citat, cum divus Hieronymus Chrysostomum prorsus ignorarit, ut taceam interim aetate divi Hieronymi non solere quemquam a communione depellere, quod novo verbo vocant excommunicare, nisi qui ad eam pertinuisset ecclesiam. Nam haec Romani pontificis monarchia post Hieronymi saeculum exorta est" (*Opera*, 2: fol. 197). Erasmus had more to say about Jerome's ignorance of Chrysostom's commentaries in ep. 1800, the preface to some translations of Chrysostom printed in March 1527 as *Chrysostomi Lucubrationes* (Allen, 6:485–86).

44. *Ep. supp.* 1, ad Demetriadem virginem de virginitate. *Inc.*: Si summo ingenio. *Censura:* "Erudita prorsus et eloquens epistola, sed quam, ut nihil aliud accedat, vel stilus palam arguat non esse Hieronymi. Praeterea consentaneum non est Hieronymum ad eandem virginem iisdem de rebus bis scripsisse. Divus Augustinus nonnihil suspicari videtur ab haeretico Pelagiano conscriptam, quod insint in ea nonnulla quae Pelagianorum dogmata resipiant, praesertim cum is Pelagius in epistola quadam testetur sese ad Demetriadem scripsisse. Beda putat esse Iuliani haeretici. Ceterum error inscriptionis hinc natus est, quod Hieronymus quoque scripserit ad hanc virginem argumento non dissimili" (*Opera*, 2: fol. 4v).

45. *Ep. supp.* 9, ad Paulam et Eustochium de assumptione beatae Mariae Virginis sermo. *Inc.*: Cogitis me. *Censura:* "Totus huius epistolae stilus sic abhorret ab Hieronymiano, ut non dubitem negare Latinum fuisse qui scripserit, sed Graecum. Resipit enim sermo totus Graecitatem quandam et balbutiem hominis in aliena lingua versantis, id quod ipse propemodum testatur cum ait: 'Latinus utens eloquio.' Quorsum enim attinebat Hieronymum praefari Paulae et Eustochio se Latine velle scribere cum quicquid scripsit Latine scripserit? Deinde cum addit 'infantium more balbutientium, qui quaecunque audierint, fari gestiunt, cum necdum possint ad plenum verba formare,' nonne palam indicat sese tentare sermonem peregrinum, in quo parum sit exercitatus, quod etiam si non fateatur, ipsa tamen dictio prae se fert? Nec enim usque adeo eloquentiae suae fuit ignarus Hieronymus, praesertim id aetatis, ut se balbutienti infantulo fuerit comparaturus. . . . Si divinare licet, suspicor esse Sophronii, quem in Catalogo scriptorum testatur fuisse virum apprime doctum, sed Graecum" (*Opera*, 2:37v).

46. *Ep. supp.* 3, ad Marcellam ut adversa toleret exhortatio. *Inc.*: Magnam humilitati nostrae. *Censura:* "Non abhorret a stilo Paulini, cuius extant aliquot ad divum Augustinum epistolae, sicuti hec superior. Verum ineptum sit in tanta scriptorum turba, quos illa ferebat aetas, divinare cuius sit, praesertim cum extent paucissima. Ut Hieronymo tribueretur, illud ansam praebuit, quod ad Marcellam scriptam sit, ad quam et alias ille scripserat"

(*Opera*, 2:15v); *Opera*, 2:3v "Quanquam ingenue fateor accidere posse, ut nonnullis tanta sit dictionis similitudo, ut modestius sit ambigere quam pronunciare."

47. Migne, *PL* 30: 391–426. Lambert, 3B, no. 560, lists ninety-three Latin manuscripts. There are many more. The date of composition is based on Lambert's list of manuscripts, none of which is earlier than the thirteenth century and only one of which he dates earlier than the fourteenth. It was unknown to Giovanni d'Andrea in 1346. In the fifteenth century, the work circulated widely in print and in vernacular translation. I am inclined to say that it was composed in Tuscany in the second half of the fourteenth century for a convent of Hieronymite nuns. Erasmus believed that the author of the fourteenth-century pseudographs also wrote the *Regula* (*Opera*, 1: fol. 48B).

48. Jerome, *Ep.* 22, 7.

49. *Regula monacharum*, 26 (*PL* 30: 414). This passage is the textual source for at least two representations of Jerome's vision of the Trinity. See E. F. Rice, "St. Jerome's 'Vision of the Trinity': an Iconographical Note," *Burlington Magazine* 125 (1983), 151–55.

50. Guido Maria Dreves, *Analecta hymnica medii aevi*, 36. *Liturgische Reimoffi-cien des Mittelalters* (Leipzig, 1897), 99.

51. *Opera*, 2: fol. 197v:
     Ipse non possum satis admirari tam insignem hominis impudentiam. Quanta cum authoriate loquitur, putas apostolum aliquem esse. Et hic impostor ipso Paulo felicior, in corpore constitutus fruitus est visione divina, totos opinor menses inter seraphim versatus. Deinde corpori redditus cum antea dixisset, in corpore cerni, redibat nobis praescius futurorum. Nam huiusmodi portenta de se scribit suppositius hic Hieronymus, qui si prodigiosam balbutiem suam et ineptissimam lo-quacitatem mutare potuisset, plane Hieronymus erat. Nunc auriculae prominentes produnt asinum, et totus sermo clamitat indignum fuisse qui in divi Hieronymi culina ministri locum teneret. Sed audi iam lector bellam praefationem, qua non Hieronymum exprimit iam senem, quemadmodum conatur, sed ebrium aliquem, vino simul et aetate de-lirantem.

52. *Opera*, 2: fol. 190:
     Caeterum in regula virginum, quam scripsit iam centenarius, totas hic furcifer hebdomadas versatur inter angelorum choros, et affatim cum divina triade confabulatus, tandem in terras devolat, iam vates factus ac futurorum praescius. Quid hac impudentius hypocrisi? Imo quid magis impium? Nam longe alium fuisse, quam videri studet, primum ipsa prodet inscitia, deinde prodigiosa sermonis balbuties, plurimis sordidis-simis et horum temporum vocabulis inquinati. Atque hic est certissimus index, et Lydius (quod dici solet) lapis. Nihil enim hic succulentum, nihil exactum, nihil elaboratum invenies, sed tumultuariam modo vulgarium verborum et ineptissimarum sententiarum congeriem.

53. *Eximii doctoris Hieronymi Stridonensis vita ex ipsius potissimum litteris contexta per Desiderium Erasmum Roterodamum*, ed. W. K. Ferguson, *Erasmi opuscula* (The Hague, 1933), 134–90. The *Vita* introduced the Froben edition of 1516 (*Opera*, 1: sig. a, 5–b, 8v). The biography has rightly attracted attention. In addition to Ferguson's introduction, see Denys Gorce, "La patristique dans la réforme d'Erasme," in *Festgabe Joseph Lortz*, 2 vols. (Baden-Baden, 1958), 1: 252–76; Peter G. Bientenholz, *History and Biography in the Work of Erasmus of Rotterdam (Travaux d'Humanisme et Renaissance*, 87) (Geneva, 1966), passim, but esp. 90–92; J. Coppens, "Le portrait de Saint Jérôme d'après Erasme," in *Colloquia Erasmiana Turonensia* (Paris, 1972), 2: 821–28; John B. Maguire, "Erasmus' Biographical Masterpiece: *Hieronymi Stridonensis Vita*," *Renaissance Quarterly* 26 (1973): 265–73; and Olin, "Erasmus and Saint Jerome," 315–21. The *Vita beati Hieronymi* of Christianus Massaeus is preserved in Grand Séminaire de Malines, MS. 37, fols. 20 ff. (see Carlo de Clercq, "Une oeuvre inédite de Chrétien Masseeuw (ob. 1546)," *De Gulden Passer* 12 [1934]: 14–19). The preface echoes Jerome and Maniacoria: "Ut ergo certa pro dubiis, ymmo vera pro falsis habeamus, omissis rivulis ex ipso nobis fonte bibendum est: et ex suisipsius libris veritas hystorie requirenda" (fol. 20).

54. *Vita*, 134–36.

55. Ibid., 136, lines 75–76.

56. Ibid., 150, lines 449–50.

57. Ibid., 140–42.

58. Ibid., 172–73.

59. Ibid., 144, lines 261–63; 154, lines 581–82.

60. Ibid., 155, lines 586–91.

61. Ibid., 157–58.

62. *Censura* of Ps.-Eusebius: "Eadem facundia, eadem eruditio, idem sermonis lepos. Illud ridiculum hominem ne tantulum quidem potuisse dictionis figuram variare. Omni, quod aiunt pedi, eundem inducit calceum. Apud hanc artificem eodem utuntur charactere omnes, Hieronymus, Augustinus, Cyrillus, Eusebius et Ambrosius; apud hunc opinor balbutiret ipse Tullius. Illud breviter admoneo pium lectorem, nihil hic esse in quo bonarum horarum ullam partem collocet, nec eget divus Hieronymus huiusmodi fucis, nec dignatur a tam insulso pingi artifice" (*Opera*, 2: fol. 209). Of Ps.-Augustine: "Deum immortalem, sic ineptiret Augustinus? Vitam impostor ille stultissime simul et indoctissime descripsit; hic seipsum ita refert, ut propemodum vincat balbutie. Neque vero solam eloquentiam requiro, hominem desidero. Mutavit personam noster hic histrio, sed vocem et gestum mutare non potuit" (*Opera*, 2: fol. 221v). Of Ps.-Cyril: "Idem et hic stilus, idem pectus, eadem insania, semper sui similis est, quocunque titulo peronatus prodeat huius actor fabulae. Quid si hic rabula valuisset literis et eloquentia, quibus ludibriis orbem implesset universum? Nunc ob insignem infantiam nulli potest imponere, nisi sit Marycho stultior aut nisi quis ultro falli cupiat" (*Opera*, 2: fol. 224). For further detail

and invective, see *Vita,* 137-38; *Opera,* 1: fol. 48B and 2: fol. 190; and Bietenholz, *History and Biography,* 105.

63. *Vita,* 139, lines 133-35.
64. *Opera,* 2: fol. 190v; ep. 396 (Allen, 2:213; *C.W.E.* 3:257).
65. *Colloquies,* tr. Craig R. Thompson (Chicago, 1965), 83-85. See also Giulio Vallese, *Erasmo e Reuchlin,* 3d ed. (Naples, 1964).
66. Jerome, Ep. 46, 10.
67. Ep. 164 (Allen, 1:374).
68. *Vita,* 145-46; *Opera,* 1: fol. 20A-B.
69. *Vita,* 148-49.
70. Ibid., 151-53.
71. *De copia,* tr. Betty I. Knott (*C.W.E.* 24:634).
72. *Vita,* 177-78; *Opera,* 1: fol. 61vC.
73. *Vita,* 181-87; *Opera,* 1: fol. 5. For an account of Gaza's *dictum celebre,* see Pietro Crinito, *De honesta disciplina,* I, 10 (ed. Angeleri, pp. 72-73). Crinito added his own judgment: "Neque prorsus negaverim quaedam esse in Hieronymo, quae non usquequaque Romanam in dicendo puritatem atque elegantiam probant. Quod equidem vitium, si id vitium est, non homini, sed tempori et professioni tribuendum existimo."
74. *Vita,* pp. 178-79; *Opera,* 4: fol. 23vD: "Neque dubito quin si divus Hieronymus hanc vidisset theologiam, Aristotelicis sententiis ac legibus undique contaminatam, vel obrutam potius, tota libertate in rem tam indignam detonuisset." Cf. ep. 456 (Allen, 2:325).
75. *Opera,* 1: fols. 66vD-67A.
76. *Vita,* 148, lines 404-11; 158, lines 673-74; 169, lines 939-40; *Opera,* 3: fol. 1v.
77. Ep. 337 (Allen, 2:105; *C.W.E.* 3:129); *Opera,* 1: fols. 6B, 41B, 62A; 3: fols. 7vC, 46A.
78. Epp. 1879, 1891, 1909, 2264 (Allen, 7:183-84, 207, 258; 8:347).
79. *Opera,* 1:6vC: "Nos scholia scribimus, non dogmata"; ibid., fol. 16A: "Licebat hoc illis temporibus, eruditionis gratia, e quibuslibet libris, si quid inesset utile, decerpere. Ita Hieronymus praeter alios multos legebat Origenem, ut interpretem, non ut dogmatisten."
80. Ep. 1841 (Allen, 7:97). Compare the views of Valla's great friend Pier Candido Decembrio. Writing to Francesco Pizolpasso in October 1438, he contrasted Jerome's reliability in matters of faith and morals with his human fallibility in matters of historical fact. Jerome misunderstood the Roman law of divorce; in *Ep.* 53, 1 he perpetuated the legend that Plato had been captured by pirates and sold as a slave to a cruel tyrant; he made mistakes in his translation of the Old Testament. "Haec non reprehendo, sed admiror ab homine docto tam multa praeter veritatem dici potuisse. An hoc sacrilegium est? . . . Puto enim sanctissimum hominem fuisse Hieronymum, sed hominem tamen, et qui didicerit, et qui erraverit, et qui correxerit, et qui mutaverit, ut caeteri solent" (R. Fubini, "Tra umanesimo e concili. Note e giunte a una pubblicazione recente su Francesco Pizolpasso (1370c.-1443), " *Studi Medievali* 7 [1966]: 363).

6: BETWEEN PROTESTANTS AND CATHOLICS

1. *Fam.* II, 9, 9, ed. V. Rossi, 4 Vols. (Florence, 1933–42), 1:92.
2. *Fam.* IV, 15, ed. Rossi, 1:189, to an unnamed "famosus vir," identified by glosses as Giovanni d'Andrea. For the correspondent and date, see E. H. Wilkins, *Petrarch's Correspondence (Medioevo e Umanesimo, 3)* (Padua, 1960), 17 and 56; for perceptive discussions of the texts, R. Fubini, "Intendimenti umanistici e riferimenti patristici dal Petrarca al Valla," *Giornale storico della letteratura Italiana* 151 (1974): 533–37, and Costanzo Di Girolamo, ed., *Libru di lu transitu et vita di Misser Sanctu Iheronimu* (Palermo, 1982), xii–xiii. Despite his dislike of the *Hieronymianus*, Petrarch may have contributed a complimentary epigram to one copy of it (P. O. Kristeller, *Iter Italicum*, 2:491, and "Petrarcas Stellung in der Geschichte der Gelehrsamkeit," in *Italien und die Romania in Humanismus und Renaissance, Festschrift für Erich Loos*, ed. K. Hempfer and E. Straub [Wiesbaden, 1983], 114).
3. *Epistolae*, bk. VI, last letter, Venice ed. (Ioannes et Gregorius de Gregoriis fratres, 24 September 1502), fol. 44v; *PL* 22:225. The letter is dated 1449.
4. Ep. 769 (Allen, 3:211; *C.W.E.*, 5:291).
5. Ep. 844 (Allen, 3:333–36; *C.W.E.*, 6:31–35); *Vita Hieronymi* (ed. Ferguson, 180–81).
6. *W.A. Briefwechsel*, no. 35 (ed. O. Clemen [1930], 1:90; *L.W.* (1963), 48:40.
7. *L.W.* (1963), 26: passim, but esp. 68, 92, 107, 111, 180–81, 249, 275–76.
8. *W.A. Tischreden*, nn. 51, 252, 445 (ed. E. Kroker [1912], 1:18, 106, 194–95; *L.W.* [1967], 54:8, 33, 72). But cf. ibid., no. 584 (*W.A.* 1:272; *L.W.* 54:104–5): "Although the fathers were often wrong, they ought nevertheless to be honored on account of their testimony to faith. So I venerate Jerome and Gregory and others inasmuch as one can sense [from their writings], in spite of everything else, that they believed as we do, as the church from the beginning believed, and as we believe."
9. *Blondi Flavii Forliviensis De Roma triumphante libri decem . . . Romae instauratae libri III. Italia illustrata. Historiarum ab inclinato Rom. imperio Decades III* (Basel, in officina Frobeniana, March 1531), sig. kk. 2v; Erasmus's ed. of Jerome's *Opera: I*, sig. gamma 6: "Scripturam divinam suae linguae hominibus tradidit, hoc est, Dalmatice vertit. At hodie piaculum existimant sacras litteras vulgata legi lingua"; E. F. Rice, ed., *The Prefatory Epistles of Jacques Lefèvre d'Etaples and Related Texts* (New York, 1972), epp. 139 and 148, pp. 470 and 516. A tradition that Jerome had devised the Glagolitic alphabet in which the earliest liturgy of Old Church Slavonic was written goes back at least to the thirteenth century. For a detailed discussion, see Craig Thompson, "Jerome and the Testimony of Erasmus in Disputes over the Vernacular Bible," *Proceedings of the Patristic, Medieval, and Renaissance Conference* 6 (Augustinian Historical Institute, Villanova University, 1981): 1–36.
10. Ep. 21, 6. "[Deus] dedit liberum arbitrium, dedit mentis propriae uoluntatem, ut uiueret unusquisque non ex imperio Dei, sed ex obsequio suo, id est

non ex necessitate, sed ex uoluntate, ut uirtus haberet locum, ut a ceteris animantibus distaremus, dum ad exemplum Dei permissum est nobis facere quod uelimus. Vnde et in peccatores aequum iudicium et in sanctos haud iniustum praemium retribuetur." Cf. *Adv. Joviniamum*, II, 3 (*PL* 23:286–87). "Liberi arbitrii nos condidit Deus, nec ad virtutes, nec ad vitia necessitate trahimur. Alioquin ubi necessitas, nec corona est. Sicut in bonis operibus perfector est Deus, non est enim volentis, neque currentis, sed miserentis et adjuvantis Dei, ut pervenire valeamus ad calcem: sic in malis atque peccatis, semina nostra sunt incentiva, et perfectio diaboli."

11. *Huldreich Zwingli's Werke*, ed. M. Schuler and Joh. Schulthess, 4 vols. (Zurich, 1828–41), 1:71: Hörend ir, wie der schülmeister heisst, nit doctores, nit patres, nit Päpst, nit stül, nit concilia; er heisst der vater Jesu Christi"; 1:81: ". . . ist das unser meinung, dass das wort gottes von uns soll in höchsten eeren gehalten werden (wort gottes verstand allein das vom geist gottes kummt) und gheinem wort sölicher gloub gegeben als dem. Dann das ist gewüss, mag nit felen, est ist heiter, lasst nit in der finsterniss irren, es leert sich selbe"; *Zwingli and Bullinger* (*Library of Christian Classics*, 24), tr. G. W. Bromiley (London, 1953), 79–80, 83–84, 87–89, 93; Rom. 3:4. On the larger problem of the attitude of the Protestant reformers toward the church fathers, see Pontien Polman, *L'Elément historique dans la controverse religieuse de XVIe siècle* (Gembloux, 1932); S. L. Greenslade, *The English Reformers and the Fathers of the Church* (Oxford, 1960); and Peter Fraenkel, *Testimonia patrum. The Function of the Patristic Argument in the Theology of Philip Melanchthon* (*Travaux d'Humanisme et Renaissance*, 46) (Geneva, 1961).

12. *Tischreden*, no. 252 (*W.A.*, 1:106; *L.W.*, 54:33–34).

13. Ibid., no. 347 (*W.A.*, 1:140; *L.W.*, 54:49).

14. *Zwingli's Werke*, 1:73, 164.

15. Ibid., 2:463; Bromiley, 231; Jerome, *Comm. in Matheum*, IV, 26, 26 (*C.C.L.* 77:251).

16. Ibid., 1:78; Bromiley, 89.

17. Melanchthon, *De ecclesia et de autoritate verbi Dei*, "De Hieronymo" (*C.R.* [1855], 23:619–20); ibid., *Vita Hieronymi* (*C.R.* [1843], 11:734–41); Jerome, *Dialogus adv. Pelagianos*, I, 13 (*PL* 23:505B). Cf. ibid., II, 7 (*PL* 23:543B): "Manifeste ostendit, non in hominis merito, sed in Dei gratia esse justitiam, qui sine legis operibus credentium suscipit fidem"; or "Non enim justificatur homo ex operibus legis, nisi per fidem Jesu Christi" (ibid., II, 9, col. 544C); or "Unde et nos dicimus esse justos sanctos viros, et post peccata placentes Deo, non suo tantum merito, sed eius clementia, cui omnis creatura subjecta est, et indiget misericordia ejus" (ibid., II, 29, col. 567A). See also Fraenkel, *Testimonia patrum*, passim, but esp. 256–93.

18. *Institutio Christianae religionis*, Praef. and II, chaps. 2, 4, 6 (*Calvini Opera selecta*, 2d ed., ed. P. Barth and G. Niesel [Munich, 1957], 3:17, line 16–22, line 15; 245, lines 18–22, 248, line 30; 249, line 1; *Library of Christian Classics*, tr. John T. McNeill and Ford Lewis Battles [Philadelphia, 1960], 20:18–19, 258–59, 263); *De aeterna Dei praedestinatione* (*C.R.* [1870],

36:266); François Wendel, *Calvin. Sources et évolution de sa pensée religieuse* (Paris, 1950) 89-92.

19. The True Partaking of the Flesh and Blood of Christ in the Holy Supper, in Calvin, *Tracts and Treatises*, tr. H. Beveridge (Edinburgh, 1849), 548-49; *Calvin's Commentaries. The Epistles of Paul the Apostle to the Romans and to the Thessalonians*, tr. Ross Mackenzie (Edinburgh, 1960), 69; *The First Epistle of Paul the Apostle to the Corinthians*, tr. J. W. Fraser (Edinburgh, 1960), 134-35, 141, 143, 161, 165; *The Epistles of Paul the Apostle to the Galatians, Ephesians, Philippians, and Colossians*, tr. T. H. L. Parker (Edinburg, 1965), 38, 58, 227. The text Calvin cited on the Supper was *Comm. in Epist. ad Ephesios*, I, 7 (*PL* 26: 451A).

20. *A Treatise of the Holy Scriptures*, in *Works of John Jewel*, 4:1173-74. Cf. Martin Chemnitz, *Examination of the Council of Trent*, 150: "For we love and venerate the testimonies of the ancient and purer church, by whose agreement we are both aided and confirmed; but our faith must rest on the word of God, not on human authority. Therefore we do not set the testimonies of the fathers over the Scripture, but subordinate them to it."

21. Emile Mâle, *L'Art religieux de la fin de XVIe siècle, du XVIIe siècle et du XVIIIe siècle. Etude sur l'iconographie après le Concile de Trente*, 2d ed. (Paris, 1951), 63-64, 458-59; E. Kirschbaum, W. Braunfels, et al., *Lexikon der christlichen Ikonographie*, 8 vols. (Freiburg-im-Breisgau, 1968-76), 5:289 and 6:439.

22. Dublin, National Gallery of Ireland, c. 1630. See Michael Jaffé, *Jacob Jordaens, 1593-1678*. Exh. cat. National Gallery of Canada, 20 November 1968-5 January 1969 (Ottawa, 1968), no. 45, pp. 96-97.

23. *The Apotheosis of St. Thomas Aquinas*. Seville, Museo Provincial de Bellas Artes, 1631. Commissioned by the Dominican College of St. Thomas Aquinas in Seville for the high altar of its church. Martin S. Soria, *The Paintings of Zurbarán* (London, 1953), no. 41, p. 142 and pls. 27-28, and Tiziana Frati, *L'opera completa di Zurbarán* (Milan, 1973), no. 76, pl. 17.

24. Athanasius, Chrysostom, Ambrose, and Augustine: Exh. cat. Vatican City, Braccio di Carlo Magno, May-July 1981. *Bernini in Vaticano* (Rome, 1981), nn. 115-17, pp. 135-37; Rudolf Wittkower, *Gian Lorenzo Bernini*, 2d ed. (London, 1966), no. 61 and pls. 93-100; H. von Einem, "Bemerkungen zur Cathedra Petri des Lorenzo Bernini," *Nachrichten der Akademie der Wissenschaften in Göttingen* (I. Phil.-hist. Klasse, 1955), 93-114.

25. *Dessins baroques florentins du Musée du Louvre*. Exh. cat. Paris, Louvre, 2 October 1981-18 January 1982 (Paris, 1981), no. 18, pp. 38-39. The subject had been represented on Giovanni d'Andrea's house facade (see above, p. 67) and in manuscript illumination, for example, Par. lat. 17.294, fol. 597.

26. *Ep.* 15, 1-2. Nefta Grimaldi, *Il Guercino, Gian Francesco Barbieri (1591-1666)* (Bologna, s.a.), pl. 132; Denis Mahon, *Il Guercino (Giovanni Francesco Barbieri, 1591-1666) dipinti*. Exh. cat. Bologna Palazzo dell'Archiginnasio, 1 September-18 November 1968 (Bologna, 1968), no. 22, pp. 55-56.

27. *Mostra dei Carracci.* Exh. cat. Bologna, Palazzo dell'Archiginnasio, 1 September–31 October 1956 (Bologna, 1956), no. 39, pp. 147–50; Richard E. Spear, *Domenichino*, 2 vols. (New Haven and London, 1982), no. 41, I, 175–78 and pl. 141. There is another early seventeenth-century *Last Communion of St. Jerome*, by Giovan Battista Paggi, in the church of S. Francesco da Paola in Genoa (c. 1620) (V. Belloni, *Pittura genovese del Seicento dal Manierismo al Barocco* [Genoa, 1969], 95–104 and fig. 27.) Some earlier examples of the subject are Botticelli, *Last Communion of St. Jerome*, c. 1494–1495 (New York, Metropolitan Museum; R. Lightbown, *Sandro Botticelli*, 2 vols. [London, 1978], 1:120–22 and pl. 45; 2[B78]: 86–87); a predella panel from an altarpiece by Bartolomeo di Giovanni, c. 1500 (Baltimore, Walters Art Gallery; F. Zeri, *Italian Paintings in the Walters Art Gallery*, 2 vols. [Baltimore, 1976], 1(65):102–3 and pl. 50); and a miniature of the school of Bourdichon, c. 1510 (Paris, Bibliothèque Nationale, MS. fr. 418, fol. 97v). The literary source is *Ep. Ps.-Eusebii*, 52 (*PL* 22:274–75; Klapper, 209–13).

28. *Divi Hieronymi epistolae selectae, et in libros tres distributae, opera D. Petri Canisii theologi* (Lyons, J. Huguetan, 1592), sig. a, v. The prefatory epistle is dated Augsburg, 1565.

29. *Les Heures du Maréchal Boucicaut,* fol. 171v, Musée Jacquemart-André, Paris. Reproduced in M. Meiss, *French Painting in the Time of Jean de Berry. The Boucicaut Master* (London, 1948), fig. 42.

30. *Ep. supp.* 9 (ed. A. Ripberger, *Spicilegium Friburgense* [1962], 9:84); *Roman Breviary,* 8 December, II Nocturne, lessons 4 and 5 (English tr. New York: Benziger Brothers, 1964), 744.

31. Johannes Cochlaeus printed the Ps.-Jerome's *Cogitis me* with a brief commentary refuting Lutherans, Zwinglians, and Erasmus's *censura de authore* (see above, chap. 5, n. 45). Erasmus's stylistic arguments are weak, wrote Cochlaeus, and his hypothesis that the author was a Greek named Sophronius is an *infirma divinatio: Duo sermones de Beata Virgine Maria, Dei genitrice, nostra Domina: unus S. Hieronymi in eius laudem [= Cogitis me]: alter Mart. Lutheri in eius iniuriam, qui divinis est scripturis confutatus* (Mainz, Franciscus Behem, September 1548), sig. B, ij–B, iij, v.

32. Pierluigi De Vecchi, *L'opera completa del Tintoretto* (Milan, 1970), no. 215, p. 115; Diane Degrazia Bohlin, *Prints and Related Drawings by the Carracci Family* (Washington, D.C.: National Gallery of Art, 1979), no. 146, pp. 252–53.

33. M. Fagiolo dell'Arco, *Il Parmigianino. Un saggio sull'eremetismo nel Cinquecento* (Rome, 1970), no. 26, 42–43, 265–66, 490 and figs. 89–91; Paola Rossi, *L'opera completa del Parmigianino* (Milan, 1980), no. 35, 95–96 and pls. 31–32; *Ep. Ps.-Augustini* (*PL* 22:287–88; Klapper, 274–81); *Ep. Ps.-Cyrilli*, 25 (*PL* 22:323–24; Klapper, 493–503); and above, chap. 3, p. 52. Why Jerome is shown asleep remains puzzling. That he had had at least one dream vision (the Ciceronian dream) was well known. Nevertheless, sleep and dream may simply be iconographic shorthand denoting a vision, a means of showing that Jerome has once again been *raptus in spiritu*. Two bits

of evidence perhaps support this view: (1) several of the preparatory drawings show Jerome awake and in postures other than lying down; (2) in a picture of Jerome's "vision" of Roman dancing girls (Aynhoe Park, Northamptonshire, attributed to Veronese), Jerome is shown lying on the ground asleep in much the same attitude as in the Parmigianino. Since Jerome's own words clearly indicate that this erotic memory tormented him as he beat his chest in the wilderness, showing him asleep should be understood as a modest instance of legendary elaboration, designed to turn a figment of the saint's heated imagination into a real vision.

34. *Oratio Angeli Bergomen. Carmelitae Doctoris, Conventus S. Martini Regentis, De divinae sapientiae et Beati Hieronymi, theologorum Bonon. protectoris piissimi, laudibus* (Bologna, Ioannes Rossius, 1574), sig. A, 4–B, 1. On Angelo da Bergamo, see Cosme de Villiers, *Biblioteca Carmelitana*, 2 vols. (Rome, 1926; reproducing the original ed. of 1752), 1:104–24 and Mazzuchelli, *Scrittori d'Italia*, 2(2):932–33.

35. Ibid., sig. C, 3–C, 4.

36. *Contenta in hoc libello. Ysidorus de sectis et nominibus haereticorum. Divi Augustini libellus aureus de fide et operibus. S. Hieronymi liber de perpetua gloriosae Virginis Mariae virginitate. Epistola eiusdem contra Vigilantium de venerandis sanctorum reliquiis,* ed. Hieronymus Gebwiler (Strasbourg, Io. Grieninger, 12 March 1523), sig. A, iij, r–v.

37. Loys Laserre, *La vie de Monseigneur sainct Hierosme* (Paris, Josse Bade for himself and Jean Petit [1529]), chap. xxxiv, fols. 125v–126.

38. Jerome, *Epistolae selectae*, ed. Petrus Canisius (Lyons, 1592), sig. a, v.

39. *Epistres familieres de Sainct Hierosme, divisees en trois livres. Traduites de Latin en François par Iean de Lavardin, abbé de l'Estoille* (Paris, Guillaume Chaudière, 1585), sig. a., ij.

40. *Epistolas de S. Hieronymo,* tr. Juan de Molina (Valencia, 1520), fol. 330.

41. *Epistolas del glorioso doctor de la yglesia San Geronimo. Repartidas en seis libros para diversos Estados. Traduzidas en lengua castellana por el Licenciado Francisco López Cuesta* (Madrid, Luis Sanchez, 1613), sig. a, 2, r–v.

42. Laserre, *Vie di sainct Hierosme,* chap. xxxiv, fols. 130–31.

43. Ibid., chaps. iii, iv, xi, fols. 11–22 and 40.

44. Ibid., chap. xxiiij, fol. 59v.

45. *Epistolae D. Hieronymi Stridoniensis et libri contra haereticos, ex antiquissimis exemplaribus, mille et amplius mendis ex Erasmi correctione sublatis, nunc primum opere ac studio Mariani Victorii Reatini emendati, eiusdemque argumentis, & scholiis, illustrati,* 3 vols. (Rome, Paulus Manutius, in aedibus Populi Romani, 1565). See also Angelo Sacchetti Sassetti, *La vita e gli scritti di Mariano Vittori* (Rieti, 1917) and Francesco Barberi, *Paolo Manuzio e la stamperia del popolo Romano (1561–1570)* (Rome, 1942).

46. Ibid., 1: sig. a, 2.

47. Ibid., sig. a, 3v–b, 5v: *Vita divi Hieronymi Stridoniensis, falso antea ab Erasmo relata, nunc per Marianum Victorium Episcopum Reatinum ex eius scriptis vere edita, et amplissimo Cardinali Carolo Borromeo dicata.*

48. Ibid., sig. b, 5v.

49. Ibid., sig. a, 2v.
50. Notices of Jerome are scattered through vols. 5–7 (Lucca, 1739–41) of the *Annales ecclesiastici*. See esp. 5: ad an. 372, xl, p. 369, col. 2 and 7: ad an. 420, xlii–l, pp. 211–13. See also C. K. Pullapilly, *Caesar Baronius, Counter-Reformation Historian* (Notre Dame, Ind., 1975).
51. Gregorio de Andres Martinez, *Proceso inquisitorial del Padre Sigüenza* (Madrid, 1975); George Kubler, *Building the Escorial* (Princeton, 1982), 131–34.
52. *La vida de S. Gerónimo doctor de la santa iglesia* (Madrid, Tomas Iunti, 1595), 250–76.
53. Ibid., 647–53.
54. Ibid., 56–71.
55. *Conciliorum oecumenicorum decreta*, ed. J. Albergio et al. (Freiburg-im-Breisgau, 1962), 751–52; J. Waterworth, *The Canons and Decrees of the Sacred and Oecumenical Council of Trent* (London, 1888), 234–36.
56. Paola Barocchi, *Trattati d'arte del Cinquecento*, 2 vols. (Bari, 1960–62); P. Prodi, "Ricerche sulla teorica delle arti figurative nella Reforma cattolica," *Archivio italiano per la storia della pietà* 4 (1965): 121–212; A. W. A. Boschloo, *Annibale Carracci in Bologna. Visible Reality in Art after the Council of Trent*, 2 vols. (The Hague, 1974), 1:121–63.
57. *De historia SS. imaginum et picturarum pro vera earum usu contra abusus Libri IV* (Louvain, Ioannes Bogardus, 1594), bk. III, chap. 42, 156–58. In the first edition, entitled *De picturis et imaginibus sacris liber unus, tractans de vitandis circa eas abusibus, et de earundem significationibus* (Louvain, Hieronymus Wellaeus, 1570) the material on Jerome is at 52–53 and 127–28.
58. *Ep.* 14, 2 and 11.
59. *Quindecim signa quindecim dierum ante diem iudicii invenit Hieronymus in annalibus Hebraeorum*, or *Hieronymus autem in annalibus Hebraeorum invenit signa quindecim dierum*. Lambert, 3B, nn. 652–55 (67 MSS.); cf. nn. 656–60. See William W. Heist, *The Fifteen Signs before Doomsday* (East Lansing, Mich., 1952) and "The Fifteen Signs before Judgment: Further Remarks," *Mediaeval Studies* 22 (1960), 192–203; Erik von Kraemer, *Les quinze signes du Jugement dernier, poème anonyme de la fin du XIIe ou du début du XIIIe siècle publié d'après tous les manuscrits connus avec introduction, notes et glossaires* (*Commentationes humanarum litterarum*, 38–39) (Helsinki, 1966).
60. *Legenda aurea*, cap. 1 (2d ed., ed. T. Graesse [Leipzig, 1850], 6–7).
61. Paris, Bibliothèque Nationale, MS. fr. 2366 (s. XV), fol. 5v. The earliest occurrence of this text known to me is in Pietro Calo da Chioggia's notice of Jerome in his *Legendae de sanctis* (before 1340) (Biblioteca Apostolica Vaticana, MS. Barb. lat. 714, fol. 323, col. 2), where it appears as follows: "Nam sive coendam sive bibam sive adfaciam, semper videtur illa tuba teribilis sonare in auribus meis: Surgite mortui, venite ad iudicium." Barb. lat. 714 was copied during Pietro Calo's lifetime and belonged to Cardinal Matteo Orsini, who died in August 1340. It is the apparent absence of the fragment in earlier accounts of St. Jerome and collections of his sayings that causes me to date it to the early fourteenth century.

62. Pseudo-Jerome's prophetic epigram is a conflation of (1) a verse from Paul's first epistle to the Corinthians (10:31), quoted by the historical Jerome (*Ep.* 127, 4) in this form: "Sive comeditis, sive bibitis, sive quid agitis, omnia in gloriam Domini facientes: Whether you eat, whether you drink, whatever you do, do it to the glory of God"; (2) a sentence from one of Jerome's authentic letters (*Ep.* 66, 10): "Sive leges, sive scribes, sive vigilabis, sive dormies, Amos tibi semper bucina in auribus sonet, hic lituus excitet animam tuam: Whether you are reading or writing, whether awake or asleep, may [the prophet] Amos always sound his trumpet in your ears, may his horn arouse your soul" (a *bucina* is a curved instrument, a *lituus* one with a long, straight tube); and (3) a passage from the *Regula monacharum*, the spurious rule for nuns in the form of a letter from St. Jerome to St. Eustochium and her nuns in Bethlehem: "Dread the coming of your spouse and judge, dearest ones, when you have been laid to rest; dread the great and terrible day of judgment, day of wrath and day of ruin . . . when the lives of each of you will be weighed in the balance and merits rewarded. *Semper tuba illa terribilis vestris perstrepat auribus: Surgite mortui, venite ad iudicium:* May that terrifying trumpet always ring in your ears, saying, Arise ye dead and come to judgment" (*PL* 30:430). Cf. Cornelius van den Steen, *Commentaria in omnes D. Pauli Epistolas* (Antwerp, heirs of Martinus Nutius and I. Meursius, 1614), 737, col. 2: "Hinc et S. Hieron. fertur hoc documentum observasse, et aliis tradidisse: Sive bibas, sive comedas, sive vigiles, sive dormias, haec tibi tuba insonet: Surgite mortui, venite ad iudicium. Quanquam in operibus Hieron. haec sententia iam non reperiatur, eius tamen quid simile inventur in Regula monachorum tom. 4. operum S. Hieron. quae collecta est ex. S. Hieron. ac conscripta a superiore ordinis Hieronymiani, quam probavit Martinus quintus Pontifex, ut habetur initio regulae" (Lope de Olmedo, *Regula monachorum*, chap. 30; *PL* 30:387). I owe much of this to the valuable paper of John Hand, "Joos van Cleve and the St. Jerome in the Norton Gallery and School of Art" (Palm Beach Art Institute, Inc., 1972) and to Jonathan Brown, *Jusepe de Ribera, Prints and Drawings.* Exh. cat. The Art Museum, Princeton University, October–November 1973 (Princeton, 1973), 41–56.

63. G. Kaftal, *Iconography of the Saints in Tuscan Painting* (Florence, 1952), 534, fig. 614. Dr. James Hankins kindly examined the fresco for me *in situ.* He reports that the inscription on the scroll, although almost unreadable, seems to contain the word *sonare* and is therefore probably a version of *Sive bibo, sive comedo.* See also Ridderbos, 63–73.

64. Mario Salmi, "Jacopo Bedi," *Art in America* 11 (1922–23):150–58. In the Galleria Nazionale delle Marche, Urbino, a panel of a polyptych by Antonio Alberti, dated even earlier in 1430, shows Jerome and the same identifying inscription (R. Longhi, *Officina Ferrarese* [Florence, 1956], 11, fig. 24).

65. Cambridge, Fitzwilliam Museum, MS. 22, p. 25. The text is Jean de Vignay's French translation of the *Golden Legend* (c. 1330). See M. R. James, *Catalogue of the Manuscripts in the Fitzwilliam Museum* (Cambridge, 1895), 43–51.

66. Pöllmann, at 468.
67. Erwin Panofsky, *Albrecht Dürer*, 2d ed., 2 vols. (Princeton, 1945), 1:211–13; 2: Handlist No. 41, p. 12 and fig. 252.
68. Julius Held, *Dürers Wirkung auf die niederländische Kunst seiner Zeit* (The Hague, 1931), 81; Georges Marlier, *La Renaissance flammande. Pierre Coeck d'Alost* (Brussels, 1966), 254–58 and figs. 198–202; Max J. Friedländer, *Early Netherlandish Painting*, ed. H. Pauwels et al., tr. H. Norden (Brussels, 1971), 7: no. 70, pl. 64; (1972), 9(1): nn. 39 and 40, pl. 57; (1975), 12: nn. 162–65, pls. 92 and 93; Exh. cat. Brussels, Palais des Beaux-Arts, 1 October–27 November 1977. *Albert Dürer aux Pays-Bas, son voyage (1520–21), son influence* (Brussels, 1977), nn. 51, 341–43, 379, pp. 66, 159–60, 177, and figs. 112, 115, 131.
69. Cf. Varro, *Res rusticae,* I, 1, 1: "si est homo bulla, eo magis senex": Petronius, *Sat.* 42: "nos non pluris sumus quam bullae"; Horace, *Carm.* IV, 7, 16: "pulvis et umbra sumus"; I Cor. 15:30: "Cottidie morior per vestram gloriam"; Jerome, *Ep.* 54, 18: "cogita te cottidie esse morituram"; *Ep.* 60, 14: "Platonis sententia est omnem sapienti uitam meditationem esse mortis. . . . Aliud est conari, aliud agere; aliud uiuere moriturum, aliud mori uicturum. Ille moriturus ex gloria est; iste moritur semper ad gloriam. Debemus igitur et nos animo praemeditari quod aliquando futuri sumus, et quod—uelimus nolimus—abesse longius non potest"; *Ep.* 60, 19: "cotidie morimur, cotidie commutamur et tamen aeternos esse nos credimus."
70. Friedländer, *Early Netherlandish Painting,* 9 (1): no. 40, pl. 57.
71. *Fundación del monasterio de el Escorial* (Madrid, 1963), Discurso XIII, 329. Sigüenza noted in the choir of the church a fresco by a certain "Rómulo, pintor italiano": "la una [obra] es cuando San Jerónimo estaba escribiendo los libros con que sirvió a la Iglesia y un ángel que le tañe al oído una trompeta para significar la memoria continua que el santo tenía del Juicio Final, y en unos lejos que se descubren se ve el mismo santo en el yermo haciendo penitencia delante de un crucifijo." For a drawing, undated, of the same subject from the circle of the Carracci see R. Wittkower, *The Drawings of the Carracci in the Collection of Her Majesty the Queen at Windsor Castle* (London, 1952), 160, no. 484.
72. *The Illustrated Bartsch* (New York, 1984), 35:221. The print carries the following inscription: "Quatuor e sacris summum doctoribus Vnus / hic toto meditans pectore Iudicium / Conspicitur: Quantum a levibus praecordia curis / Separat, est tantum proximus ille Deo."
73. Brown, *Ribera Prints and Drawings,* no. 4, p. 66.
74. Mahon, *Guercino dipinti,* no. 39, pp. 88–90, dated "intorno al 1619–20." Professor Juergen Schulz has called to my attention a fictive painting of Jerome hearing the trumpet call, once on a wall of the "Stanza di Paolo Veronese" in the Villa Barbaro at Maser, but removed by a restorer named Ottorino Nonfarmale when the room was "restored" in 1955. The picture reproduces, much enlarged and in reverse, and with some variations,

Guercino's *St. Jerome.* The variations appear to derive from Ribera's 1621 prints.

75. Frati, *L'opera completa di Zurbarán,* no. 338, p. 110 and pl. 63. A. Pigler, *Barockthemen,* 2d ed., 2 vols. (Budapest, 1974), 1:435–36, lists thirty seventeenth-century examples of the subject. There are many more.

76. *Commentaria in omnes D. Pauli Epistolas,* 737, col. 2.

7: THE TRANSLATOR OF THE VULGATE BIBLE

1. Vienna, Kunsthistorisches Museum, 1631–35; E. Baccheschi, *L'opera completa di Guido Reni* (Milan, 1971), no.189a, p.11; Exh. cat. Vienna, Albertina, 14 May–5 July 1981. *Guido Reni Zeichnungen* (Vienna, 1981), nn. 121–23, pp. 168–69. There is a variant, later in date, in Detroit. See D. Stephen Pepper, "*The Angel Appearing to Saint Jerome* by Guido Reni, a New Acquisition," *Bulletin of the Detroit Institute of Arts* 48(2) (1969): 28–35.

2. *Vita Hieronymi (PL* 22: 186–87 and 196).

3. *Speculum historiale,* XVI, xix (Venice, ed. September 1494, fol. 199).

4. *De scriptoribus ecclesiasticis,* 2d ed. (Paris, Berthold Rembolt, 16 October 1512), fol. 27.

5. Hody, 430–33.

6. *Opus Minus,* in *Fr. Rogeri Bacon opera quaedam hactenus inedita,* ed. J. S. Brewer (Rolls Series, 15) (London, 1859), 330–49.

7. *Summa Domini Armacani in questionibus Armenorum,* ed. Joannes Sudoris (Paris, Ponset le Preux for Jean Petit, 1511/12), XIX, 18–42, sig. C, i-C, iii.

8. *Annotationes in Novum Testamentum,* in *Opera* (Basel, Henricus Petrus, March 1540), 843, col. 1 ("semibarbarus"); 844, col. 1 ("Inepte translatum et idcirco inepta sententia"); 849, col. 2 ("Nimis inculta oratio, nec plane graeco vocabulo respondens"); 862, col. 1, ad I Cor. 2:9: *"Nec in cor hominis ascendit, quae praeparavit deus, qui diligunt illum.* Interpres non animadvertit verbum graecum, etsi numeri singularis, tamen fuisse transferendum pluraliter, ut facit Hieronymus in epistola super pentateuchum, *nec in cor hominis ascenderunt;* ut appareat aut non esse hunc interpretem Hieronymum, aut eius interpretationem fuisse corruptam. Idem vitium paulo post." For more examples see S. Garofalo, "Gli umanisti italiani del secolo XV e la Bibbia," *La Bibbia e il Concilio di Trento (Scripta Pontificii Instituti Biblici,* 96) (Rome, 1947), 44–55, and Jerry H. Bentley, *Humanists and Holy Writ. New Testament Scholarship in the Renaissance* (Princeton, 1983), 32–69.

9. *Johann Reuchlins Briefwechsel,* ed. Ludwig Geiger (Bibliothek des Litterarischen Vereins in Stuttgart, CXXVI) (Tübingen, 1875), ep. 15, p. 16; *De rudimentis Hebraeicis* (Pforzheim, Thomas Anshelm, 27 March 1506), 549; and Werner Schwartz, *Principles and Problems of Biblical Translation. Some Reformation Controversies and Their Background* (Cambridge, 1955), 61–91.

10. *Des. Erasmi Roterodami in Novum Testamentum ad eodem denuo recognitum Annotationes* (Basel, Johann Froben, March 1519), sig. aa2, v; p. 131, *in margine;* p. 135, *in marg.;* p. 236. See also Schwarz, op. cit., 92–166, and J. H. Bentley, "Erasmus' *Annotationes in Novum Testamentum* and the Textual Criticism of the Gospels," *Archiv für Reformationsgeschichte* 46 (1976): 33–75.

11. "Apologia quod vetus interpretatio epistolarum beatissimi Pauli quae passim legitur non sit tralatio Hieronymi," in *Contenta. Epistola ad Rhomanos. Epistola prima ad Corinthios . . . Commentariorum libri quatuordecim. Linus de passione Petri & Pauli* (Paris, Henri Estienne, 15 December 1512), sig. a, ii, v–a, iiij, v.

12. E. F. Sutcliffe, "The Name 'Vulgate'" and A. Allgeier, "Haec vetus et vulgata editio," *Biblica* 29 (1948): 345–52, 353–90.

13. Lefèvre, "Apologia," concluding (sig. a, iiij, v): "plane intelliget ex eodem non modo epistolarum Pauli, sed nec evangeliorum traductionem qua nunc utuntur ecclesiae esse Hieronymianam." Many modern scholars think that Jerome revised only the Gospels and use arguments very similar to Lefèvre's to show that he did not revise the rest of the New Testament. The Vulgate of the Pauline and Catholic epistles (and probably of Acts and Revelation also) is likely the work of an editor active in Rome at the end of the fourth century. He has recently been identified, very plausibly, as Rufinus the Syrian, a priest and monk from Jerome's own monastery in Bethlehem, sent by him on a mission to the imperial court c. 398. See F. Cavallera, "Saint Jérôme et la Vulgate des Actes, des Epîtres et de l'Apocalypse," *Bulletin de littérature ecclésiastique* 21 (1920), 269–92; H. J. Frede, *Ein neuer Paulustext and Kommentar,* 2 vols. (Freiburg-im-Breisgau, 1973), 1: 253–55; H. J. Frede, ed., *Vetus Latina* 25/2, *Epistulae ad Thessalonicenses, Timotheum, Titum, Philomenem, Hebraeos* (Freiburg, 1976), 99–100 and 155, n. 49. Cf. Gerald Bonner, "Rufinus of Syria and African Pelagianism," *Augustinian Studies* 1 (1970): 31–47; Eugene TeSelle, "Rufinus the Syrian, Caelestius, Pelagius: Explorations in the Prehistory of the Pelagian Controversy," *Augustinian Studies* 3 (1972): 61–95; and O. Wermelinger, *Rom und Pelagius. Die theologische Position der römischen Bischöfe in pelagianischem Streit in den Jahren 411–432* (Stuttgart, 1975), 12–15.

14. *Paulina de recta paschae celebratione: et de die passionis domini nostri Iesu Christi* (Fossembrone, Octavianus Petrutius, 8 July 1513), bk. II, chap. 1, sig. B, vi–vi, v: "Ex quibus constare arbitror beatum Hieronymum novum testamentum prout in ecclesia canitur non traduxisse. Posset quoque id plurimis exemplis probari quibus idem in suis commentariis hanc ipsam damnat translationem ab ecclesia usu habitam, et quasi ab alio factam carpit, et interpretem reprehendit. . . . Apparet ergo quod haec usitata aeditio non est a Hieronymo translata. . . . Nobis autem impraesentiarum sat est Hieronymum hanc nostram translationem damnare et a se factam negare, quod et plurimis aliis locis deduci potest."

15. Ibid., sig. B, vii–B, viii, v: "Redeuntes ergo ad primum nostrum propositum satis constare arbitror translationem nostram usitatam a Hieronymo

minime factam esse, quandoquidem eam damnans plurimis in locis corruptam docet non solum in novo, sed etiam in veteri testamento. . . . Praeterea Augustinus libro .18. de civitate dei docet Hieronymi ex Hebraica veritate aeditionem ab ecclesia non fuisse receptam, sed Septuaginta interpretum translationem in usu ecclesiae duntaxat haberi. . . . Ex quibus apparet Hieronymi interpretationem ab ecclesia non fuisse acceptam. . . . Satis itaque constare arbitror usitatam translationem non esse ipsius Hieronymi, licet eius praefatiunculae in ipsius exordiis sint praemissae.''

16. So in the "Apologia" prefacing the New Testament (Basel, Froben, 1516): "Iam illud quemadmodum extra controversiam est apud eruditos, ita indoctis etiam multorum libris persuasum esse reor hanc novi testamenti editionem Hieronymi non esse; tametsi nos nec hanc, qualiscunque est aut cuiuscunque est, neque convellimus ullo modo neque calumniamur" (ed. Holborn, 165, lines 26–31). See also Epp. 326, 337, 456, 843 (Allen, 2:57–58, 110–11, 324–25; 3:313, lines 17–24; *C.W.E.* 3:71, 134–35; 4:45; 6:5–14).

17. *Biblia* (Lyons, Antoine du Ry, 29 January 1527/28), sig. d, iij, v.

18. *En tibi lector Hebraica Biblia Latina planeque nova Sebast. Munsteri tralatione*, 2 vols. (Basel, H. Bebelius for Michael Isingrinius and Henricus Petrus, 1534–35), 1:sig. a, 5v–b, 1v.

19. *Psalmorum omnium iuxta Hebraicam veritatem paraphrastica interpretatio* (Paris, Claude Chevallon, 1533), sig. a, ij, a.

20. *Annotationes Iacobi Lopidis Stunicae contra Iacobum Fabrum Stapulensem* (Alcalá, Arnaldus Guilielmus de Brocarius, 1519). See H. J. de Jonge's notice of Stunica in the introduction to his edition of Erasmus's *Apologia ad Annotationes Stvnicae* (*Opera Omnia*, 9 (2) [Amsterdam-Oxford, 1983], 13–43).

21. *Collationes quinque super Epistolam ad Romanos beati Pauli Apostoli* (Antwerp, Guilielmus Vorstermanus, May 1529). On Franz Titelmans see H. de Jongh, *L'ancienne faculté de théologie de Louvain au premier siècle de son existence, 1432–1540* (Louvain, 1911), 249, n. 1; Allen, 7:69; Leopold von Ebersberg, in *Lexikon für Theologie und Kirche* (1965), 10:210–11; and J. H. Bentley, "New Testament Scholars at Louvain in the Early Sixteenth Century," *Studies in Medieval and Renaissance History*, n.s. 2 (1979): 69–79.

22. *Ioannis Driedonis a Turnhout theologiae professoris apud Lovanienses, De ecclesiasticis scripturis et dogmatibus Libri.4.* (Louvain, Rutgerius Rescius, 10 June 1533). See also de Jongh, op. cit., 156–60; H. de Vocht, *Monvmenta Hvmanistica Lovaniensia. Texts and Studies about Louvain Humanists in the First Half of the XVIth Century (Hvmanistica Lovaniensia, 4)* (Louvain, 1934), 344–45; R. Draguet, "Le maître louvaniste Driedo inspirateur du décret de Trente sur la Vulgate," in *Miscellanea historica in honorem Alberti de Meyer*, 2 vols. (Louvain, 1946), 2:836–45; B. Emmi, "Il posto del *De Ecclesiasticis Scripturis et Dogmaticis* nelle discussioni tridentine," *Ephemerides Theologiae Louvanienses* 25 (1949): 588–97; and J. Etienne, *Spiritualisme érasmien et théologiens louvanistes* (Louvain, 1956), 105–60 (bibliography).

23. In his *Opera omnia*, ed. Ambrosius Morandus, 3 vols. (Venice, Dominicus

Nicolinus, 1591), 1:239–48; Th. Freudenberger, *Augustinus Steuchus aus Gubbio, Augustinerchorherr und päpstlicher Bibliothekar (1479–1548) und sein literarisches Lebenswerk* (Münster, 1935).

24. Titelmans, *Collationes,* sig. d, 4v–e, 1; Driedo, *De eccl. scrip.,* 85–87, 89.

25. Titelmans, *Collationes,* sig. a, 4v–a, 5v and a, 7v; Steucho, *Opera,* 1: fols. 244v–248.

26. Driedo, *De eccl. scrip.,* 81:

Quamquam probabile est vulgatam aeditionem, qua in novo Testamento Ecclesia nunc utitur, non esse pure Hieronymianam ac castigatam ad veritatem Graecae fidei, sed mixtam quandam, partim ex illa, partim ex editione quadam olim vulgata, non sunt tamen ulla neque evangelica praecepta neque fidei mysteria in hac aeditione nostra vel praetermissa vel obscure designata, quae non in eadem apertissimis locis sunt declarata. . . . Ex cuius [aeditionis] sive soloecismis, sive sententiis minus forsitan apte versis neque comprobatur, neque fovetur ulla haeresis, in qua fidei nostrae mysteria sufficienter declarantur, in qua neque sit quicquam quod praestet occasionem errandi pernitiose. Unde credimus neque in Graecis Hebraicisque exemplaribus esse ullum Christianae fidei mysterium, ullumve salutis humanae dogma necessarium, quod hactenus aut fugerit aut latuerit Latinorum Ecclesiam, aut si omissum aut contrarie positum in aeditione nostra Latina, quanvis in ea sint loca nonnulla aut ambigue aut obscure aut minus congrue posita, quae hactenus etiam eruditissimi patres tollaverunt, non quod ignoraverint aut approbaverint errores, sed quia viderint nihil periculi in fede et moribus pendere ex huiusmodi locis, vel non prorsus a suo fonte deviis, vel etiam aut sic aut aliter interpretatis.

Also, ibid., 90: "Nam fidei et morum praecepta aliaque ad salutem utilia sufficienter sunt expressa et declarata in aeditione nostra Latina, eaque in quibus discrepat aeditio nostra Latina a veritate Graeca non multum iuvare possunt haereticos. Quamobrem non oportet nos turbari, si quibusdam in locis aeditionis nostrae scriptura sit vel ambigua vel obscura vel suspecta tanquam aliquantulum devia a mente scriptoris."

27. Ibid., 82, 96–100.

28. *De recta paschae celebratione,* sig. C, iii: "Ex hac et tanta translationum diversitate inferri potest aeditionem non debere dici autenticam ex hoc solo quod in usu ecclesiae extitit, maxime si ab originali fuerit discrepans; vel saltem originalia et prototypa ab apostolis et evangelistis vel a prophetis conscripta magis erunt autentica. Praeterea veritas evangelii est una et aeterna, translationes vero sunt multae et temporales, pro beneplacito summi pontificis mutabiles et abolendae, originale vero semper unum et idem manet; ergo translationes non debent dici simpliciter autenticae, nisi fuerint originali conformes." A lively advocate of the more radically conservative inspirational view was Petrus Sutor (Pierre Cousturier), who in his *De tralatione bibliae et novarum reprobatione interpretationum* (Paris, 1525) argued not only that Jerome had translated the entire Vulgate under the

direct inspiration of the Holy Spirit but that in order to prepare him for the task God had carried him off to the third heaven. For a full account see Heinz Holeczek, *Humanistische Bibelphilologie als Reformproblem bei Erasmus von Rotterdam, Thomas More, und William Tyndale* (Leiden, 1975), 186–245.

29. *Praef. in Pentateuchum (PL 28: 151A)*.

30. *Comm. in Galat.* I, 11 *(PL 26: 447A)*: "Nec putemus in verbis scripturarum esse Evangelium, sed in sensu; non in superficie, sed in medulla; non in sermonum foliis, sed in radice rationis."

31. Titelmans, *Collationes,* sig. c, 6v–d, 4.

32. Ep. 844 (Allen, 3:331–33; *C.W.E.* 6:28–30).

33. Driedo, *De Eccl. scrip.*, 72, 87–90. The church thus ratifies Jerome's translation, not because it is in perfect consonance with the originals, "sed tanquam omnibus aeditionibus tunc factis praeferendum, et in regulis fidei et morum nusquam deviam, et tanquam talem quae publice legatur et recipiatur in usum, quae et ad scripturas in suo fonte diligenter collata, excussa, et examinata nihil contineat subdole vel adiectum vel immutatum" (ibid., 96).

34. Steucho, *Opera,* I, 241–241v; Freudenberger, *Augustinus Steuchus,* 171–72.

35. Steucho, *Opera,* I, fols. 247v–248.

36. Stunica, *Contra Fabrum,* sig. A, 5-5v.

37. Driedo, *De eccl. scrip.,* 79–80, 87. Cf. above, n. 26.

38. *Praef. in Tobit (PL 29: 23–26); Praef. in Judith (PL 29: 37–40)*.

39. R. Weber, ed., *Le psautier Romain et les autres anciens Psautiers latins (Collectanea Biblica Latina,* 10) (Rome, 1953); *Liber Psalmorum ex recensione S. Hier.* (= vol. 10 of the Benedictine Vulgate) (Rome, 1953); and H. de Sainte-Marie, ed., *Psalterium iuxta Hebraeos (Collectanea Biblica Latina,* 11) (Rome, 1954). Triple Psalters survive from the ninth to the thirteenth century containing all three versions in parallel columns. Quadruple Psalters are also known; a particularly fine one was copied at St. Gall in 909, with the three versions of Jerome plus the Septuagint Greek transcribed in Latin characters. See V. Leroquais, *Les Psautiers manuscrits latins des bibliothèques publiques de France,* 2 vols. (Macon, 1940–41), 1:153–54; 2:18, 78–91, 119–20. The first part of the *Quincuplex Psalterium* of Lefèvre d'Etaples (1509) reproduces a typical triple Psalter (E. F. Rice, ed., *Prefatory Epistles of Jacques Lefèvre d'Etaples* [New York, 1972], ep. 66, 192–201).

40. Titelmans, *Collationes,* sig. a, 7v.

41. *Concilium Tridentinum,* ed. Societas Goerresiana (Freiburg-im-Breisgau, 1911), 5: 91–92. The translation is by E. F. Sutcliff, "The Council of Trent on the *Authentia* of the Vulgate," *Journal of Theological Studies* 49 (1948): 35–36.

42. H. Höpfl, *Beiträge zur Geschichte der Sixto-Klementinischen Vulgata* (Freiburg-im-Breisgau, 1913), 4–8; G.-M. Vosté, "La Volgata al Concilio di Trento," *La Bibbia e il Concilio di Trento (Scripta Pontificii Instituti Biblici,* 96) (Rome, 1947), 1–19; Sutcliffe, "Council of Trent," 35–42; H. Jedin,

Papal Legate at the Council of Trent. Cardinal Seripando, tr. F. C. Eckhoff (London, 1947), 295–99; ibid., *A History of the Council of Trent,* tr. E. Graf, 2 vols. (London, 1961), 2:58–97.

43. *Acta Concilii Tridentini, anno M.D. XLVI celebrati: una cum annotationibus piis ac lectu dignissimis* (N.p., 1546), sig. h, 1v–h, 3v.

44. *Acta Synodi Tridentinae. Cum antidoto* (N.p., 1547), 98–99, 102.

45. *Examination of the Council of Trent,* tr. Fred Kramer, 2 vols. (St. Louis, 1971), 1:201–2.

46. *De editione latina Vulgata, quo sensu a Concilio Tridentino definitum sit, ut pro authentica habeatur,* in X.-M. LeBachelet, *Bellarmine et la Bible Sixto-Clementine* (Paris, 1911), 107.

47. Hody, 510–39.

48. *Biblia Sacra vulgatae editionis,* ed. Monachi abbatiae pontificiae Sancti Hieronymi in Urbe (Rome, 1959), x–xi. The text will be found in almost any other edition of the Vulgate Bible as well.

49. Hody, 531–32, 541.

50. Bologna, S. Martino Maggiore, 1598; H. Bodmer, *Lodovico Carracci* (Burg b.M., 1939), no. 45 and pl. 47.

51. London, National Gallery, 1602; Michael Levey, *National Gallery Catalogues. The Seventeenth and Eighteenth Century Italian Schools* (London, 1971), 95–96; Richard E. Spear, *Domenichino,* 2 vols. (New Haven, 1982), 1:126(2) and pl. 3. This is one of two of Domenichino's earliest surviving documented pictures; it is recorded in an inventory of 1603 in the collection of Cardinal Pietro Aldobrandini.

52. Madrid, Prado, c. 1603. Illustrated by H. Voss, *Die Malerie der Barock in Rom* (Berlin, 1924), 198. Traditionally attributed to Domenichino, but ascribed to Albani by Donald Posner (*Arte Antica e Moderna* 12 [1960]: 411, n. 66) and Denis Mahon (Exh. cat. *L'ideale classico del seicento in Italia e la pittura di paesaggio.* Bologna. V Mostra biennale d'arte antica [Bologna, 1962], no. 18, pp. 97–98).

53. Potsdam-Sanssouci, Bildergalerie, c. 1609; Hans Vlieghe, *Corpus Rubenianum Ludwig Burchard, 8. Saints,* tr. P. S. Falla, 2 vols. (New York, 1973), 2:97–99 and fig. 65.

54. (a) Rotterdam, Museum Boymans-van Beuningen and (b) Stockholm, Nationalmuseum, 1620–21; Alan McNairn, *The Young van Dyck.* Exh. cat. National Gallery of Canada (Ottawa, 1980), nn. 74 and 75, pp. 160–65.

55. Washington, National Gallery, c. 1625; W. R. Crelly, *The Painting of Simon Vouet* (New Haven, 1962), no. 153, fig. 25.

56. Venice, S. Niccolò da Tolentino, c. 1627; Exh. cat. Augsburg, Rathaus and Cleveland Museum of Art, 2 August 1975–7 March 1976. *Johann Liss* (Augsburg, 1975), no. A39 and color pl. 9. The pictures carry various titles at present: *The Vision of St. Jerome, The Angel Appearing to St. Jerome, St. Jerome in His Study, St. Jerome with the Angel, St. Jerome and the Angel, The Inspiration of St. Jerome,* or simply *St. Jerome.* A more accurate title for all such pictures would be *The Inspiration of St. Jerome.*

57. Par. lat. 1141, fol. 3 (Amédée Boinet, *La miniature carolingienne. Planches* [Paris, 1913], pl. 131); Cambridge, Corpus Christi College, MS. 389, fol. 1v (Francis Wormald, *English Drawings of the Tenth and Eleventh Centuries* [London, 1952], 61 and pl. 36); and Lambert, 4A, pl. 3.

58. M. Meiss, *French Painting in the Time of Jean de Berry. The Limbourgs and Their Contemporaries,* 2 vols. (London, 1974), 2: fig. 357; ibid., "French and Italian Variations on an Early Fifteenth-Century Theme: St. Jerome in His Study," *Gazette des Beaux-Arts* 62 (1963): 147-50. In an *Inspiration of St. Jerome* in an early fifteenth-century Hours of the Virgin (British Library, MS. Royal 2 A. VIII, 113v), rays of golden light play around Jerome's head as he turns to listen to the dove of the Holy Spirit murmuring in his ear.

59. M. Bucci et al., *Mostra del Cigoli e del suo ambiente* (San Miniato al Tedesco, 1959), no. 26, pp. 76-78; Exh. cat., Paris, Louvre, 2 October 1981-18 January 1982. *Dessins baroques florentins du Musée du Louvre* (Paris, 1981), no. 18, p. 38.

60. H. van de Waal, "Rembrandt's Faust Etching, a Socinian Document, and the Iconography of the Inspired Scholar," *Oud Holland* 79 (1964): 39, n. 83, lists examples of the *Inspiration of St. Matthew.* The earliest he illustrates is a sculpture from Chartres. See also the important article by Irving Lavin, "Divine Inspiration in Caravaggio's two St. Matthews," *Art Bulletin* 56 (1974): 59-81, to which I owe much.

61. On the various pairings of the four evangelists and the four doctors of the Latin church, see Barbier de Montault, "Le culte des Docteurs de l'Eglise à Rome," *Revue de l'art chrétien* 41 (1891): 116. Although Jerome was eventually paired with Mark because each had a lion, he was also frequently paired with Matthew: for example, in a frescoed pendentive in the church of S. Maria in Porto fuori città at Ravenna (c. 1350) or Correggio's pendentive in S. Giovanni Evangelista in Parma (1520-24). The key passage in Jerome's preface to his Commentary on Matthew is the following: "[Ecclesia] quattuor flumina paradisi instar eructans quattuor et angulos et anulos habet, per quos quasi arca testamenti et custos legis Domini lignis inmobilibus uehitur. Primus omnium Matheus est, publicanus cognomine Leui, qui euangelium in Iudaea hebreo sermone edidit. . . . Haec igitur quattuor euangelia multo ante praedicta Hiezechielis quoque uolumen probat, in quo prima uisio ita contexitur: *Et in medio sicut similitudo quattuor animalium, et uultus eorum facies hominis et facies leonis et facies uituli et facies aquilae.* Prima hominis facies Matheum significat" (ed. E. Bonnard, *S.C.* 242 [Paris, 1977], 1:62 and 64.

62. Paris, BN., Ms. lat. 13.285, fols. 17v-18 (*Horae,* English, s. XV; V. Leroquais, *Les Livres d'Heures manuscrits de la Bibliothèque Nationale* [Paris, 1927], 2: 88-99, no. 212):
    Sanctus Ieronimus in hoc modo disposuit hoc Psalterium, sicut angelus domini docuit eum per spiritum sanctum. Et propter hoc abreviatum est, quod illi qui solitudinem habent seculi, vel qui infirmitatibus iacent, vel qui operibus occupantur, vel qui iter longum agunt, vel qui navigio

navigant, vel qui bellum commissuri sunt contra hostes, vel qui contra invidiam diabolorum militant, vel qui votum voverunt domino cantare magnum psalterium et non possunt, vel qui ieiunant fortiter et debilitatem habent, vel qui solempnia festa custodiunt et non possunt cantare magnum psalterium, istud cantent. Et qui animam suam salvare voluerit secundum misericordiam dei assidue cantet istud et possidebit regnum dei.

For the same text, see also BN., MS. fr. 24.748, fols. 140–140v; British Library, King's MS. 9, fols. 238–238v; Royal 2.A. VIII, fols. 111v–112; Cambridge, Fitzwilliam Museum, MSS. 49, fol. 86; 51, fol. 130v; 52, fol. 118; 54, fol. 163; 153, fol. 280. For Ficino's translation see P. O. Kristeller, "Marsilio Ficino letterato e le glosse attribuite a lui nel codice Caetani di Dante," *Quaderni della Fondazione Camillo Caetani* (Rome, 1981), 3: 30–31.

Bibliography

Note: The Bibliography lists secondary works selected from those cited in the Notes. Ancient, medieval, and Renaissance texts and authors can be retrieved through the Index.

Abel, E. "Isota Nogarola." *Vierteljahrschrift für Kultur und Literatur der Renaissance* 1 (1886): 323-55, 440-73.

Aigrain, René. *L'hagiographie. Ses sources, ses méthodes, son histoire.* Paris, 1953.

Albert Dürer aux Pays-Bas, son voyage (1520-1521), son influence, Exh. cat. Brussels, Palais des Beaux-Arts. 1 October–27 November 1977. Brussels, 1977.

Allerit, Odette d'. "Hiéronymites." In *Dictionnaire de spiritualité,* vol. 7, 451-62. Paris, 1969.

Allgeier, A. "Haec vetus et vulgata editio." *Biblica* 29 (1948): 353-90.

Andres Martinez, Gregorio de. *Proceso inquisitorial del Padre Sigüenza.* Madrid, 1975.

Antin, P. *Recueil sur Saint Jérôme* (*C.L.* 95). Brussels, 1968.

Arns, E. *La technique du livre d'après Saint Jérôme,* Paris, 1953.

Babinger, F. *Laudivius Zacchia, Erdicter der "Epistolae Magni Turci."* Sitzungsberichte der Bayer. Akad. d. Wissenschaften, Philos.-hist. Kl. Jahrg. 1960, Heft 13. Munich, 1960.

Barbier de Montault, A. "Le culte des Docteurs de l'Eglise à Rome." *Revue de l'art chrétien* 43 (1893): 106-18.

Bardenhewer, O. *Geschichte der altkirchlichen Literatur.* 2d ed. 4 vols. Freiburg-im-Breisgau, 1913-24.

Bartelink, G. J. M. *Hieronymus. Liber de optimo genere interpretandi (Epistula 57). Ein Kommentar* (*Mnemosyne,* Supplement, 61). Leiden, 1980.

Baxandall, Michael. *Giotto and the Orators.* Oxford, 1971.

Béné, Charles. *Erasme et Saint Augustin ou influence de Saint Augustin sur l'humanisme d'Erasme* (*Travaux d'Humanisme et Renaissance,* 103). Geneva, 1969.

Bentley, J. H. "Erasmus' *Annotationes in Novum Testamentum* and the Textual Criticism of the Gospels." *Archiv für Reformationsgeschichte* 66 (1976): 33–75.

———. *Humanists and Holy Writ. New Testament Scholarship in the Renaissance.* Princeton, 1983.

Bergström, I. "Disguised Symbolism in Madonna Pictures and Still Life." *Burlington Magazine* 27 (1955): 303–8, 340–49.

———. "Medicina, Fons et Scrinium: A Study in Van Eychean Symbolism and Its Influence in Italian Art." *Konshistorisk Tidskrift* 26 (1957): 1–20.

Biasiotti, G. "La reproduzione della grotta della Natività di Betlemme nella basilica di Santa Maria Maggiore in Roma." *Dissertazioni della Pontificia Accademia Romana di Archeologia* 15 (1921): 95–110.

La Bibbia e il Concilio di Trento (Scripta Pontificii Instituti Biblici, 96). Rome, 1947.

Bietenholz, P. G. *History and Biography in the Work of Erasmus of Rotterdam (Travaux d'Humanisme et Renaissance, 87).* Geneva, 1966.

Bonner, G. "Rufinus of Syria and African Pelagianism." *Augustinian Studies* 1 (1970): 31–47.

Boon, A. *Pachomiana Latina.* Louvain, 1932.

Boschloo, A. W. A. *Annibale Carracci in Bologna. Visible Reality in Art after the Council of Trent.* 2 vols. The Hague, 1974.

Braverman, J. *Jerome's Commentary on Daniel: A Study of Comparative Jewish and Christian Interpretations of the Hebrew Bible.* Washington, D.C., 1978.

Brown, Jonathan. *Jusepe de Ribera. Prints and Drawings.* Exh. cat. The Art Museum, Princeton University. October–November 1973. Princeton, 1973.

Brown, Peter. *Augustine of Hippo.* London, 1967.

———. *The Cult of the Saints.* Chicago, 1981.

Brunori, D. *L'Eremo di S. Girolamo a Fiesole.* Fiesole, 1920.

Cavallera, F. "Saint Jérôme et la Vulgate des Actes, des Epîtres et de l'Apocalypse." *Bulletin de littérature ecclésiastique* 21 (1920): 269–92.

———. *Saint Jérôme, sa vie et son oeuvre.* 2 vols. Louvain, 1922.

Cividali, Pia. *Il beato Giovanni dalle Celle (Memorie della R. Accademia dei Lincei,* ser. 5, vol. 12, fasc. 5). Rome, 1907.

Colloquia Erasmiana Turonensia. Douzième stage international d'études humanistes: Tours 1969. 2 vols. Paris, 1972.

Colloquium Erasmianum. Actes du Colloque international réuni à Mons du 26 au 29 octobre à l'occasion du cinquième centenaire de la naissance d'Erasme. Mons, Centre Universitaire de l'Etat, 1968.

Contardi, Bruno, and A. Gentili, eds. *Il S. Girolamo di Lorenzo Lotto a Castel S. Angelo.* Rome, 1983.

Courcelle, Pierre. *Les lettres grecques en Occident de Macrobe à Cassiodore.* Paris, 1943.

———. *Recherches sur saint Ambroise. "Vies" anciennes, culture, iconographie.* Paris, 1973.

Courcelle, P., and Jeanne Courcelle. *Iconographie de St. Augustin. Les cycles du XIVe siècle.* Paris, 1965.

———. *Iconographie de St. Augustin. Les cycles du XVe siècle.* Paris, 1969.

D'Amico, J. F. "Beatus Rhenanus, Tertullian, and the Reformation." *Archiv für Reformationsgeschichte* 71 (1980): 37–63.

Delcorno, C. "Per l'edizione delle *Vite dei santi Padri* del Cavalca. La tradizione manoscritta: i codici delle biblioteche fiorentine." *Lettere italiane* 29 (1977): 265–89; 30 (1978): 47–87, 480–524.

Delehaye, H. *Sanctus, essai sur le culte des saints dans l'antiquité.* Brussels, 1927.

———. *Les origines du culte des martyrs (Subsidia Hagiographica, 20).* Brussels, 1933.

———. *Les Légendes hagiographiques.* 4th ed. Brussels, 1955.

Dell'Osta, R. *Un teologo del potere papale e suoi rapporti col cardinalato nel secolo XV, ossia Teodoro de' Lelli.* Belluno, 1948.

Di Girolamo, Costanzo. *Libru di lu transitu et vita di Misser Sanctu Iheronimu (Collezione di testi siciliani dei secoli XIV e XV, 15).* Palermo, 1982.

Dondaine, A. "Le Dominican français Jean de Mailly et la Légende dorée." *Archives d'histoire dominicaine* 1 (1946): 53–102.

Draguet, R. "Le maître louvaniste Driedo inspirateur du décret de Trente sur la Vulgate." In *Miscellanea historica in honorem Alberti de Meyer.* 2 vols. vol. 2, 836–45. Louvain, 1946.

Dufner, Georg. *Geschichte der Jesuaten (Uomini e dottrine, 21).* Rome, 1975.

Eisenberg, M. "The Penitent St. Jerome by Giovanni Toscani." *Burlington Magazine* 118 (1976): 275–83.

Emmi, B. "Il posto del *De ecclesiasticis scripturis et dogmaticis* nelle discussioni tridentine." *Ephemerides theologiae Louvanienses* 25 (1949): 588–97.

Etienne, J. *Spiritualisme érasmien et théologiens louvanistes.* Louvain, 1956.

Fagiolo dell'Arco, M. *Il Parmigianino. Un saggio sull'eremetismo nel Cinquecento.* Rome, 1970.

Fahy, E. "A Portrait of a Renaissance Cardinal as St. Jerome." *Minneapolis Institute of Arts Bulletin* 59 (1970): 1–19.

Faloci-Pulignani, M. *Delle profezie del beato Tommasuccio. Saggio bibliografico.* Foligno, 1881.

———. *Le Profezie del beato Tommasuccio da Foligno.* Foligno, 1887.

———. "La leggenda del beato Tommasuccio." *Miscellanea francescana di storia, di lettere, di arti,* n.s. 21 (1931): 149–51, 244–51.

Favez, C. *Saint Jérôme peint par lui-même* (C.L. 33). Brussels, 1958.

Ferrara, P. *Luci ed ombre nella christianità del secolo XIV. Il beato Pietro Gambacorta da Pisa e la sua Congregazione (1380–1933).* Vatican City, 1964.

Ferri, G. "Le carte dell'archivio Liberiano dal secolo X al XV." *Archivio della R. Società Romana di Storia Patria* 30 (1907): 153–64.

Festugière, S.-J. *Antioch paienne et chrétienne. Libanius, Chrysostome et les moines de Syrie.* Paris, 1959.

Fischer, B. *Verzeichnis der Sigel für Kirchenschriftsteller. Vetus latina,* 1(1), 2d ed. Freiburg-im-Briesgau, 1963.

Fraenkel, P. *Testimonia patrum. The Function of the Patristic Argument in the Theology of Philip Melanchthon* (*Travaux d'Humanisme et Renaissance,* 46). Geneva, 1961.

Frede, H. J. *Ein neuer Paulustext und Kommentar.* 2 vols. Freiburg-im-Breisgau, 1973.

Frere, W. H. *Studies in Early Roman Liturgy,* 3. *The Roman Epistle-Lectionary.* Oxford, 1935.

Freudenberger, Th. *Augustinus Steuchus aus Gubbio, Augustiner-Chorherr und päpstlicher Bibliothekar (1479–1548) und sein literarisches Lebenswerk.* Munster, 1935.

Friedmann, H. *A Bestiary for Saint Jerome. Animal Symbolism in European Religious Art.* Washington, D.C., 1980.

Fubini, R. "Intendimenti umanistici e riferimenti patristici dal Petrarca al Valla." *Giornale storico della letteratura italiana* 15 (1974): 520–78.

Gaiffier, B. de. "Un thème hagiographique, le pendu miraculeusement sauvé." *Revue Belge d'archéologie et d'histoire de l'art* 13 (1943): 123–48.

Gajano, Sofia Boesch, ed. *Agiografia altomedievale.* Bologna, 1976.

Garin, E. "La *dignitas hominis* e la letteratura patristica." *La Rinascita* 1 (1938): 102–46.

Geary, P. J. *Furta sacra. Thefts of Relics in the Central Middle Ages.* Princeton, 1978.

Gijsel, J. *Die unmittelbare Textüberlieferung des sog. Pseudo-Matthaeus.* Brussels, 1981.

Gorce, D. *La lectio divina des origines du cénobitisme à St. Benoît et Cassiodore,* 1. *St. Jérôme et la lecture sacrée dans le milieu ascétique romain.* Paris, 1925.

———. "La patristique dans la réforme d'Erasme." In *Festgabe Joseph Lortz,* 2 vols. Vol. 1, 233–76. Baden-Baden, 1958.

———. "St Jérôme et son environnement artistique et liturgique." *Collectanea Cisterciensia* 36 (1974): 150–78.

Gordan, Phyllis W. G. *Two Renaissance Book Hunters. The Letters of Poggius Bracciolini to Nicolaus de Niccolis.* New York, 1974.

Gray, Hanna H. "Valla's *Encomium of St. Thomas Aquinas* and the Humanist Conception of Christian Antiquity." In *Essays in History and Literature Presented by Fellows of the Newbury Library to Stanley Pargellis,* edited by H. Bluhm, 37–51. Chicago, 1965.

Greenslade, S. L. *The English Reformers and the Fathers of the Church.* Oxford, 1960.

Grützmacher, G. *Hieronymus. Eine biographische Studie.* 3 vols. Berlin, 1901–8.

Hagendahl, H. *Latin Fathers and the Classics.* Göteborg, 1958.

Halkin, F. "Un émule d'Orphée. La légende grecque inédite de saint Zosime, martyr d'Anazarbe en Cilicie." *Analecta Bollandiana* 70 (1952): 249–61.

Hall, Edwin. "Cardinal Albergati, St. Jerome, and the Detroit Van Eyck." *Art Quarterly* 31 (1968): 2–24.

———. "More about the Detroit Van Eyck: The Astrolabe, the Congress of Arras, and Cardinal Albergati." *Art Quarterly* 34 (1971): 181–201.

Hand, John. *Joos van Cleve and the "St. Jerome" in the Norton Gallery and School of Art.* Palm Beach Art Institute, 1972.

Hay, Denys. *The Church in Italy in the Fifteenth Century.* Cambridge, 1977.

Heist, W. W. *The Fifteen Signs before Doomsday.* East Lansing, Mich., 1952.

Henderson, John. "The Flagellant Movement and Flagellant Confraternities in Central Italy, 1260–1400." *Studies in Church History* 15 (1978): 147–60.

Hennecke, E. *New Testament Apocrypha,* edited by W. Schneemelcher, translated by R. M. Wilson et al. 2 vols. Philadelphia, 1963–65.

Hermann-Mascard, Nicole. *Les reliques des saints.* Paris, 1975.

Highfield, J. R. L. "The Jeronimites in Spain, Their Patrons and Success, 1373–1516." *Journal of Ecclesiastical History* 34 (1983): 513–33.

Holeczek, H. *Humanistische Bibelphilologie als Reformproblem bei Erasmus von Rotterdam, Thomas More, und William Tyndale.* Leiden, 1975.

Höpfl, H. *Beiträge zur Geschichte der Sixto-Klementinischen Vulgata.* Freiburg-im-Breisgau, 1913.

Husner, F. "Die Handschrift der Scholien des Erasmus von Rotterdam zu den Hieronymus-Briefen." In *Festschrift Gustav Binz,* 132–46. Basel, 1935.

Ignacio de Madrid, O. S. H. "La Orden de San Jerónimo en España. Primeros pasos para una historia critica." *Studia Monastica* 3 (1961): 409–27.

Jaarinen, Matta. *Die mittelniederdeutsche Uebersetzung der sogenanten Hieronymus-Briefe.* Helsinki, 1944.

Jay, P. "Sur la date de naissance de Saint Jérôme." *Revue des études latines* 51 (1973): 262–80.

Jedin, H. *A History of the Council of Trent,* translated by E. Graf. 2 vols. London, 1961.

Jongh, H. de. *L'ancienne faculté de théologie de Louvain au premier siècle de son existence, 1432–1540.* Louvain, 1911.

Jungblut, Renate. *Hieronymus: Darstellung und Verehrung eines Kirchenvaters.* Tübingen, 1967.

Kaftal, George. *Saints in Italian Art. Iconography of the Saints in Tuscan Painting.* Florence, 1952.

———. *Iconography of the Saints in Central and South Italian Schools of Painting.* Florence, 1965.

———. *Iconography of the Saints in the Painting of North East Italy.* Florence, 1978.

Kelly, J.N.D. *Jerome: His Life, Writings, and Controversies.* London, 1975.

Kessler, Herbert. *The Illustrated Bibles from Tours (Studies in Manuscript Illumination,* 7). Princeton, 1977.

King, Margaret. "The Religious Retreat of Isotta Nogarola (1418–1466)." *Signs* 3 (1978): 807–22.

———. "Book-lined Cells: Women and Humanism in the Early Italian Renaissance." In *Beyond Their Sex. Learned Women of the European Past,* edited by Patricia Labalme, 66–90. New York, 1980.

Klapper, J. "Aus der Frühzeit des Humanismus. Dictungen zu Ehren des heiligen Hieronymus." In *Bausteine. Festschrift Max Koch zum 70. Geburtstage dargebracht*, edited by E. Boehlich and H. Heckel, 255–81. Breslau, 1926.

———. *Johann von Neumarkt, Bischof und Hofkanzler. Religiöse Frührenaissance in Böhmen zur Zeit Kaiser Karls IV.* Leipzig, 1964.

Knauber, A. "Die patrologische Schätzung des Clemens von Alexandrien bis zu seinem neuerlichen Bekanntwerden durch die ersten Druckeditionen des 16. Jahrhunderts." In *Kyriakon. Festschrift Johannes Quasten*, edited by P. Granfield and J. A. Jungmann. 2 vols. Vol. 1, 289–308. Munster i. W., 1970.

Koska, G. *S. Girolamo degli Schiavoni.* Rome, 1971.

Krautheimer, R. *Rome. Profile of a City, 312–1308.* Princeton, 1980.

Kristeller, P. O. "Augustine and the Early Renaissance." In *Studies in Renaissance Thought and Letters*, 355–72. Rome, 1956.

———. "Marsilio Ficino letterato e le glosse attribuite a lui nel codice Caetani di Dante." *Quaderni della Fondazione Camillo Caetani* (Rome, 1981), 3:1–76.

———. "Petrarcas Stellung in der Geschichte der Gelehrsamkeit." In *Italien und die Romania in Humanismus und Renaissance. Festschrift für Erich Loos*, edited by K. Hempfer and E. Straub, 102–21. Wiesbaden, 1983.

Kunze, Gerhard. *Die gottesdienstliche Schriftslesung.* 2 vols. Göttingen, 1947.

Kuretsky, S. "Rembrandt's Tree Stump: An Iconographic Attribute of St. Jerome." *Art Bulletin* 56 (1974): 57–80.

Kuttner, S. "Cardinalis: The History of a Canonical Concept." *Traditio* 3 (1945): 129–214.

Lambot, C. "L'Homélie du Pseudo-Jérôme sur l'Assomption et l'Evangile de la Nativité de Marie d'après une lettre inédite d'Hincmar." *Revue Bénédictine* 46 (1934): 265–82.

Lanzoni, F. *Genesi, svolgimento e tramonto delle leggende storiche* (*Studi e testi*, 43). Rome, 1925.

Lavin, I. "Divine Inspiration in Caravaggio's Two St. Matthews." *Art Bulletin* 56 (1974): 59–81.

LeBachelet, X.-M. *Bellarmine et la Bible Sixto-Clementine.* Paris, 1911.

Leff, Gordon. *Heresy in the Later Middle Ages.* 2 vols. Manchester, 1967.

Leroquais, V. *Les Livres d'Heures manuscrits de la Bibliothèque Nationale.* 2 vols. Paris, 1927.

———. *Les Psautiers manuscrits latins des bibliothèques publiques de France.* 2 vols. Macon, 1940–41.

Levi d'Ancona, M. *The Garden of the Renaissance. Botanical Symbolism in Italian Painting.* Florence, 1977.

Lorenz, R. "Die Anfänge des abendländischen Mönchtum im 4. Jahrhundert." *Zeitschrift für Kirchengeschichte* 76 (1966): 1–61.

Lubac, Henri de. *Exégèse médiévale. Les quatre sens de l'Ecriture.* 2 vols. in 3. Paris, 1959–64.

McManamon, J. M. "Innovation in Early Humanist Rhetoric: The Oratory of Pier Paolo Vergerio the Elder." *Rinascimento* 22 (1982): 3–32.

Maguire, J. B. "Erasmus' Biographical Masterpiece: Hieronymi Stridonensis Vita." *Renaissance Quarterly* 26 (1973): 265–73.

Mâle, Emile. *L'Art religieux de la fin du XVIe siècle, du XVIIe siècle, et du XVIIIe siècle. Etude sur l'iconographie après le Concile de Trente.* 2d ed. Paris, 1951.

Manser, A. "Von heiligen Rufe des Hieronymus und seine frühe Ehrung im Martyrologium vorab des abendländischen Mönchtums." *Benediktinische Monatschrift* 2 (1920): 363–80.

Marrou, H.-I. *Saint Augustin et la fin de la culture antique.* Paris, 1938.

Mattioli, N. *Il beato Simone Fidati da Cascia dell'ordine romitano di S. Agostino e i suoi scritti editi ed inediti.* Rome, 1898.

Meershoek, G. Q. A. *Le Latin biblique d'après saint Jérôme. Aspects linguistiques de la rencontre entre la Bible et le monde classique* (*Latinitas Christianorum Primaeva,*20). Utrecht, 1966.

Meiss, Millard. "French and Italian Variations on an Early Fifteenth-Century Theme: St. Jerome and His Study." *Gazette des Beaux-Arts* 62 (1963): 147–70.

———. "Scholarship and Penitence in the Early Renaissance: The Image of St. Jerome." *Pantheon* 32(2) (1974): 135–40.

———. *French Painting in the Time of Jean de Berry. The Limbourgs and Their Contemporaries.* 2 vols. New York, 1974.

Metzger, B. M. "St. Paul and the Baptized Lion." *Princeton Seminary Bulletin* 39(2) (1945): 11–21.

———. *The Early Versions of the New Testament.* Oxford, 1977.

Mione, E. "Le 'Vitae patrum' nella traduzione d'Ambrogio Traversari." *Aevum* 24 (1950): 319–31.

———. "Il Pratum spirituale di Giovanni Mosco." *Orientalia Christiana Periodica* 17 (1951): 61–94.

Miscellanea Geronimiana. Scritti varii pubblicati nel XV centenario dalla morte di San Girolamo. Rome, 1920.

Monfasani, John. *George of Trebizond. A Biography and a Study of His Rhetoric and Logic (Columbia Studies in the Classical Tradition, 1).* Leiden, 1976.

Moorman, John. *A History of the Franciscan Order from Its Origins to the Year 1517.* Oxford, 1968.

Murphy, F. X., ed. *A Monument to St. Jerome.* New York, 1952.

Murphy, J. J. *The Notion of Tradition in John Driedo.* Milwaukee, 1959.

Musto, Ronald G. "The Letters of Angelo Clareno." Ph.D. diss., Columbia University, 1977.

―――. "Angelo Clareno's 'Preparantia Christi Iesu habitationem et mansionem ineffabilem et divinam in nostris.'" *Archivium Franciscanum Historicum* 73 (1980): 69–89.

Nimmo, D. "Poverty and Politics: The Motivation of Fourteenth-Century Franciscan Reform in Italy." *Studies in Church History* 15 (1978): 161–78.

Olin, John C. "Erasmus and Saint Jerome." *Thought* 54 (1979): 313–21.

O'Malley, J. W. *Praise and Blame in Renaissance Rome: Rhetoric, Doctrine, and Reform in the Sacred Orators of the Papal Court, c. 1450–1521 (Duke Monographs in Medieval and Renaissance Studies, 3).* Durham, N.C., 1979.

Opelt, I. "Das Bienenwunder in der Ambrosius-Biographie des Paulinus von Mailand." *Vigiliae Christianae* 22 (1968): 38–44.

―――. *Hieronymus' Streitschriften.* Heidelberg, 1973.

Oswald, F. "Die Darstellungen des Hl. Hieronymus beim Meister des Bartholomäusaltares." *Wallraf-Richartz-Jahrbuch* 33 (1961): 342–46.

Pächt, O. "Zur Entstehung des 'Hieronymus im Gehaus.'" *Pantheon* 21 (1963): 131–42.

Panofsky, E. *Albrecht Dürer.* 2d ed. 2 vols. Princeton, 1945.

―――. "A Letter to St. Jerome: A Note on the Relationship between Petrus Christus and Jan van Eyck." In *Studies in Art and Literature for Belle da Costa Greene,* 102–8. Princeton, 1954.

Parshall, Peter W. "Albrecht Dürer's St. Jerome in His Study: A Philological Reference. *Art Bulletin* 53 (1971): 303–5.

Penna, A. *S. Gerolamo.* Turin, 1949.

―――. *Principi e carattere dell'esegessi di S. Gerolamo.* Rome, 1952.

Pepper, D. S. "The Angel Appearing to Saint Jerome by Guido Reni, a

New Acquisition." *Bulletin of the Detroit Institute of Arts* 48(2) (1969): 28–35.

Peri, V. "Notizia su Nicola Maniacutia, autore ecclesiastico Romano del XII secolo." *Aevum* (1962): 534–38.

Pillion, Louise. "Trois faits de la légende de saint Jérôme illustrés dans une prédelle de Signorelli." *Revue de l'art chrétien* 53 (1910): 35–36.

Poncelet, A. "Le Légendier de Pierre Calo." *Analecta Bollandiana* 24 (1910): 5–116.

Post, R. R. *The Modern Devotion (Studies in Medieval and Reformation Thought*, 3). Leiden, 1968.

Prodi, P. "Ricerche sulla teorica delle arti figurative nella riforma cattolica." *Archivio italiano per la storia della pietà* 4 (1965): 121–212.

Pullapilly, C. K. *Caesar Baronius, Counter-Reformation Historian.* Notre Dame, Ind., 1975.

Quadrio, G. *Il trattato "De assumptione Beatae Mariae Virginis" dello Pseudo-Agostino e il suo influsso nella theologia assunzionistica latina (Analecta Gregoriana*, 52). Rome, 1951.

Quentin, H. *Les martyrologes historiques du Moyen Age.* Paris, 1908.

Revuelta, J. *Los Jerónimos, fundación y primera expansión (1373–1414).* Guadalajara, 1982.

Reynolds, R. E. "The Pseudo-Hieronymian De septem ordinibus ecclesiae." *Revue Bénédictine* 80 (1970): 238–52.

Rice, E. F. "The Humanist Idea of Christian Antiquity: Lefèvre d'Etaples and His Circle." *Studies in the Renaissance* 9 (1962): 126–60.

———. "St. Jerome's 'Vision of the Trinity': An Iconographical Note." *Burlington Magazine* 125 (1983): 151–55.

Ridderbos, Bernhard. *Saint and Symbol. Images in Early Italian Art.* Groningen, 1984.

Ring, Grete. "St. Jerome Extracting the Thorn from the Lion's Foot." *Art Bulletin* 27 (1945): 188–96.

Ripberger, A. *Der Pseudo-Hieronymus-Brief IX "Cogitis me." Ein erster marianischer Traktat des Mittelalters von Paschasius Radbert (Spicilegium Friburgensis*, 9). Freiburg-Schweiz, 1962.

Roberts, H. I. "St. Augustine in 'St. Jerome's Study.' Carpaccio's Painting and Its Legendary Source." *Art Bulletin* 41 (1959): 285–303.

Robey, David. "P. P. Vergerio the Elder: Republicanism and Civic Values in the Work of an Early Humanist." *Past and Present* no. 58 (1973): 3–37.

Rossi, G. "Contributi alla biografia del canonista Giovanni d'Andrea." *Rivista trimestrale di diritto e procedura civile* 11 (1957): 1451–1501.

Sabbadini, R. *Le scoperte dei codici latini e greci ne' secoli XIV e XV. Nuove ricerche.* Florence, 1914.

Sagmüller, J. B. *Ein Traktat des Bischofs von Feltre und Treviso Teodoro de' Lelli über das Verhältnis von Primat und Kardinalat (Römische Quartalschrift für christl. Alterthumskunde und für Kirchengeschichte.* 2. Supplement Heft). Rome, 1983.

Sajanello, G. B. *Historica monumenta Ordinis S. Hieronymi Congregationis B. Petri de Pisis.* 2d. ed. Venice, 1759.

Saltman, Avrom. *Pseudo-Jerome Quaestiones on the Book of Samuel (Studia Post Biblica, 26).* Leiden, 1975.

Schär, Max. *Das Nachleben des Origenes im Zeitalter des Humanismus (Beiträge zur Geschichtswissenschaft, 140).* Basel, 1979.

Schucan, Luzi. *Das Nachleben von Basilius Magnus "Ad adolescentes." Ein Beitrag zur Geschichte des christlichen Humanismus (Travaux d'Humanisme et Renaissance, 133).* Geneva, 1973.

Schwarz, Werner. "The Meaning of *Fidus interpres* in Medieval Translation." *Journal of Theological Studies* 45 (1944–45): 73–78.

————. *Principles and Problems of Biblical Translation. Some Reformation Controversies and Their Background.* Cambridge, 1955.

Scrinium Erasmianum. Mélanges historiques publiés sous le patronage de l'Université de Louvain à l'occasion du cinquième centenaire de la naissance d'Erasme, edited by J. Coppens. 2 vols. Leiden, 1969–70.

Semple, W. H. "St. Jerome as a Biblical Translator." *Bulletin of the John Rylands Library* 48 (1965): 227–43.

Sicroff, A. "The Jeronymite Monastery of Guadalupe in 14th- and 15th-Century Spain." In *Collected Studies in Honor of Américo Castro's Eightieth Year,* edited by M.P. Hornick, 379–422. Lincombe Lodge Research Library, Boars Hill, Oxford, 1965.

Siegmund, A. *Die Ueberlieferung der griechischen christlichen Literatur in der lateinischen Kirche bis zum zwölften Jahrhundert (Abhandlungen der bayerischen Benediktiner-Akademie, 5).* Munich-Pasing, 1949.

Spear, Richard. *Domenichino.* 2 vols. (New Haven, 1982).

Stinger, C. L. *Humanism and the Church Fathers. Ambrogio Traversari (1396–1439) and Christian Antiquity in the Italian Renaissance.* Albany, N.Y., 1977.

Strümpell, A. "Hieronymus im Gehäuse." *Marburger Jahrbuch für Kuntwissenschaft* 2 (1925–26): 173–252.

Studia Hieronymiana. VI. Centenario de la Orden de San Jerónimo. 2 vols. Madrid, 1973.

Sutcliff, E. F. "The Name 'Vulgate.'" *Biblica* 29 (1948): 345–52.

Thomson, D. F. S., and H. C. Porter. *Erasmus and Cambridge.* Toronto, 1963.

Töth, Paolo de. *Il beato Cardinale Nicolo Albergati e i suoi tempi, 1375–1444.* 2 vols. Acquapendente, 1934.

Trimpi, Erica. "'Iohannem Baptistam Hieronymo aequalem et non maiorem': A Predella for Matteo di Giovanni's Placici Altarpiece." *Burlington Magazine* 125 (1983): 437–66.

Trinkaus, Charles. *In His Own Image and Likeness. Humanity and Divinity in Italian Renaissance Thought.* 2 vols. Chicago, 1970.

Turcan, M. "Saint Jérôme et les femmes." *Bulletin de l'Association Guillaume Budé* (1968): 259–72.

Ullman, B. L. *The Humanism of Coluccio Salutati.* Padua, 1963.

Ullman, B. L., and Philip Stadter. *The Public Library of Renaissance Florence. Niccolo Niccoli, Cosimo de' Medici, and the Library of San Marco.* Padua, 1972.

Usener, H. *Der heilige Tychon.* Leipzig, 1907.

Uttenweiler, J. "Zur Stellung des hl. Hieronymus im Mittelalter." *Benediktinische Monatschrift* 2 (1920): 522–41.

Vaccari, A. "Le antiche vite di S. Girolamo." In *Scritti di erudizione e di filologia.* 2 vols. Vol. 1, 31–51. Rome, 1958.

Vauchez, André. *La sainteté en Occident aux derniers siècles du Moyen Age d'après les procès de canonisation et les documents hagiographiques (Bibliothèque des Ecoles françaises d'Athènes et de Rome, 241).* Rome, 1981.

Venturi, A. *L'arte a San Girolamo.* Milan, 1924.

Vocht, H. de. *Monumenta Humanistica Lovaniensia. Texts and Studies about Louvain Humanists in the First Half of the XVIth Century (Humanistica Lovaniensia, 4).* Louvain, 1934.

Waal, H. van de. "Rembrandt's Faust Etching, a Socinian Document, and the Iconography of the Inspired Scholar." *Oud Holland* 79 (1964): 7–48.

Weinstein, Donald, and R. M. Bell. *Saints and Society. The Two Worlds of Western Christendom, 1000–1700.* Chicago, 1982.

Wermelinger, O. *Rom und Pelagius. Die theologische Position der römischen Bischöfe in pelagianischem Streit in den Jahren 411–432.* Stuttgart, 1975.

Weissman, Ronald. *Ritual Brotherhood in Renaissance Florence.* New York, 1982.

Wendel, François. *Calvin. Sources et évolution de sa pensée religieuse.* Paris, 1950.

Wind, E. "Studies in Allegorical Protriture. I–II. Albrecht von Brandenburg as St. Erasmus." *Journal of the Warburg and Courtauld Institutes* 1
(1937–38): 142–62.

Wittkower, R. "Desiderio da Settignano's *St. Jerome in the Desert*." In
U.S. National Gallery of Art. Studies in the History of Art (1971–72): 7–
37.

Index

ACCIAIUOLI, ZANOBI, 88–89
Acta Pauli, 40, 213 n. 46
Ado of Vienne, 32; *Martyrologium,* 208 n. 1, 211 n. 28
Aelian, *De nat. animalium,* 213 n. 40
Aeneas Silvius. *See* Pius II (pope)
Aesop, 39, 139; *Fables,* 39, 90, 212 n. 39
Aesticampianus, Johannes, 90–91
Agucchi, Girolamo (cardinal), 8
Alaric, 20
Albani, Francesco, 189, 282 n. 52
Albergati, Nicolò, 108–9
Albert of Brandenburg, 108, 119
Alberti, Antonio, 255 n. 62
Albertus Magnus, 188
Alcibiades, 88
Alcuin, 47, 188, 199; *Comm. in Joan.,* 214 n. 76
Aldobrandini, Pietro, 262 n. 51
Aldus Manutius, 88, 154
Alexander of Aphrodisias, 3
Alexander the Great, 41, 97, 214 n. 50
Altichiero da Verona, 106, 111
Amboise, Georges d', 241 n. 16
Ambrose, Saint, 11, 32, 35, 46, 48, 85, 89, 118, 125, 136, 140, 143–44, 151, 178, 181, 218 n. 1, 251 n. 24; *De mysteriis,* 210 n. 13
Amerbach, Basilius, 118
Amerbach, Boniface, 118
Amerbach, Bruno, 118–19
Amerbach, Johann, 118; *Amerbachkorrespondenz,* 241 n. 8
Anacharsis, 97
Anastasius, Saint, 44
Andrea, Giovanni d' (Johannes Andreae), 64–65, 67–68, 74, 81, 108, 121–24, 137, 219 n. 1, 228 n. 66, 230 n. 82, 242 n. 22, 246 n. 47, 249 n. 2;

Hieronymianus, 64, 66, 120–22, 124, 137, 219 n. 1, 220 n. 17, 221 n. 18, 224 n. 34, 225 nn. 36, 37, 40, 226 nn. 41, 42, 241 nn. 15, 17, fig. 25
Andrea de' Bussi, Giovanni, 122, 124, 234 n. 34
Androclus, 39, 213 n. 40
Angelico, Fra, 99
Angelo da Bergamo, 151; *De b. Hier. laudibus,* 253 nn. 34, 35
Anne de Bretagne, 232 n. 20
Anne de France (duchess of Bourbon), 89, 232 n. 20
Anselm, Saint, 188
Anthony, Saint, 43, 228 n. 66
Anthony of Padua, Saint, 81
Antonino Pierozzi, Saint, 108, 123–24; *Chronicon,* 123, 242 nn. 23–25
Antoninus of Piacenza, 24; *Itinerarium,* 24, 210 n. 8
Apion, *Aegyptiaca,* 213 n. 40
Apollinarius (bishop of Laodicea), 11, 19
Apollonius of Tyana, 88, 97, 103, 237 n. 61
Apuleius, 209 n. 2; *Met.,* 215 n. 56
Aquila, 15
Aquinas, Thomas, Saint, 47, 106, 135, 144, 188; *Summa con. gentiles,* 223 n. 32; *Summa theologiae,* 47, 223 n. 32
Aristides, 5, 103, 237 n. 61
Aristophanes, 88, 119
Aristotle, 3, 4, 87, 89, 92, 97, 99, 102–3, 125, 134–35, 137–38, 237 n. 61; *De anima,* 92; *Poetics,* 119
Asella, 12
Astemio, Lorenzo, 90, 232 n. 22
Athanasius, Saint, 3, 251 n. 24; *Life of Anthony,* 3, 45
Attilius Regulus, 97
Augustine, Saint, 17, 18, 24, 32, 35, 47,

CPSIA information can be obtained at www.ICGtesting.com
Printed in the USA
LVOW06s0513130813

347532LV00002B/16/A